GUANTÁNAMO

AMERICAN CROSSROADS

Edited by Earl Lewis, George Lipsitz, Peggy Pascoe, George Sánchez, and Dana Takagi

Guantánamo

A Working-Class History between
Empire and Revolution

JANA K. LIPMAN

UNIVERSITY OF CALIFORNIA PRESS   Berkeley   Los Angeles   London

University of California Press, one of the most distinguished
university presses in the United States, enriches lives around
the world by advancing scholarship in the humanities, social
sciences, and natural sciences. Its activities are supported by
the UC Press Foundation and by philanthropic contributions
from individuals and institutions. For more information, visit
www.ucpress.edu.

University of California Press
Berkeley and Los Angeles, California

University of California Press, Ltd.
London, England

Library of Congress Cataloging-in-Publication Data

Lipman, Jana K.
  Guantánamo : a working-class history between empire and
revolution / Jana K. Lipman.
     p.   cm.—(American crossroads ; 25)
  Includes bibliographical references and index.
  ISBN 978-0-520-25539-5 (cloth : alk. paper)
  ISBN 978-0-520-25540-1 (pbk. : alk. paper)
    1. Guantánamo Bay Naval Base (Cuba)—Employees—
History.   2. Civil-military relations—Cuba—Guantánamo
Bay.   3. Navy-yards and naval stations, American—Cuba—
History.   4. Caimanera (Cuba)—History.   5. Guantánamo
(Cuba)—History.   I. Title.

VA68.G8L57   2009
359.7097291'67—dc22   2008021092

Manufactured in the United States of America

17   16   15   14   13   12   11   10   09
10   9   8   7   6   5   4   3   2   1

This book is printed on Natures Book, which contains 50%
postconsumer waste and meets the minimum requirements of
ANSI/NISO Z39.48–1992 (R 1997) (Permanence of Paper).

For Eli

Contents

Illustrations

FIGURES

MAPS

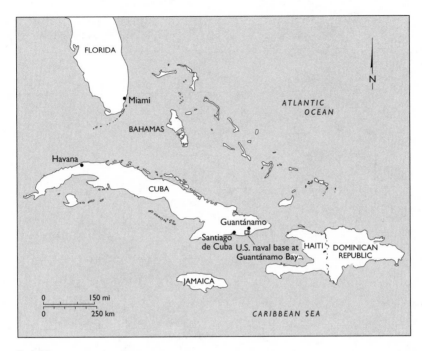

Map 1. Cuba.

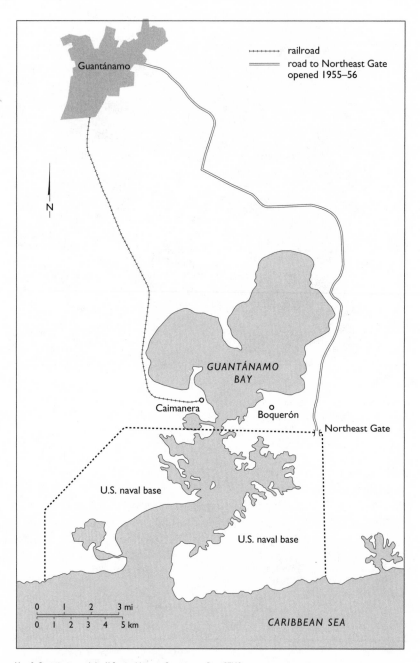

Map 2. Guantánamo and the U.S. naval base in Guantánamo Bay (GTMO).

Introduction
Between Guantánamo and GTMO

I met Robert Duncan in Havana at a Cuba-Jamaica World Cup soccer qualifying match in 2001. I was conducting research on exchanges between Cuba and Jamaica in the 1950s and 1960s, and the Jamaican Embassy staff had invited me to the game. At halftime, I was introduced to Robert, an older Cuban man who spoke perfect English with a Jamaican accent. I told Robert that I was interested in learning about Jamaican descendants living in Cuba before and after the Cuban revolution. Without further prompting, he shared his story.

Robert's parents were born in Jamaica and, like thousands of British West Indians in the early twentieth century, they migrated to Cuba looking for work. In the end, his father and mother both found positions on the U.S. naval base in Guantánamo Bay. Robert explained that his parents were apolitical and conservative and, like many West Indians of the era, opted to remain outside of Cuban politics. In contrast, Robert was eager to take part in the fight against Fulgencio Batista's corrupt and illegitimate government. In 1958 Cuban rebels camped out in the nearby hills surrounding the city of Guantánamo. Sixteen-year-old Robert decided to run off and join the revolutionaries. His choice caused discord and debates within his family, but Robert insisted. He was born in Cuba, and he wanted to join the struggle. Despite his family's initial anger and

1

political neutrality, Robert's father clandestinely pilfered boots, backpacks, and supplies from the base to help his son. Robert could rattle off a list of his *compañeros* who were also descendants of West Indians with ties to the base. He commented that he and his friends were more professional than the other rebels, because they had regular contact with the naval base and were accustomed to military culture and discipline. The rest, as they say, is history: Batista fled, Robert marched with the rebel forces into Havana, and the revolution triumphed. Robert remained a career army officer, training in Moscow and serving with distinction as a lieutenant colonel in Angola.[1]

Robert's testimony intrigued me because it so gracefully revealed a multinational community within Guantánamo where Cubans, West Indians, and North Americans lived in close proximity. It also suggested a local history of the U.S. naval base in Guantánamo that I had never imagined, and one that pointedly demonstrated the limits of U.S. imperial power. Even along the perimeter of its naval base, the United States could not stop the Cuban revolution, nor could it prevent men like Robert from joining the rebel forces or, in the case of his father, from stealing U.S. supplies.

On this same research trip, I traveled to Guantánamo, Cuba, to meet with members of the British West Indian Welfare Centre. There, too, men and women told me how their families had worked on the U.S. military base. As most North Americans might be, I was startled to learn there was a relatively large Cuban city named Guantánamo, with more than a hundred thousand people, an active city center, two movie theaters, and a network of horse and buggy routes that looped through the city. There was no immediate evidence that we were just over a dozen miles away from a U.S. military base, and only the overwhelming heat reminded me that, for all intents and purposes, Guantánamo was landlocked. From the city, Guantánamo Bay and the base were invisible and inaccessible.

One month after I returned from Cuba, Al Qaeda terrorists attacked the United States on September 11, 2001. With the subsequent invasions of Afghanistan and Iraq, the U.S. government made the unprecedented decision to imprison alleged Al Qaeda members on the U.S. naval base in Guantánamo Bay. The former nineteenth-century Caribbean military outpost had a newfound purpose in the War on Terror. Notwithstanding more than one hundred years of occupation, the U.S. government claimed that the U.S. Constitution did not extend to the base, and "ultimate sovereignty" remained with the Cuban government. This legal fiction created the perfect prison. It enabled the United States to detain individuals indefinitely, withhold legal support, and if circumstances dictated, intimidate prisoners without judicial review or restraint. Despite lawsuits and international outrage, as of this writing 275 men remain captive inside the naval base without due process and in blatant disregard of U.S. legal principles and the Geneva Conventions. Among public intellectuals, "Guantánamo" has become a symbol of U.S. hubris, shame, and utter disregard for human rights and the rule of law.[2]

With international attention focused on the detainees, I decided to learn more about the sleepy Cuban city I had visited the summer before 9/11. I returned to Guantánamo, Cuba, in 2004 for five months of field and archival research to study the social history of the city's relationship to the base. In my many conversations with local men and women, no one once initiated a conversation about Al Qaeda. Only with prompting did anyone mention the naval base at all. And when I explained my project, I was not met with bitterness or outrage at the United States. Instead, most people immediately commented that their father, uncle, or neighbor used to work on the base, and if he or she was still alive, many of them promptly offered to introduce me. In these interviews and conversations, I heard very little that was directly anti-imperialist or hostile about the base. The only palpable resentment was economic: the United States had callously fired hundreds of workers in the early 1960s and cut off their U.S. government pensions. Many urged me to lobby for their pensions when I returned home, insisting that with more pressure the United States might restore these desperately needed dollars to its former employees. Buried in this resentment was a call to older U.S. pledges of good neighborly behavior as well as the immediate need for cash in contemporary Cuba. The men and women I spoke with were not concerned with international controversies or human rights abuses but instead honed in on the particular circumstances of workers in Guantánamo.

Thousands of local men and women have worked for the U.S. military and private contractors on the naval base in Guantánamo Bay since the early twentieth century. These men and women worked in construction, maintenance, offices, supply depots, clubs, bars, golf courses, and private homes. In Guantánamo, the local population referred to all of these employees as *los trabajadores de la base* (the base workers), and this generalization often implied that they were all male. However, alongside the men, many women labored on the base. In the Cuban racial schema, the workers included black, white, and mixed race individuals. Base workers also came from a range of national backgrounds. Many were Cuban, while others were British West Indians. Plus, there was generally a handful of Puerto Ricans, Spaniards, Chinese, and South Asian workers as well. Base workers spoke Spanish, and they often spoke English or learned it on the job. From World War II until the years following the Cuban revolution, social contact and exchange between North Americans and *guantanameros* was common. In the 1950s, many base workers supported Fidel Castro's anti-Batista 26 of July Movement, while another cohort rejected the revolution and sought exile on the base. As of April 2006, there were three Cuban employees who still commuted to the base each day. Collectively, base workers' stories are laced with anger, ambivalence, and compromise, demonstrating the contradictions embedded in neocolonial relations.

With ongoing debates about U.S. detention policies and the looming uncertainty of a post-Castro Cuba, labor history grounds Guantánamo in its Cuban geography. When political leaders, including former President Jimmy Carter, former UN Secretary General Kofi Annan, former Secretary of State Colin Powell, and even Secretary of Defense Robert Gates urge the Bush administration to "close Guantánamo," they are referring to the detention camps, and not to the base itself.[3] "Guantánamo" has come to signify unchecked detention and interrogation. But by critiquing the camps and not the naval base, these leaders miss the foundation that allows the United States to exercise unchecked authority—the legacy of U.S. imperialism in Cuba, the complete rupture with the Cuban government after the revolution, and the base's subsequent isolation from the surrounding community.

In response to the present situation, left-wing scholars are just as likely as the U.S. administration to ignore the local specificity of Guantánamo. In her essay, "Where Is Guantánamo?" Amy Kaplan describes how the U.S. Supreme Court's 2004 *Rasul v. Bush* decision evaded the question of whether the base was a domestic or foreign entity. She concludes that this legal dodging "creates a world in which Guantánamo is everywhere." Likewise, social theorists have dubbed Guantánamo a "space of exception" or an "anomalous zone" where the absence of law systematically dehumanizes its residents and expands the scope of U.S. power.[4] Through legal and literary analyses, these scholars examine the 1903 and 1934 lease agreements governing U.S. control over Guantánamo Bay, as well as the precedents established in the Haitian and Cuban refugee crises during the 1990s. They end pessimistically with a chilling portrait of the U.S. naval base as a place devoid of law or accountability.

Although I agree with many of their conclusions, these scholars have divorced the naval base's legal history from its social and political context. The exchanges between Cubans and North Americans in Guantánamo remain invisible and anonymous. In contrast, I argue that the base workers are critical to the evolution of the base. Rather than conceptualizing "Guantánamo" as a theoretical or constitutional dilemma, this history grapples with the local legacies of U.S. neocolonialism and military occupation in Cuba. It recognizes Guantánamo's political economy and its population. Guantánamo is exceptional in many ways, but I offer a more straightforward answer to Kaplan's central question. Guantánamo is in Cuba.

Rooting the history of the U.S. naval base firmly in its local environs, I demonstrate how base workers and military personnel wielded and managed power on the margins of the Cuban nation and U.S. empire. In the terminology of recent scholarship, the U.S. naval base in Guantánamo Bay is a transnational space, a geographic locale that operated and operates outside traditional nation-state norms and borders. Many historians have gravitated to the term *transnational,* which signals "how people and ideas and institutions and cultures moved above, below, through, and around, as well as, within the nation-state," thus studying topics that "spill over and seep through national borders."[5] This scholarship decenters the nation-state as the primary area of historical analysis and expands the scope of U.S. history outside its continental boundaries.[6] Diasporas, new technologies, and nonelite actors benefit from this shift in attention. The transnational turn has significantly broadened the purview of what *counts* as U.S. history to include Mexican Americans along the southwestern border, black musicians, athletes, and intellectuals who crisscrossed the Atlantic, and Dominican migrants who maintained financial and familial ties across two countries.[7] My research draws on this scholarship, and the base workers in Guantánamo Bay belong to this cohort. However, the term *international,* the history between states, does not lose its value. If anything international relations were magnified in Guantánamo, a region where friction between Cuba and the U.S. military dominated the local landscape. Base workers had to navigate and travel *between* these two poles; there was nothing *transcendent* about it. In fact, "politically bounded territories" defined base workers' experiences.[8] As nonstate actors, they were keenly aware of the international border that constituted their daily reality. Disputes over hiring practices, wages, and labor law were international, rather than transnational, clashes, often encapsulating the contradictions of U.S. foreign policy and military occupation.

In this vein, I argue that social history is diplomatic history and that local and international histories meet on the ground. Base workers were international actors, and their stories reshape our understanding of U.S. foreign relations. The labor history of the U.S. naval base in Guantánamo Bay demonstrates how neocolonialism, empire, and revolution functioned in working people's lives.

THE COLD WAR, NEOCOLONIALISM, AND WORK

The U.S. occupation of Guantánamo Bay began in 1898. At first, the number of local workers and U.S. military personnel numbered in the hundreds; for example, in the 1930s, the base housed only 345 enlisted men and 22 officers. World War II marked a dramatic change. During the war, the Marine Corps alone stationed 1,200 men and trained an additional 6,000. The upsurge in local base employment was similar. At its peak between 1940 and 1943, there were approximately 13,000 government and contract workers.[9] This exponential increase in individuals, activity, and exchange created a new era in Guantánamo's political economy. From the close of World War II until 1964, the U.S. Navy, private contractors, and individual families regularly employed 3,500 men and women. The 1959 Cuban revolution triggered a dramatic change in affairs. Fidel Castro became an enemy of the United States, and base workers found themselves on the front lines of a Cold War no-man's-land. The tradition of local employment ended in 1964, five years after the Cuban revolution, due to a minor Cold War scuffle between Castro and President Lyndon Johnson. As a result, 1964 marked the end of regular contact between Guantánamo and the base and the decline of a Cuban working-class population on the naval station.

In the Caribbean, the Cold War and neocolonialism worked hand in hand to consolidate U.S. power, affecting not just national politics but everyday encounters. With its emphasis on base workers, this history intervenes in Cold War historiography and studies of U.S. empire. It takes the era between World War II and the mid-1960s as its primary area of inquiry. By exploring the period of maximum exchange, this study offers an alternative chronology of U.S.-Cuban relations and an analysis of labor and empire.

An emphasis on the World War II years through the mid-1960s reframes the traditional periodization of the Good Neighbor policy and the Cold War. President Franklin Roosevelt's 1933 declaration of the Good Neighbor policy halted the myriad of U.S. military invasions in Latin

America that had marked the early part of the century. It replaced U.S. brute force with the less martial, although not necessarily more subtle, tools of economic, cultural, and political persuasion and coercion.[10] In Guantánamo, the United States was more than just a rhetorical neighbor. With the promise of friendship and reciprocity embedded in the diplomatic language, Guantánamo businesspeople, workers, and politicians appropriated the idiom of neighborliness for their own ends. They lobbied for more jobs for Cuban workers, more customers for local businesses, and more cordial relations with the U.S. military base. Neighborliness was also used euphemistically to describe U.S. liberty parties (military shore leave) and the ensuing sexual encounters with local women. Cuban officials employed this language heavy with neocolonial obligation throughout the 1940s, 1950s, and even in the months following the Cuban revolution. Through geography and political discourse, Guantánamo tested the U.S. commitment to and definition of neighborliness.

The focus on midcentury events also backdates the importance of the Cold War in Cuban history. With good reason, most historians of the Cold War have concentrated on Fidel Castro's rise to power and the Cuban revolution.[11] This scholarship is valuable, but it ignores the decade of U.S.-Cuban Cold War politics before the revolution. Base workers witnessed and experienced a range of Cold War conflicts between World War II and the 1960s. Their ability to critique the base, organize collectively, and form alliances were all contingent on Cold War politics. Although few base employees cared about "communism" per se, they recognized that international forces could dictate whether they could join a union or keep their jobs. Adding yet another variable, base workers did not necessarily recognize a contradiction in working for the U.S. military and participating in the nationalist struggle. Many continued living in revolutionary Cuba and working on the base even during the Bay of Pigs invasion and the 1962 Missile Crisis. Base workers' decisions and crises did not mirror the international drama, but instead laid bare the tangible twists and turns of the Cold War in a specific place. By taking a local perspective, Cuba's Cold War history no longer appears bipolar or defined only by Fidel Castro and the Cuban revolution.

Readers will note that I use the term *neocolonial* when discussing the U.S. presence in Guantánamo. I employ the term because it best describes the asymmetrical power dynamic in the United States' political, cultural, and economic influence in the Guantánamo region. The United

States controlled territory within the naval station, but its legal authority did not extend outside the base's boundaries. After 1902, the U.S. occupation was contingent on at least a formal recognition of Cuban national sovereignty. Despite the glaring political imbalance within the relationship, Guantánamo, Cuba, was never a direct colony of the United States, nor were its workers ever legally defined as U.S. colonial subjects. Relying on the base for financial stability and enjoying a degree of social prestige, base workers' dilemmas were as often *neo*colonial as they were anticolonial. Furthermore, the U.S. naval base in Guantánamo Bay is anything but *post*colonial. It remains firmly stationed there. I draw from postcolonial scholarship and its anti-imperial critique, but postcolonial does not describe the terrain in Guantánamo.[12] Instead, I prefer to use the term neocolonial and expand its scope to include a myriad of daily interactions, relationships, romances, assaults, protests, friendships, and betrayals between U.S. actors and local men and women in Guantánamo.

The histories of base workers also contribute to the growing body of scholarly work on the "cultures of U.S. imperialism."[13] A new generation of academics has demonstrated that empire is integral to U.S. history, instead of merely an aberration or momentary stage. Nontraditional approaches to diplomatic history have opened up dynamic areas of investigation, emphasizing the power of cultural production and representation. Scholars such as Amy Kaplan, Mary Renda, Laura Wexler, Christina Klein, and Ann Laura Stoler have offered potent analyses of how race and sex have worked to export and, sometimes subvert, U.S. imperial power structures.[14] Their work emphasizes the construction of white manhood and womanhood along with the ramifications of the U.S. imperial gaze. In turn, Mark Bradley and Seth Jacobs have used cultural analyses to demonstrate how the Cold War and U.S. empire intersected as the United States responded to decolonization and Third World nationalism.[15] While providing valuable critiques of U.S. imperialism, these scholars still privilege elites at the expense of working people.[16] Film, photography, theater, literature, and museum exhibits provide innovative alternatives to the State Department archives, but they do not necessarily capture how U.S. empire was encountered by non-U.S. actors. This scholarship analyzes representations of empire, rather than the experiences of empire for Cubans, Filipinos, Puerto Ricans, Middle Easterners, Pacific Islanders, and other populations outside the United States. As such, U.S. men and women and U.S. cultural production remain at their center.

The following history analyzes the culture of empire through the vector of labor and work. Base workers are the key protagonists. The possibility of employment, steady pay, and U.S. pensions far surpassed most workers' resentment against U.S. imperialism. At the same time, base workers actively fought against U.S. abuses, unfair wage scales, and arbitrary governance. In the years leading up to World War II and the Korean War, workers' central anxieties focused on *gaining* a job on the base; after 1959, they hinged on the politics of *keeping* one's job. The result was international relations and political exchange on a local, and often individual, level.

The naval base in Guantánamo Bay remains iconic as a symbol of late nineteenth-century U.S. imperial conquest. Throughout the century, U.S. basing policy made the military's strategic priorities visible to the world. From early twentieth-century imperial outposts in Cuba and Hawaii to the massive postwar installations in Germany, Japan, and later Korea, the U.S. military left its "footprint" across the globe.[17] Although the particularities of each base were unique, the social, economic, and sexual consequences of U.S. militarism often produced similar results in vastly different regional settings.[18] Prostitution, economic dependence, and environmental destruction were the norm. These military bases also resembled U.S. rule in other Caribbean locales, particularly the Panama Canal Zone and Puerto Rico.[19] The men and women who lived alongside these bases had to balance between the prerogatives of the U.S. military and their own governments.

Given U.S. military geography, the naval base in Guantánamo Bay stands out. It was the first U.S. overseas base on foreign territory, and after the Cuban revolution, its labor structure unwittingly made it a model for the twenty-first century. Cuban workers tenaciously clung to base employment after the revolution, but by the mid-1960s, the base reduced its local workforce by more than seventy percent. The U.S. government no longer trusted the majority of local men and women from Guantánamo. To replace these Cuban workers, the U.S. military re-imagined its neocolonial networks. It initiated an overseas contract labor program from Jamaica and later the Philippines. Military officials also stopped direct government hires, and in the process, removed the navy from many political and monetary obligations. Today the vast majority of base workers, the cooks, gardeners, and laborers, are foreign nationals who work for private contractors.

In 2004, Secretary of Defense Donald Rumsfeld proposed revamping the U.S. military's global posture for the first time in fifty years, including the size, scope, and location of its overseas bases. The Department of Defense prioritized cooperative security locations (bases with few permanently stationed U.S. military personnel in peripheral regions such as Senegal, the Gulf states, and Djibouti) over the more traditional main operating bases in Okinawa, Germany, and South Korea. The seemingly less obtrusive, "cooperative" sites were dubbed "lily pad" bases, and they were touted for their flexibility, strategic capabilities, and potential power. Rumsfeld admitted that large bases in Okinawa and Korea had become an "irritant" to those governments, and lily pads offered a new model.[20] With smaller bases in critical geopolitical regions, the U.S. military hopes to circumvent the political, sexual, and environmental controversies that have arisen on the borders of U.S. military bases. Moreover, alliances can shift rapidly, and sovereign states can say no. The United States does not want its military capabilities dependent on a single base or a single host country.

Isolated, remote, and "self-sufficient," the U.S. naval base in Guantánamo Bay appears to be a prototype in the U.S. military's contemporary quest for more lily pads. The base's decades-long reliance on privatized labor predates the recent turn to subcontracting with all its benefits and pitfalls. Although it does not resemble a lily pad with its permanent status and long history, the naval base in Guantánamo Bay gives military officials the ability to act with complete independence from the Cuban government and the "flexibility" to do what they want. In this case, the U.S. government has violated basic principles of due process dating back to the Magna Carta, creating a distressing precedent for other U.S. military installations.[21]

The severance of local relations with Guantánamo, Cuba, and the outsourcing of labor contribute to and enable this political calculus. Before the Cuban revolution, base employees negotiated, individually and collectively, with the U.S. military and the Cuban government. Local commuters set limits to the U.S. military's control. Neocolonialism always defined the parameters, but base workers' agency, struggles, and compromises demonstrated that the U.S. military could not ignore the local community or its Cuban environment. In the years after the Cuban revolution, the U.S. government successfully redefined the naval base as an island unto itself. Although this is accurate in today's geopolitics, it was not inevitable, nor was it the case for many decades. And base workers would have disagreed. Between the tumults of empire and revolution, the U.S. naval base in Guantánamo Bay has always been in Guantánamo, Cuba.

POLITICS OF LANGUAGE: GUANTÁNAMO AND "GITMO"

When I tell people I conducted research in Guantánamo, they immediately assume I have been on the U.S. naval base. I have not. I am asked about the detainees, human rights abuses, and the question of U.S. law and constitutional overreach. Each time, I must explain that I was in Guantánamo, Cuba, and it was impossible for me to cross the military border and enter the base. It was not until my fourth visit that I even visited the designated tourist lookout station, the Mirador de Malones, finally viewing the base from afar. My disclaimers are usually met with confusion, because although the naval enclave of "Guantánamo" produces immediate recognition, Guantánamo, Cuba, does not. Because "Guantánamo" can signify both the base and the city, the shared name allows for a blurring of identities and territories.

Throughout the 1940s and 1950s, the Guantánamo press fastidiously maintained language that differentiated the base from the neighboring city. "Guantánamo" referred to the city of Guantánamo, and no further explanation or description was needed. The press referred to "Guantánamo" as "Guantánamo City" only when it was writing for an English-speaking public. For example, *La Revista Oriental,* a magazine for eastern Cuba's aspiring elite, occasionally published features in English for the North American and British expatriates in the region. In these instances, "Guantánamo" became "Guantánamo City."[22] The editors recognized that they needed to distinguish the city from the base for its English-speaking audience. In contrast, when writing in Spanish, the local press never referred to the base as simply "Guantánamo"; rather, it was the "naval station," "the North American naval station in the bay," or the "U.S. operating and supply base in Guantánamo Bay."[23] Interestingly, the press often included a subtle critique, referring to the naval station as *"la base naval en nuestra bahía,"* or the naval base in *our* bay.[24] Although the "our" was neither emphasized nor commented upon, its repetitive appearance underscored that the base was in Cuba— *nuestra*–territory.

In fact, Guantánamo was not the closest Cuban city to the naval base. That somewhat dubious privilege belonged to Caimanera and Boquerón. Caimanera and Boquerón bordered Guantánamo Bay and existed on opposite sides of the U.S. territory. Journalists dubbed Caimanera the *antesala,* or the reception hall, for the U.S. Navy.[25] This designation invoked a mixture of pride and shame among the local press corps. Regional boosters emphasized Caimanera's national importance as the only town in Cuba with an international border. They lobbied for national investments and public works, such as water and public health services, to offer a respectable first impression and welcome for U.S. sailors on leave. Yet the reality was that Caimanera and Boquerón had constant water shortages, no public schools, unpaved roads, and were renowned only for their brothels and bars. Salt mines, fishing, and a railroad depot for the Guantánamo Sugar Company helped diversify the economy, but the bulk of commercial activity depended on the base. These towns became known as centers of prostitution and excess in both Cuba and the U.S. Navy, but the name Caimanera never gained the same familiarity or symbolic resonance as Guantánamo.[26]

The U.S. Navy and its men baptized the base, "Gitmo," according to its military acronym GTMO. The *New York Times* generally referred to the "U.S. naval base in Guantánamo Bay," maintaining a distinction between the base and the Cuban city. However, most North Americans linguistically merged "Guantánamo" and the naval base. U.S. military geography was reinforced in the media's representation of the Caribbean. For example, the *New York Times* featured "Fifteen News Questions" to test its readers' attention to weekly events. Questions included: "In his trip beginning this Friday, President Truman will visit Key West, San Juan, Charlotte Amalie, and Guantánamo. Where are these places?" or "Among the key United States bases in the Caribbean area are Guantánamo Bay, Roosevelt Roads, and Trinidad. Where are they?"[27] As the Cuban revolution advanced, U.S. popular magazines were even more likely to ignore the Cuban community. Headlines proclaimed, "Guantánamo: Keystone in the Caribbean," "Guantánamo: Ours or Castro's?" and "Clouds over Guantánamo."[28] By using "Guantánamo" to signify the naval base, the popular press generally ignored the presence of the Cuban city. In this manner, the U.S. marines and military forces were the only actors visible to a U.S. audience.

Much to the chagrin of the Guantánamo elite, many Cubans in Havana were equally ignorant of Guantánamo. Located in eastern Cuba, more than five hundred miles from Havana, *habaneros* always considered Guantánamo to be in the proverbial boondocks, far from the political, economic, and cultural center of the island. As recently as 1985, Guantánamo's official historians within the Cuban Communist Party felt the need to emphasize that "the history of Guantánamo province is one of the least known in the entire country, although not because it is the least important."[29] Guantánamo achieved its greatest fame through the verses of José "Joseito" Fernández Díaz, a Havana singer who immortalized the girl from Guantánamo in the song "Guantanamera." Composed in 1928, "Joséito" Fernández adapted José Martí's *Versos Sencillos* and paired it with the chorus of "Guantanamera." The song became the theme for one of Havana's most popular radio programs, *El Suceso del Día.*[30] *El Suceso del Día*, accompanied by "Guantanamera," aired every day at 3:30 P.M. from the late 1930s until 1954. With more than a decade of repetition, the lilting melody of *"guantanamera, guajira, guantanamera"* cemented the national association of Guantánamo with the *guajira*, the simple, country girl.

Along with this image of the *guajira*, the national press identified Guantánamo with bordellos, North American debauchery, and the U.S. base. Just like North Americans, Havana reporters ignored the distinction between the base and the city. After the Cuban revolution, this became politically significant since "Guantánamo" came to symbolize the enemy and the reputed home of U.S. espionage and counterrevolutionary activity. In the earliest editions of *Venceremos*, the post-1962, state-run Guantánamo newspaper, the editor, Idilio Isaac Rodríguez, confronted the Cuban government's identification of "Guantánamo" with the "naval base" head-on. As a local, he righteously defended Guantánamo's revolutionary credentials and railed against Havana journalists for equating the naval base with the people of Guantánamo and Caimanera. "Our newspapers only inflame the error: they [have] identified the naval base with Guantánamo and Caimanera . . . although we are sure this was not the intention of our brother journalists. To say 'Guantánamo is a nest of enemy agents' is not only to commit a grand injustice against this city, but also to cede to the enemy a force that it does not have, nor ever will have in this city."[31] Rodríguez insisted that the Havana journalists apologize for denigrating the local community's revolutionary fervor. This exchange is telling, for just as the U.S. national press erased the distinction between Guantánamo and the naval base, so did the Cuban national press. This left local *guantanameros* in a defensive position, one which, after the revolution, was potentially suspect.

The city and people of Guantánamo are at the center of my analysis. Guantánamo could never fully escape its economic reliance on and geographic definition by U.S. military power. The Cuban city grew in size with the expansion of the U.S. base, and its economic fortunes fell when jobs and commercial activity ceased after the Cuban revolution. Still, the distinction between the city and the base is central. To clarify my linguistic choices, I will refer to the U.S. naval base in Guantánamo Bay either by its military acronym, GTMO, or as the U.S. naval base. The city of

Guantánamo will be called "Guantánamo," without the English "city" to qualify it.[32] I do this to recognize that the community deserves recognition on its own terms.

ARCHIVES AND INTERVIEWS

In the pursuit of this project, I have traveled between the United States and Cuba on several occasions. I have leafed through countless U.S. diplomatic cables and reports, and I have sat over coffee with elderly, retired base workers, listening to their stories of work and life in Guantánamo. The range of sources, written and oral, U.S. and Cuban, state-preserved and private papers, illustrates my contention that Guantánamo was a place where diplomats, political leaders, military personnel, and working people interacted and constructed the region's social landscape.

Undertaking a multiarchival approach, I conducted research in Washington DC, Havana, Santiago de Cuba, and Guantánamo. I began by reviewing materials preserved by the U.S. government in the U.S. National Archives (NARA) in Washington DC. These archives yielded U.S. government reports, lengthy descriptions of the military's labor relations, and otherwise unavailable regional newspaper articles and radio broadcasts. My research was aided by state-of-the-art facilities, copy machines, and air-conditioning. In Cuba, I consulted records in the national and regional archives, the provincial libraries' extensive newspaper and periodical collections, and church and mutual aid society records. Almost stalling my research, in Guantánamo, the provincial library was closed to the public and undergoing renovations during my entire stay. Thankfully, the unparalleled understanding of the library staff and the good nature of the security guards allowed me to peruse the newspaper collection as construction workers painted walls and repaired the building.

Along with archival research, I conducted more than a dozen personal interviews with former and current base workers in Cuba.[33] These men and women generously offered detailed information, including wry accounts tinged with nostalgia, humor, and anger regarding their experiences with the U.S. naval base. Like all of Cuba, present-day Guantánamo suffers from food shortages, electric outages, low wages, and minimal government support for elderly retirees. My informants' memories were influenced by their experiences with the Cuban revolution, but just as importantly, their accounts reflected the contemporary hardships and daily struggles of Cuban life forty-five years later. In addition, these interviews were inevitably shaped by my own, foreign presence. I became *la rubia bajita* (the short little blonde woman), knocking on doors and asking for people's time, stories, and trust. The barriers were significant. I was a North American; I was white; I was at least two generations removed; and I was asking questions about the base.

I was cognizant of these divides of race, class, nationality, and age as I conducted my research; however, it was Rosa Johnson, a seventy-eight-year-old woman who alerted me to how much my race and nationality influenced the interviews. Rosa was of West Indian descent, and she spoke fluent English. She was also blind. We had been talking for close to an hour about her job as a maid for an officer's family when she began to discuss the conflicts between Cuban and West Indian domestic servants. Before she spoke, she asked, "Because what color you is, black?" It had never occurred to me that because she was blind, she had been assuming that I was a black U.S. researcher. This was no time for a discussion on the social construction of race, and I quickly responded that I was white. She looked surprised and a bit disappointed. She said the last U.S. academic who had interviewed her was a black North American studying Jamaican descendants in Cuba. She continued, but was concerned about hurting my feelings. As she criticized white U.S. officers' wives, she would add, "Don't get vexed over that. Don't get mad over what I'm telling you."[34]

In spite of these barriers and caveats, most of the men and women I met were willing to sit down and tell me about their experiences on GTMO. I interviewed thirteen men and five women. The eldest was ninety-three and the youngest were in their mid-seventies. Three of the men had been members of Fidel Castro's 26 of July Movement who later left the base because of their revolutionary activity, and two of the men were still commuting and working for the U.S. Navy when I met them.[35]

These interviews reflect the contradictions and ambiguities of memory, and they provide a powerful counterpoint to U.S. and Cuban state narratives.[36] Workers' memories were permeated with ambivalence, and their testimonies were far from univocal. For example, I met a stalwart Communist Party member who was fired for his commitment to the revolution, yet he spoke perfect English and expressed pride and joy in his twenty years on the base. It was a far less overtly "revolutionary" woman who complained she felt stifled by the military rules on the base and disliked the North American presence in Guantánamo. And as in all oral testimony, the present is often as important as the past. Elderly men and women framed their experiences in relationship to their current economic situations. Thus, base workers' testimonies alternately refuted, complemented, and complicated written sources and accounts. And written sources, in turn, refuted, complemented, and complicated individuals' personal memories. Through the interplay of workers' memories alongside archival sources, I hope to invoke the complexities of individuals' choices and options in the fraught political landscape between Guantánamo and GTMO and between empire and revolution.

It is impossible to develop an analysis of Guantánamo, Cuba, without a discussion of the base's early twentieth-century imperial origins. The prologue provides a brief introduction to Guantánamo's regional history, the legal foundations of the U.S. naval base, and the imposition and abrogation of the Platt Amendment.

My narrative proper begins with the preparation for World War II. Chapter 1 investigates the competition for base jobs sparked by the expansion of the military base during the 1940s. World War II marked the U.S. military's newfound reliance on private corporations, and the U.S. government subcontracted the majority of GTMO's construction to the Frederick Snare Corporation. This created a divide between secure, well-paid government positions and insecure, temporary, private hires. As men and women commuted back and forth between Guantánamo and GTMO, divisions between private and public employment and rivalries based on national identity increased the levels of insecurity among the local workforce.

Chapter 2 explores the postwar era in Guantánamo and the role of Cold War politics in pre-Castro Cuba. This chapter examines the formation of a labor union on the base that initially had the blessing of the Cuban Confederation of Workers (CTC) and the American Federation of Labor (AFL). The union prospered because of a convergence of anticommunist unionism in Cuba and the United States, and it collapsed when the base union's leadership militantly defended a worker who was detained on the base without trial. More than the Cuban state, workers desired clarity of their legal status, and the base union demonstrated the strengths and limits of worker agency.

Chapter 3 traces the contours of the Good Neighbor policy in Guantánamo during the 1940s and 1950s. By analyzing prostitution, dancing, and marriages between Cuban women and U.S. men, I explore class and racial divisions within the Guantánamo community and the U.S. military. This chapter also analyzes the gendered and racial experiences of local workers on the base. Through the constant crossings between Guantánamo and GTMO, base workers could also adopt a subversive role. From 1956 through 1958, the 26 of July Movement organized cells within the base. Workers smuggled arms, supplies, and petrol off the base, reportedly with the knowledge of at least low-level U.S. military personnel. This political activity turned the base's military function on its head, and tested just how good a neighbor the United States had become.

Chapter 4 analyzes the consequences of the Cuban revolution on the local population and workforce. Suddenly suspect as possible spies, base workers suffered constant surveillance on both sides of the "cactus curtain." The revolutionary government stigmatized base employees, and U.S. officials questioned the loyalty of their Cuban workforce. Local workers had to choose whether to leave their base jobs, continue commuting, or seek asylum on the base. By narrating this drama in Guantánamo, Cuba, the chapter reframes U.S.-Cuban relations through the anomalous experience of the men and women who depended on both governments.

Chapter 5 explains how the United States replaced the majority of local workers with private, Jamaican contract workers in 1964. No longer able to assert political power over the Cuban government, GTMO officials sought to become independent of Cuban labor and resources. This newfound "independence" still rested on a U.S. neocolonial network, and the U.S. Navy began hiring hundreds of Jamaican contract workers. As private employees, physically removed from their own nations, these workers could not leave the base and had far fewer strategies to negotiate their work lives. In contrast, a small cohort of two to three hundred Cuban workers continued to make the daily commute to GTMO. In 1979, the remaining commuters successfully lobbied the U.S. military and won valuable U.S. pensions. Only base workers who were still employed in 1979 could claim this benefit, but for the first time since the revolution, Cuban workers could retire in Cuba and retain their right to a U.S. pension. Thus, U.S. officials preserved elements from their prerevolutionary neocolonial practices, while they simultaneously restructured the base as a postmodern, deterritorialized workplace.

The epilogue argues that the U.S. naval base in Guantánamo Bay is a harbinger of twenty-first-century U.S. military geography. Workers are still key actors in international relations. Third Country Nationals work as private contractors in GTMO, Iraq, and Afghanistan, and their presence underscores the critical relationship between the military, labor, and empire. GTMO deserves its notoriety as a detention camp, and it also deserves notice for its labor practices before and after the Cuban revolution.

Military bases require more than soldiers and sailors; they also need workers. In Guantánamo, base workers navigated the conflicts between U.S. neocolonialism and Cuban nationalism first-hand. Their decisions, tragedies, and victories were both on the margins of the state and tied to international affairs. They forced the U.S. military to grant consideration to its local workforce, to Guantánamo, and to Cuba. In essence, base workers' journeys between Guantánamo and GTMO embodied how empire *worked* in local men and women's daily lives.

Prologue
Regional Politics, 1898, and
the Platt Amendment

I n 1952 the GTMO base commander wrote, "The naval base is essentially U.S. territory, under the complete jurisdiction and control of the United States. There is no other area like it in Cuba—perhaps not in the world. In a word, it is unique, and therefore requires unique treatment."[1] The U.S. base in Guantánamo Bay may have been unique, but it did not emerge in a vacuum. Instead, it followed years of Spanish colonial neglect in eastern Cuba, as well as the U.S. military's successful invasion in 1898.

Imposing colonial rule, Spain divided Cuba into three provinces: Occidental, Central, and Oriental. Then in 1878 it redivided the island into six provinces with Oriente being the largest. Santiago de Cuba was Oriente's capital and Guantánamo was a smaller provincial city fifty miles farther to the east. In the eighteenth and nineteenth centuries, Spain invested heavily in Havana and in western Cuba's sugar industries; however, it concentrated far fewer resources in the eastern provinces. Although Spanish influence dominated the island, the Guantánamo region also hosted a flood of French colonial elites who had fled the Haitian revolution in the early nineteenth century. These counterrevolutionary Creoles brought their designs for coffee plantations and their commitment to slave labor. This led to a more diverse but less

Figure 1. Early twentieth-century postcard representing local fruit sellers in Guantánamo Bay. Published by H. H. Stratton, Chattanooga, TN.

profitable economy, which included coffee, cattle, and chocolate dispersed among small sugar plantations.[2] One of Cuba's most noted historians, Juan Pérez de la Riva, divided colonial Cuba into two distinct regions: Cuba A (Havana and western Cuba) and Cuba B (Santiago de Cuba, Guantánamo, and eastern Cuba). He attributed Cuba's "extraordinary development" and wealth solely to Cuba A. Moreover, he argued that the eastern provinces were doubly colonized, first by Spain, and then by Havana.[3] From a national perspective, Guantánamo was a marginal region at best.

Guantánamo's proximity to Haiti and its own population of color marked Guantánamo and Oriente as a distinctly "darker" region in the national imagination. Eastern Cuba as a whole has been characterized as "Caribbean," a not-so-subtle reference to its black population, as opposed to Havana's "European" and presumably whiter culture.[4] For example, a U.S. diplomat compared Santiago de Cuba to Havana: "Havana is all right, but Santiago is as different from Havana in environment as night is from day, and I believe I can say the same about the color of a large majority of the people."[5] In mid-nineteenth-century Guantánamo, slavery dominated the local economy. Slaves comprised 44.5 percent of Guantánamo's population, and free people of color accounted for an additional 28 percent. Thus, people of color were a majority in Guantánamo.[6]

In 1868, Cuban Creoles began a ten-year military campaign for Cuban independence, which left the Spanish state weakened, but in power.[7] Insurgents challenged Spain again in 1879 in *La Guerra Chiquita,* and yet again in the 1895–98 War of Independence. The black Cuban population, both enslaved and free, served as the base of the Liberation Army in Oriente, often provoking racial anxieties among white Cuban Creoles nervous about the future complexion of the nation. The Liberation Army promoted men of color into leadership positions, most famously, Antonio Maceo, Flor Crombert, and Guillermo Moncada. Despite Spanish propaganda and the resistance of Oriente elites, this multiracial Liberation Army gained strength and won military victories, building toward an independent Cuba. This revolutionary spirit was not just one of rhetoric, but arguably engendered a popular consensus in eastern Cuba for the inclusion of black Cubans into the civic body, along with the promotion of women's rights and collective land ownership.[8]

Fundamentally changing the political equation, the United States entered the Cuban War of Independence and rechristened it the Spanish-American War.[9] U.S. marines landed in Guantánamo Bay on June 10, 1898, and raised the first U.S. flag on Cuban soil. The *New York Times* boldly proclaimed, "Our Flag Flies at Guantánamo," ignoring more than thirty years of Cuban battles and heralding the "first successful landing of the war."[10] From this incipient moment, the history of Guantánamo Bay became entangled with U.S. military power. There are hints of the U.S. Navy's acquisitive desire even at the outset. Within days of the initial U.S. invasion, the *New York Times* reported that "the fine harbor there [Guantánamo] will make a good American base."[11] The U.S. Navy maintained its enthusiasm for Guantánamo Bay in the weeks following Spain's defeat, and it "advocate[d] the retention by the United States of this bay [Guantánamo] as a permanent naval base."[12]

As many historians have documented, the U.S. military deftly leapfrogged over the Cuban Liberation Army and prevented its general, Calixto Garcia, from entering Santiago de Cuba to accept Spain's surrender. Instead, Spain handed its colony over to the United States rather than grant Cuba independence. In this manner, the United States erased more than thirty years of Cuban struggle and disingenuously positioned itself as Cuba's liberator.[13] The dominant ideology of the era precluded acceptance of Cuban independence or multiracial democracy. The U.S. press depicted the men and women who fought for independence, the *mambises,* as simple, barbaric, and black. For example, the *New York*

Figure 2. "Hoisting the Flag at Guantánamo, June 12, 1898." Library of Congress, Prints and Photographs Division, Detroit Publishing Company Collection, LC-D4–21495.

Times described the long-fighting Cuban soldiers as "the little black Cuban warriors" who "waved their machetes and howled curses at the Spanish in savage fashion." Yet military realities also forced the U.S. military to adopt a grudging respect. Although the marines "were inclined to discount them, this morning they spoke enthusiastically of the auxiliaries [Cuban *mambises*] for their daring." By the end, "the little black warriors . . . proved their worth."[14] These vivid tropes of civilization and savagery complicated the U.S. imperial role. The United States could not allow Cuba to be independent, but neither could it completely deny the Cuban role in the victory against Spain. An even more delicate problem, it could not embrace Cuba's "little black warriors" nor integrate them into U.S. politics. This contradiction extended to Guantánamo, where even as the U.S. naval officers were eyeing Guantánamo Bay, they wanted little to do with Guantánamo, Cuba. In referring to the risk of tropical illness for U.S. marines, the officers reported that "with proper sanitary precautions, there need be no fear of sickness, and it is evident that sickness among the resident population in the cities near here [Caimanera and Guantánamo] is mainly due to the lack of sanitary precautions and the filthiness of the natives."[15] Thus, the U.S. officers imagined the possibility of possessing Guantánamo Bay without possessing *guantanameros*.[16]

After Spain's defeat, the United States gained military control and governed Cuba from 1899 to 1902. From the outset the Cuban population, from elites to the popular classes, protested U.S. military occupation and demanded independence. The United States was in a neocolonial bind because, before entering the war against Spain, the Senate had attached the 1898 Teller Amendment to President McKinley's request for military action. The Teller Amendment had specifically eschewed formal annexation and prohibited permanent U.S. rule over Cuba. At the same time, U.S. leaders feared an independent Cuba that was not subservient to U.S. interests. To solve this conundrum, the United States presented Cuba with the Platt Amendment, a U.S.-written platform that fundamentally compromised Cuban sovereignty. The Platt Amendment enabled the U.S. military to invade Cuba whenever it believed it necessary to "preserve" Cuban independence and restore stability. It limited Cuba's ability to make treaties with foreign governments, prevented the Cuban government from acquiring debt, and insisted Cuba maintain the sanitation programs the United States had imposed. It also required a U.S. naval base in Cuba: "That to enable the United States to maintain the independence of Cuba, and to protect the people thereof, as well as for its own defense, the government of Cuba will sell or lease to the United States land necessary for coaling or naval stations at certain specified points, to be agreed upon with the president of the United States."[17]

The United States recognized a Cuban constitutional committee, but insisted that it would not grant Cuba formal independence without the new Cuban government's acceptance of the Platt Amendment. Not surprisingly, the Cuban public widely rejected the Platt Amendment as an affront to its decades-long nationalist struggle. The United States remained adamant: It would not withdraw unless Cuba incorporated the Platt Amendment into its constitution. In this manner, the U.S. government devised a legalistic formula whereby it continued to exercise military and economic control over Cuba without formally governing it. On June 12, 1901, the constitutional delegates voted to accept the Platt Amendment, sixteen to eleven, with four abstentions. The vast majority of the "no" votes came from Oriente.[18] These opposition votes may have been rooted in the stronger *independista* spirit in Oriente, but they were also a vote against the U.S. naval base, which would be a physical as well as symbolic injury to the region.[19]

On May 20, 1902, the United States military withdrew from Cuba, and Tomás Estrada Palma became the first president of Cuba. Estrada

Palma now had the task of implementing the Platt Amendment and designating territory for the U.S. coaling and naval stations. He negotiated that Cuban land would be "leased," not "sold," but this legal distinction merely constituted a neocolonial linguistic trick that did not effectively limit U.S. power.[20] In his work on early twentieth-century naval history, Richard Challener suggests that Cuba's elite sacrificed Guantánamo's sovereignty to save Havana's.[21] The United States had lobbied hard for a military base in Havana so as to be in range of Cuba's political capital. Not surprisingly, the provisional Cuban government was "dead set against yielding a base at Havana."[22] In contrast, Guantánamo Bay was in the hinterlands. Its deep, protected harbor and strategic position within the Caribbean was attractive to the U.S. Navy, even if its location within Cuba was not. In the end, the Estrada Palma government sanctioned two U.S. military bases, yielding control over Bahía Honda in the west and Guantánamo Bay in the east. In many ways, it was Guantánamo Bay's peripheral location that allowed the United States to maintain its grip so firmly over this maritime port.

The 1903 Lease Agreement between the United States and Cuba spelled out the United States' subsequent control over Guantánamo Bay. The lease granted the U.S. military forty-five square miles, including the mouth of Guantánamo Bay and territory to its east and west. The United States also gained complete jurisdiction. "While on the one hand the United States recognizes the continuance of the ultimate sovereignty of the Republic of Cuba over the above described areas of land and water, on the other hand the Republic of Cuba consents that during the period of the occupation by the United States of said areas under the terms of this agreement the United States shall exercise complete jurisdiction and control over and within said areas."[23] It was with this statement that the semantics of "ultimate sovereignty" and "complete jurisdiction and control" were established in opposition. According to this legal invention, a territory could be under the ultimate sovereignty of one nation, but a second nation could have complete jurisdiction and control over the same territory. The United States also agreed to pay Cuba the nominal sum of two thousand dollars in gold coin a year, to construct a fence along the base's boundary, and to prevent commercial or industrial enterprises from within the base. Finally, it established guidelines for extradition if Cuban fugitives sought refuge on the naval base, or if North Americans attempted to escape Cuban law. Significantly, Cuban politicians recognized the base for the embarrassment it was, and they quietly boycotted the official ceremony. Even the *New*

York Times admitted, "Nobody is anxious to appear conspicuously in the turnover."[24]

A termination date was noticeably absent from the lease. In fact, no date was written into the lease at all. This omission has led to confusion and, over the years, both Cuban and North American writers have mistakenly assumed the lease ended after ninety-nine years. For example, in June 1959 *La Voz del Pueblo* critiqued anti-American sentiments in Guantánamo and justified the treaty's validity for ninety-nine years.[25] More recently, a Canadian journalist reiterated that the lease lasted for ninety-nine years.[26] Even the Cuban Communist Party's Historical Committee in Guantánamo mistakenly stated that the treaty was signed for one hundred years.[27] The absence of an end date magnified the United States' power over GTMO. As one GTMO commander admitted, "In the annals of leases between two sovereign nations, there is probably no lease in which the terms are so favorable to the lessee and the rights granted so complete as at Guantánamo Bay."[28]

GTMO provided the U.S. military with mobility, flexibility, and power inside Cuba and throughout the Caribbean. In Cuba, the most brutal example occurred in 1912, when Cuban veterans of color formed the Independent Party of Color (PIC) and demanded greater black representation in the Cuban government.[29] Although never gaining a significant electoral base, the PIC mobilized in Oriente. The United States threatened to invade if the Cuban government, under President José Miguel Gómez, did not crack down on black protest and protect U.S. property. The *New York Times* reported, "Bands of discontented negroes are stealing and pillaging small stores. . . . The orders are out to show the negroes no mercy."[30] Although to this point no U.S. property had been touched, seven U.S. battleships patrolled Cuba's southeastern coast, and approximately 1500 marines entered and occupied Guantánamo, ostensibly to protect U.S. economic interests.[31] This program was a deliberate one of intimidation: "A thousand bluejackets will impress the negroes with the fact that the power of the United States is near by, and that further acts of lawlessness on their part will lead to their ultimate punishment." The *New York Times* continued, "The sailors will be given liberal shore leave so that the negroes as they come into the towns to get supplies may see them and carry back word to their associates that the forces of 'North Americanos' have arrived and are on the alert."[32] Along with the "negro rebels," the Cuban government also took notice of the U.S. troops. The U.S. military presence signaled that if the Cuban government did not crack down on insurgents, the U.S. military would. To prevent U.S. intervention and to demonstrate the Cuban state's authority, President Gómez sanctioned a brutal repression. The Cuban Army proceeded to massacre between 2,000 and 5,000 black Cubans in eastern Cuba. The official Cuban Army casualties numbered only sixteen.[33] The U.S. military had encouraged this excessive violence, and it resonated with the tolerated racial terror in the U.S. South in the same era.

The U.S. marines were not the only North Americans in eastern Cuba. U.S.-owned sugar companies, such as the Cuban American Sugar Company, the United Fruit Company, and the Guantánamo Sugar Company, invested heavily and dominated the geographic and economic landscape in Cuba's eastern provinces. In 1902 Oriente and Camagüey produced only 15 percent of Cuban sugar; by 1924 the proportion had increased to 54 percent.[34] These beacons to U.S. economic wealth defined a region populated by Cuban and West Indian sugar workers. U.S. plantations and company towns represented the economic might of U.S. neocolonialism and, like the base, resulted in enclaves, separate, yet within Cuba.[35]

This capital investment demanded labor. With a booming sugar economy in the 1920s, close to three hundred thousand migrant workers from Haiti, Jamaica, Barbados, and the smaller West Indian islands flocked to Cuba for economic opportunities on U.S.-owned sugar plantations in Camagüey, Holguín, Santiago de Cuba, and Guantánamo.[36] Cuban immigration policies in the early twentieth century encouraged white Spanish workers while limiting entrance to West Indian workers. By privileging Spaniards over West Indians, the Cuban government made its preference clear in its hope to "whiten" the population. It was only after intense lobbying by U.S. companies, which desired steady access to migrant workers, that the Cuban government lifted restrictions against West Indian migration in 1913.[37] Thus, black West Indian and Haitian migrants entered Cuba's historically contested racial topography as cheap labor for U.S. economic interests. British West Indian migrants also worked in disproportionate numbers on the U.S. naval base.[38] This served to further "color" Guantánamo black in the Cuban political imagination. As a result, Cubans often conflated blackness with West Indian migrants, erasing the reality that many Cuban citizens were also people of color. Despite the falseness in this distinction, popular discourse and racial antagonism coded Caribbean migrants as black and damaged the possibility of coalitions between working-class Cubans and migrants.

GTMO's legal status was not an issue again until 1934. In 1933 in the midst of the Great Depression, a popular movement toppled Gerardo Machado's repressive government. After strikes, protests, and a "Sergeants' Revolt" led by Fulgencio Batista, the civilian leader Ramón Grau San Martín became the head of a provisional revolutionary government. In this moment of change, Grau San Martín instituted a reformist and nationalist agenda. He unilaterally abrogated the hated Platt Amendment. He also issued a set of decrees, including women's suffrage, labor protections, and lower utility rates. The United States feared that these measures would be hostile to its economic and political interests and refused to recognize Grau San Martín's government. Rather than plan a U.S. military invasion, U.S. Ambassador Sumner Welles encouraged Batista to throw his weight behind the revolutionary government's opponents. In January 1934, Batista orchestrated a coup, placing Colonel Carlos Mendieta at the head of the civilian government, while he maintained control over the military. The United States immediately recognized this new government. Sumner Welles's artful manipulation of Cuban domestic politics underscored President Franklin D. Roosevelt's new strategy in Latin America, the Good Neighbor policy. With power concentrated in its economic investments, the United States shifted from the precedent of military invasion under Woodrow Wilson's watch to a policy of intervention through diplomatic and economic channels.[39]

By May 1934, the U.S. government accepted Grau San Martín's abrogation of the Platt Amendment and formally annulled it. However, the United States also renegotiated and maintained its lease over the naval station in Guantánamo Bay. From the Roosevelt administration's point of view, the Platt Amendment was no longer worth the acrimony it aroused in the Cuban population. As the *New York Times* explained, "The Platt Amendment has become a stone of stumbling and a rock of offense not only to Cubans but to many Central and South Americans. To make an end of it is an act of wise policy."[40] In Cuba, this was a moment of celebration. The Santiago de Cuba press announced "[t]he Platt Amendment has died" and reported on the capital's festivities, fireworks, and military bands.[41] Understated in this triumphant moment was the maintenance of the U.S. naval base in Guantánamo Bay. Havana's conservative and often pro-American newspaper, *Diario de la Marina*, minimized this remaining exception to Cuba's sovereignty. It reported briefly that the U.S. naval base in Guantánamo was the only component of the Platt Amendment to remain in force, "but absolutely all the rest, including the coaling station in the Bahía Honda, disappear today."[42] After thirty years of delayed sovereignty, the remaining U.S. military presence in Guantánamo was not the point to emphasize. In Guantánamo, the leading newspaper, La Voz del Pueblo, seemed to concur. In contrast to Havana's reported jubilation, the Guantánamo press was at best subdued in reporting the "death of the Platt Amendment." Although there was a perfunctory article about its abolition, La Voz del Pueblo did not mention the U.S. naval base at all.[43] The silence was telling. For the men and women who lived in Guantánamo very little had changed. The symbolic political victory was minor given the base's tangible, ongoing presence and the city's reliance on the base for jobs, North American tourism, and commerce.

In 1934 the United States renegotiated the 1903 Lease Agreement, and the resulting treaty cemented U.S. authority over the naval station. First, the 1934 agreement continued all of the policies and conditions from the 1903 accords. Second, it added a clause that enabled either government to "suspend communications" due to contagious diseases in the region. Third, and most importantly, it articulated a formula whereby Cuba could never force the United States to leave its territory unilaterally: "So long as the United States of America shall not abandon the said naval station of Guantánamo or the two Governments shall not agree to a modification of its present limits, the station shall continue to have the territorial area that it now has."[44] With these words, the United States' unfettered control was inscribed into the 1934 Lease Agreement. Again, there was no date for termination or for renewed negotiations.

This treaty provides the legal framework that, according to the United States, still governs the base. As Rear Admiral Marion Emerson Murphy succinctly stated in 1952, "For all practical purposes, [GTMO] is American territory. Under the foregoing agreements, the United States has for approximately fifty years exercised the essential elements of sovereignty over this territory, without actually owning it."[45]

1

The Case of Kid Chicle
Military Expansion and Labor Competition,
1939–1945

In December 1940, Lino Rodríguez Grenot decided to try his luck on the base. A boxer known as "Kid Chicle," Rodríguez was twenty-seven years old, black, and unemployed. Born in Santiago de Cuba, he lived a marginal existence in Guantánamo. He supported himself by boxing whenever he could, but he was just as likely to be selling lottery tickets and trinkets in the streets. In the only known photo of Rodríguez, he wore a panama hat and a white suit with a jaunty pocket handkerchief. He stared at the camera in a self-conscious projection of youthful ambition and style. With the surge in World War II military construction, there were thousands of new jobs on the U.S. military base, and Lino Rodríguez wanted one.[1]

In Caimanera, Rodríguez's best hope for work was with the Frederick Snare Corporation, a private company that had won the U.S. government contract to enlarge the base. At first, the Snare Corporation had ferried workers back and forth between Caimanera's docks and GTMO on its own private launches, but job competition and barely suppressed violence made this untenable. Frustrated, unemployed workers had jumped onto the boats and even attacked a Snare operator, creating disruptions and "unmanageable conditions." To alleviate the situation and ensure a steady stream of laborers, the U.S. Navy decided to assist the

Snare Corporation. It agreed to carry workers on a "Navy boat manned by two unarmed marines with the [U.S.] colors flying."[2]

On December 17, Lt. Kenneth M. West was the ranking officer on the ferry. Lt. West had previously worked for the sugar behemoth, the United Fruit Company in eastern Cuba. The navy placed him in charge of transporting workers for the Snare Corporation "due to his experiences in Cuba." The navy and the Snare Corporation also required all workers to obtain a special pass before they could enter the base. Like many hopeful workers, Rodríguez arrived in Caimanera without the coveted pass, and so he waited jobless on the docks.

On this December day, Lt. West selected twenty-nine men on the wharf to work on the base.[3] Angry that they had not been chosen, more than four hundred unemployed men reportedly rushed at Lt. West. Quickly, Lt. West led his contingent to a privately owned dock several hundred feet away and helped his chosen workers onboard. Lino Rodríguez stood nearby and observed the workers entering the launch. He seized his chance. Unauthorized, he leapt into the boat, presumably believing he could force his way onto the base without a pass and gain a job on his own merits. Lt. West did not welcome the intruder. As the launch pulled away from the dock, he struck Rodríguez with a "blackjack" and threw him out of the boat. Rodríguez fell into the bay and died.

Rodríguez's death spurred public outrage and unprecedented protests against the naval base throughout eastern Cuba. The crime had taken place in Guantánamo Bay, and hundreds of workers on the docks had witnessed it.[4] After several men fished his corpse out of the water, local unions and the Communist Party argued that Lt. West must be tried for murder in Cuban territory. Rodríguez's family came forward, and his aunt expressed her desire to see justice done under Cuban law. Workers wore black arm bands in protest; locals marched to the cemetery and demanded justice; and several newspapers predicted there might be a strike.[5]

Guantanameros maintained that Lt. West's blow killed Lino Rodríguez. Drowning might imply that some of the fault lay with Rodríguez and relieve Lt. West of culpability. Four Guantánamo doctors performed an autopsy and concluded that Rodríguez's lungs were not filled with water. Therefore, they ruled out drowning as the cause of death.[6] Not surprisingly, U.S. officials did not accept this conclusion, and they insisted Rodríguez had "drown[ed] under regrettable circumstances."[7] Regardless, beaten or drowned, Rodríguez's death was tragic.

Given the local outrage, the U.S. Navy's principal objective was to keep any lawsuit out of the Cuban court system. Acting Secretary of the Navy James Forrestal believed it would be impossible to conduct a "reasonable and fair trial" in Santiago de Cuba or Guantánamo.[8] To avert a Cuban trial, U.S. officials parsed the scene of the crime in dispute, distinguishing between the bay and the boat. According to the 1903 and 1934 lease agreements, the waters in Guantánamo Bay remained under Cuban jurisdiction. About this, there was no dispute. However, the U.S. Navy argued that the scene of the incident was the boat, not the bay, and that U.S. law governed U.S. vessels. Through this logic, the United States argued that the U.S. legal system had jurisdiction over Lt. West. From the capital in Havana, the Cuban Ministerio de Justicia agreed that crimes committed on foreign ships remained within the jurisdiction of the foreign nation.[9] The U.S. ambassador noted that the Cuban government "had taken a very correct attitude" by allowing the United States to handle the matter.[10] The consequent U.S. court-martial tried Lt. West for "involuntary manslaughter" and "conduct to the prejudice of good order and discipline." He was found not guilty.[11]

In Guantánamo, the case of Kid Chicle captured the desperation of unemployed workers, the precariousness of crossing *la frontera* (the border), and the unchecked power of the U.S. military. The story of Lino Rodríguez embodied the anxieties and competition for World War II–era workers. His death also revealed the growing chasm between government and private base employment and Guantánamo's complex social fabric. As the U.S. military geared up for World War II, the Guantánamo region acted as a border between civilian and military zones, between government and private sectors, between North American and Cuban cultures, and even between Caribbean national groups. Lino Rodríguez was just one of thousands of workers who migrated to Guantánamo and hoped to take advantage of GTMO's growth.

WORLD WAR II, NAVAL POWER, AND GUANTÁNAMO BAY

During World War II the U.S. militarized the Caribbean, creating a defensive perimeter that would outlast the German threat and solidify U.S. power in the region. Since the 1934 Lease Agreement, the United States had not significantly modified its force or its mission at GTMO. World War II changed that. In a 1938 report written under the shadow of European and Japanese mobilization, the U.S. Navy conducted an extensive survey of its bases in the United States and its territories. The report clearly predicted an emergency and the need for military preparedness on a global scale. Although the Caribbean was far from the anticipated theater of war, the naval officers maintained that GTMO would increase in strategic importance. Atlantic outlying possessions offered key facilities for training and maintenance. GTMO was earmarked as an "intermediate station between the Panama Canal and stations to the east."[12] World War II became the turning point in the U.S. Navy's commitment to GTMO.

In 1939 the U.S. military began actively demonstrating its naval superiority in the Caribbean, staging large, dramatic, and extensive war games between Cuba and Puerto Rico. Headlines like "Navy to Build Up Atlantic Squadron," "Navy Board Urges 41 Defense Bases for Entire Nation," and "Congress to Vote Navy Equal to Any," heralded the growing commitment to U.S. mobilization.[13] On the editorial page, the *New York Times* lamented that the U.S. bases in Key West, Guantánamo Bay, and Puerto Rico had been ignored for too long, and it stressed that the Caribbean was now more strategically significant than it had been since 1898.[14] The U.S. naval expansion would have short- and long-term consequences for the Caribbean. In the immediate future, it meant rapid military construction, an increased U.S. military presence, and Latin American nations' participation, even if marginally, in World War II. For the long-term, it meant an established and developed U.S. naval force that could monitor the Western Hemisphere. As retired Rear Admiral Yates Stirling Jr. commented in 1940, "It is gratifying that the United States at last is learning of the vital necessity for bases in strategically important defense areas. . . . Naval bases for warships and airplanes in Guantánamo, Puerto Rico, Jamaica, together with those in the Lesser Antilles would enable the United States to command the Caribbean and maintain a watchful eye over the north coast of South America whose great oil production makes it vital that we permit no enemy to gain a foothold."[15] Rear Admiral Stirling connected the war against Germany and the protection of oil in South America with the underlining presumption that the U.S. military presence would continue after the war. Yet before the United States could execute this plan, it needed to modernize its navy and prepare for the immediate fight.

In 1939 President Roosevelt monitored the massive war games being staged in the Caribbean on board the USS *Houston*. In a mock battle, 150 warships carrying sixty thousand officers and enlisted men practiced maneuvers from the eastern seaboard to northern Brazil with the largest concentration of U.S. ships in Guantánamo Bay.[16] The sheer number of military personnel stationed at GTMO created a spectacle of U.S. power. After the war games, U.S. ships welcomed a small contingent of the Santiago de Cuba Lion's Club to visit and admire the fleet. As a local *santi-aguerro* journalist recounted, "We went over to the ship in groups and admired the high technology, the power of these machines, and their defensive weapons."[17] The navy may have impressed the Santiago Lion's Club, but it was still not prepared to fight a war in two oceans.

Over the next two years, the U.S. government invested heavily in the U.S. Navy, and its installations in the Caribbean were no exception. In 1939 the U.S. Congress granted $89,478,000 for expanding existing naval stations. This budget increased exponentially as the war in Europe intensified. The First Supplemental National Defense Appropriation Act of 1941 added more than one billion dollars to the army and navy's yearly budgets, and the Second Supplemental National Defense Appropriation Act of 1941 requested nearly five billion more. By the end of the war, the Bureau of Yards and Docks had spent an unprecedented $9,250,000,000.[18] Through the Lend-Lease Agreement with the United Kingdom, the United States provided fifty destroyers in exchange for military bases in Britain's Caribbean colonies, including Trinidad, Jamaica, Bermuda, St. Lucia, the Bahamas, and Antigua. By connecting bases in Guantánamo Bay, Puerto Rico, the British Lend-Lease bases, and the Panama Canal Zone, the United States fashioned a formidable chain of bases throughout the Caribbean.

Under President Batista, the Cuban government became a staunch ally against the Axis powers. In response to Pearl Harbor, the Cuban Congress declared war against Japan on December 9, and war against Germany on December 11, 1941. Throughout World War II, the United States and Cuba signed nine military agreements and, in addition to GTMO, the United States gained access to air bases in San Antonio, San Julián, and Pinar del Rio. Its rights to these bases extended for six months after the formal conclusion of World War II, and the United States returned them to Cuba in 1946. In return for this cooperation, the United States agreed to purchase Cuban sugar at fixed rates, which profited Cuban growers. Batista also negotiated a twenty-five million dollar U.S. loan for public works. The U.S. Navy believed it too could gain long-term benefits from wartime conditions, and it proposed extending GTMO's boundaries to include additional territory and exclusive control over the Yateras River (the source of GTMO's water supply). The Cuban government had been willing to contemplate a cooperative defense zone with joint control, but it was unwilling to discuss a unilateral U.S. plan. After more than a year of negotiations, the navy dropped its request and GTMO's borders remained fixed at their original points.[19]

During World War II, GTMO served three main military functions: (1) it belonged to the network of Atlantic bases that protected merchant ships and the Atlantic from German U-Boat attacks; (2) it provided an ample training ground for U.S. sailors and marines; and (3) it offered entertainment, recreation, and a bit of debauchery far from direct combat.

Throughout the war, German U-Boats targeted U.S. merchant ships delivering crucial supplies to Great Britain. Although the North Atlantic was the central stage for these conflicts, U.S. Navy and Coast Guard convoys also patrolled the eastern coast and the Caribbean. From 1942 to 1943, Germany sent U-Boats to the Caribbean to stifle shipping and supplies originating in Latin America. This campaign was more successful than is often acknowledged and, in 1942, 36 percent of all allied merchant ship losses occurred in the Caribbean.[20] The risk of German U-Boat attacks loomed large in the U.S. Navy's early planning, and GTMO became a key base in this defense.

As the war progressed and the risks to the Atlantic decreased, GTMO became a central training ground where military personnel prepared for combat as they waited for deployment to Europe or the Pacific. Training officer Colonel Bernard Dubel insisted, "The lads . . . are anxious to go places where there's more action," and gain the glory of Guadalcanal, Wake Island, Guam, and Midway.[21] GTMO became known as a tropical paradise, where sailors could jump off cliffs, splash into the water, drink rum, and play baseball far from the risks of war.[22] The military's increased size also meant that there were more U.S. sailors and marines in Guantánamo than ever before. U.S. officers socialized with Guantánamo's elite, and the influx of military personnel resulted in substantial profits for merchants and restaurant proprietors in the region. Through ongoing social and commercial ties, Guantánamo's political economy became firmly tied to the base.

GUANTÁNAMO'S SOCIAL LANDSCAPE: COMMERCE, THE *ZAFRA*, AND THE BASE

Guantánamo never approached the same level of wealth or cultural prestige as Havana or Santiago de Cuba. However, its proximity to the base resulted in an aggressive commercial class that defined Guantánamo's elite. The local press referred to this community as *las fuerzas vivas*, or the city's "vibrant forces." They became the public spokespeople in Guantánamo who advocated for public works, improved sanitation, and greater national investment in Guantánamo's tourist potential.[23]

Sugar and coffee plantation owners and administrators would have held the highest positions in Guantánamo's class structure, but their numbers were small. For example, William G. Osment was born in England, traveled to the United States in the late nineteenth century, and enlisted in the U.S. Army to fight in the Spanish-American War. After the war, this Anglo-North American became the vice president and director of the U.S.-owned Guantánamo and Western Railroad Company. Osment was known as a "lavish entertainer" in Guantánamo.[24] The Guantánamo Sugar Company was also a U.S. corporation, and the chief administrator, William Crosby, occupied an equally powerful position in town. U.S. businesspeople involved with the sugar industry, along with U.S. naval officials, added a North American element to Guantánamo's upper classes.

In contrast, Guantánamo's *fuerzas vivas* were overwhelmingly Cuban. They were hotel owners, restaurateurs, café proprietors, and beer, rum, and soft drink distributors. In 1939 there were already 150 eating and drinking establishments.[25] Antonio Jané Civit, the president of Guantánamo's tourist bureau; José "Pepito" Alvarez, a prominent club owner; and Alfredo Oslé Correa, a promoter for better roads, were all leading members of the *fuerzas vivas*. These ambitious men and women socialized with U.S. officials, maintained close contacts with North American customers, and depended on U.S. dollars for their prosperity. They also welcomed liberty parties and remarked on the uninhibited, carefree, and spendthrift ways of the U.S. sailors and marines. They called these men *francos,* possibly stemming from the term *día franco,* or day off. Moreover, the Guantánamo commercial elite depended on the *francos* to spend money in local bars, clubs, and less reputable establishments. The *fuerzas vivas* included members of the Union Club, the Colonia Español, Block Cataluña, the Lion's Club, the Rotary Club, and later the United Service Organization (USO). These key organizations were where Guantánamo's elite socialized and did business. The *fuerzas vivas* also advocated for better public health standards and infrastructure in Guantánamo and Caimanera. From their perspective, more hospitable conditions for U.S. military personnel equaled greater prosperity for Guantánamo.

Cuban social clubs were segregated by race and nationality, and the prominent civic organizations accepted white Cuban and Spanish members. Cubans of color belonged to a parallel set of organizations, including Siglo XX, Club Moncada, and La Nueva Era, but these societies did not play an equivalent role in Guantánamo's commercial structure.[26]

Guantánamo's West Indian and Chinese members established yet another tier of nationally and racially based mutual aid societies, such as the Masonic Lodge, the West Indian Democratic Association, La Nueva China, and Hoy Yui Kong Sol.[27] These organizations fostered a middle-class sensibility that veered away from political activism. Many of the West Indians worked on the U.S. naval base or in other service occupations, and most Chinese were small business owners, running restaurants, cafés, and laundries.

Guantánamo's working class included white Cubans, Cubans of color, West Indians, and Haitians, all who predominantly worked in the sugar industry. Before World War II, the Guantánamo Sugar Company and the United Fruit Company were the dominant employers in the region. For example, the Guantánamo Sugar Company hired 4500 workers during the *zafra* (harvest) and 2000 during the *tiempo de muerto* (dead period).[28] These jobs offered irregular, seasonal employment and were marked by their brutal physicality. In addition, U.S.-controlled plantations existed as self-sufficient enclaves almost entirely "outside and above [Cuban] law."[29]

During World War II, GTMO opened up thousands of new opportunities. For workers accustomed to the neocolonial control of U.S. sugar companies, the leap to employment on the U.S. military installation may not have been particularly great. GTMO could be seen as just one more branch of the United States' political and economic control in the region.[30] Moreover, U.S. government jobs on GTMO often appeared more attractive than the sugar *centrales*. GTMO offered security, steadier wages, and a level of prestige. Men and women who worked on the base were part of the "aristocracy of labor."[31] As a result, with the sudden increase in base employment, workers throughout the country traveled to Guantánamo and Caimanera in search of these jobs. What they did not know was that the U.S. Navy had subcontracted the majority of new construction work to the Frederick Snare Corporation.

PASSES, LAUNCHES, AND THE FREDERICK SNARE CORPORATION

The rapid development and growth of the U.S. naval base was a joint effort of the U.S. Navy and its private-sector partner, the Frederick Snare Corporation. The navy granted the Snare Corporation a U.S. government contract and with that delegated authority over the majority of the workforce. At the same time, the navy was more than willing to assist the Snare Corporation with materials, labor, and security information.

With this hedging of responsibility, the navy's reliance on the Snare Corporation raised the question of accountability in public-private enterprises.

Prior to World War II, the United States had relied on private companies in Guantánamo, but on a small scale and at least nominally under Cuban jurisdiction. For example, GTMO lacked its own water supply, and the dry, almost desert-like conditions in the region made it impossible for the base to be self-sufficient. The base relied on water from the nearby Yateras River outside its borders. After experimenting with water delivered by train, the United States initiated a competition for an aqueduct. To minimize complications with Cuban law and governance, the United States insisted that the aqueduct could only transport water to the base; it could not service any of the surrounding Cuban communities. The United States rejected outright a bid from the Guantánamo municipal government, which had hoped to use the U.S. contract to improve local public health and access to clean drinking water. Instead, the U.S. Navy granted the contract to Henri Schueg Chassin, based in the Bacardi Company in 1938.[32] This created a precedent whereby a private entity within Cuba worked solely for the U.S. Navy on Cuban soil.

With the urgent need to develop GTMO, the United States again turned to a private corporation. This policy was part of a much larger pattern whereby the federal government increased its reliance on private business during World War II. Under President Roosevelt and Secretary of War Henry Stimson, the U.S. government entered more than 7,400 private contracts to expedite military construction. These contracts cost more than fifty times the equivalent World War I–era ones and signaled the extent to which the federal government allied itself with corporate capital.[33] In the rush to war, the U.S. government entered an unprecedented number of "cost-plus" contracts. Under "cost-plus," each company would recoup their entire "cost," and then receive an additional "plus" for profit, thereby creating an incentive for corporations to participate in the military build-up. Stimson argued the private sector needed a guaranteed profit. The military situation necessitated immediate action and stimulation, regardless of the price.[34]

The U.S. Navy awarded the Frederick Snare Corporation government contract NOy-4162 to expand GTMO's facilities, and over the next five years it spent thirty-four million dollars. At its peak, the Snare Corporation employed 9,000 local workers, and the U.S. Navy employed an additional 4,000 civil service employees. In his *History of Guantánamo Bay*, Admiral Murphy wrote, "The history of Contract NOy-4162 is virtually the history of the World War II buildup of Guantánamo Bay."[35] The prominence of the Snare Corporation elevated the role of a private, nongovernment employer on the base.

The Frederick Snare Corporation was a U.S.-owned company that operated in New York, Havana, Buenos Aires, and the Panama Canal Zone. It constructed much of early Havana's infrastructure, including highways and the national baseball stadium. Frederick Snare was a well-known figure in Havana's social scene and, according to *Time,* "Father Snare" changed the "mores of Havana's better classes." Most notably, he designed the Havana Country Club, which contained Cuba's first golf course and "the most lavish and expensive swimming pool in any Caribbean country." He was the president of the country club until 1946.[36] Already established in Cuba, the Snare Corporation could quickly shift its operations east and modernize the base. The U.S. Ambassador to Cuba George S. Messersmith described the relationship between the U.S. Navy and the Snare Corporation as "desirable." He had confidence the company's familiarity with Cuba would make it well suited to the challenge.[37]

Between 1940 and 1943, the Snare Corporation's presence on the base was massive and unprecedented. Snare built a new self-contained Marine Corps base, new airfields on McCalla Hill and Leeward Point, ninety-two magazines, and a variety of social and recreational facilities, including a chapel and a school. Efficiency was critical, and military and private materials became indistinguishable. As Admiral Murphy recorded, "Due to the speed with which construction was begun, the contractors had no opportunity to make preliminary preparation; therefore all available equipment of the station was turned over to the Frederick Snare Corporation for their use."[38] In the expediency of war, the Snare Corporation occupied a newly defined niche between private and public entities, which allowed the U.S. Navy to erase, or emphasize, this distinction as it best served U.S. interests.

The United States granted the Snare Corporation broad leeway in its employment practices and recognized that it would employ thousands of local workers. This created a two-tier workforce where the U.S. Navy offered permanent employment at steady wages, even as the Snare Corporation paid workers much less for temporary jobs. Lino Lemes García, a local journalist, reported, "There are more than two thousand men working on the base today, some are working for the [U.S.] administration and the others for the Frederick Snare Corporation. Those working directly for the [U.S.] government are earning a higher daily wage and are paid in U.S. dollars."[39] Snare jobs were also time-sensitive, construction-related, and short-term. As a result, many men and women gained employment for a brief time, to be laid off and then rehired later. Cuban workers quickly recognized that U.S. government civil service positions came with far better benefits and salaries than the more temporary, contract jobs offered by the Snare Corporation. The Havana-based Communist Party periodical, *Hoy,* paid close attention to the Snare Corporation in eastern Oriente. In a pointed critique, *Hoy* recognized the consequent politics of a private corporation building a military base: "A problem is created when a foreign company insists on . . . discriminating and paying ridiculous salaries for the benefit of military activities put in practice by the government of the United States."[40]

The U.S. Navy had no qualms about assisting the Snare Corporation in its hiring procedures or blurring the line between government and private employer. The U.S. Navy insisted that it did not have jurisdiction or control over the Snare Corporation's labor practices; however, it was still involved in its employment policies. Distrusting the Snare Corporation's ability to weed out potential security threats, the United States gave direct aid and advice. For example, U.S. officials feared that fascist Falangists (Franco supporters) would be able to infiltrate the base and, on this premise, they banned all Spanish employees from working there.[41] The U.S. base intelligence officer investigated Spanish employees for the Snare Corporation and for the U.S. government alike, making no distinction between the two. Even as the Snare Corporation expanded its purview to other regional projects, the U.S. Navy maintained an interest in its hiring practices. For example, the United States also contracted the Snare Corporation to excavate a nickel mine in Mayari, Oriente. To prevent "employment of suspicious persons," U.S. naval intelligence shared GTMO's list of "undesirable workers" and effectively created a blacklist. The U.S. Navy listed close to two hundred employees it considered to be a security risk. If the Snare Corporation decided to hire one of these workers, the U.S. Navy volunteered to continue the investigations.[42]

Workers recognized the precariousness of contract employment, but they desperately wanted and needed base jobs. Cuba was just recovering from the Great Depression, and men and women from Santiago de Cuba, Holguín, Camagüey, and even Havana traveled to Guantánamo looking for work and opportunities. By 1940 the local press complained that Guantánamo was overrun with potential criminals, prostitutes, and desperate men and women who were willing to do anything to get a job. As a result, thousands lingered in Caimanera unemployed and hungry.

Figure 3. World War II-era postcard of downtown Caimanera. Photo by Aguirre.

Local journalist Lino Lemes cautioned these migrants to come only if they had an invitation: "I am going to give this advice to the thousands of unemployed in Cuba: Don't come looking for work on the naval base if you aren't bringing a letter from the Frederick Snare Corporation in Havana."[43] In subsequent columns, Lemes referred repeatedly to the "invasion of workers" in Caimanera.[44]

In the initial stages from 1939 to 1940, the hiring process was informal, unregulated, and largely dependent on family connections. First, all workers had to secure a "pass." The former workers I spoke with remembered getting a pass from a friend or relative who already had a job on the base. For example, Santiago Ruiz was born in Gíbara, a small community in northeastern Oriente. He worked as a musician and barber, but in 1940 he came to Guantánamo in search of better living conditions. He recounted how he originally got a job on the U.S. naval base:

> A musician friend of mine came to my barber shop one day for a haircut and shave. He wanted—he had an idea—to start an orchestra. He already knew me, although I didn't know him. . . . He said to me that he thought we could form an orchestra. . . . I told him, yes, I was interested. . . . He was a boss on the base, and therefore could find me a job. Many days passed, almost like two months after our conversation. . . . Then one day he told me, "Now I've managed to get a 'pass' so you can work on the base." I went to the base the next day with him. He spoke English, and he spoke there with the *marino* who was in the port. . . . I ran to complete the paperwork . . . and I achieved a positive result. I began to work on the base in 1944.

During the days, Santiago worked as a mechanic, and in the evenings he performed at the Officers' Club, playing Cuban music and learning North American–style tunes like "In the Mood," and "Moonlight Serenade."[45]

Santiago Ruiz's neighbor and *compañero,* Ricardo Baylor, had a considerably more fraught and anxiety-ridden time acquiring a pass and finding work at GTMO. His parents were Jamaican migrants, and Ricardo grew up in Preston, a United Fruit Company town with a large West Indian community. He had a cousin who worked as a domestic servant on the base, and he recalled somewhat resentfully that she was "a little indifferent" when it came to helping his family make contacts. His brother went to Guantánamo first. He told Ricardo stories about the boss coming out onto the docks in Caimanera, shouting "Ten carpenters! Eight workers!" The laborers waiting on the wharves would then rush and jump into small, crowded launches, pushing their way through for the opportunity to work on the base. "I had to work to help my family, because my mother, you know, she raised us and there were four of us, and so I had to work. . . . And then my brother was able to obtain a 'pass' for me." With the pass in hand, Ricardo moved to Guantánamo in 1945 and began to work on the U.S. military base.[46]

Even a self-conscious anti-imperialist could reconcile his ideology with working for the U.S. *marinos.*[47] For example, as a young boy Alberto Torres admired his father, who was among the founders of the Cuban Communist Party in Caimanera, and he in turn headed the local chapter of the Young Communist League. Despite this political education, Alberto recalled working on the base as a golf caddy. "Yes, in World War II, I began to work on the base before I was eighteen years old. . . . They selected persons of my age, sixteen, fifteen, in order to carry the officers' bags when they played golf. And then the officer would choose me, and they paid two dollars and eighty-eight cents. . . . They couldn't get the ball in the hole, because they were so drunk." He later gained a permanent job in the Supply Department in 1940: "All of my brothers spent time and worked there, because work in Cuba was scarce. Because of this the Americans could assert themselves. . . . The sugar harvest lasted only two months and then there was unemployment."[48] In Guantánamo, the base offered one of the clearest paths to individual economic security, regardless of its ramifications for national sovereignty or Cuban nationalism. Although GTMO was a direct affront to Cuban self-determination and a tangible reminder of U.S. dominance, for most workers, economic need far outweighed any possible political objections.

In Guantánamo, these informal family networks were powerful, and workers without these ties often felt desperate. A black market quickly emerged. Most notoriously, Francisco Ochoa, the chief of inspectors in the port, began selling passes to workers who wanted to enter the naval station.[49] Security measures were haphazard and easily manipulated, and so Cuban officials were able to initiate this clandestine business and profit from the unemployed migrant population.

Once workers obtained passes, they could travel to the base, apply for jobs, undergo health and security checks, and with luck, begin work. Every potential worker was screened by the base doctor for tuberculosis and other infectious diseases. In addition, base officials measured, weighed, photographed, and fingerprinted prospective employees. Finally, after all these tests, the workers received a number and badge, or *chapa,* enabling them to enter the base. The *chapa* identified workers as men or women of good repute and health and, much like a passport, it was the physical artifact of the workers' privileged travel. These security checks and *chapas* loomed large in Cuban memories. The Guantánamo Municipal Museum has a display case devoted to workers' identification badges, and workers recounted the clearance process in oral and written accounts.[50] In effect, these badges clearly and uncritically marked the Cubans as "foreigners" in their own country.[51]

Not only did workers need a pass and then a *chapa,* but they also had an expensive and physically arduous commute. Some workers, particularly female domestic servants, lived on the base and traveled to Guantánamo only on the weekends. Many more undertook the daily commute from Guantánamo to the base, spending an average of two hours each way. There were no direct roads between Guantánamo and Caimanera, so workers had to travel by railroad. This cost not only time, but money. Transportation cost $.30 a day, which added up to $1.50 to $1.80 a week. Workers' salaries could be as low as $14.30 a week, and the average laborer earned $17.68 a week.[52] With these wages, transportation took a significant chunk out of workers' salaries. Once they arrived in Caimanera, workers would then jump on a ferry and travel by water to the base. These launches also cost a daily fee. Lemes reiterated that the boats were overcrowded and potentially unsafe. Workers did not know how to swim, and the boats were not equipped with life jackets or first aid kits.[53] In 1943 a launch actually hit a sunken ship, and several workers were wounded and needed medical attention.[54] This commute ingrained itself in base workers' memories. For example, Walter Knight explained there were large crowds of people clamoring on the docks and waiting for the launches. Finally, someone would shout "It's here!" and everyone would rush for the boat.[55] Another worker, Maria Boothe, remembered being afraid: "In the early years there was a launch . . . but me, I didn't like that much [laughs], I was afraid of the sea. It was about a fifteen minute trip."[56]

This physical journey to the base was not an accident. For more than thirty years, Guantánamo's *fuerzas vivas,* and Alfredo Oslé Correa in particular, lobbied, cajoled, and advocated for a direct road between Guantánamo and Caimanera. Although Oslé began his campaign in 1920, he did not see the road completed for more than twenty-five years. It also took until the mid-1950s for a second road to be built directly to GTMO's northeast gate. This improvement finally allowed base workers to travel by car or bus, rather than by train and launch. The *fuerzas vivas* blamed the delay on the Cuban national government, which generally ignored the needs and the economies of the eastern provinces. In the weeks following the nuclear blasts in Hiroshima and Nagasaki, *La Voz del Pueblo* sarcastically observed: "And to think we started the campaign for the road to Caimanera before they started studying the atomic bomb!"[57] Clearly, neither the U.S. Navy nor the Cuban national government wanted to facilitate easy access to the base.[58] If the U.S. Navy had wanted greater contact with Guantánamo, it could have easily financed it. Instead, it forced workers to travel for several hours each day to reach *la frontera.* By requiring a long commute and holding workers at the docks (instead of at an overland checkpoint), the navy emphasized the distance between Guantánamo and GTMO.

Traveling across Guantánamo Bay was not the workers' only journey. Many were migrants, either internal migrants from within Cuba or foreign workers who came to Cuba before the Great Depression. In close proximity to Haiti and Jamaica, eastern Cuba acted as a Caribbean crossroads, with a rich history of Spanish, English, and Creole-speaking people. Guantánamo's multinational community of Cubans, West Indians, Haitians, Chinese, Puerto Ricans, and Spaniards led to competition and demands for jobs based on nationality. Each population had a distinct status in Cuba and a distinct historical relationship to the U.S. government. Officially, the U.S. Navy ignored the national divisions in Guantánamo's workforce and treated all non-U.S. workers as local hires. Unofficially, the U.S. Navy took full advantage of nationalist animosity among its labor pool. GTMO's hiring practices inverted Guantánamo's social structure. Manipulating racial and national hierarchies, U.S. officials often rebuffed Cuban nationals and Spanish migrants and favored West Indians. In response, prospective employees called on a spectrum of linguistic, legal, and nationalist strategies to gain access to base jobs. Workers argued alternately that language, race, or neocolonial obligation should lead to preferential employment for their nationality. In the process, the military border not only separated North Americans from Cubans, but it also revealed a multinational population defined by disparate legacies of neocolonialism.

NATIONALITY AND LABOR

GTMO's expansion followed years of national Cuban debates over the role of foreign labor. During the early twentieth century, more than seven hundred thousand Spaniards and three hundred thousand West Indians and Haitians migrated to Cuba. The cumulative total constituted a substantial percentage of the national population, which was just shy of four million people in 1931.[59] The vast majority of the Caribbean migrants worked in the U.S.-dominated sugar industry. Native-born workers resented the competition presented by migrants, and this hostility reached its nadir during the sugar industry's crash and the Great Depression. With the 1933 overthrow of the Machado dictatorship, the new revolutionary government led by Ramón Grau San Martín responded to Cuban workers' long-standing frustration with foreign labor. Under the slogan "Cuba for the Cubans," the government passed a decree on October 18, 1933, authorizing the deportation of unemployed foreigners, and issued a second decree on November 8, 1933, declaring that 50 percent of all jobs must go to native Cuban workers, known as the Law of 50 Percent.[60]

These nationalist and xenophobic measures had a great deal of popular support throughout Cuba. Organized dissent ironically came from opposite sides of the political divide: U.S. corporations, which relied on flexible migrant labor, and the Cuban Communist Party, which valued class over race and nationality. These discriminatory laws delineated who was included and who was excluded from *cubanidad*. Plus, they served as an official reminder that foreign workers were not welcome. The Law of 50 Percent was initially aimed at the disproportionate numbers of Spaniards in the commercial sector, but it also carried a racist tenor. Spaniards lost jobs and returned to Spain, but West Indians and Haitians suffered the brunt of discrimination, job loss, and repatriation. Because of their English-speaking skills and relatively high literacy levels, West Indians sought alternate employment in the service industry, in urban centers, and on the U.S. naval base in Guantánamo. As subjects of the British Empire, West Indians petitioned the British consul for protection and support. Haitians had no such recourse, and almost forty thousand were forcibly deported.[61] The 1940 Cuban Constitution did not codify the Law of 50 Percent, but it continued to promote nationalist hiring practices that favored Cuban citizens. Thus, national rivalries defined Cuban labor debates before World War II, and these antecedents shaped the environment of worker competition in Guantánamo as the U.S. Navy hired thousands of men and women.

This same era coincided with the United States' proclamation of the Good Neighbor policy. With the onset of World War II, this rhetorical friendship solidified into a hemispheric alliance. The United States employed the mutual language of neighborliness and masked its continued imperial and neocolonial presence in Latin America. Through the Good Neighbor policy, the United States presented its foreign policy as a beneficial partnership, and it sought to escape the obligations that accompanied modern empire. Despite these intentions, in Guantánamo, GTMO's "neighbors" argued that the United States had concrete and direct commitments to the Cuban community. The trope of neighborliness resonated more than many U.S. diplomats realized, and Cubans used it to appeal to U.S. ideals, rights, and responsibilities.

Guantánamo's politicians, journalists, and workers all believed that the Good Neighbor policy compelled U.S. officials to provide material benefits to Cuban workers. Individual Cubans wrote plaintive letters to the U.S. consulate, essentially begging for a recommendation, a pass, an "in" onto the base, and what they hoped would be a steady job and economic security. They directed their pleas to the U.S. consul and even to the president. For example, José Clemente composed a heartfelt plea to President Roosevelt: "As you see, I've always wanted to work there [GTMO], and I have done everything I can, for I like and have always admired American customs and specially your democracy. . . . There would be nothing that would satisfy me as much as working for Americans. . . . I want to work for Americans. Even when I've been born in Cuba my heart and sympathies are toward the States. Do it and God will choose you as His everlasting President."[62] Clemente drafted his appeal in English and, on the face of it, represented the ideal neocolonial subject who admired and articulated loyalty to U.S. democracy and values. Yet, Clemente's language came full circle, assuming U.S. patronage to the Cuban people in general, and to him, as a loyal subject, in particular. This was exactly the kind of demand the United States had hoped to avoid.

The governor of Oriente Province, Dr. Angel Pérez, a native of Guantánamo, specifically asked the U.S. consul to designate base jobs for *guantanameros.* The base commander's response was terse and negative: "We are unable *in accordance with law* to give the governor of Oriente Province any assurance that employment will be given to Cubans at this station." This answer was harsh and evasive, for within a year of this correspondence, the United States had hired several thousand workers. The U.S. officials' key point was that "in accordance with law," the United States had no responsibility to hire Cubans.[63] The Guantánamo mayor also lobbied the navy to give jobs to its immediate neighbors, insisting that Guantánamo workers should be hired before migrants from Havana.[64] Workers themselves clamored for *guantanameros* to have the first stab at base jobs. In 1941 five hundred unemployed workers from Guantánamo protested that they had been waiting for work while the base hired people from other *pueblos* or cities.[65]

Even more galling, the navy hired large numbers of foreign migrants to work on the base. In a nationalist critique, Guantánamo journalist Lino Lemes García emphasized GTMO's presence in Cuba. Co-opting the language of neighborliness, he argued that the base needed to result in benefits for Cubans: "The Yankee government could practically demonstrate the Good Neighbor policy by giving preference to the natives in building the public works."[66] He was angry that the base operated outside Cuban jurisdiction—it did not have to adhere to the Law of 50 Percent or Cuban labor laws. As a result, foreigners could seek employment on the base on the same terms as Cubans and often found jobs ahead of Cuban *guantanameros.* Lemes proposed that if the United States did not hire more Cuban workers, then Cubans must modify the 1934 treaty agreement to include labor protections: "It is a sad and embarrassing fact that while foreigners find work easily on the base, natives must do incredible things to work on the base, even though the U.S. base is in Cuba." It was only by protecting Cuban workers that the United States could truly call itself a "good neighbor."[67]

Lino Lemes García was the most vocal critic of the working conditions on GTMO. He wrote regularly for Guantánamo's leading daily, *La Voz del Pueblo,* and the less established, *El Vigilante,* while also freelancing for Santiago and Havana papers. His constant editorials and letters to Cuban and U.S. officials made him persona non grata to the U.S. diplomatic corps, who dismissed him as "irresponsible," "shoddy," "discredited," and went as far as placing him on the list of Cubans whose "entry into the United States would be contrary to the

Figure 4. Caricature of Lino Lemes García. The word written on his pencil means "truthful." *La Revista Oriental,* August 1955. Courtesy of the Elvira Cape Provincial Library, Santiago de Cuba.

public interest."[68] From World War II through the Cuban revolution, Lemes addressed almost every issue related to GTMO and Guantánamo, including wages, pensions, public health, prostitution, commercial relationships, customs, and U.S. sailors' liberty parties in town. And despite U.S. officials' patronizing criticism and studied indifference, Lemes wrote for the Guantánamo press for more than twenty years, becoming the most consistent advocate for Cuban workers on the naval base.

In his promotion of Cuban workers, Lino Lemes often singled out West Indians for critique, claiming they garnered jobs on the base at the expense of local Cubans. Many Cuban workers saw West Indians as their direct rivals, and competition for jobs emerged along national lines. From the beginning of the twentieth century, West Indians had been part of Guantánamo and GTMO's social fabric. Most came to work in Oriente's

U.S.-controlled sugar industry. Facing discrimination and economic hardships, West Indian migrants adopted a range of strategies to survive and build communities in Cuba. In the early decades of the twentieth century, Marcus Garvey's United Negro Improvement Association (UNIA) and its internationalist black nationalism attracted a large following in Oriente among the migrant community. Some West Indian migrants participated in the Cuban labor movement and even organized the Antillean Workers' Union. Still, others responded to prejudice by replacing their English names for Spanish monikers to escape dismissal and integrate more easily. And many West Indians also turned inward, to the Episcopal Church, to fraternal organizations, and to private associations such as the Catalina Lodge and the British West Indian Welfare Centre.[69] These individuals were generally literate English speakers who valued social propriety. For example, in 1943 base workers formed the British West Indies Democratic Association in Caimanera. It welcomed workers from the Frederick Snare Corporation and "everyone of sufficient morality who asks to join." The founders depoliticized their aims, renouncing any discussion of race or politics within "the bosom of the Association."[70] This policy was indicative of West Indians' middle-class aspirations and reluctance to engage in Cuban politics or affiliate themselves directly with black Cubans, Haitians, or other Cubans of color.

West Indians held a disproportionate number of base jobs, working as cooks, chauffeurs, office workers, manual laborers, and domestic servants. Because gaining a job often depended on one's internal connections, West Indians were also in an advantageous position in the run-up to World War II. Lemes went so far as to describe Jamaicans as "good diplomats" for their ability to obtain passes for their relatives and West Indian community members.[71]

GTMO acted as an oddly protective work space for West Indian migrants and their descendants. Their English-speaking skills meant they held numerous supervisory and white collar positions and had direct contact with U.S. personnel. Moreover, all aliens were required to register on the List of Foreigners. The Cuban government made several attempts to force the U.S. base to cooperate with this practice and register West Indian workers on GTMO. The U.S. government was reluctant to participate because it did not want to administer Cuban law within the base. As a result, foreign nationals could "evade Cuban laws," because the U.S. administration ignored the policy.[72] The boundaries of the base stymied Cuban efforts to register West Indians and offered a shield from Cuban labor laws.

Not surprisingly, West Indians' private organizations, coupled with their favored positions, made them targets within Guantánamo. Cubans often ignored West Indians' vulnerability in the general workforce and viewed their lack of formal political activity as a sign of passivity. There were almost no positive images of West Indians in the press; instead, most references appeared in the crime reports.[73] Although these accounts did not explicitly racialize or disparage West Indians for their blackness, they repeatedly referred to them as foreigners and *jamaiquinos*. In eastern Cuba, there was a clear linguistic distinction between *jamaicano* and *jamaiquino*. To the West Indian community, *jamaicano* implied respect, but *jamaiquino* was insulting and derogatory.[74] The normalized use of *jamaiquino* in the press reflected the derision aimed at the migrants.[75]

In Lino Lemes's campaign for more Cuban workers, he also emphasized what he saw as West Indians' "submissive" personalities, opining that if the United States preferred "the Jamaicans, the Chinese, the Indians, and other foreigners who were not protected by the American Flag, maybe it is because these workers are more docile."[76] In the Santiago de Cuba paper, *Oriente*, José Octavio Muñoz also argued that West Indian workers had an unfair advantage at GTMO because they "subject themselves more docilely to the anti-Cuban procedures that are prevalent here."[77] Juan Carlos Pulsara, a former base worker, bluntly articulated this common sense notion that West Indians were "mild," "submissive," and had an "obedient character." He commented that they were often given supervisory positions because they did not "revolt or make demands. . . . The Jamaicans had this defect: [they were] very submissive, you understand me? . . . They were very, very submissive, and they liked to denounce the Cubans for whatever irregularities they committed."[78]

West Indian workers navigated a precarious landscape defined by British imperialism in their home islands and U.S. neocolonialism in Cuba.[79] As black men and women, they often asserted their *Britishness* to distinguish themselves from Cubans of color, even as they too were excluded from the upper echelons of Oriente society. This attachment to a British identity sometimes resulted in isolation from Cuban politics and national debates.[80] Significantly, GTMO also mimicked U.S. strategies in Panama, which had also relied on West Indian migrants to build the canal. In both the Canal Zone and in GTMO, the United States elevated the status of West Indians and created a new class of favored workers who gained their privilege precisely for being outside the national politic.[81] As a result, in the 1940s U.S. officials could effectively take advantage of these English-speaking workers and the division in the labor force. The naval base elevated the positions of West Indians and effectively transformed the social order of Guantánamo.

The United Kingdom was not the only country with Caribbean colonies, and the small Puerto Rican community in Guantánamo occupied a peculiar position between U.S. citizenship and U.S. subjecthood. Puerto Ricans' status was multiple and ambiguous. Puerto Ricans were technically U.S. citizens, but this citizenship claim was diminished by Puerto Rico's colonial position vis-à-vis the United States.[82] Puerto Ricans also shared many cultural ties to Cubans, including language, religion, and historic links to both Spain and the African Diaspora. But, Puerto Ricans were also migrants and excluded from Cuban citizenship. Puerto Rican workers found themselves vying for jobs on GTMO, a place equally anomalous and laced with questions of sovereignty and citizenship as Puerto Rico itself.

In the context of World War II, the United States required all U.S. citizens in Cuba, including Puerto Ricans, to register with the U.S. Selective Service. In a letter written in Spanish to the U.S. consulate, Juan Almodóvar Sánchez requested what was required of him, as a U.S. citizen, regarding military inscription. The U.S. consul responded in Spanish, informing him that he had to register at the Guantánamo Sugar Company.[83] Not only did this again conflate U.S. military and economic power in eastern Cuba, it also revealed a North American community with Spanish surnames. When U.S. consul Gordon Burke made his report to the State Department regarding the distribution of selective service cards, almost all of those registered had Spanish names: Mario Almenares, Eduardo Alvarez, Ignacio Ávila, Antonio Balaguer, Armando Benítez, and Horacio Modesto.[84] Many of these men might have been U.S. citizens of Cuban descent, but this population also undoubtedly included numerous Puerto Ricans.

Puerto Rican migrants lobbied for their rights to work on the U.S. military base, and they pointed to their U.S. citizenship and loyalty to the United States in making these claims. For example, Eddy Pagán, a Puerto Rican worker, wrote two letters to the U.S. consul complaining that officials favored non-U.S. workers on the base. Pagán went out of his way to declare that he was "born under the American Flag," remained loyal to the U.S. Congress and Constitution, and considered himself a child of Washington and Lincoln. He criticized U.S. officials for dismissing Puerto Ricans before Cuban, Jamaican, or Chinese workers.[85] As a Puerto Rican, he was a U.S. citizen and deserved preferential treatment for base employment. Pagán called on his colonial position within the U.S. empire to gain status, even though his letters and claims to "America" also revealed his tenuous claim to U.S. citizenship.

Puerto Ricans' status as U.S. citizens was contested, and many petitioners used the word *subdito,* or subject, alongside or instead of *ciudadano,* or citizen. This slippage shows the duality of Puerto Ricans' claims to U.S. citizenship and their status as colonial subjects. For example, Juan Martínez Lugo wrote to the U.S. State Department in 1940. "I write to you in order to say that I am Juan Martínez Lugo, an American citizen of the United States. I came from Puerto Rico . . . but now I can't find work in any places. I have a big family and our life is to [sic] difficult now. I beg you some recommendation to Military Chief of Guantánamo Navy Army. If you need some reference of mi, I can send to you my passport and other documents."[86] Although the letter was written in English, his Spanish spelling of "mi" reflected his mixed sensibility. For his efforts, the U.S. consulate in Santiago de Cuba answered his letter without acknowledging his claims to U.S. citizenship and denied any knowledge of GTMO's activities: "In reply you are informed that this consulate has no jurisdiction over the naval station, and for this reason has no official information as to the work that is being done there."[87] In another example, Santos Lugo wrote to the U.S. consulate asking for employment on GTMO in 1939. Unlike Pagán and Martínez, Lugo did not define himself as a U.S. citizen, but rather as a *subdito,* a North American subject.[88] This word choice unintentionally undercut his claim to full U.S. benefits, equality, and preferential employment status. Pagán too concluded his epistle stating that he was a U.S. citizen *and* a "subject of the great nation." Although these linguistic differences may seem minor, they accurately reflected Puerto Ricans' ambiguous position and the second-class nature of their U.S. citizenship.

Puerto Ricans were also sidelined because they were arguably indistinguishable racially or culturally from the general Cuban population. In their letters to U.S. officials, Puerto Ricans often asserted their experience as veterans of the U.S. Army and their rights as U.S. subjects or citizens; however, many wrote to the U.S. Consulate in Spanish, identifying themselves linguistically with Cuba rather than the United States. In an angry and detailed complaint, Pedro Salgado and José Fernández identified themselves as "Puerto Ricans, who are American subjects," and they allied themselves with their Cuban counterparts. "We must clarify that this Company [Frederick Snare Corporation] wants to employ foreign personnel. . . . This Company is pleased to employ Spaniards, Jamaicans, and other foreigners who can bully their way in, while Puerto Ricans and

Cubans are treated and seen as if they were dogs."[89] Salgado and Fernández claimed Puerto Ricans and Cubans held equal rights vis-à-vis the U.S. government as colonial *subditos*. They pointed to their competition as the "foreign" Jamaicans. The U.S. officials translating their missive ignored or failed to recognize Salgado and Fernández as Puerto Ricans or as U.S. citizens (or subjects). The translator's summary simply stated: "[A]ccording to these writers, the Cubans are not getting their share of it [work]. . . . The writers complain that Jamaican negroes are being favored, etcetera."[90] In this conclusion, Salgado and Fernández "became" Cubans in the diplomatic record without any particular privileges to base employment. Cubans and Puerto Ricans both believed their claims should supersede groups they saw as foreign. They lobbied the U.S. government alternately as "good neighbors" and U.S. citizens, but both populations still found themselves in a subordinated neocolonial position, dependent on the U.S. military.

Finally, World War II changed the politics of loyalty on the base. Despite the minimal threat of a German invasion, U.S. officers kept a vigilant eye on possible German, Japanese, and Spanish spies. The war was on, and the base was protecting U.S. interests in the Western Hemisphere.[91] The Cuban government and U.S. investors had welcomed Spanish workers throughout the early twentieth century for their whiteness and for their labor, but now the United States feared Spanish fascists might infiltrate the base. On this premise, they banned all Spaniards. As Captain George Weyler explained: "About that time [1942], all employees known to be Spanish citizens were discharged for the reason that it was believed that the majority of these employees were associated with 'Falangistas' and entertained pro-Axis sympathies."[92] The base also canceled its contracts with Spanish merchants, including one of Guantánamo's leading elites, José "Pepe" Alvarez.[93] This defensive strategy reversed decades of preferential treatment of Spanish migrants in Cuba based on their perceived "whitening" of the population.

However, nationality was not as clear-cut as the U.S. officials imagined or desired. Spanish workers promptly went to the municipal judge of Caimanera, Juan Pérez Pérez, and bought doctored birth certificates "proving" their Cuban nationality. Through this legal sleight of hand, they planned to regain their jobs on the base. Loyalty became a matter of paperwork, and to the chagrin of U.S. officials, Judge Pérez Pérez happily obliged. U.S. officials angrily stated, "There is conclusive proof that Juan Pérez has been engaged over a period of time in a false birth certificate racket."[94] José Fernández Pérez, José Pereira García, José López

Rodríguez, Manuel Rodríguez López, Antonio Dalmau Vicons, and Ismael Fernández Paradela, all born in Spain, worked on the U.S. naval base before 1942. After being laid off in 1942, these men paid Judge Pérez between twenty-five and thirty-five dollars for false birth certificates, claiming that they were born in Guantánamo or Caimanera, so they could then reapply for base jobs.[95] These incidents infuriated U.S. officials, perhaps out of fear that military security had been breached or simply embarrassment at being duped by a corrupt local judge. These Spanish workers had demonstrated the limitations of U.S. security and surveillance in the region. Proof of loyalty and *cubanidad* could easily be bought and sold in the local marketplace.

Of course this deception was the last thing the U.S. Navy wanted or anticipated. Its military authority was rooted in its power to maintain borders and monitor who could and could not enter the base. The base intervened in Guantánamo's social hierarchy and gained power by ignoring, or manipulating, local norms, laws, and prejudices. In the process, the naval base magnified national divisions and the tangled histories of neocolonialism and migration within Guantánamo. And yet the Spanish case is telling, for it deflates the U.S. military's appearance of omnipotence. Cubans, Puerto Ricans, West Indians, and Spaniards used the political and cultural tools available to them to navigate and take advantage of the U.S. imperial outpost. The rush for jobs and economic competition created an environment of instability and flux, where workers did almost anything they could to get to GTMO.

KID CHICLE: DEATH AND MEMORY IN GUANTÁNAMO BAY

The case of Lino "Kid Chicle" Rodríguez represented the culmination of unemployment and disorder in Guantánamo during World War II. The tragedy placed work and labor at the center of diplomatic relations and exemplified the contradictions of neocolonialism. In Guantánamo, locals responded to Rodríguez's death with a decidedly regional perspective, whereas national actors had more freedom to downplay or overplay the story depending on their political allegiances. And by 1941 the U.S. and Cuban governments hoped to sweep the case away. It was not until after the Cuban revolution in 1959 that the anti-imperialist, Castro government revived the Caso del Chicle and reframed it as a demonstrative example of Yankee aggression in Guantánamo Bay.[96]

Before the death of Rodríguez and throughout the autumn of 1940, the Guantánamo press had repeatedly hammered away at the unfair pass system. Rodríguez's death crystallized the complaints and injustices with the subcontracting system locals had already identified. In fact, on the day of Rodríguez's death, Lino Lemes reported that the Snare Corporation had refused to open a local employment office to standardize the application process, and so workers had to bribe the contractors.[97] In the aftermath of the tragedy, the local community blamed Sr. Francisco Ochoa, a Cuban official, and designated him as a key villain in the event. The Santiago de Cuba daily, *Diario de Cuba*, reported that local workers wanted to "lynch" Sr. Ochoa, judging him responsible for Rodríguez's death and believing he had given passes only to workers who came with influence or paid a bribe.[98]

Anger at U.S. economic and military power intersected, particularly given that the main aggressor, Lt. West, had worked for the United Fruit Company before becoming an officer in the U.S. Navy. Lino Lemes called attention to Lt. West's earlier history with the UFC in Preston and concluded: "Lt. West was responsible for the premature death of the boxer Lino Rodríguez Grenot, the defenseless victim of the savage Yankee marine, who maybe thought that a man of color did not merit the same consideration or respect as a white man."[99] From a Guantánamo perspective, the distinction between U.S. private capital and U.S. military power collapsed. Lt. West was a former UFC employee, an officer in the U.S. Navy, and working to supply labor for the Frederick Snare Corporation. In this instance, Lemes identified all three with patronizing and racially biased attitudes toward Cubans. It is not surprising that local workers did not consider the U.S. military and the Frederick Snare Corporation as separate, independent entities.

From the U.S. Navy's perspective, it was imperative to maintain the division between military and private operations, even when admitting a mutually beneficial relationship. In a confidential memo after the event, Acting Secretary of the Navy James Forrestal identified earlier labor disputes on the docks as the impetus for the U.S. Navy's assistance to the Snare Corporation.[100] By sending U.S. launches captained by U.S. Marine Corps officers, the U.S. Navy strengthened the public-private arrangement, even as it sought to delineate where the private corporation's responsibilities began and where the U.S. Navy's ended.

After the immediate shock and public clamor over Rodríguez's death, the leading Guantánamo newspapers, *La Voz del Pueblo* and *El Vigilante*, downplayed the protests and minimized the disruption. *La Voz del Pueblo*, the region's most prominent paper, tempered its reporting and hoped that the judicial authorities would quickly intervene.[101] Even the more populist *El Vigilante* advised, "Calm, people, calm," voicing its faith that Lt. West would be punished.[102] The Santiago de Cuba paper, *Diario de Cuba*, also cautioned, "We all must cooperate to re-establish the normal, cordial relations between the people of Caimanera and Guantánamo, and the authorities on the naval station, because our economic life greatly benefits from this exchange."[103] Despite the tragedy, Guantánamo's economic well-being necessitated amicable, not hostile, relations with the base.

The Havana press, from the conservative *Diario de la Marina* to the Communist *Hoy*, also reported on the Kid Chicle case, putting local Guantánamo politics and the U.S. military base in the national news. The *Diario de la Marina*, known for its sympathetic ear to the U.S. government, reluctantly covered the event with minimal attention to detail. The paper waited several days to publish an account, never mentioned Rodríguez or West by name (instead saying a Cuban worker had lost his life at the hands of a U.S. lieutenant), and emphasized that U.S. authorities had begun an investigation.[104] Still, news from Oriente rarely appeared in the *Diario de la Marina*, and the brief article attested to how base workers' travails could affect U.S.-Cuban relations and play to a national audience. On the opposite end of the political spectrum, *Hoy* articulated an anti-imperialist analysis of the Rodríguez case. The paper predicted energetic protests would paralyze the base if legal charges were not brought against West.[105]

In several editorials, *Hoy* framed Rodríguez's death as one of many events in a long list of neocolonial outrages. The U.S. disregard for human life was apparent and inexcusable. The United States continued to treat Cuba like a "conquered country."[106] In its most vitriolic language, an editorial thundered, "This act occurred easily, because to the Yankee officer it appeared a normal thing to end the life of a Cuban worker. Surely this Señor had the discriminating conscience of a colonialist like all imperialist agents. They believe our people are inferior. . . . To them, it is like liquidating a dog." In this tenor, *Hoy* railed against the Snare Corporation for devaluing the lives of Cubans, Africans, Chinese, and all people of color.[107] Unlike the Guantánamo *fuerzas vivas*, who lived in the shadow of economic dependence on the U.S. military, the national Communist Party was able to denounce the U.S. military as imperialistic.

Along with the national press attention, worker organizations throughout eastern Cuba sent telegrams in rapid succession to the national government in Havana. Unions and guilds in Caimanera, Las Tunas, Antilla,

Santa Clara, Camagüey, Central Miranda, Holguín, and Santiago de Cuba called on the Cuban government for "justice," to "save Cuban dignity," and to ask "for severe punishment for the guilty party."[108] Because of the foreign status of the naval base, this incident of brutality had the possibility of becoming a national, or even an international, crisis. The Cuban government responded, and President Batista commissioned Cuban investigators to visit Caimanera almost immediately.

Not surprisingly, the U.S. Navy and State Department officials hoped the case would disappear as quickly as possible and refused to term the event a "murder" or a "crime." The story barely registered in the U.S. press. It did appear in the *New York Times,* but only for a day.[109] It also ran in the *Chicago Defender,* indicating black North Americans' interest in U.S.-Cuban relations and the U.S. military's treatment of people of color outside its borders. Unlike Cuban or mainstream U.S. accounts, the *Defender* explicitly labeled Lt. West as a *white* officer and reiterated Cuban accounts that the blackjack, and not drowning, had caused Kid Chicle's death.[110] This example aside, the majority of U.S. commentary and reports remained sterilized of all guilt or remorse. The U.S. Navy referred to Rodríguez's death as the "incident involving a lieutenant at the U.S. naval station at Guantánamo and a Cuban workman."[111] Admiral George Weyler explained without admitting any responsibility: "Lino Rodríguez died as a result of an accident sustained by one of our boats."[112]

That said, the navy did conduct a court-martial, and the U.S. ambassador was even a bit "embarrassed" when Lt. West was acquitted of all charges. Although pleased to learn the United States did not have to "assume any responsibility for the loss of this man's life," he did suggest an "act of grace" of five thousand dollars to Rodríguez's family.[113] U.S. officials felt guilty enough to search out Rodríguez's aunt and offer her a lump sum in compensation for the death of her nephew, but only after several weeks of agonizing and debating the merits of his aunt as a "legitimate" caretaker. They did not want to appear as if the monetary compensation was a sign of guilt or responsibility.[114] As the case continued to linger, the U.S. officials' disdain for Rodríguez's life became palpable and less discreet, and by 1942 the U.S. consul described Rodríguez as "that worthless Cuban boxer."[115] But with the money distributed, the case was closed and, for the most part, it was forgotten. Even the otherwise exhaustive account by Admiral Murphy, the 1953 *History of Guantánamo Bay,* erased all memory of Lino Rodríguez.

This incident did not appear again in Cuban accounts until after the Cuban revolution, when Lino Rodríguez was resurrected as one of the first martyrs of the base. Rodríguez's death so clearly demonstrated the U.S. military's unchecked power in Guantánamo that revolutionary historians revived the events and created an official history. In a 1964 article in *Venceremos,* the state-run newspaper, Kid Chicle's death was featured prominently as an early example of U.S. aggression and as an event that fostered an "anti-imperialist conscience" in the public.[116] And, as recorded in Rigoberto Cruz Díaz's 1976 exposé on the U.S. naval base, many local informants remembered Kid Chicle.[117] In the Guantánamo Municipal Museum, there are several display cases recounting the events of Kid Chicle, including an example of a "blackjack." School children visit the museum and learn about Lino Rodríguez and U.S. violence. In this way, Rodríguez has been remembered, and his death has been given new meaning. In light of the Cuban revolution, Kid Chicle became the archetypal Cuban worker struck down by U.S. imperialism.

However, Lino Rodríguez was not the only Cuban worker to die in the construction frenzy during World War II. These other casualties did not generate publicity, nor were their stories passed down to later generations. Instead, they remain forgotten by the U.S. and Cuban governments and by Guantánamo historians. For example, in the weeks before Rodríguez's death, another Santiago worker, Agustín Alvarez, died on the base in an automobile accident. Again, Alvarez worked for the Snare Corporation, not the U.S. military. Lino Lemes chastised the U.S. government for not intervening in this case and for avoiding responsibility. Lemes pointed out that if the U.S. government insisted "only the American flag flies" on the base, then it should be accountable for what happened there. If U.S. law governed the base, Lemes wanted to know why the United States did not investigate the accident or the Snare Corporation.[118] Months later, Lemes again penned, "Another Worker Dies on the Yankee Base." He attributed this work-related death to the lack of medical attention on the base for Cuban workers, and he sent a letter and his article to President Roosevelt.[119] In May 1941, there was another death due to the Snare Corporation. Master Carpenter Venancio Hechavarría went to work on the base in the morning, "strong," "healthy," and "robust," but by the end of the day he left in agony, without his full mind or the ability to speak. Later that day, he died. The local doctor believed that his death was due to exposure to toxic conditions. Lino Lemes hoped the Snare Corporation would compensate Hechavarría's widow, but he doubted this would take place: "We know that there can be no justice with this company." Lemes urged an active press campaign and a photographic display of Hechavarría's corpse and funeral.[120]

U.S. brutality and violence did not define these deaths as it did with Kid Chicle, but these incidents similarly begged the question of employment and the U.S. responsibility to its Cuban workforce. The problem was two-fold. First, the U.S. military did not want to accept responsibility for work-related accidents or deaths on the base, for to have done so would have been an admission of wrong-doing or weakness. Second, as a private employer, the Snare Corporation had incredible flexibility and could guard the U.S. government from direct accountability. In these conflicts between workers and the base, the Snare Corporation offered the U.S. military more than just speed, efficiency, and lower costs; it offered pro-tection against direct liability.

Finally, there was at least one other case where a Cuban man died at the hands of a U.S. marine. Manuel Luís Rodríguez González was a twenty-nine-year-old Cuban who worked for the Snare Corporation in the employees' canteen. On a late October evening, a U.S. sentry on guard shot and killed Rodríguez González. According to Captain George L. Weyler, there was a U.S. marine posted on the leeward point who ac-knowledged Rodríguez González's death. The body was identified, em-balmed, and returned for burial in Guantánamo. Weyler indicated that the circumstances surrounding the shooting were unknown.[121] A young marine appeared too quick to pull the trigger, and he shot Rodríguez González without any provocation or known cause.

Unlike Kid Chicle Rodríguez's death, the death of Rodríguez González garnered almost no attention in the local press. There was a single article in *Hoy*. It blamed the incident on a drunken *marino* and de-manded urgent action to protect Cuban lives. There was no subsequent clamor or uproar, and the press accounts did not come close to match-ing the publicity surrounding Kid Chicle.[122] Instead, Rodríguez González's common-law wife, Luisa Hernández Vásquez, went to a local attorney and inquired about compensation for herself and her child "who had been legitimated according to the laws of Cuba."[123] Captain Weyler distanced himself and the U.S. Navy from the Rodríguez González case: "As you know, the U.S. government is in no way re-sponsible nor liable for the criminal acts of its employees, including the personnel of the armed forces. It is my understanding that the employ-ees of the *fonda* [canteen] in which Rodríguez worked are covered by in-surance and that any indemnity or claim will be paid from the social in-surance company." What happened next is unclear. Captain Weyler noted, "The Court of Inquiry recommended further judicial action against the marine sentry and this tribunal is now in session."[124] The name of the marine sentry appears nowhere in the documents, nor does the result of his tribunal, nor any records of compensation paid to Manuel Rodríguez González's family. There is also no further information in the Guantánamo press or historical accounts.

It is difficult to reconcile these silences with the tumult of activity and protest in the case of Kid Chicle. In many ways, Manuel Rodríguez González's death was equally violent, and the U.S. military equally culpable. In this instance, a U.S. marine shot Rodríguez González on the base. The U.S. consul attributed the subdued response to fears of economic retaliation if there was another public uproar: "The incident [Manuel Rodríguez González's death] was given very little publicity in the local papers, doubtless due to the fact that the belief is prevalent here that it would perhaps contribute to the definite withdrawal of all liberty and visits in Santiago by the personnel at the base."[125] This analysis does not seem sufficiently compelling. While the commercial elite was indeed dependent on U.S. liberty parties, it does not explain the lack of outrage from labor unions, the Communist Party, or journalists like Lino Lemes in the aftermath of this tragedy.

Unlike Rodríguez González, who died on the job, Kid Chicle died trying to get a job. Moreover, Kid Chicle's death was public and occurred in the waters between Guantánamo and GTMO. Unemployed workers on the docks and the twenty-nine Cuban workers in the launch all witnessed his death. The United States could not separate this incident from the memories of insecurity and worker competition, or minimize its symbolism for the men and women who jumped on launches and crossed Guantánamo Bay. In contrast, Rodríguez González's death, although also violent, happened within the territory of the base and without witnesses. Taking place away from the docks and the boundary lines, Rodríguez González's death was forgotten. Kid Chicle alone became the symbol of Guantánamo's victimization and U.S. aggression memorialized in state-sponsored accounts and local memory. He represented the unemployed worker who looked for economic opportunity and struggled to make his way to the base during the World War II boom. For a community so close to the U.S. border, Kid Chicle's death signified the journey, psychological and physical, between Guantánamo and GTMO.

In the weeks following Kid Chicle's death, the Frederick Snare Corporation opened an employment office in Guantánamo to help facilitate the passes and avoid future conflicts. Employment on the base was not steady, and by 1942 the base renovations had been completed. In short order, the Snare Corporation closed its Guantánamo office and layoffs were endemic. From a peak of 13,000 workers, the U.S. Navy decreased its civilian workforce to approximately 3,500 by 1945. After the early years of World War II, the military risks to the base decreased and the main arena of the naval war moved to the Pacific, far from the Caribbean. But the military establishment remained long after the fighting ended. Modernized and expanded, GTMO maintained its reliance on local workers. These men and women continued to negotiate their working conditions between Guantánamo and GTMO as the United States redefined its mission in the Cold War.

2

"We Are Real Democrats"
Legal Debates and Cold War Unionism
before Castro, 1940–1954

L orenzo Salomón Deer was twenty-four years old and a first generation, Cuban-born, West Indian descendant. In 1951 he found a job on
the base in the Navy Exchange, also known as the *tiendacita,* which
sold personal items, such as cigarettes, brushes, toothpaste, and hair gel.
On September 15, 1954, eight cartons of Lucky Strike and Camel cigarettes were empty. The cigarette packs had been stolen, and Salomón was
the prime suspect. Salomón proclaimed his innocence and explained that
there had not been enough time to check the merchandise. His supervisor
did not believe him. Cigarettes were commonly smuggled off the base and
sold on the black market in Guantánamo. The supervisor doubted that,
after three years of experience, Salomón would be unable to recognize the
weight and size of a typical cigarette carton. In short order, base officials
accused Salomón of stealing $1543.26 in cigarettes.[1]

Reaction to this alleged theft was immediate. Typically, when base officials believed a local civilian had committed a crime, they fired the
worker and pressed charges in Caimanera or Guantánamo. In this instance, they took a more punitive course and detained Salomón on the
base without notifying his family, a lawyer, or the base union. Rumors
spread when workers realized that Salomón had been thrown in jail without trial or inquiry. José Repilado Pérez, a delegate of the base workers'

union, described the crisis in almost biblical language: "Lorenzo Salomón disappeared as if he had been swallowed by the earth."[2]

On release two weeks later, Salomón claimed that he had been wrongfully accused, beaten, and tortured until he signed a false confession. *Avance,* a Havana-based periodical, followed the story, sent a correspondent to Guantánamo, and published a sympathetic profile of Salomón. In an interview, Salomón described his ordeal in detail, "Immediately they imprisoned me. . . . I was forced to stand on my feet the entire time. There I was incommunicado for fifteen days. . . . Lovell Irving [the intelligence officer] hit me with his open hand on the nape of the neck. When I fell to the floor, a *marino* who came with Irving clubbed me in the stomach and liver. I fainted with pain and woke up in a hospital. There the doctor massaged my wounds and gave me injections. Then they put me back in jail." He elaborated that he had been forced to stand for fourteen to fifteen hours each day, could not change his clothes, received rotten potatoes and dirty water, and was beaten regularly. He believed the base officials wanted him to die. In the end, he signed a confession that he had stolen the cigarettes. "Many times I refused to sign the paper that they brought to me in English. They told me if I signed it, they wouldn't keep me any longer and would send me back to Cuba. I wanted to get out of there in any way possible, and I couldn't tolerate any more beatings. Finally, I signed what they wanted. Many days later, they told me that I had signed a confession that said I had robbed money in order to go to the United States." Salomón added that his confinement was so brutal that if the officials had asked him if he had killed Abraham Lincoln, he would have confessed to that too.[3]

When Salomón was released, the base union's leadership announced that he looked like a "Zombie from Haiti." His eyes were "empty and lacking expression and life," he walked and moved in a "terrifying[ly] slow" manner, and his cadaverous face was evidence of "mental and physical tortures."[4] The union spokesmen insisted that Salomón's detention fell outside the boundaries of U.S. and Cuban law and democratic governance. In their opinion, Salomón's treatment went beyond the pale. If the U.S. Navy could detain a local worker without trial, workers would be vulnerable to unchecked U.S. military abuses. The union's vocal critique worried Cuban politicians and U.S. officials, for its anger and hostility could be interpreted as veering toward a radical, nationalistic position. The U.S. Navy's Office of Industrial Relations even concurred that the detention had been "excessive," particularly because there was no evidence of violent crime. It urged the State Department to

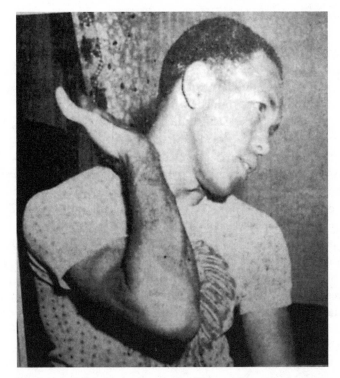

Figure 5. Lorenzo Salomón describing being struck by a U.S. base intelligence officer "on the nape of his neck." *Avance*, October 15, 1954. Courtesy of the Institute of Literature and Linguistics, Havana, Cuba.

"handle foreign nationals accused of crimes against the United States with extreme care."[5]

On the naval base, the work of diplomacy and international relations became a matter of day-to-day economic affairs. Base employees had to navigate their nebulous legal status each time they crossed the *frontera*: Were working conditions governed by Cuban labor law or by U.S. labor law? Did workers on the U.S. naval base deserve U.S. government salaries and pensions, or were they covered by the Cuban welfare system? If a worker committed a crime on the base, was he or she tried under Cuban law or by U.S. military codes of justice? On the surface these concerns were local and provincial, but each in its own way challenged the boundaries of U.S. power and begged the question of law, jurisdiction, and sovereignty. Although the Cuban government occasionally came to the defense of base workers, it did not challenge the United States' underlining authority on the naval base. In contrast, throughout the 1940s and 1950s, base workers agitated for better conditions, respect, and higher wages, compelling the U.S. Navy to recognize their concerns and make compromises. Because international standards between Guantánamo and GTMO affected their personal well-being, base workers, far more than the Cuban government, fought to clarify the rule of law. In the decades framed by promises of "good neighborly" relations and fears of the Cold War, the U.S. Navy had to finesse legal questions and respond to the local community.

The Salomón case erupted in the mid-1950s and revealed the collision of U.S. neocolonialism, worker activism, and Cold War politics outside the main stage of U.S. foreign relations. U.S. neocolonial economic policies were coterminous with its Cold War military objectives, and the base workers' union demonstrated the interplay of international, national, and local politics. The base union emerged because of a variety of factors that included an opportunistic Guantánamo politician, an anti-communist, internationalist American Federation of Labor (AFL), and activist base workers, as well as an accommodating U.S. naval administration. In this era, the United States generally defined all dissent as potential "communism," dismissing the importance of domestic dynamics and nationalism. The Cold War framed the parameters of how much leeway the United States would tolerate in its workforce and, ironically, provided both the opening for the base workers' union and the reason for its eventual demise.

Base workers' agency encompassed an array of strategies, from denouncing U.S. officials as fascists to clandestinely stealing cigarettes to acquiescing to U.S. power structures. This is not to attribute an ahistoric revolutionary agency to GTMO employees or provide an inevitable prelude to the Cuban revolution.[6] In the few post-1959 Cuban accounts of the Salomón case, the base union is posited as a forerunner to the 26 of July Movement (M-26-7) and the Cuban revolution.[7] This contention is not without merit, for several union leaders joined the early M-26-7 cells in Guantánamo and Caimanera. Yet this celebratory and teleological analysis does not grapple with the complexity of 1950s U.S.-Cuban politics. It ignores the anti-communist Cold War forces that originally promoted the union, national leaders' neocolonial ambitions, and base workers' own ambivalence toward their U.S. employers.

Vibrant local nationalism and 1950s Cold War politics have been forgotten in the wake of the far more dramatic showdown between the United States and Fidel Castro. The written and oral evidence about the base union often contradicted each other, underscoring the ambiguities of base employment. In my conversations with elderly base workers, a few reveled in their former union days, but many more dismissed the importance of the base union as ineffective, conservative, and inappropriate. In contrast, the archival record is bursting with incendiary language, evidence of local frustrations, and thinly veiled anti-Americanism.[8] This discrepancy points to the popular erasure of Cold War politics in U.S.-Cuban relations before the revolution. The base union and Salomón case counter this assumption. Collectively, they illustrate how the Cold War and neocolonialism framed worker activism and legal debates in post–World War II, pre-Castro Guantánamo.

GTMO AND COLD WAR MILITARY STRATEGY

The United States did not demobilize after World War II. Instead, the U.S. military emerged strong and intact, and its archipelago of bases was well equipped to defend against communism and to maintain U.S. military and economic dominance. The Navy Civil Engineer Corps', or Seabees', account of *Building the Navy's Bases in World War II* described the construction of bases throughout the world, listing its accomplishments: "Bases in the North Atlantic," "Construction Battalions in France and Germany," "Bases in Alaska," "Bases in the Philippines," and "Okinawa."[9] These bases did not disappear at the end of the war. Instead, the structure and network of U.S. bases morphed into a defensive perimeter against the Soviet Union. The U.S. government feared Soviet expansionism and militarism, and it actively sought to support anti-communist governments and protect U.S. economic interests on a global scale.[10] The U.S. military infrastructure that had developed during World War II began to articulate a new Cold War geography.

In fact, the bases became valuable in and of themselves. As early as 1946, Admiral Chester W. Nimitz argued that the "surest defense against atomic bombardment" was a strong navy and a sufficient number of bases to protect against missiles and attack: "Future warfare may for us resolve itself largely into a struggle for the possession of air bases—bases from which an enemy might bomb us effectively and from which we might effectively bomb an enemy."[11] The U.S. Navy prioritized the Pacific Rim and located the central commands in Guam and Hawaii. The Caribbean would be a secondary region; however, it too never demobilized. And GTMO was no exception. Admiral Murphy noted that "unlike the period between World War I and World War II when the [GTMO] naval station had been reduced to a stand-by status," there was no equivalent reduction after World War II.[12] Through a strong military and sense of purpose, the U.S. Navy chose to maintain and expand its international reach and, correspondingly, its funding never receded back to pre-war levels.

The stated mission of the Caribbean Command was to protect the United States, guard the Panama Canal, and defend the naval bases in Puerto Rico, Cuba, and Trinidad. In the Caribbean, preparation and readiness for war coexisted alongside the U.S. Navy's own assessment that the U.S.S.R. would *not* launch a major strike so near the United States.[13] This created a contradictory scenario. On the one hand, U.S. military intelligence concluded that the U.S.S.R. would not initiate a preemptive attack in the Caribbean. On the other hand, Cold War logic presupposed a Soviet threat and the constant need for preparedness. Taking the lessons it had learned from World War II, the U.S. Navy believed oil tankers would be the primary targets for Soviet submarine attacks.[14] It also prioritized protecting shipping routes and preventing anticipated sabotage in Venezuela's oil fields, the Panama Canal, and U.S. military bases. Throughout the late 1940s, the U.S. Navy conducted several war games in the Atlantic to simulate attacks on U.S. bases and hostile Soviet actions. These exercises included anti-aircraft practice, submarine warfare, massive deployments, and even preparations against atomic bombings.[15] The cost of all of these exercises was high, and some military officers argued that having so many expensive and well-developed bases was not necessary. The *New York Times* reported that the Caribbean bases replicated facilities already available on the mainland. GTMO was singled out as being potentially "over-developed."[16]

Despite the submarines and expensive war games, the Cold War in Latin America was only superficially a defensive war against the Soviets; the real fear was of local radicalism, redistribution of wealth, and organized opposition to U.S. capitalist interests. The United States promoted dictatorships in the Caribbean as part of a Cold War strategy to prevent internal radicalism. It was only with military strongmen at the helm that the United States could practice a policy of "non-interventionism" and still rest assured its investments were safe. In the wake of U.S.-sponsored authoritarian militarism, all that remained were dictators, formalistic democracies, and so-called stability.[17]

BATISTA, COMMUNISM, AND THE CUBAN CONFEDERATION OF LABOR, 1940–1945

The U.S. relationship with Fulgencio Batista followed a trajectory of U.S.-backed Cold War dictatorships, albeit with an alternate revolutionary conclusion. Fulgencio Batista was the dominant Cuban figure between 1933 and 1958. Far more than a caricatured dictator, Batista's ideology, allegiances, and relationship with the United States transformed over the decades. Born to a poor family of mixed racial heritage in Oriente, Batista joined the army as a young man. He became prominent as a leader in the coup against Gerardo Machado in 1933. When the United States refused to recognize the 1933 revolutionary government led by Ramón Grau San Martín, Batista threw the military's support behind a civilian president, Carlos Mendieta. Batista wielded significant power as the military might behind a series of "puppet presidents," including Mendieta, José A. Barnet, Miguel Mariano Gómez, and finally Federico Laredo Bru. Each of these men owed their position to Batista, and he remained the driving force in Cuba's political scene. In opposition to this regime, Grau San Martín formed the Auténtico Party, invoking his own "authentic" revolutionary past and attracting nationalist student leaders, such as Eduardo Chibás. However, Batista too embraced many of the principles of 1933, instituting programs for public healthcare, rural community schools, and land reform. Through these populist measures, Batista gained a broad following, and he was elected president of Cuba in 1940 in a relatively free and competitive election.[18]

Batista also forged a strategic alliance with the Unión Revolucionaria Communista, or the Cuban Communist Party, in 1938.[19] In conjunction with the Popular Front, the Cuban Communist Party sought partners and coalitions during the 1930s. It had initially opposed Batista, but after being firmly rejected by Grau San Martín's Auténtico Party, its leadership initiated a dialogue with Batista. Batista needed a popular base to solidify his political support, and he believed he could benefit by a relationship with the Communists. Batista agreed to legalize the party and to allow it to freely publish its newspaper *Hoy* and reorganize the Cuban labor movement under its mantle. As a result, Batista gained a political apparatus to support his presidential bid, and the Communist Party found itself a legitimate player within the Cuban government. In Cuba, the Communist leadership supported union organization and social welfare programs, but because it relied on the government (rather than opposing it), it did not develop a radical character. This collaboration with the government resulted in dependence that later defanged the Cuban labor movement.[20]

The Communist Party had its greatest success when it sponsored the 1939 nation-wide labor coalition, the Confederación de Trabajadores de Cuba (CTC), or the Cuban Confederation of Workers. By 1940 the CTC was the umbrella organization for 537 unions and counted approximately 350,000 members. A significant percentage of CTC members were Cubans of color who benefited from successful strikes and the government's new sympathetic approach to sugar and tobacco workers. Lázaro Peña, a black Cuban tobacco worker, became the CTC's first secretary general and public spokesperson. Because the vast majority of agricultural workers labored for U.S.-owned sugar companies, strikes and labor demands also took on a nationalist tenor. Most CTC members were not Communists, and did not identify as such, but they were more than willing to associate with an organization that looked out for their interests and had a direct line to the national government.[21]

By 1940 Cuban workers had won stronger labor protections than almost any workers in the Western Hemisphere, including those in the United States. The 1940 Cuban Constitution provided workers with unprecedented rights, including the right to participate in collective bargaining, to strike, to a forty-four–hour work week at forty-eight hours of pay, to a minimum wage, to equal pay for men and women, to one month of annual leave, and to paid maternity leave. Peña's leadership accentuated the role of Cubans of color as well as of agricultural workers. In contrast, U.S. labor legislation, including the 1935 National Labor Relations Act and the 1937 Fair Labor Standards Act, explicitly excluded farm workers and domestic servants. The result of a "Southern Compromise," U.S. labor law prevented the majority of black workers from unionizing. Thus, the 1940 Cuban Constitution provided workers, at least on paper, with an exceptionally protective and receptive social welfare state.

Because its leadership included many Communist members, the U.S. government disliked negotiating with the CTC, and it most emphatically did not want its influence on the U.S. naval base in Guantánamo Bay. However, the CTC held a critical role in Batista's coalition and popular politics. So much so that in 1940, U.S. Ambassador George Messersmith agreed to meet with Lázaro Peña about the Frederick Snare Corporation and working conditions on the naval base. Peña hoped to negotiate a contract that would protect workers against arbitrary dismissal and hold the Snare Corporation accountable to Cuban labor law. Messersmith refused. He believed the Communist Party was trying to "create labor trouble at Guantánamo station," describing Peña as a "virulent Communist leader," and "an exploiter of labor." He feared collective bargaining would weaken U.S. authority, disrupt its relationships with private contractors, and allow Communists to enter the base. According to

Messersmith, a labor contract at GTMO was "unnecessary" and "undesirable."[22] Despite Messersmith's repudiation of Peña and his *compañeros*, it remains notable that the U.S. ambassador spoke with them about employment issues on GTMO at all. Batista's support for the Allied cause meant that the United States had to accept an active Communist-led labor union in Cuba. Still, communism was an anathema to U.S. diplomats, and they refused to permit the CTC onto the military base. By 1943 the U.S. State Department and the AFL joined forces to initiate an anticommunist labor movement in Cuba.[23]

World War II's conclusion marked the beginning of the Cold War, and U.S. hostility against communism became even more pronounced. On GTMO, base intelligence officers fired known Communist employees. Cuban domestic politics also became less welcoming to the Communist Party. In 1944 Batista's hand-picked successor Carlos Saladrigas lost the presidential election to Ramón Grau San Martín and the Auténticos. When the Auténticos came to power in 1944, the Communists lost much of their authority. In line with red scares and the Cold War, the Auténticos purged the labor unions of their Communist leadership, censored the Communist Party's newspapers and radio stations, and even sanctioned the murders of Communist labor leaders. The Auténticos presided over an anti-communist government as well as unprecedented corruption.[24]

On the naval base, the United States stood guard against Communist threats. GTMO officers remained on the lookout for "enemy infiltration into Cuba," and believed that attacks were as likely to be domestic as foreign. Cuba's failing political economy could encourage local "armed bands" to attack "with little or no warning."[25] The most likely destabilizing forces would be organized labor in Oriente or workers who traveled between Guantánamo and GTMO. During World War II, fascist workers had been seen as the greatest danger. Now, vigilance against Communists and Communist sympathizers took on a new urgency.

Alberto Torres's father was a founding member of the Communist Party in Caimanera. Alberto and his brothers worked on the U.S. naval base and were also members of the Party's youth wing. However, at the war's conclusion, Alberto was promptly fired for his political activities. Alberto associated the giant and drunken victory celebrations at the end of World War II with a renewed vigor against communism. "At eight or nine at night there was an announcement, and they declared a national holiday for the victory against Japan. . . . We enjoyed a vacation for one week in honor of the U.S. victory, and then we returned to the base. And when we returned that week, they were already spreading rumors—rumors about who the

North Americans were going to get rid of—that they were going to throw the Communists off the base." Alberto remembered that U.S. officials soon picked him up for questioning. The base intelligence officers did not speak Spanish, so they relied on a Cuban translator to interrogate Alberto. In retrospect, Alberto found the dialogue quite comic. He had known the translator personally, and he remembered how the translator tried to cajole him to renounce (or at least hide) his Communist sympathies. To soften him up, the translator asked innocuous questions about movies, melodramas, and John Wayne. But after trying to get Alberto on his side and convince him to give in to the U.S. officials, he finally proceeded with political questions. The interrogation shifted, and he asked Alberto what he thought of the war and the United Nations. Then, he asked if he was a member of a political party: "Republican Party, Conservative Party, Liberal Party, PRC, Communist Party? . . . And I said, 'Come on, you know better, tell *Johnny* that I've always been a Communist.' " With this, Alberto acted out how he was physically attacked and thrown off the base. " 'Ay! Communist!' And they took me like this—Pa! Pa! Pa!—and they threw me and, damn, there was the door. . . . Yes, yes, yes, they threw me against the door. . . . Then they threw me, expelled me from the base. . . . You know, the employees had to form a line and lift up their arms, as they registered you and let you exit. . . . But me, no, to me, they put me in the front of the line and threw me out the door. . . . Then I felt the blows that they had given me."[26] Given the eventual institutionalization of the Communist Party in Cuba in the years following Castro's 1959 victory, Alberto took a great deal of pride in recounting this story. More than fifty years later, Alberto Torres could assert that he had always been a Communist and that he had never hidden his affiliation.

However colored by time, Torres's narrative invoked the new tenor of Cold War politics on GTMO. U.S. officials no longer had to negotiate with the CTC or Lázaro Peña, and they most certainly were not going to tolerate avowed Communist Party members as base employees. Still, the naval officials proceeded somewhat cautiously to avoid outright conflict with its workforce. For example, in 1951 the base commander discharged twenty-four local workers for allegedly being Communist Party members. They were not given hearings or advance notice and were dismissed immediately. However, the base commander did not want to publicize why these workers had been fired and euphemistically declared they were "general[ly] unsuitable for further employment." Any reference to their Communist activities was to be publicly silenced.[27] The aversion to making an example of these employees suggests that base workers were not as outraged or concerned about the ideological purity of their coworkers as their U.S. superiors. In this era, Cuban Communists were not particularly radical, oppositional, or anti-American; instead, their leaders cooperated with government partners and the Ministry of Labor. While U.S. officials worried about Communist infiltration and the Cold War, workers were far more preoccupied with wages and job security. There is no evidence that workers mobilized to support Torres or the other allegedly Communist employees, but they repeatedly protested unfair layoffs and unexplained dismissals. Rather than being attracted to the Communist Party, base workers championed the U.S. rule of law and U.S. principles to improve their neocolonial position. To the best of their abilities, they insisted that GTMO recognize a single legal standard and respect workers' rights in this Cold War context.

SOCIAL LAW ON GTMO: CUBAN OR NORTH AMERICAN?

Although operating in Cuban territory, the U.S. Navy recognized that it was against U.S. interests to follow any Cuban laws on the base. There was power in jurisdiction. Conceding to Cuban labor demands could create a slippery slope and erode U.S. authority. As one base commander stated, if Cuban labor laws applied to workers on the base, it "might easily progress to the application of other Cuban laws" on GTMO. He feared that any adherence to Cuban law would "nullify" the United States' "complete jurisdiction." Still, the base was clearly in Cuba, and officials had to recognize Cuban workers' expectations and the local political economy. The U.S. Navy's strategy for navigating between U.S. law and Cuban workers' demands was to grant the substance of the demands without conceding to the letter of Cuban law.[28]

At GTMO, U.S. officers often took advantage of the discrepancies between U.S. and Cuban law, deliberately choosing the law that best suited management. Because of GTMO's anomalous position and unique legal status, these nitty-gritty labor decisions became a concern for the diplomatic corps and the State Department. For example, in the early 1950s local workers claimed that the base had followed the Cuban standard for annual leave, even though U.S. law had provided more generous benefits. But when the Cuban law changed to allow for more time off, base officials switched course and decided to follow the now more stingy U.S. standard.[29] GTMO officials also compared U.S. and Cuban maternity policies and concluded that female employees received fewer benefits under U.S. Navy regulations than under Cuban law. They dismissed this concern, because few Cuban employers provided the legislated support and base workers did not prioritize women's issues.[30] In each instance, the United States had to consider Cuban norms and laws, but it did not have to replicate them.

Guantánamo journalist Lino Lemes was the most persistent advocate for base workers' rights. His critique did not challenge the United States' right to operate the naval station; instead, he consistently harped on the fact that base workers had no legal protections. As soon as the base expansion began Lemes wrote, "Right now two thousand workers on the U.S. naval station . . . do not receive benefits under Cuban social law nor under U.S. social law." He repeated this sentiment time and again, declaring, "The workers on the U.S. naval base are not protected by the American social laws nor by the Cuban social laws."[31] When Lemes called for "social laws," he was referring to minimum wage, maximum hours, pensions, leave policies, and job security. Lemes challenged the U.S. government to live up to its democratic principles. He not only wrote editorials, but also composed letters to the president of the United States, the secretary of the navy, the secretary of state, the governor of Santiago de Cuba, and the president of Cuba.[32] If the U.S. Navy studiously refused to accept Cuban social laws, Lemes demanded they enforce U.S. labor laws. In letters to President Roosevelt, he suggested that the United States disingenuously applied "whichever [law] happened to be more convenient."[33]

Throughout the 1940s, base workers participated in protests, wrote letters to U.S. officials, and in a variety of ways made their concerns heard. For example, in 1940 workers complained that "the food is very bad," and even worse, water was turned off in the base camps after seven o'clock at night, forcing workers to buy soft drinks and beers at the company store.[34] In 1945 a group of workers protested their low salaries and claimed they earned well below the Cuban minimum wage.[35] Transportation continued to be a concern for workers, and in 1947, 150 workers rallied against increased railroad fees and demanded corresponding raises.[36] Workers also took umbrage at the extravagant lifestyles of North Americans on the base. For example, Pedro Peres Ruiz wrote to the U.S. Office of Inter-American Affairs: "I am sure there are things being done here which are not in accordance with the laws of the United States." He outlined his concerns about low wages and long hours and contrasted base workers' labor with U.S. officers' privileges. "The bosses of this base spend weekends banqueting and dancing, throwing away in riotous living . . . the fruits of our labor. This money they throw away has been exploited from the workers of an American naval base. . . . Please do something for the workingmen of this base, or if that is not possible, please pass this on to some of the labor unions in the United States."[37] After a brief review, the U.S. Navy concluded that no one by the name of Pedro Ruiz worked on the base, and no one of that name was listed on the Guantánamo voting rolls. As a result, the base commander concluded that the letter was a "crank." Whether "Pedro Peres Ruiz" was a pseudonym, a composite of several workers, or a worker lost in administrative files, his letter voiced the contrast between Cuban working-class standards and the display of North American luxury on the base.

Such missives and demonstrations also illustrated a certain attraction to and faith in U.S. ideals and U.S. institutions. Workers used the rhetoric of U.S. democracy to request benefits from their U.S. employers. As neocolonial subjects, they believed they were entitled to the protection of U.S. rights and had no qualms about soliciting the U.S. government. Although there is no evidence that the United States responded to these requests directly, the perusal and collection of these epistles indicates a keen interest in keeping a close watch on its workforce.

Workers could also take a far more hostile tone with the U.S. military. For example, Angel Calzado, a base worker, sent a scathing note to the U.S. State Department. He believed that U.S. officials showed "Olympic scorn" toward base workers, asserting "that we, all the workers and employees of the base, do not leave our status as free men and citizens of a civilized country in the courtyard of our homes when we arise at half-past four in the morning" and travel to the base. In the most vitriolic passage, Calzado compared the treatment of base workers as the "same treatment that the Nazis gave the prisoners in the concentration camps."[38] The anger embedded in his words unmasked Cuban nationalism and resentment against GTMO. Written just days before Germany's total surrender, Calzado identified GTMO officials with Nazis rather than with good neighbors. Unlike the elusive Ruiz, Calzado signed his letter with his name and badge number—more than willing to be recognized and named. However, base officials did not fire Calzado, and he continued to work at GTMO until 1954. He later became active in the base workers' union, which formed in 1950, and to which he was elected secretary general.

These critiques reveal the ways in which workers lobbied the U.S. Navy to live up to U.S. principles and the rule of law. This is not to overstate the case or argue for a direct popular challenge to the U.S.

military occupation of Guantánamo Bay. Instead it shows how workers believed they could improve their conditions by holding the U.S.
Navy accountable to U.S. and Cuban standards. Their daily grievances
brought to light base workers' understandings of and frustrations with
the U.S. military. Throughout the 1940s, base workers did not have a
union or a collective voice, and so they petitioned the U.S. government
individually with or without success. By 1950 Cuba's national labor
movement and the Cold War converged to allow a base workers'
union.

THE COLD WAR, THE CTC, AND THE AFL, 1946-1948

The control of the national Cuban labor movement became a political
battle in the years following World War II. The spring of 1946 saw a
wave of strikes in the sugar industry, and in the immediate post-war
months, the CTC continued to wield significant power. Grau San Martín
initially tolerated the Communist-controlled CTC, but the U.S. State Department and the AFL pressured the administration to reorganize the
CTC as an anti-communist organization. In addition, democratic reformers were disillusioned by the Auténtico government's corrupt practices. In 1947 Eddy Chibás, who entered politics as a charismatic student
leader in 1933, split with Grau and formed the oppositional, nationalist
Ortodoxo Party. Chibás attracted a middle-class following and represented the ideals of the 1933 revolution: social justice, integrity, and national sovereignty. He was also an anti-communist who did not welcome
the Communist Party or the CTC to be part of his coalition. These
schisms radically reconfigured the CTC.

In 1947 the CTC split into two opposing camps: a Communist-led coalition, still led by Lázaro Peña, and an anti-communist Auténtico branch.
The AFL and the U.S. State Department had been intimately involved
with this division, and they had encouraged anti-communist union leaders to oppose Peña. In fact, the AFL and the State Department worked together to promote anti-communist unions throughout Latin America, and
Cuba was one of their first successes. Grau's government acknowledged
only the anti-communist CTC and began an aggressive anti-communist
purge, which included persecuting Communist members. Without support from the socially progressive Ortodoxos, the Communist Party no
longer had a government partner, and it dwindled in numbers and influence. The CTC was now led by opportunist Auténtico leaders, such as Eusebio Mujal, Juan Arévalo, and Francisco Aguirre.[39]

In 1948 Carlos Prío, the Auténtico candidate, won the presidency. His government was noted for its corruption and *gangsterismo*. He reportedly embezzled ninety million dollars of government funds for his own personal wealth.[40] These years of Auténtico rule did not result in much aid or investment in the eastern provinces. With little success, the *fuerzas vivas* in Guantánamo clamored for government funds for public health, clean water, and roads. In 1948 Guantánamo students led a hunger strike to compel the government to construct local schools.[41] The lack of government services provoked mass protests and strikes throughout the region, which even reached the U.S. media and the *New York Times*.[42]

In Guantánamo, labor became a key wedge whereby Cuban CTC officials could negotiate with the U.S. naval base. The advent of the Korean War led to a new spike in government and contract base jobs. With the Cold War escalating and heightening concerns about domestic nationalism and regional protests, U.S. officials agreed to work with the anti-communist CTC. This resulted in the emergence of a base workers' union, which U.S. and Cuban officials hoped would channel workers' grievances in a manageable and conservative direction.

COLD WAR UNIONISM

In 1950 the U.S. Navy took a rare step and recognized a union of base workers and employees on the U.S. naval base in Guantánamo Bay. Without the Cold War, the union would never have been organized or accepted by Cuban politicians or U.S. officials. National leaders from the AFL and the now anti-communist CTC supported the union as a measure against potential radicalism. The union's stated goals were relatively non-threatening; it gave up the right to strike and was charged to support bread and butter issues like wages, benefits, and safety concerns. However, the presence of an organized and mobilized workforce could not be completely constricted by Cold War norms, and Cuban nationalism was never far below the surface of the local rank-and-file leadership.

The base workers' union was strongest during one of Cuba's more volatile political eras, the years immediately preceding and following Batista's 1952 *golpe del estado,* or coup d'état. The union's rise and fall mapped the peculiarities and limitations of U.S.-Cuba, pre-Castro Cold War relations. In 1950 the Auténtico Party was in power, but rapidly losing credibility with the general population. A presidential election was scheduled for May 1952, and the Auténticos, Ortodoxos, and Batista were all in the race. Eddy Chibás's suicide in 1951 left the Ortodoxos in disarray, but if the 1952 elections had been held, it is possible the Ortodoxo Party might have won based on its nationalist appeal and commitment to root out corruption. Instead, Batista took no chances and conspired with the army to overtake the Prío government. With almost no government resistance, Batista announced himself Cuba's ruler on March 10, 1952. Identifying Batista as a dictator with whom it could do business, the United States government granted Batista's new regime official recognition on March 27, 1952. In turn, Batista knew to burnish his Cold War credentials. He promised the United States he would respect U.S. capital, and this time around he severed all ties with the Soviet Union and outlawed the Communist Party. From 1952 through 1958, Batista continued to work with the CTC as a corporatist labor base, but now the CTC was stripped of its progressive tendencies and dedicated organizers.[43]

The dominant CTC leader after World War II was Eusebio Mujal Barinol, an opportunistic and ambitious politician from the Guantánamo region with a shady history. Mujal switched parties as the political winds dictated and gained a reputation as a particularly corrupt and dishonest player in a world of much corruption and dishonesty.[44] He began his political career as a Communist, only to repudiate the party a few years later. He then joined the nationalist, militia-like Joven Cuba in opposition to Batista's rule in 1934. By 1938 he allied himself with the Auténticos and the anti-communist labor movement. Elected senator from the Guantánamo region, Mujal became the most prominent *guantanamero* in national Cuban politics, wielding significant power as the secretary general of the CTC under the Auténtico government from 1949 until 1952. After Batista's 1952 *golpe del estado*, Mujal again chose the winning side. Rather than call for national strikes to protest this assault on democratic elections or support his own Auténtico Party, Mujal joined forces with Batista and maintained his position in the CTC. Under Mujal, the CTC became a symbol of co-opted, corporatist unionism in both the Auténtico and the Batista eras. Even U.S. diplomats searching for anti-communist allies in the Cuban labor movement distanced themselves from Mujal in the late 1940s. His stewardship was characterized by fraud, theft, and cronyism, and alleged murders of rival Communist union leaders.[45] With the triumph of the 26 of July Movement and Fidel Castro in 1959, the revolutionary government vilified Mujal, who exiled himself to the United States.

Mujal had Guantánamo origins. He was from a Spanish immigrant family that settled in Guantánamo in the early twentieth century. His fa-

Figure 6. Eusebio Mujal, political advertisement. *La Voz del Pueblo*, May 1948. Courtesy of the Guantánamo Provincial Library.

ther owned the local bakery, and Mujal grew up in Guantánamo, where he launched his political career. In the 1940s Mujal retained local support among the Guantánamo elites who lauded him for protecting workers' rights and guarding against communism.[46] Since that time, Mujal's reputation has not held up as well. In interviews with former base workers, they described Mujal as a reactionary and untrustworthy. Former base worker Juan Carlos Pulsara commented that even before 1952, Mujal had an "imperialist ideology" and was already an "agent of U.S.

politics." Walter Knight stated that Mujal was interested only in collecting union dues and robbing them from the workers. He described Mujal as a "bandit." He concluded by reluctantly admitting that for better or worse, Mujal was a *guantanamero*.[47]

Despite, or perhaps because of his duplicity, Mujal was an excellent ally for the AFL's anti-communist foreign policy in the 1940s and 1950s. In the United States, the AFL had always championed conservative trade unionism, which accepted the corporate capitalist economy, and in the 1930s it had shunned the more progressive Congress of Industrial Organizations (CIO). With the end of World War II, the AFL and the CIO competed for alliances in Europe and Latin America. With the domestic red scare in the United States and the 1947 Taft-Hartley Act's demand for loyalty oaths, the AFL remained committed to a capitalist economy and government-sanctioned unionism. The AFL spent considerable resources undermining Communist-affiliated unions in Latin America and pressuring Latin American trade unions to adhere to the United States' Cold War position.[48] By taking this hard-line stand, the AFL hoped to defuse international radicalism and curry favor at home as labor's Cold Warriors. Serafino Romualdi, an Italian immigrant and unionist, was the AFL's leading ambassador in Latin America. He credited the Communist Party's failure to gain power in Latin America as the direct result of the AFL-supported trade union movement.[49] From World War II through the 1960s, Romualdi directed the AFL's Latin American program and reportedly worked hand in hand with the CIA.[50] In Cuba, Romualdi found his anti-communist partner in Mujal, and the two worked closely together in the late 1940s and 1950s.

In 1950 Mujal and Romualdi joined forces in a surprising joint venture: the base workers' union in Guantánamo Bay. Mujal began to speak publicly of a base workers' union in Guantánamo in the spring of 1950, and he sent an official proposal to the AFL's 1950 national convention.[51] In this proposal, he asked for AFL sponsorship and spelled out the base workers' concerns: local workers' salaries were inferior to U.S. workers' salaries, local base workers earned less than the U.S. minimum wage of seventy-five cents an hour, workers had to travel up to four hours a day commuting to and from the base, and GTMO workers did not have "an efficient mechanism to regulate their relations with the base or fix their complaints."[52] The AFL supported Mujal's platform and endorsed the base workers' rights to organize a union. The AFL offered more than just symbolic support. Romualdi agreed to act as a mediator between the local workers and the U.S. Navy, and he traveled to Guantánamo to meet with local labor leaders.[53] Spearheading a base workers' union allowed Mujal and Romualdi direct access to U.S. diplomatic officials and the U.S. Navy.

The goals of the new union were to resolve ongoing issues between the workers and the base authorities and to prevent base workers from gravitating to radical or Communist organizations. Lino Lemes lauded the emergence of organized labor on the base as "another triumph for Mujal." Lemes imagined that the base union would finally clarify workers' legal status. And Lemes made no bones about the union's position in the Cold War. His column's headline in *El Vigilante* on October 4, 1950 announced, "Unionization, Better Pay and Other Measures for the Base Workers is a Mortal Blow against Communism." He believed that the U.S. acceptance of the base workers' union would be a strong measure in the anti-communist campaign.[54]

The U.S. Navy grudgingly accepted this trade union as a control measure against worker agitation. Admiral Murphy, who wrote *The History of Guantánamo Bay,* was the commanding officer when the union organized itself on the base.[55] Of all the base commanders, Admiral Murphy made the most concerted effort to improve relations between Guantánamo and GTMO. To this end, he recognized the base workers' union. Even so, a union on a military base was such an unusual phenomenon that Lemes noted, it "seemed incredible." The union opened a hall in Guantánamo and communicated directly with base officials, including Admiral Murphy. Admiral Murphy also presented the union leadership with a U.S. flag to display alongside its Cuban flag at the union hall's opening ceremonies, and the base newsletter, *The Indian,* publicized this event.[56] Throughout these ceremonies, Murphy's attitude remained that of a benevolent colonial benefactor. As long as the union remained in line and did not air its grievances publicly, Murphy could accept it.

Quite noticeably, the U.S. Navy avoided using the word "union" in its official employee handbook, *Your Navy Job.* Instead, it sidestepped the debate over a "union," while stating respect for employees' right "to join, or refrain from joining, organized *employee groups.*" It continued that this group did not have the right to strike and needed to recognize it was dealing with the military and not a private company.[57] Despite this linguistic slippage, in all diplomatic correspondence U.S. officials recognized and called the new organization a "union." In Murphy's opinion, the base union representatives were "excitable Latin Americans inexperienced in union leadership" prone to "immature conduct." He could permit negotiations and dialogue as long as they did not create a public outcry.[58]

Under the Cold War bargain, the union was not supposed to disrupt the balance of power or embarrass the base. However, Mujal and Romualdi were not simply puppets or beholden to GTMO officials. They recognized that through targeted publicity, they could gain leverage over the U.S. government. For example, in April 1952, in the weeks following Batista's *golpe del estado,* the base union took a more aggressive, rather than a more passive, posture. Frustrated at being stonewalled by base officials in their campaign for more equitable working conditions, the union leadership went to *Prensa Libre,* a Havana newspaper. When the base officials asked them to retract their statements, the union leadership refused, repeating that they had spoken the truth. The base officials were outraged that this "local" conflict had become national, and they cut the union leaders' salaries and disciplined them. Faced with U.S. opposition, Mujal and Romualdi backed the base union's leadership. Mujal went so far as to promise that "the whole labor movement of Cuba will stand behind the union at the Guantánamo naval base."[59] Mujal's reaction appears somewhat surprising, given that he had just agreed to support Batista and, in doing so, had prevented the "whole labor movement of Cuba" from protesting the coup. Yet in this instance, Mujal seems to have enjoyed the clout and sway he gained by pushing U.S. officials to recognize "his" union. Presumably, Mujal believed that the union was under his control, and that he could press GTMO officials, engage with State Department diplomats, and increase his own foreign influence through sponsoring the base union. On a certain level, the United States had to negotiate with the partners it had designated as acceptable. The Cold War allowed a certain flexibility for anti-communist unionists and dictators, in this case, Mujal and Batista.

Thus, the origins of control in the base workers' union were top-down. On their own, the local workers did not have enough political clout to demand recognition from the base authorities and from the outset the base union was nationally directed. Still, workers' concerns were real, and they began to use the union as an effective tool to voice their grievances.

Workers joined, or did not join, the union for a range of reasons. Of the approximately 3,200 employees on the base, U.S. officials estimated that approximately 1,300 were on the union rolls.[60] The union defined its membership as "native and alien" employees, and not just "Cubans." The "alien" designation encompassed West Indians, Spaniards, and other non-US, non-Cuban nationals, including all *no americanos.* The leadership was mostly Cuban, but at least one worker with an English name, Cornelius Lewis, belonged to the executive board, suggesting his West Indian heritage.[61] The union represented only government civil service employees. Private contract employees and privately hired domestic servants were not allowed to join. It was also predominantly male and, although some women did work as civil service employees, the term "base worker" became normalized as male. For the most part, workers did not choose to join the union out of an oppositional stance or latent anti-Americanism. Rather, workers chose to join out of self-interest and because trade unionism played an established role in Cuban political culture.[62] As Walter Knight, a West Indian descendant, commented: "Yes, I was a member, about everyone was in it. . . . [It was] normal, you know, every sector here [in Cuba] had a union, and we [the base workers] didn't have one. We thought that we needed to have a union too."[63]

The base union sought to rectify the disparities between local and U.S. employees on the base, and to clarify workers' positions between Cuban and U.S. legal norms. Its first priority was to advocate for raises and a more equitable pay scale. There were two principal concerns with wages. First, there was discrimination evident in the gap between what Cubans earned and what U.S. civilian employees earned, and second, base workers claimed their salaries were not even up to local standards. Several workers remembered earning far less than their U.S. counterparts. For example, Juan Carlos Pulsara described the bifurcated wage system: "For example, I am going to give you a comparison, I earned . . . as a mechanical drawer . . . one dollar and forty cents an hour. . . . But the U.S. citizen doing equivalent work earned six dollars and a bit an hour. . . . That is five times more. And the U.S. citizens who worked on the base received a 20 percent bonus from their boss. They earned more for being overseas, for being away from the continental territory. . . . This was terrible. This bonus for being overseas was more than my salary, more privileges and that gave them power to acquire everything that they needed in the navy stores, . . . imagine."[64]

Like Juan Carlos, Santiago Ruiz had similar memories of earning far less than the North Americans with whom he worked. Santiago was more resigned to the situation and laughed a bit in retrospect: "I worked as a *plantillero*. . . . Each of the Americans earned, for example, more or less $4.00 an hour. I earned $1.48 an hour. . . . I had to accept it, had to accept it."[65] This salary pattern was far from unusual. Throughout the U.S. network of bases and overseas projects, in particular the Panama Canal, the United States had profited from paying local workers on a native pay scale, rather than paying U.S. wages.[66] This was an effective strategy that kept U.S. costs down and maintained a hierarchy whereby U.S. employees were consistently in superior positions over local workers.

The union campaigned for equal wages for U.S. and local civil service employees. Although it did not achieve this goal, base officials took notice.[67] In radio broadcasts, the union became more aggressive and defined the wage discrepancy as "discrimination." The leadership also pointed out that one U.S. salary was equivalent to three native salaries. This made layoffs appear even more unfair, especially when the U.S. Navy explained it was laying off local workers for budgetary reasons.[68] By 1954 the base union's radio broadcasts were demanding "equal pay for equal work" and decrying the differential between U.S. civil service and local workers' salaries.[69]

The disparities between government and private contract jobs provided yet another opening for the base union. By all accounts, government civil service positions provided higher wages and better benefits than contract work. Civil service employees contributed a percentage of their salaries to a fund, which would later be used for annuities distributed on retirement. For example, Ramón Sánchez contributed six and a half cents a week to the retirement fund. Government positions also created opportunities for advancement and offered English and evening classes.[70] In contrast, private contract jobs did not offer pensions, leave, or other benefits. The U.S. Navy supported this division, because it did not want to face competition from its own contractors. As a result, the average worker saw four (and sometimes more) unequal pay scales. At the top were U.S. civil service employees, second were local workers with civil service positions, third were workers employed by private contractors, and finally there were domestic workers. Moreover, although the U.S. Navy tolerated the union, it had no intention of foisting a similar body onto its private contractors.

Private contractors operated outside of Cuban labor law and U.S. labor law. The contractors were under no obligation to match the Cuban minimum wage nor the civil service employee pay scale. When the United States was negotiating its first contract with the Snare Corporation, Ambassador George Messersmith articulated the fine balance contractors would have to walk: concede to most Cuban labor demands even though it was not "essential that every single requirement of the Cuban labor laws be carried through."[71] To base workers this distinction was acute. For example, in 1940 the Puerto Rican workers Pedro Salgado and José Fernández wrote to President Roosevelt: "In reality, this company [Frederick Snare] sometimes followed Cuban laws and other times American laws, from our perspective mocking the laws of both nations."[72] Salgado and Fernández believed private contractors insulted the rule of law, resulting in a hypocrisy of U.S. principles.

Private contract employees looked to the government base workers' union as a model. Although they never had the same support from the CTC or the AFL, they too wanted to form their own union. In 1950, with the growing militarization for the Korean War, the U.S. Navy contracted the Drake Winkleman Corporation to build an airstrip on the Leeward Point, also known as Tres Pierdas. A subset of these contract workers sent their demands by telegram to President Harry Truman: "We, 500 laborers working for the American base at Guantánamo with the Drake Winkleman Co. request your immediate intervention in dispute caused by failure of said company to comply with social laws in Cuba." In subsequent telegrams they denounced the Drake Winkleman Corporation as "criminal," called on "democratic Cuban workers" for support, and demanded higher salaries. They also wanted vacation time, the standard Cuban work week of forty-eight hours of pay for forty-four hours of work, sick days, and time off for Cuban national holidays. The United States response was brief: Cuban law was not recognized on the base and increasing the contractor's costs would be "disastrous." Naval officers also noted that Juan Zarran Treas, who signed the telegram, no longer worked for the Winkleman Corporation, and they doubted he represented the five hundred workers he claimed. The Winkleman Corporation saw little to gain and much to lose in recognizing a union. It refused to yield on any of the principal issues and defended itself as living up to its U.S. contract. It hired workers only on a daily basis, and therefore had no obligation to pay for vacation or sick leave. Although the Winkleman Corporation agreed to meet with a contingent of workers, it offered no concessions.[73]

However, the precedent of state-sponsored unionization had been set, and contract workers hoped they could spur Cuban national politicians from Mujal to Batista to intervene and defend their cause. In his many editorials, Lino Lemes advocated for the CTC to support the private employees. He reported that the Winkleman Corporation had unjustly fired a group of workers who had protested the overpriced and poor food on the work site. Moreover, he railed against the lack of legal protections for contract workers: "It will be necessary for the U.S. government to intervene, in order for these powerful companies to follow either American or Cuban social law, because right now they follow whichever one is most convenient."[74] Lino Lemes also argued that this new union would be another "blow against communism."[75] *La Voz del Pueblo* encouraged Batista to initiate a dialogue with the U.S. ambassador in Havana to resolve the private employees' predicament through diplomatic channels.[76] Workers occupied a politically charged territory, and if they garnered the right allies, they could provoke national leaders to defend their platform before the U.S. government.

The government employees' union, now led by Angel Calzado and José Pérez Repilado, committed its solidarity to the contract workers. Mujal and Romualdi also threw their support behind Zarran and the private employees, warning the U.S. government to concede to these workers' demands rather than risk an international conflict. On the radio, the base union broadcast editorials that backed the contract workers. Calzado even made an argument with a sly and knowing twist on U.S. labor practices; because private employers generally paid better salaries than the government in the United States, he argued that the private contract workers should actually earn higher salaries than the civil service employees.[77] Mujal also voiced his support for the Winkleman employees and threatened that it was in the U.S. Navy's interest to resolve labor conflicts. He went so far as to suggest that a labor problem on the base could make it "necessary for Cuba to reconsider the entire question of the base."[78] For Mujal to even infer that labor concerns could jeopardize U.S. military control in GTMO was eyebrow-raising. Romualdi seconded this threat and concluded that any conflicts with the base union would provide the Communists and "extreme nationalists" with a "ready-made issue." He noted that "there is already talk of initiating a nationwide campaign for the revision of the treaty between Cuba and the United States."[79]

Romualdi's conflation of the Communists and extreme nationalists was indicative of the United States' myopic Cold War vision, whereby all dissent was labeled as Communist. Although in 1952 the Cuban Communist Party was weaker than it had been since the early 1930s, U.S. officials still defined workers' agency as another brand of communism. The base commander admitted, "There is nothing to indicate any connection between the base union and the Communist Party." Even so, he went on to connect the two: "It is noteworthy that the tactics being employed by the union are those normally used by Communists, and the end effect (planting the seeds of distrust, suspicion, and hatred of the United States) is the same."[80] Rather than interpreting the resurgence of worker activism as a sign of Cuban nationalism or legitimate frustration with an unequal wage structure, the U.S. naval officials could not escape the dominant belief that any critique of U.S. policy was akin to communism.

In their most potentially damaging challenge to U.S. authority, Lino Lemes and the base workers suggested renegotiating the 1903 and 1934 lease agreements. As early as 1940, Lino Lemes had argued that the lease agreements needed to be revamped: "It is necessary to modify the treaty because it does not protect the native worker."[81] He viewed the 1953 anniversary as the perfect opportunity. To protect local workers, the United States and Cuba should renew the treaty with additional language regarding workers' rights, benefits, and pensions. Regardless of the fact that he repeatedly called for a new treaty for close to fifteen years, he couched this proposal in conservative language. He framed a renewed lease agreement as an anti-communist, not an anti-American, endeavor: "I am fighting for a new treaty between the United States and Cuba in relation to the personnel who work on the base, and this new treaty will be another violent strike against communism."[82] Lemes implicitly recognized that U.S. officials might interpret his nationalism and dedication to base workers' rights as a communist or radical measure, and so he emphasized his anti-communist credentials along with his petition to renew the lease agreements.

US officials ignored Lemes's requests and hoped to ignore GTMO's fiftieth anniversary altogether. They knew that despite relatively friendly relations and economic commerce between Guantánamo and GTMO, it was impossible to escape the fact that GTMO's legacy was enmeshed in the Platt Amendment and Cuba's limited independence after 1902. A high-profile ceremony could "result in undue publicity and undesirable public reaction in Cuba." The State Department believed it was necessary to keep the celebration within "moderate limits" that should not include President Batista or any of his cabinet, so as not to put them in an awkward position.[83] Quite bluntly, the U.S. government did not want to draw attention to fifty years of U.S. occupation in Guantánamo Bay.[84]

In contrast, the base workers' union called on the CTC and the Cuban government to initiate a "Revision of the Treaty," to obtain better working conditions.[85] The union radio broadcasts took on an increasingly nationalist tenor: It was "imperative" to revise the treaty to protect "this piece of land which belongs to the Cubans." The leadership argued that "the $2000 per year paid as rent for this land do[es] not give rights of life and death upon the workers."[86] In this manner, the base union publicized the U.S. Navy's low rent and asserted that this sum should not result in arbitrary power over Cuban workers.

This rhetoric was exactly what base officials had hoped to avoid. As the union leadership grew more confident, it made stronger and more strident claims against the U.S. government. The union was beginning to overstep its initial role as an antidote to radicalism. Base officials had to weigh how much public acrimony they could tolerate and at what point the union crossed the line and became a threat itself. The union broadcast two weekly radio spots in Guantánamo on channel CMKS. The radio announcements often attacked unequal pay scales and discrimination against Cubans in "promotion, housing, and transportation." The chief of industrial relations charged that the programs contained "highly inflammatory propaganda" and were filled with "half-truths" and "distortions."[87] For example, José Pérez Repilado described the scenario of a base worker, with a wife and two children, who had been dismissed after nine years of service. Repilado doubted the U.S. Navy's claim that it "had no money." According to the base official who recorded and translated the broadcast, Repilado said:

> This is unjust and discriminatory. . . . [I]t seems impossible that the men be treated as savages (sons of the jungle, he said) just five miles away from their own country, being discriminated and looked at contemptibly in this piece of land which is very much their own. [Repilado] said that the medals, diplomas, and commendations given to the men here, are as good to them as if they were thrown into the garbage can . . . that they expect the intervention of the Cuban government, civic organizations, and others, to prevent continuation of the despicable moral and economical discrimination which has been strangling them for so many years.[88]

Repilado's claim to the land that was "very much their own" was the closest the union came to protesting the U.S. occupation of Cuban territory outright. The union leadership under Calzado and Repilado was growing more confident.

The base union now sought to champion workers' rights through a nationalist critique, while still existing within the parameters of a Cold War organization. This would become an increasingly difficult balancing act. On the one hand, Calzado and Repilado's broadcasts unearthed hostility against the U.S. military and frustration with base workers' neocolonial position. On the other hand, Calzado and Repilado relied not only on grassroots support, but also the continued patronage of Mujal, the CTC, Romualdi, and the AFL. In the 1950s U.S. officials did not often distinguish between nationalism and communism, and this trait predated Castro's 1959 rise to power. Paradoxically, the radicalism that the United States, along with Mujal and Romualdi, had hoped to stymie now gained momentum and a bold voice, albeit still through an anti-communist organization they themselves had sponsored.

PETTY THEFT, SMUGGLING, AND JURISDICTION

Not all protest was as blatant and public as the base union's radio broadcasts. Political scientist James Scott's theory of "weapons of the weak" and "every day acts of resistance" also resonates in the neocolonial confines of the base. Scott expands the definition of agency to less blatant political acts, which lie outside normally sanctioned channels, such as union activity and writing letters to President Roosevelt. Instead these "weapons of the weak" include a wide swath of activities, from workers taking long breaks to helping themselves to their employers' possessions.[89] The base union leaders did not publicly condone petty theft, but from all accounts, base workers smuggled and stole commercial items on a widespread basis, pilfering everything from cigarettes to small boats. This was not an overt challenge to U.S. authority, but it demonstrated a general disregard for U.S. property rights. Given the U.S. occupation of Cuban territory and U.S. displays of wealth, many workers might have believed that this additional compensation was their due. As long as it did not threaten their jobs, workers either participated or looked the other way when it came to small-scale robbery. Moreover, the Caimanera and Guantánamo courts displayed little interest in prosecuting these cases and provided ample cover for alleged thieves. This situation created a legal crisis for GTMO. Base officials believed they needed to enforce the base's boundaries and punish perpetrators outside the Cuban judicial system.

After labor law, criminal law had the most direct impact on workers' daily lives. In Cuba, customs officials wanted to prevent untaxed, contraband goods from entering Cuba. For base officials, theft disrupted law and order on the base and, at an official level, simply could not be tolerated. Monitoring and preventing these crimes provoked a debate about whether U.S. or Cuban law governed those charged. According to the 1903 treaty, "fugitives from justice" who were subject to Cuban law could not "take refuge" on the base, nor could persons subject to U.S. law seek refuge in Cuba.[90] Nevertheless, this clause did not clarify the fate of workers charged with crimes *on* the base. Typically, the United States and Cuba maintained a mutual policy whereby U.S. sailors and marines who found themselves in legal difficulties, often related to drunken brawls, were remanded to the naval station, and

Cuban workers charged with theft were brought to trial in the Cuban court system. In most instances, nationality trumped geography, and neither country tried to enforce its criminal legal system on citizens from the other nation. This practice generally resulted in the United States' favor, as it did in the Kid Chicle case.

In my interviews, all the former workers remembered stories about robbing items from the base. My questions were generally met with smiles and knowing nods, although only one worker admitted to being complicit in a theft. He confessed that his wife, a domestic servant, had been fired from an officer's home for stealing.[91] Juan Carlos Pulsara denied ever participating in petty theft before the revolution, but he essentially justified the practice as a critical component of the moral economy, where contraband compensated for low salaries.[92] Other informants denied any direct participation, but almost all had a story about a friend, or a friend of a friend, who filched goods off the base. For example, Victor Davis, who began working on the base in 1944, recalled a lot of "tricky" business: "We had guys there, they were genius. I don't know where they put things. . . . They had some trousers, with two or three or four pockets and them fill the thing, and they carry big things out, you understand." Victor added that this was a common occurrence for some time until the men with large pockets were finally caught and fired for their actions.[93]

Or take the case of Rosa Johnson, a woman who worked as a domestic servant. She had been forced to sever a friendship with a neighboring maid who had been accused of stealing. She recalled that she and her friend would visit each other in their off hours, and one day her friend stole her employer's silverware. The friend then turned on Rosa, "She tell her mistress, that it is I who did it, the action, that bad action." Rosa continued that her employers did not believe she was guilty because they trusted her and had been testing her. Her employers saved their money in their underwear and sock drawer, and this meant that every time Rosa put away their underwear she would come across "a pack of money . . . hundred dollar, fifty dollar, five dollar, ten dollar . . . and I close that drawer. . . . I don't have nothing to do with that drawer no more." Her employers told her they checked the drawer every night to make sure she had not touched their money. In the end, Rosa's employers barred her from speaking with the friend. When I asked Rosa if she continued her friendship, she said, "No, no, I couldn't because they would blackball me."[94] These examples suggest widespread theft and an underground economy where employees attempted to increase their salaries by taking small items from the U.S. Navy and hoping their employers either failed to notice or pretended not to see.

The archival record provides a glimpse at the materials workers stole from the base. Items ranged from those that could be hidden in a pocket to those that must have taken a good deal of coordination, planning, and plotting to extract. The confiscated goods ranged from the valuable to the seemingly inconsequential. For example, base officials charged Modesta Mesa García and Mario Miranda for stealing thirty-five pine lumber planks and one small boat, and Pedro Crespo allegedly stole one spoon and thirty-six feet of unused rope. An incomplete list of stolen items included: a Fairbanks 6 HP engine, penicillin, soap, three bicycles, a fifteen gallon water tank, a bottle of gasoline, a pair of black shoes, a pair of yellow work gloves, three sailors' caps, four truck tires, a reel of copper wire, a fifty-five gallon gasoline drum, an aluminum teapot, one blanket, five forks, four spoons, and a bottle of Tabasco sauce.[95] A case that took advantage of "US independence" was a robbery against the Chapman family who lived on GTMO. The thieves planned and executed a robbery for the Fourth of July, when they knew the Chapman family would be out celebrating. The loot was considerable: a ring, a gold reliquary, a GE radio, an Airline radio, a Kodak camera, a check for one hundred and twenty dollars, black shoes, tennis shoes, and a pair of scissors. One of the robbers gave himself away when he tried to sell the stolen items in the market, after which the Cuban police apprehended the eight men involved.[96] However, these men, and others charged with theft on the base, were tried in Guantánamo and were not extradited to the base.

Frustrating the base authorities, the local Guantánamo court often delayed these cases, refused to prosecute them, or acquitted the defendants. Judge Juan Pérez Pérez (the same judge accused of doctoring Spanish birth certificates) gained a reputation of impeding prosecutions and assisting men and women accused of thefts. Essentially, he provided them with enough time to hide the suspected items.[97] Moreover, U.S. officials were angered when acquitted defendants were allowed to keep U.S. government property or, even when convicted, the property was put up for public auction, rather than returned directly to the U.S. government. As Franklin Hawley, the U.S. consul in Santiago de Cuba remarked, even the Cuban judicial system's general disarray and inefficiency could not account for the long delays in cases involving the base.[98] Although some of these "delays" may have been due to judicial corruption or incompetence, they may also have been due to a systematic, and relatively sympathetic, hearing the Guantánamo courts gave to base employees. Whether siding with the Cuban workers' conception of moral economy or deciding that part of the base's "rent" included pilfered goods, the courts were generally reluctant to punish those who stole items from the base.

Angry with the Guantánamo court's lackadaisical response, base authorities toyed with the idea of disciplining Cuban workers on the base itself. In the early 1950s, the base commander noted that the Cuban courts had been "unsatisfactory" in resolving the problem of petty theft. Cases lingered for three to four years, most suspects were acquitted despite hard evidence, and those convicted received only "light sentences."[99] Feeling impotent in the face of the local court system, the base authorities suggested overturning several decades of precedent and cracking down on employee theft. In 1952 the base commander requested authorization from the U.S. State Department to try an employee on the base for stealing approximately four hundred dollars from the Naval Exchange.[100] The State Department's legal advisor agreed that the 1903 Lease Agreement's clause governing "fugitives from justice" left the door open to detain Cubans who committed crimes on the base. They worked under U.S. jurisdiction and were not "fugitives." Therefore, the "US military authorities have the right, if they choose to exercise it, to try the Cuban for the violation of the Code."[101] This change in legal strategy would be far more likely to deter crime; however, it carried serious political ramifications. The Guantánamo municipal authorities were reluctant to challenge GTMO's status, but holding Cuban citizens without a trial was an offense to Cuban nationalism, jurisdiction, and sovereignty.

The GTMO military officers who dealt with the problem of petty crime on a daily basis wanted an immediate solution. In contrast, the State Department viewed U.S.-Cuban relations in a more global context. The State Department suggested that greater vigilance, rather than punitive measures, be considered to minimize the political fallout.[102] It insisted that in the greater international scheme, these crimes were insignificant. It did not want the base authorities to threaten U.S.-Cuban relations over the question of stolen cigarettes or paint. There was nothing to gain in demonstrating U.S. jurisdiction and undercutting Cuba's limited sovereignty over the territory. Such an affront, even with a friendly government in Havana, had the possibility of backfiring and encouraging the Cuban government to challenge the lease agreements and GTMO's territorial rights. For U.S. Ambassador Willard Beaulac, it was just not worth the risk.[103] Given the State Department's concerns, Admiral Murphy agreed to "drop the matter."[104]

In fact, the U.S. State Department's fears were on the mark. Both Cuban and U.S. archival records remain somewhat unclear about the extent to which GTMO's new detention policy was executed, and there is no record of it in the local press. However, in the spring of 1953, Guantánamo student groups began vigorously protesting the detention of local base employees. Presumably, the base authorities decided to ignore the State Department's warnings and had detained a worker. The Guantánamo Student Federation sent a telegram to Secretary of State John Foster Dulles protesting the "illegal detentions" on the base.[105] Their complaints only intensified. "Today we step forward to denounce before the public conscience, the outrages and illegal detentions committed against the Cubans who, for unfounded suspicions, are incarcerated for agonizing days in the famous prisons at Carabela Point [GTMO's brig], without having been previously submitted to trial, permitted counsel, permitted to produce evidence, and other guarantees that the Penal Code of the liberal-democratic system have established to safeguard human rights."

The students went on to say that the penal system on the base was worse than that of either the Spanish colonial system or the Soviet Union. They believed that the illegal detention of Cuban workers was similar to fascism. The student organization charged that the detainees had been beaten and tortured, and it concluded by calling on the United States to live up to its stated principles of democracy.[106] The students' language was harsh, and it damned GTMO as not much better than a concentration camp. The fury revealed a deep anti-Americanism in Guantánamo that could define the U.S. military alongside totalitarian communism and fascism. The U.S. Cold War promises of democracy and freedom rang false in this context, and the students rejected U.S. hypocrisy along with Soviet alternatives. Defending the base workers was a way *guantanameros* could vent their anger and resentment against the U.S. military.

Inexperienced with oppositional student groups, Rear Admiral C. L. C. Atkenson responded to the students and urged them to stop spreading misinformation. In his rebuttal, Atkenson did not deny the detentions; rather, he asserted they were not illegal. He explained that any worker who admitted guilt or accused another worker as an accomplice was confined under the Uniform Code of Military Justice.[107] U.S. Ambassador Beaulac, more practiced in dealing with volatile student groups, chastised Atkenson for responding and acknowledging that the workers were in fact being detained. Atkenson's actions had legitimized the students' attack and verified their central complaint. In Havana, Ambassador Beaulac had the advantage of perspective. Conflicts between Guantánamo and GTMO simply were not worth the energy and served only to provide fresh material for United States' enemies and critics. He suggested that all local workers suspected of any crime be remanded back to the Cuban courts as "proof of good relations."[108]

The question of petty crime had moved far beyond how to account for missing paint, cigarettes, spoons, or radios and into the realm of human rights, torture, and fascism. This ideological journey resulted from workers' unusual position of traversing between national legal spaces on a daily basis. In fact, crime tested the boundaries of the base, because workers had to smuggle their contraband, not merely out of their worksites, but also across the *frontera*. This disrespect for U.S. property and military boundaries unsettled, although it did not seriously challenge, U.S. authority. When base officials decided to take a stand against this low-level yet constant theft, they upset the sensitive balance between GTMO and Guantánamo. For this reason, the 1954 detention of Lorenzo Salomón created an uproar, displaying the limitations and contours of U.S. military authority and Cold War unionism.

THE CASE OF LORENZO SALOMÓN

The Lorenzo Salomón case unfolded more than a year after U.S. military officials first suggested detaining base workers for criminal offenses. Apprehending Salomón for allegedly stealing more than fifteen hundred dollars of merchandise, base intelligence officers clearly hoped to make an example of him. His detention also corresponded with the union's growing strength and combativeness. Under Angel Calzado and José Repilado, the union denounced this arbitrary detention and ratcheted its rhetoric to new heights. This time, however, Calzado and Repilado's challenge went beyond what base authorities were willing to tolerate. The Cold War forces that had initially allowed the union to organize and grow now turned against it.

Calzado and Repilado began an intense and vocal campaign. Through radio programs, union bulletins, and direct communication with the U.S. State Department, they portrayed U.S. officials as "fascists" and "torturers." In a newsletter, they publicized the Salomón story and compared the U.S. base intelligence officers to Communists and Nazis. Like the students before, the union leadership concluded by calling on U.S. ideals: "We could not conceive that in a naval establishment of the most powerful nation in the world, champion of democracy, things like this could happen and much less [that it could] use methods and systems of terror."[109] In a similar vein, Calzado and Repilado wrote to the U.S. ambassador. They noted that the base workers had nicknamed Lovell Irving, the base intelligence officer, "the torturer," "the executioner," and "the Himmler of the naval base." Calzado and Repilado tempered their complaint with a nod to the United States' historic benevolence and commitment to democratic principles, but their accusation was clear. In the Salomón case, the U.S. officials had been no better than the Nazis.[110]

In the wake of these incendiary descriptions of U.S. brutality, GTMO officials fired Calzado and Repilado for their public protests. They adamantly denied mistreating or torturing Salomón, and they could no longer condone such a hostile or mobilized union leadership within the base. Base officials, along with the AFL, had previously admonished the union leaders to stay out of the pubic eye and to recognize the difference between a private employer and a military installation. To GTMO officials, Calzado and Repilado's radio broadcasts were the "straw that broke the camel's back."[111] The union's position had shifted since its inception in 1950 as an organization that shared the stage with the base commander under the U.S. and Cuban flags to an organization that publicly compared U.S. officials to Nazis. As the union leadership grew more aggressive and independent, it appeared less and less controlled by the AFL or by Eusebio Mujal's CTC.

The U.S. Navy's Office of Industrial Relations convened a meeting with Romualdi, and all agreed that a new leadership with more moderate goals and methods needed to be installed.[112] The union had exceeded the mandate permitted by base officials and the AFL. Moreover, the Batista regime had no interest in perpetuating direct conflicts with the U.S. government. By 1954 the CTC under Mujal's leadership rubber-stamped Batista's programs, and Mujal prohibited local syndicates from taking political stands or opposing the government. Even a few years earlier, Mujal had chosen to stand back as the base union leadership took its grievances to the press; now he organized its demise. Mujal and Romualdi found their experiment in base unionism had run out of control. The base union exerted far more independence than either anti-communist labor leader had ever intended, and now the United States called on them to quiet the local scene.

Mujal traveled to Guantánamo to mediate between the union leadership and base officials and to prevent further mobilization. As the head of the CTC and the initiator of the union, he had to calm U.S. officials and reconfigure the base workers' union.[113] GTMO officials insisted that they were not in the "union busting business," and that they were more than willing to cooperate with "any reasonable union leadership."[114] The union had an election scheduled for December 1954, only eight weeks after the Salomón affair and the subsequent dismissals. Mujal wanted to ensure that more moderate leaders won.[115] The U.S. Navy stated that Repilado and Calzado were no longer eligible to hold leadership positions within the union, as they were no longer base employees. Filiberto Ferrer became the acting secretary general of the base workers' union. Mujal backed Ferrer, but even he admitted that Ferrer was a weak leader compared to Repilado and Calzado and might "not be strong enough to control extremist elements in the union."[116]

When GTMO officials fired Repilado and Calzado, the publicity shifted away from Salomón and onto the union leadership's right to employment and free organization. Repilado and Calzado were not Communists, but they acknowledged the Cold War politics that governed the U.S. worldview. Fired and expelled from GTMO, Repilado and Calzado advocated for their jobs and their right to head the union from Guantánamo. There they engaged in a hunger strike, initially supported by the Guantánamo mayor, and they asserted that they were the true leaders of the union.[117] As late as August 1955, close to a year after the Salomón incident, Angel Calzado was still publishing bulletins and backing possible alternatives to Ferrer. He urged base workers to keep paying their dues to the original union that had won "prestige and so many victories." In a nationalist vein, he condemned the base for discriminating against Cuban workers and usurping Cuban land. Calzado denounced Mujal as a "scoundrel." Pointedly, he also inverted the U.S. Navy's Cold War logic. He realized U.S. officials labeled all critics as Communists, and so he openly addressed their fears:

> It is not by caressing the RED DEVILS that peace for the civilized world will be achieved; no, it is by practicing SOCIAL JUSTICE; it is by practicing the magnificent postulates of democracy, of which our employers boast themselves to be the champions when in reality the only thing they do is to show their contempt for the things which are really vital to the greatness and sovereignty of our countries. To say all of this is not COMMUNISM, no. . . . We who speak thus are enemies of Iron Curtains but we are also enemies of any type of oppression harming human dignity, and hence, the dignity of the country we belong to. WE ARE REAL DEMOCRATS.

Calzado concluded that he and Repilado had been "expelled" in an "anti-democratic" manner, simply because they had been speaking out against the "oppressors" of "our poor natives." In his view, the United States did not respect the rights of those who were not U.S. citizens.[118]

Calzado and Repilado had broken out of the confines of the anti-communist AFL-CTC collaboration. They were anti-communists, but also nationalists and independent activists. This is not what the U.S. Navy, Eusebio Mujal, or Serafino Romualdi had intended, and it was not an acceptable alternative. Throughout the aftermath of the Salomón case, the union leadership became more and more antagonistic, not only toward the U.S. government, but also against Mujal and the corporatist CTC.

The base union declined in effectiveness and importance after the Salomón case. Throughout the mid-1950s, Repilado and Calzado continued to hold considerable sway in Guantánamo, and they supported a variety of candidates to recapture the base union under independent leadership. Their supporters even succeeded in winning the 1956 election, but Mujal refused to recognize the results and installed an "Intervention Commission." This "intervention" team effectively marked the end of an independent union within GTMO. The U.S. Navy noted that "there has been practically no union activity by the group during the past six months, and it is possible that it is being maintained as a 'paper' organization to strengthen the position of Eusebio Mujal Barinol." Despite the obvious anti-democratic nature of this turn of events, GTMO officials welcomed the change: "The lack of union activity is considered more desirable than the vicious type of union activity which was carried on under former union leaders Calzado and Repilado."[119] GTMO's experiment in negotiating and meeting with the base workers' union had ended.

In my conversation with base worker Walter Knight, he blamed the Cuban government almost as much as he blamed the U.S. authorities for the Salomón case. Batista and Mujal had not stood up for the union leadership and had allowed the United States to abuse base workers: "Yes, there was a Salomón. I believe he robbed and was put in prison. . . . It happened that the government here [in Cuba] at this time allowed these things to occur. Many things weren't only the North Americans' fault. The government here permitted all these things [the detentions]." He noted that Mujal had just "taken all of the money," and that the union ceased to be effective after the Salomón case.[120]

As Calzado and Repilado emerged as the dominant players, Salomón himself became secondary to the case. The union mobilized in Salomón's support, but according to all accounts, he had never been a member. He was a Jamaican descendant, and the press referred to him sometimes as a Cuban and sometimes as a *jamaiquino*. His national background underscored the union leadership's willingness to represent all local workers, Cubans and West Indian descendants alike. Salomón's innocence or guilt was also in question. Although he proclaimed his innocence and the union genuinely backed him, everyone acknowledged the prevalence of theft on the base and thought there was enough evidence to suggest his guilt. Even Calzado and Repilado did not insist on Salomón's innocence. Rather, they maintained, they objected to the U.S. Navy's practice of unauthorized detention and abuse: "The base officials have every right to clarify whatever event happened on the base, but we don't believe that they have the right to physically and mentally mistreat a single Cuban citizen or any of the other nationalities who work on the base."[121] Former base union member Juan Carlos Pulsara believed that Salomón was in fact guilty, "Salomón? . . . From the moment that it happened, I already felt no sympathy for Salomón." However, he believed the base union had to defend his rights, even if he had committed the crime.[122] After his release, the U.S. Navy pressed charges against Salomón in Santiago de Cuba, and the local court found in GTMO's favor. Salomón served six months in jail.[123]

CONCLUSION

When I would initiate a conversation about the base union or the Salomón case with former base workers, most of them had vague memories of the union, but almost none of them granted it much importance. For example, in my conversation with Ramón Sánchez, I asked him if he had been a member of the base workers' union. He quickly replied that he had never been involved in it. Later, when he sifted through his files looking for old documents, he came upon his old union card, complete with his photograph and the symbol of two hands shaking from U.S. and Cuban portholes.[124] Ramón had completely forgotten he had ever been a member. In another conversation, Miguel Gómez remembered he had been a member and recalled the formation of the union, but his tone was somewhat despondent: "Someone spoke to us from the CIO—the big organization—someone named Romualdi, an Italian, of Italian origin, who was the leader of the CIO, and he wanted to unite us . . . but it was very difficult on a naval base to have a union."[125] Miguel wrongly identified Romualdi with the CIO instead of the AFL but, more importantly, he spoke of Romualdi without prompting and clearly remembered the AFL leader's visits to Guantánamo. Yet despite these recollections, Miguel Gómez emphasized the union's ineffectiveness and did not recall it as successful or strong.

If anything, the weakness of the union dominated workers' memories. As Santiago Ruiz described it, "The thing was that the union was . . . a very weak organization in front of the U.S. government. . . . It existed, but it was only a passing thing."[126] Yet another base worker, Derek Stedman, concurred. He did not even remember the union having been officially sanctioned: "Well, there was a union there but it didn't work much. It worked for a time, but it wasn't recognized on the base . . . and the union didn't have any . . . power. . . . No, no, no, I was never a member of the union . . . because I don't like the system of the union."[127] And Juan González recalled bluntly, "The union didn't have any validity . . . because it couldn't resolve anything. . . . It wasn't recognized here in Cuba, and much less on the naval base. On the naval base the unions didn't work."[128] Even Juan Carlos Pulsara, who was proud of his union membership, concluded that the union had been "conservative."[129]

How to account for these narratives of weakness and impotence given the base union leaders' aggressive words? My informants' silences and dismissals contrasted starkly with the hostile diatribes in the written record. A Cuban historian suggested to me that my interviewees, elderly in 2004, would have been relatively young during the 1950s, and they may not have seen the value of the union.[130] She explained that older workers at the time would have been more invested in campaigns for better pensions and salaries, but this generation has since passed away. Also, there might have been a divide between the strident union leadership and the rank and file. The union membership may have shied away from Angel Calzado and José Repilado's increasing rancor. Workers had joined the union when the risk was low, and the U.S. admiral himself had sanctioned it. It is also possible that elderly retirees have forgotten their youthful expectations and the possibility of activist unions. As Walter Knight noted, unions had played a central role in Cuban political culture; every sector had a union. Yet, the experience of Mujal's corporatist and corrupt unionism followed by socialist, state-controlled syndicates under Castro may well have buried contemporary expectations for independent unions.[131]

Even more likely, the Cuban revolution overshadowed this moment of worker mobilization and nationalism to the point where it appeared insignificant. With the 26 of July Movement and the victory of Castro's rebels only a few years later, for elderly men looking back, the union appeared hopeless, weak, and a feeble attempt at self-determination. The tensions between Cuba and the United States after 1959 far exceeded any of the earlier local conflicts of the 1940s and 1950s. There was no risk the Salomón case would trigger a U.S. invasion, initiate a nuclear war, or result in a debilitating economic embargo. The intense animosity between the United States and Cuba after the revolution served to erase prior controversies between Guantánamo and GTMO. In addition, the majority of base workers lost their jobs in the early 1960s, and so many have idealized their previous economic status and minimized earlier conflicts. As a result, the early 1950s have been reimagined as an era of amicable relations and without independent organizations or anti-American mobilization. In this way, the history of the base union has been lost and transformed into a faded memory at best.

In this analysis, I respectfully disagree with my Cuban informants' interpretation of the base union. I think that rather the base union epitomized the contradictions of Cold War unionism. The base union took advantage of a Cold War opening whereby anti-communist national figures backed local workers' demands, and U.S. officials agreed to make concessions. At the most basic level, the union improved salaries for workers, established a principle of equal work for equal pay, and questioned the right of private contractors to disregard workers' needs for benefits and pensions. Although I would not suggest that the union achieved major victories in any of these categories, its presence pushed base officials to conduct salary surveys, offer incentives, and institute wage increases. The U.S. Navy had to confront the local terrain of Guantánamo politics, encompassing corrupt local judges, opportunistic politicians, student groups, and union leaders. Moreover, after the Salomón case there is no evidence that additional workers were ever detained on the base. Although it is possible other cases were censored in the press, removed from the U.S. archives, or ignored by the base workers, it is also quite possible that GTMO officials decided their detention policy was simply not worth the effort. Most likely base officials took heed of the State Department's warnings and did not continue the practice.

As importantly, base workers, far more than the Cuban government, addressed and negotiated the boundaries of U.S. jurisdiction and sought to protect workers in what was otherwise a legal vacuum. Mujal, and by extension the Batista regime, were willing to support the union, but only when it was under their influence. When the base union leadership overstepped the CTC and AFL's narrow objectives, neither Mujal nor Romualdi defended base workers' rights or fight for a single legal standard. For workers, this was a betrayal. Jurisdiction and sovereignty were not just abstract principles. Instead, the interpretation of international law determined their salaries, benefits, and rights to due process.

The base union was a pivotal organization, because it allowed base workers the opportunity to make claims on the U.S. and Cuban governments and thereby participate in international relations. However, it also laid bare the contradictions and ambiguities of worker activism on the base. At times, base workers heralded U.S. principles of democracy and liberty, emphasizing the benevolence and strength of the United States. When GTMO officials' actions did not meet the United States' rhetorical ideals, base workers condemned U.S. hypocrisy and arbitrary power. But workers' protests could only go so far. Once they became too vocal, they lost their national and international allies. Even more, the workers needed the base. Although students and the union leadership described the U.S. government as fascist and totalitarian, they did not demand that the U.S. Navy withdraw from Guantánamo Bay. Workers' livelihoods depended on base jobs. As a result, base workers often navigated the politics of neocolonial Cold War Cuba with ambivalence. And ambivalence pervaded not just workers' legal struggles, but also their social encounters with their North American neighbors in Guantánamo.

3

Good Neighbors, Good
Revolutionaries, 1940–1958

Rosa Johnson, a seventy-eight-year-old woman of West Indian descent, worked as a domestic servant for a U.S. naval officer's family in the 1950s. She was born in rural Oriente, and her family worked in Central Miranda. When she was in her mid-thirties, she traveled to Guantánamo to seek work on the base.

Forty years later, she still resented how her former employers had taken advantage of her. Unlike other workers who refrained from criticizing their North American supervisors, Rosa listed her complaints: low pay and unremitting work. Her wage, fifteen pesos, "was like an insult," and she had an endless array of responsibilities: "taking care of children, cooking, ironing, cleaning, and giving 'wax' to the floor." Even more than the low pay, Rosa resented that her "mistress" refused to respect her time or her day off. In most families, Rosa explained, the officer's wife and the domestic servant alternated nights for child care: "But her, she gave me all her nights. . . . Babysit. All the nights. Babysit. . . . I didn't complain. . . . She went out Thursday for the night. She went on Friday, Saturday, and Sunday to Haiti to spend the weekend. . . . Then I took care of the children."[1]

Rosa's entrapment in the house was not romanticized, and she expressed no affection for the children, nor respect for her mistress. If not resistance and nationalism, her narrative reflected a discontent, anger, and aggression that was anything but nostalgic. She also spoke bluntly of North American racism, noting that U.S. women preferred white over black maids. "Some of them [U.S. military wives] don't take the maids black. No. They look for the white, and the white ones don't understand the English. You get me?" In this formulation, Rosa defined bilingual West Indian women as black, and Cuban women as white. Maid-swapping must have been a common occurrence, because the U.S. Navy's *Guide to Living* suggested it as a pleasant solution to U.S. wives' language barriers: "You will be surprised and delighted to find your household running smoothly with the help of your neighbor's English-speaking maid acting as interpreter."[2] Rosa, however, did not find the situation "delightful." She resented being rejected because of her color, and then asked to do additional work as an interpreter. She attributed the U.S. wives' prejudices to their southern backgrounds and being "puffed up." In direct contrast to these experiences of discrimination, Rosa romanticized the Cuban revolution's commitment to racial equality. Identifying with Fidel Castro, albeit in a religious idiom, she espoused, "God is our father. And all of us is his children. No matter the color. That is why I like Fidel Castro. Because he . . . doesn't look if you're black or white."

Despite Rosa's distaste for U.S. racism and her harping employer, her relationship with a U.S. family also gave her an entrée into U.S. culture that she clearly embraced. As Rosa spoke about her mistress, she became more animated, using dramatic tones and multiple voices: "I was in the house of an American woman, and she drank too much. . . . She sat on the sofa with her beer. A lemonade here, and a bottle of whisky and a glass, and the cigarettes . . . and I was in the kitchen, cooking." Although our interview began in Spanish, by this point Rosa had switched completely to English. She gave her best imitation of her North American employer and her younger self: "She asked, 'Rosa.' 'Yes, Mistress.' 'Come here.' 'Mistress, I'm cooking.' 'Rosa, I said to come here.' I went. 'Sit down.' I said, 'Mistress?' 'I said to sit down, and let's have a drink. [Rosa used a drawl here and rolled her 'r's for a dramatic drrrriiiink.] Go here and get me the cigarettes. Salem. Take a cigarette.' I said, 'I don't smoke.' 'Drink and take a cigarette and smoke.' And from that time, I was smoking. . . . And she says to me, 'I'm going to learn you a song.' 'Ah Mistress, I'm cooking.' 'Ohhh Rosa, forget it. Come here.' Let's see. . . . Let's see if I remember—Love me tender, Love me true . . . " At this point, Rosa reached back into her memories and belted out the Elvis Presley standard for me in its entirety.[3]

Working for a U.S. family, Rosa resented her employer and judged her for drinking, smoking, and shirking her child-rearing duties. Rosa's narrative unsettles. On the one hand, Rosa still seems traumatized by the long hours and her subservient, abused position within the household. On the other hand, she clearly enjoyed her exposure to and knowledge of U.S. culture, music, and mores. Working in a private home, isolated from her friends, with her daily life ruled by commands to "wax the floor" and "babysit," Rosa's experience was quite different from that of her male counterparts who had greater access to white collar jobs and advancement on the base. Her testimony fell into neither nostalgia nor a state-imposed, anti-imperialist narrative. Instead, her memories remained a muddle of anger and hurt alongside a clear joy and affinity for U.S. popular culture. Rosa did not define herself or her employment as political, but her intimate experiences with U.S. families underscored an ambivalent, neocolonial critique.

Rosa's account comments on the complex interplay of gender, race, and nationality in North American–Guantánamo encounters. In the 1940s and 1950s, the ongoing exchange of men and women across the *frontera* intertwined Guantánamo and GTMO's social hierarchies with mixed, and often ambivalent, results. Wielding economic and military power, North Americans generally considered themselves in a superior, paternalist (or in Rosa's case maternalist) position over the local population. However, the U.S. Navy had to take Guantánamo social norms and communities into consideration, even if dismissively, because they shared a common geography. When on leave, U.S. sailors and marines, colloquially known as *francos,* enjoyed their liberty parties in Guantánamo and Caimanera. In turn, the commercial elite parleyed social ties and profits from these excursions. Although welcoming *francos* into their bars and hotels, these proprietors also expected the U.S. Navy to recognize Guantánamo's class and racial distinctions. Just as importantly, Guantánamo was quite simply where GTMO's workforce lived. Base workers brought their own attitudes toward gender, class, and race onto GTMO, evaluating Cuban and U.S. forms of discrimination depending on their own work and social experiences. These neocolonial encounters revealed layers of ambiguity, contradiction, and division on both sides of the bay.[4]

Throughout the 1940s and 1950s, U.S. officials and Guantánamo boosters continued to tout Guantánamo-GTMO relations through the rhetoric of the Good Neighbor policy. Most historians have situated the Good Neighbor policy firmly in President Franklin D. Roosevelt's presidency and in World War II. They have defined it almost solely as a diplomatic overture, without considering the social, economic, sexual, or racial consequences of U.S. citizens in Latin America.[5] In contrast, in Guantánamo, "good neighborliness" was a constant trope well into the 1950s. It carried an overtly sexual and gendered resonance, for in practice the Good Neighbor policy equaled thousands of U.S. sailors and marines frequenting Guantánamo and Caimanera's bars and brothels. Uncle Sam's paternalist generosity could take on a sinister veneer, as the U.S. Navy regulated prostitution and looked the other way when Cuban women were disrespected or molested. As a result, the Good Neighbor policy created considerable anxiety among *guantanameros* and *guantanameras* who felt it imperative to protect "decent" women from their "neighbors."

Guantánamo had a complex social hierarchy, and Rosa Johnson's allusion to black and white maids only touches on how racial, national, and class backgrounds intersected in the local topography. Race became another point of contestation, particularly when it came to sexual and romantic partners between North American men and *guantanameras*. These relations delineated how U.S. and Cuban patterns of racial prejudice continued to value whiteness, even as they revealed multiracial populations on both sides. The U.S. Navy included African Americans, Puerto Ricans, and Filipinos, as well as northern and southern whites. Its own nonwhite members contradicted the U.S. projection of white supremacy and emphasized potentially undesired similarities between the United States' and Cuba's racial compositions. Good neighborliness went only so far, and the Cuban and U.S. populations were culturally and racially closer than many U.S. military officials may have desired.

Finally, the U.S. military had to confront Guantánamo's political culture and the growing nationalist, anti-Batista movements in the late 1950s. By 1958 Guantánamo and the base became key locales for Fidel and Raúl Castro's 26 of July Movement. For workers sympathetic to the rebel cause, GTMO's plentiful resources provided a welcome supply of gas, oil, boots, backpacks, and arms. They took advantage of GTMO's permeable borders and facilitated a supply chain to the guerrillas. Rather than merely submitting to neocolonial hierarchies, base workers became emboldened by their access to the base and the strengthening revolutionary movement. For GTMO, sexual, racial, and now political proximity came with the risk of becoming too engaged with Guantánamo's local affairs.

In short, by 1958, how good a neighbor had GTMO become?

GOOD NEIGHBORS, GOOD IMPERIALISTS

The U.S. Navy and the Guantánamo elite invoked "good neighborliness" throughout the 1940s and 1950s. This slogan framed the neocolonial give-and-take between the U.S. military and Guantánamo's commercial sectors. The U.S. Navy injected North American superiority and benevolence into the "neighborly" rhetoric, while *guantanameros* hoped appeals to "neighborliness" would result in ever greater U.S. dollars, investments, and patronage.

Notably, both U.S. and Cuban officials pointed to the Cuban War of Independence and the subsequent 1898 U.S. invasion as the foundation for this friendship. In the process, they cemented the parameters of a neocolonial relationship. Oriente, and Guantánamo in particular, occupied a contradictory position in the Cuban national imagination. It had been the heart of Cuban nationalism, and yet after independence it became the region most heavily controlled by U.S. capital interests. GTMO remained the clearest symbol of Cuba and Oriente's sacrificed sovereignty and the unfulfilled promise of independence. U.S. officials often articulated Cuban independence as only a derivative of U.S. military power. For example, on July 4, 1949, a U.S. diplomat visited Guantánamo's War of Independence veterans and expressed his deep friendship and admiration for the "old liberators." However, he did not honor these *mambises* on the day of Cuban independence, but rather that "most glorious date in the United States," July Fourth.[6] In the process, the U.S. official marked the neocolonial status of Cuba's liberation and its honored veterans. U.S. independence trumped and superseded any Cuban claim to self-rule, particularly in Guantánamo.

Given the reality of U.S. economic and political power, the Guantánamo elite often followed suit and articulated a U.S.-scripted fantasy of mutual friendship. For example, in 1951 the city of Guantánamo, led by Mayor Dr. Ladislao Guerra, celebrated Cuban-American Friendship Day. In this ceremony, Dr. Guerra presented the keys of the city to Admiral Marion Emerson Murphy.[7] *La Voz del Pueblo* noted that the Cuban people, and *guantanameros* specifically, recognized a special feeling of gratitude toward the United States. The United States had been a "friendly nation" since the War of Independence, when it had fought alongside the heroic *mambises* for the "liberty and independence of our nation."[8] In a neocolonial sleight-of-hand, the Guantánamo elite expressed a strong bond with the United States, precisely because of the U.S. military intervention in the War of Independence. In this single ceremony, Cuban nationalist pride and independence became subservient to U.S. military power.

In another poignant example, Colonel Coruthers waxed nostalgic about the long history of Cuban and North American friendship during the inauguration ceremony of José Martí Park. In all of Cuba, he believed, this "friendship" expressed itself most "eloquently" between Guantánamo and the U.S. naval base. "Permit me to say that we are invited to this country, but we do not feel the sensation of strangeness that we feel when we are on foreign soil. Instead, there is the cordiality between friends."[9] Colonel Coruthers's language belied the reality of GTMO's occupation of Guantánamo Bay. In his words, Cuba "invited" the U.S. military, an exceptionally inaccurate, if not deliberate, misreading of the Platt Amendment and lease agreements. The park itself was named after José Martí, modern Cuba's nationalist icon and life-long critic of U.S. imperialism. The irony appears to have been lost on all or, at the very least, on Colonel Coruthers.

From the U.S. Navy's perspective, being a good neighbor was defined by paternalism and imperial privilege. The U.S. Navy presented itself as a benevolent, fatherly figure, granting favors to the less developed Guantánamo. Neighborliness was essentially charity. Almost any topic could fall under the rubric of good neighborliness, including aid for public works, public health, road maintenance, commerce, liberty parties, baseball games, Christmas celebrations, cocktail parties, and Boy Scout excursions. For example, Admiral Murphy pointed to how quickly the navy came to Caimanera's defense during a destructive fire as proof of U.S. friendship. He emphasized that this aid was given "as a matter of course," and prevented even greater damage.[10] The U.S. Navy also regularly donated money to local institutions, distributed gifts at Christmas time, and hosted a Caribbean carnival on the base to raise funds for charity.[11] These acts were not about mutual friendship, but instead solidified the U.S. Navy's superior position. Through typical colonial tropes, U.S. officers played the role of gracious, colonial benefactor and expected the Guantánamo community to be grateful for GTMO's largess.

For Guantánamo's *fuerzas vivas,* the Good Neighbor policy was good business. Second only to the sugar industry, commerce with the base was the foundation of its economy. U.S. liberty parties were the "second *zafra,*" "a river of gold" and "a bridge of money," which improved relations between Cubans and the base authorities.[12] U.S. consumer culture mapped the local landscape with undeniably North American names, for example, Club Nevada, Hotel Washington, Hotel Miami,

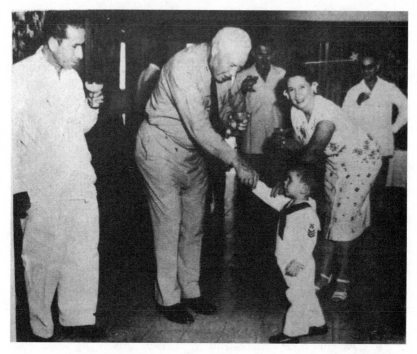

Figure 7. U.S. Admiral Taylor at a local Guantánamo function. *La Revista Oriental,* June 1955. Courtesy of the Elvira Cape Provincial Library, Santiago de Cuba.

Club Arizona, Yusimi (you see me), and Yusnavi (U.S. Navy). Although in popular memory and revolutionary Cuban discourse, U.S. sailors and marines relentlessly ran rampant through Caimanera and Guantánamo, archival accounts describe a more tenuous economic picture. Some months a steady stream of *francos* visited but, other times, the U.S. Navy limited the number of *francos,* which damaged the local economy.[13] Guantánamo elites and journalists would then cajole the navy to increase the number of U.S. military personnel allowed on leave. Repeatedly, they called on the Good Neighbor policy in their pleas. For example, in 1955 José Vázquez Pubillones, the editor of *La Voz del Pueblo,* lamented the dip in U.S. liberty parties and appealed to the Good Neighbor policy to encourage more.[14] Juan González García, a member of the Caimanera Chamber of Commerce, also cited the Good Neighbor policy when he pleaded for additional liberty parties: "We hope that you will not forget our neighboring town. Friend, give your approval in order that every weekend we can enjoy the visits of your young men."[15] And Angel Fer-

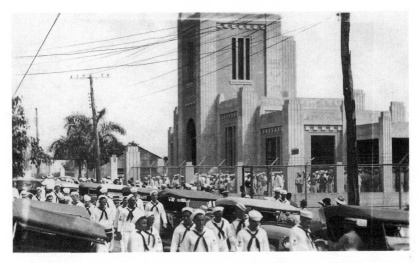

Figure 8. World War II–era postcard of U.S. sailors on liberty arriving at the Guantánamo train station. Photo by Aguirre.

rand Latoisón, a leading columnist in *La Voz del Pueblo*, described Caimanera as a community that had developed a "North American spirit" based on the longevity of the Good Neighbor policy. Liberty parties were essential to the economy and, without them, the city was doomed. In Ferrand's opinion, more *francos* would be a sign of "the good will and friendship that have always existed between their neighbors and the Americans who visited."[16]

In Guantánamo, the press redefined the military *francos* through the language of tourism. If Havana was populated by U.S. tourists on vacation, in Guantánamo, U.S. military occupation and U.S. tourism merged into a single and uniquely *guantanamero* configuration: "military tourism."[17] Reporters described Guantánamo as a "natural" zone of tourism where "military tourists strengthen[ed] . . . the cordial relations between the United States and Cuba."[18] Throughout the years, Lino Lemes described Guantánamo as a "Natural Zone of Tourism" countless times.[19] Through these appeals, he strategically lobbied the Cuban government for better roads, infrastructure, and public health programs for Guantánamo. He was outraged that the Cuban Ministry of Tourism overlooked Guantánamo and dedicated all of its investments in Havana and Varadero.[20] The naturalization of North American military tourists functioned rhetorically and physically—as the years progressed, fewer and fewer people could imagine Guantánamo without the base and *francos*. The language of military tourism merged the objectives of mid-twentieth-

Figure 9. World War–II era postcard of a bar in Caimanera. Photo by Aguirre.

century U.S. neocolonial capitalism and the more starkly imperial presence of the U.S. military base.

Buried in these constant calls for *francos* and military tourists, the commercial elite erased the reality of sex, prostitution, and brothels that U.S. liberty parties meant for Guantánamo and Caimanera. Because if military personnel on leave were "tourists," sex with Cuban women was the key purchase *francos* made. In the local press, only *El Vigilante* confronted prostitution directly, while the more staid and respectable *La Voz del Pueblo* refused to comment on the vulgar and impolitic presence of brothels in its city. Some journalists just ignored the U.S. military base, describing Guantánamo as a place marked by harmony, peace, clear waters, vibrant citizens, and spiritual serenity.[21] A second technique was to deplore the grime, waste, and public health hazards in Guantánamo, but again, without ever mentioning GTMO. For example *La Voz del Pueblo* proclaimed, "Guantánamo and Caimanera are the two dirtiest cities in the world." This editorial never once mentioned the base.[22] It condemned the cities' filth and unhygienic streets, but did not point its finger at the U.S. military or the liberty parties. Perhaps the editors recognized that in the constant refrain for more *francos*, the city was essentially prostituting itself figuratively and literally to the base and the *marinos*.

Regardless of the flowery language invoking Cuban-American friendship and commerce, the reality was physical and sexual. The U.S. sailors and marines were not just buying rum, souvenirs, and cigars. Rather, the "rivers of gold" flowed into gambling dens, bars, women's beds, and pimps' pockets. One catchy North American ditty chimed:

> Guantánamo City has hundreds of doors
> And every one's jammed with hundreds of whores
> They hang from the window with stark naked chests
> They knock out your brains with their low hanging breasts.

> Here's to Old Gitmo on Cuba's fair shore
> The land of the cockroach, the flea, and the whore
> We'll save our pennies and wait for the day
> We get the hell out of Guantánamo Bay.[23]

In this musical rendition, the singer defined Guantánamo by its sexual commerce and mocked Guantánamo's women as sexual but undesirable. The lyrics captured the *fuerzas vivas'* worst fears; North American *francos* saw the city as nothing more than a cesspool of pests and prostitutes. Even more troublesome, this song encouraged sailors to "save their pennies" and avoid even the most minimal expenditures in town. Despite the song's exhortations, large numbers of *francos* ignored its advice and visited the "hundreds of whores" to be found in Guantánamo and Caimanera. Uncle Sam morphed from the benevolent and charitable figure presented by Admiral Murphy into a scornful and soused suitor. "Neighborliness" and "friendship" equaled prostitution, venereal disease, and exploitation, defining the contradictory reality of the Good Neighbor policy on the ground.

MILITARY TOURISM AND ZONES OF TOLERANCE

Like the hundreds of men who migrated to Guantánamo in search of base jobs, women also came to Guantánamo and Caimanera in search of work. While some women found employment as domestic servants or in civil service positions, others became entertainers, waitresses, and prostitutes. Lino Lemes counted more than one thousand prostitutes in Guantánamo and Caimanera.[24] A 1988 analysis of prostitution by La Federación de Mujeres Cubanas (FMC), or the Cuban Women's Federation, claimed there were more than one hundred brothels in Caimanera: "Prostitution was practiced throughout the country, but the most frank and degrading exploitation was in Caimanera."[25] The local press and later post-revolutionary accounts reported that these women came from Havana, Santiago de Cuba, Matanzas—anywhere, that is, but

Guantánamo.[26] This emphasis worked to label prostitution as separate and distinct from Guantánamo. For example, *La Voz del Pueblo* reported five women were arrested for "scandalous" behavior, and they were from all over Oriente: Holguín, Manzanillo, Santiago de Cuba, and Gíbara.[27] Although certainly not all prostitutes came from outside the region, internal migration was significant. Herminia, a former prostitute from Camagüey, explained why young women left the countryside for Guantánamo and Caimanera. "There was so much poverty. The majority of the girls felt obligated to help their families, but there wasn't any work, and when there was, you would earn only a pittance. What can a *campesino* earn? Five *reales*. . . . And so they saw prostitution as an opportunity to change their lives and leave all of that misery. There were many motivations, but necessity was the main one."[28]

Fictional accounts reiterated this pattern. In Nicolás Dorr's 1984 theatrical work, *El Barrio Chino*, Violeta and Lucrecia both travel from Havana to Caimanera to work as "waitresses" near the base.[29] There is limited archival information about Guantánamo and Caimanera's prostitutes, who they were, where they worked, or what their personal experiences were.[30] Perhaps these women came to Guantánamo to escape the sugar cane fields, or perhaps they came to work on the base and found lucrative opportunities more easily in the brothels, or perhaps they came because of a sister or friend who came before them. And very likely the women circulated between occupations and between informal and formal economic sectors.

Access, control, and regulation of women's bodies and sexuality were central, not secondary, to the consolidation of colonial and military power.[31] It was the way in which the U.S. military presence exerted its strength on a daily basis and intervened in Guantánamo's social fabric. Women entertained, served, slept with, and sometimes even married the foot soldiers (or, in this case, foot sailors) of imperial power. In so doing, the U.S. military reinforced its position of authority, presuming access not only to Cuban soil, but also to Cuban women's bodies. This military presence framed Guantánamo's social norms and threatened to mark all local women, not just designated prostitutes, as sexually available.

As shown in table 1, U.S. Navy venereal disease reports provide an impersonal window onto Guantánamo and Santiago de Cuba's sexual economy. In these medical documents, the sailor reported the name, age, and race of his sexual contact. He also provided a physical description of the local woman, recalling if she were thin, fat, or medium, with blond, brown, or red hair. The sailor then indicated if he met the woman

TABLE 1. U.S. NAVY VENEREAL DISEASE CONTACT REPORTS, MARCH 1946

U.S. Male Race	U.S. Male Age	Female Race	Female Age	Female Height	Female Build	Female Hair	Type	Place	Procured by	Fee in Dollars
White	22	White	23	Avg.	Med.	Dark	Prostitute	Bar	Self	2.00
White	18	White	23	Avg.	Thin	Dark	Prostitute	Brothel	Pimp	2.00
White	18	White	21	Avg.	Med.	Light	Prostitute	Brothel	Pimp	2.00
White	18	White	20	Avg.	Med.	Dark	Prostitute	Brothel	Pimp	2.00
White	18	White	20	Short	Med.	Dark	Prostitute	Hotel	Pimp	5.00 + 13.00 for drinks, etc.
White	21	White	18	Short	Med.	Dark	Prostitute	Brothel	Pimp	15.00 + 20.00 for drinks, etc.
White	18	White	20	Short	Med.	Dark	Prostitute	Home/Apt.	Pimp	2.00
White	18	White	27	Short	Med.	Dark	Prostitute	Brothel	Self	2.00 + 1.50 for drinks, etc.
White	18	White	19	Short	Thin	Light	Prostitute	Brothel	Self	2.00 + 3.00 for drinks etc.
White	18	White	17	Avg.	Thin	Dark	Prostitute	Home/Apt.	Self	1.40
White	18	White	26	Short	Fat	Dark	Prostitute	Brothel	Self	2.00
White	18	White	21	Avg.	Med.	Light	Prostitute	Home/Apt.	Pimp	2.00 + 8.00 for drinks, etc.
White	23	White	16	Short	Med.	Dark	Prostitute	Brothel	Pimp	12.00 + 10.00 for drinks, etc.
White	20	White	16	Short	Med.	Dark	Prostitute	Brothel	Pimp	5.00
White	20	White	19	Avg.	Med.	Dark	Prostitute	Home/Apt.	Self	15.00
White	20	White	35	Short	Med.	Dark	Prostitute	Home/Apt.	Self	None

SOURCE: Data from Medical Department, U.S. Navy, Venereal Disease Contact Reports, March 1946, U.S. National Archives and Records Administration, College Park, MD, RG 84, Foreign Service Posts of the State Department, Santiago de Cuba Consulate, General Records, 1946, 820–842.6, Box 41.

through a "pick-up," a friend, a streetwalker, a hostess, or another prostitute. The medical officer also asked whether the woman was "procured" through the sailor's "own effort," or through a pimp, cab driver, bellhop, or waiter. And while there was a space for the woman's name, the U.S. serviceman's name was discreetly absent from the medical form.[32]

These records document the stark specifics and economics of individual sexual encounters. For example, a twenty-two-year-old, white sailor had a sexual contact with a white woman at the Moonlight Bar in Guantánamo for two dollars. In another instance, an eighteen-year-old, white sailor used a pimp, Albert Ellis, to meet a young woman for two dollars. This same man used a "navy tube" as a prophylaxis. Albert Ellis seems to have been a popular pimp for this group of sailors, and he introduced another eighteen-year-old sailor to a Señorita Susana Derez *[sic]*, who also charged $2.00. Food, drinks, and room were often additional costs not included in the "sexual" fee. For example, one young sailor described his partner as a short, dark-haired, medium-sized prostitute. He paid $5.00 for sex at a local hotel in Santiago de Cuba, but he also shelled out an additional $13.00 in entertainment and drinks. In 1946 the cost of an evening with a Cuban prostitute ranged from $1.40 to $15.00[33] All of the U.S. military personnel indicated that they were white and that they had slept with a white woman, illustrating a notable uniformity given the high percentage of Cubans of color. Whether this statistic reflected white U.S. men's preference for white Cuban women, their ignorance of Cuban racial taxonomies, or a concealment of their interracial exploits is unknown. These standard forms and matter-of-fact medical exams indicate the U.S. Navy's acquiescence with local prostitution and its prevalence in a sailor's life.[34]

Recognizing the high rates of venereal disease and public health threats, some U.S. officials tried to prevent U.S. sailors from entering Caimanera and Guantánamo. Even by the U.S. Navy's standards, Caimanera stood out as particularly rife with waste, garbage, and general disrepute.[35] Captain Roland W. Faulk, who served as a U.S. chaplain at GTMO in 1949, believed the U.S. Navy had sacrificed its commitment to U.S. public health norms. He wanted to put a stop to liberty parties, for in his mind, Caimanera had only one purpose: prostitution. Captain Faulk worried that his protests fell on deaf ears. Faulk's commanding officer refused to halt the liberty parties, because the Cuban government would then claim the navy was withholding dollars from the local community. In his superior's opinion, holding the *francos* on the base was not worth the "international diplomatic hassle." As a result, Captain Faulk concluded, "The policies of the Navy medicine [department] were in fact aiding and abetting prostitution. . . . In GTMO I did a study of 188 cases of men who had been infected by venereal disease at Caimanera and my conclusion then was that if this is all the [U.S.] Navy can do in this area—it is an abysmal failure."[36] Faulk's testimony demonstrated the degree to which the U.S. Navy tolerated prostitution in foreign ports. Just as notably, the superior officer connected the raucous and sexually promiscuous liberty parties with international and diplomatic relations. He recognized that Cuba expected the base to contribute to Guantánamo's economy. He cared about maintaining good relations with Cuba far more than he cared about the sailors' chastity. Using the neocolonial leverage available, the Cuban national and local governments had exerted some pressure on the U.S. Navy. If the U.S. Navy was stationed in Guantánamo Bay, it had better spend its dollars in Guantánamo.

Since the Cuban revolution, state-sponsored accounts and popular memory depict prostitution as widely practiced and legal throughout Guantánamo before 1959. "Zones of tolerance," or red-light districts, were designated areas where prostitution, drug use, and gambling were "tolerated." In Guantánamo, the streets in the southeastern quadrant housed the city's zone of tolerance, and in Caimanera, the entire town was dominated by it. Most Cuban histories as well as individual testimonies recount that after the revolution, prostitution disappeared. This is seen as one of the victories of the Castro era.[37] Whereas the broad sweep of this narrative is accurate, the easy dichotomy of before and after the revolution erases a more contested sexual landscape in the years before the Cuban revolution.

The legal status of Guantánamo's zone of tolerance was far from clear-cut in the 1940s and 1950s. For example, journalist Lino Lemes insisted, "They [the government] must *bring back* the zones of tolerance."[38] Why was Lino Lemes asking for a return of the zones of tolerance when, according to public memory and state discourse, they were an accepted and legal part of pre-revolutionary Guantánamo and Caimanera? In fact, both *La Voz del Pueblo* and *El Vigilante* referred to an "ex-zone" or an "extinguished" zone in Guantánamo.[39] The Cuban Congress had passed a 1919 tourism law in response to speculators' interests in enticing tourists and their dollars. This decision had opened the door to legalized gambling and casinos on Cuba's waterfront. The law stipulated that companies able to invest more than one million dollars could develop official "tourist zones," resulting in the proliferation of the burlesques, casinos, and spectacles that came to define Havana and Varadero. Lacking wealthy investors and national attention, Guantánamo and Caimanera did not seem to have benefited from this explicit designation. By the 1940s, Lemes's writings implied that a zone of tolerance had once been legally sanctioned, but that this status had since been revoked. Lemes advocated for renewed, and official, zones of tolerance, so that prostitution could be properly monitored in Guantánamo and Caimanera.[40]

Lino Lemes proposed several mechanisms to regulate prostitution. He believed legalizing prostitution would protect the "decent" women in Guantánamo, guard against the spread of venereal disease, and prevent minors from entering brothels. As early as 1940, Lino Lemes suggested a boldly visual solution: "We need zones of tolerance. The houses in it should be painted all the same color in order that they [the *marinos*] are not confused with decent houses. This is very necessary." He suggested yellow.[41] Lemes also championed free venereal disease screening and treatment for all local prostitutes. In 1942 the Guantánamo municipality established a contagious disease clinic, Patronata contra la Lepra, Enfermedades Cutáneas, y Sífilis (PLECS), or the Board against Leprosy, Skin Diseases, and Syphilis. Through PLECS, local medical officers tested prostitutes once a week. However, the scans cost each prostitute eight dollars, plus additional funds for treatment if she was infected. Lemes believed these costs were prohibitive, so he advocated, "It is necessary to create an anti-venereal dispensary of Guantánamo that would be *completely free* for the victims of what we call social diseases." In Lemes's mind, prostitution was a necessary evil and a general societal problem, only exaggerated by the U.S. naval station. In an unknowing nod toward the future, Lemes added, "It may appear immoral, but to those who think this, I will tell them that prostitution is a necessary evil, and it is inevitable. No government, not even the Communists, have been able to eliminate it."[42]

By accepting vice in a designated district, Lino Lemes and the Guantánamo commercial elite hoped to regulate the U.S. military's drinking and sexual appetites and, just as importantly, keep this depravity away from Guantánamo society. The zone of tolerance's main function was to presumably restrict sexual commerce to a lower class of people and neighborhood, all while maintaining good relations with the U.S. military and its lucrative commerce. However, the U.S. *francos* were not so easy to contain. Although never mentioned explicitly, rape and assault lurk at the corners of people's memories and accounts. In their drunken states and presumptuousness, U.S. sailors and marines acted as if all women in Guantánamo and Caimanera were available for their sexual advances.

The local population's greatest anxiety was that U.S. sailors and marines could not distinguish between "decent" women and "women of pleasure." These fears appear justified. In fact, their privileged presence as "military tourists" had the power to erase carefully constructed class divisions in Guantánamo. As journalist Lino Lemes wrote, "Now, when these military tourists are drunk, they can constitute a serious menace to the families of Caimanera and Guantánamo. When they don't meet prostitutes, they often offend the ladies. . . . [T]hen Cuban gentlemen can be very violent in order to stop them from disrespecting Cuban woman. Much blood could run and men could lose lives, putting the friendship between the United States and Cuba in danger."[43] *Guantanameros* feared that the North American *marinos* would not frequent prostitutes, but would instead harass their mothers, sisters, and daughters. One base worker, Walter Knight, remembered that when the sailors came into town, they would look for sex and bother local women of "decent families." The U.S. *marinos* were "drunk" and "half-savages," going into "whatever house [they wanted]." Walter concluded that despite this disrespect and abuse, the U.S. sailors spent plenty of money in town and "that was what interested many people."[44] According to Ramón Sánchez, "On Saturdays, especially Saturdays . . . the trains would have ten cars full of sailors and marines from the base. And they'd come here. Know why they'd come here, they'd drink, drink, drink, all day and all night." He explained that the *marinos* would ride horses around town and make advances at Cuban women. This led to fights with "her husband, or her fiancée. . . . There would be many troubles."[45] The repetition of U.S. licentiousness and aggression was constant in individuals' personal testimonies. These bitter memories underscored that many U.S. *marinos* saw all Cuban women, and by extension all of Cuba, as fair game.

Calls to respect local women may not seem radical or anti-American, yet this is how the U.S. consular office interpreted the complaints. For example, *Libertad,* a Santiago de Cuba paper, ran the article "Objectionable Tourists," which criticized U.S. *marinos* for "habitual drunkenness," "brawling in public places," and "arrogance." More to the point, the author objected to U.S. military personnel disrespecting and cavorting with Cuban women: "Many of these visitors give the impression that they are privileged to do anything that strikes their fancy. They should be taught by those competent to do so that our women are as worthy of respect and consideration as their own mothers and sisters." On reading this article, a U.S. diplomat refused to recognize the poor conduct of North American *francos*. He instead asserted that the journalist was anti-American and a homosexual.[46] In one fell swoop, the U.S. consul smeared the author as sexually deviant, ignored the complaints against Cuban women, and rhetorically emasculated the local community even further.

In another incident involving the Cuban–Anglo-American Club, the U.S. consul was again sympathetic to the U.S. *francos*. This time U.S. Navy "boys" had been "unjustly" charged with "bad behavior and disrespect" to "Cuban custom, its women, and their families." Examples of this "bad behavior" included two enlisted men at the club raiding the "ladies toilet" and breaking a mirror. Other U.S. sailors on leave were believed to have been "molesting pedestrians, particularly young women" and throwing small firecrackers at them.[47] Again, the U.S. consul downplayed these charges and chalked the criticism up to anti-American sentiments.

Despite this general dismissiveness, the U.S. Navy recognized that sailors and marines' unchecked sexual presumption created animosity and anger within Guantánamo, Caimanera, and Santiago de Cuba. The U.S. officials generally resolved these conflicts by putting a halt to local liberty visits. The U.S. Navy would then send military *francos* to Jamaica, Haiti, and Puerto Rico, rather than Caimanera and Guantánamo, thus exchanging one neocolonial territory for another.[48] In turn, this deprived Caimanera, Guantánamo, and Santiago de Cuba of much needed commerce and cash, and forced the elite to beg for their return. The Guantánamo businesses proprietors were in a compromised, classically neocolonial bind. Even as they might protest how U.S. *marinos* disrespected Cuban women, they were financially dependent on their dollars.

Although U.S. sailors and marines might have ignored the distinction between Guantánamo's decent families and its prostitutes, they may have been more attuned to Guantánamo's multiracial population. Brothels were segregated by class and race, and this was as much a legacy of Spanish colonialism and Cuban social mores as it was a gesture to U.S. Jim Crow. For example, Alberto Torres recalled that there were hierarchies for prostitutes, with "blond," "beautiful," and "olive-skinned" girls for lawyers, politicians, and base officials, and far more common brothels for the average sailor. He laughed, explaining there were bars where a woman cost "one hundred, three hundred dollars. And then you went to other bars . . . and it was like one dollar, fifty cents."[49] This privileging

of whiteness and blondness was a matter of both U.S. and Cuban prejudice. Former base worker Juan Carlos Pulsara emphasized not only the
race of the Cuban women, but also the race of the U.S. men, comment-
ing that the madames had to separate their black and white prostitutes
to cater to their North American customers' desires.[50] While white U.S.
sailors slept with Cuban women of color, they would not sleep with the
same women who slept with black U.S. *francos*. In these accounts, Pulsara and Torres observed how U.S. and Cuban racial prejudices and
norms intermingled in the brothel.[51]

Prostitution was a fact of the local political economy, and U.S. *marinos* were objectionable, not so much because they paid for sex, but because they did not recognize Guantánamo social standards. The nebulous and permeable zones of tolerance embodied the Good Neighbor
policy's seedier, but more tangible, side. It was in these social and sexual
exchanges that local people experienced the concrete effects of U.S. neocolonialism and competed for U.S. dollars. Throughout the 1940s and
1950s, sexual and social encounters remained key sites of racial and class
anxieties among both the Guantánamo population and the U.S. military.

RACE AND CLASS: DANCING BETWEEN BLACK SAILORS AND WHITE CUBANS

The U.S. Navy and the Guantánamo elite attempted to neutralize the
sexual excesses of *marinos* by sponsoring social functions outside the
brothels. Whether U.S. sailors and marines paid for sexual services,
danced with selected *damitas,* or married local women, they were navigating a social terrain influenced, but not fully defined, by the U.S. military presence. In 1943 the U.S. Navy in conjunction with Guantánamo's
fuerzas vivas inaugurated the United Service Organization (USO) in an
effort to moderate the sexual nature of visits from *francos*. The USO became the public site where U.S. sailors danced with local women under the
good graces of the U.S. military and the local elite. The USO established a
dance hall where "respectable" Cuban women could seek North American
mates. In full social view, the USO also drew attention to Cuban and U.S.
racial dynamics; Cubans of color and nonwhite North Americans were not
welcome. Racial difference became pronounced in this context of sexual
and social exchange, intertwining Cuban and North American prejudices.
The resulting collision of U.S. and Cuban class and racial norms identified
two multivocal, stratified populations.

Race and class defined Cuban society, and Guantánamo was no exception. Cuba's multiracial population constantly tested the bounds of

citizenship and inclusion. To be sure, Cuba's racial taxonomies included far more variation than the U.S. "one drop rule" and, throughout the island, race encompassed a spectrum of *mestizos* and *mulattos*. Yet despite this continuum, Cuban society continued to privilege whiteness, while blackness (*negro* or *prieto*) remained stigmatized. José Martí's ideal of a raceless *cubanidad* collided with, and ironically could reinforce, traditional racial hierarchies. The Cuban government's official commitment to "racelessness" enabled it to outlaw political organizations based on racial identity. This eliminated the possibility for Cubans of color to organize against discrimination as such.[52] Because of Oriente's history of black leadership and nationalist ideals during the Cuban War of Independence, the challenge of racial inclusion and social equality was even more acute in the eastern province.

In Guantánamo, racial identity was marked by far more than phenotype, and national background and professional status were key components in how race was classified and defined.[53] The Spanish Association and the Union Club catered to members of the upper class, most of whom traced their heritage directly to Spain. These men and women claimed a Cuban whiteness, which denied black or African backgrounds. Black Cubans belonged to separate voluntary associations, including Siglo XX, the Club Moncada, and La Nueva Era.[54] Organized and controlled by black professionals, these societies hoped to advance economic and social mobility for black Cubans.[55] Although also defined as black, West Indians formed separate mutual aid organizations, including the British West Indian Centre and Masonic lodges. Thus, nationality and class status intersected to define Guantánamo's racial geography. This topography was not neutral; whiteness was valued and interracial socializing and marriages were still rare. However, unlike the United States, exclusion was not policed by legal codes or public segregation. Instead, the local racial hierarchy was based on social stratification and nationality rather than law.

Despite these racial divisions, from a U.S. perspective, Cuba could be romanticized as a racial paradise or feared as a black republic. Without a doubt, Cubans of color wielded far greater political power than African Americans did in the United States. As a result, the African American press and community looked to Cuba as a country that promised full black citizenship, and they cheered for Cuban baseball stars and listened to Cuban music.[56] Even more importantly, Cubans of color had suffrage rights, and their votes were often the key in Cuban elections.[57] U.S. diplomats in Oriente rued the fact that they had to negotiate with a black community, and even worse, one that was enfranchised. One U.S. official guessed that 75 percent of Oriente's population possessed "various portions of negro blood," and on Election Day, he noted somewhat hostilely, "the negro was the man of the day."[58] The high levels of political participation particularly rankled U.S. military officers when they had to negotiate with black Cubans in leadership positions. For example, in a case of drunken *francos* being held by municipal authorities, U.S. officials complained that the Guantánamo judge who had jurisdiction over the case was a "nigger."[59] Having to negotiate and accept people of color in authority challenged U.S. officers' racial privilege over a neocolonial population. Even more unsettling, Guantánamo offered a model in which people of color could vote and hold public positions, potentially exposing white and black U.S. sailors to a more racially open society.

African American, Puerto Rican, and Filipino sailors all served in the U.S. Navy. Up until World War II, most military personnel of color were kept in subservient positions and not allowed to rise in rank. Black men served almost exclusively in the U.S. Navy's mess halls as cooks and waiters, and Filipinos were the traditional porters and butlers to U.S. naval officers.[60] However, during the 1940s, African American mobilization within the United States created limited but new spaces for black military service and the consequent claims to U.S. citizenship. This recognition of people of color within the U.S. military was problematic for U.S. officials. First, it fractured the U.S. identification with whiteness and power. Second, it opened the possibility of African Americans, Filipinos, and U.S. Latinos meeting Cuban men and women. The U.S. Navy ironically provided black sailors the opportunity to witness a society where people of color held positions of respect and a public tradition of nationalism and multiracial citizenship.

A 1943 intelligence report laid out U.S. racial fears in clear language and displayed evidence of U.S. officials' surveillance of black sailors. In August 1943 L. I. Bowman, a naval intelligence officer, reported that a group of "negro enlisted men" attacked two white sailors "without provocation." He stated that this animosity between white and black sailors was habitual, even admitting, "at times, the white enlisted men have been at fault." Morale among black sailors was low, because they believed discrimination kept them in the mess hall. Bowman defended this practice. "[They] are possibly the victims of racial propaganda. They are disgruntled because they have been led to believe that they are being discriminated against and fail to take into consideration that they do not have the educational qualifications and mental stamina to fill the ratings in other departments."[61]

He also noted that many of the African American messmen displayed a pattern of misbehavior and insubordination. For example, one African American sailor, George Silvester Cox, had tried to promote himself. On his own initiative and without authorization, he donned a chief petty officer emblem and tried to sit in the chief petty officer's section. Although appearing only fleetingly in the archives, Cox's protest and self-promotion characterized the frustration and anger many African Americans felt at their second-class status in the U.S. military.

This same document provided information of racial unrest in Guantánamo. "Reliable confidential informants in Guantánamo City, Cuba, have reported several instances indicating racial unrest there. . . . Alicia Magoon and Bonani, both colored, were known to be drunk and disorderly, making statements to the effect that the present war [WW II] was a 'white man's war,' with which the colored people had no concern." Intelligence Officer Bowman cautioned that José Medina, a black Cuban and one of the "radical labor leaders" of the Guantánamo Railroad workers, was a potentially volatile personality. He noted that Medina and other "radical leaders" had been "fanning" the "fire of racial consciousness," and suggested that they might even be agents of an enemy government. Moreover, he attributed this newfound racial antagonism to the 1943 Detroit riots.[62] Bowman never directly commented on the connection between his scrutiny of black sailors at GTMO and his reports on black Cubans in Guantánamo; however, he categorized the two incidents together. This juxtaposition was not random, but rather invoked the possibility that George Cox, the black messman who had tried to promote himself, could come into the vicinity of José Medina, the black Cuban labor leader. The U.S. imperial project could quite inadvertently be subverted by its own, not Cuba's, multiracial and black population.

The USO also revealed racial divisions within the U.S. Navy. During World War II, the U.S. Armed Services with the cooperation of local counterparts established USO clubs nearby foreign and domestic military bases to provide, monitor, and control recreational alternatives for U.S. sailors and marines.[63] In Guantánamo, Dr. Antonio Jané Civit was the Cuban chairperson of the USO, and he championed regular contact between U.S. military personnel and the Guantánamo commercial elite. Middle- and upper-class Guantánamo girls attended the USO dances in great numbers. At the opening ceremonies, *El Vigilante* reported that there were enough prestigious ladies and *damitas* for more than one hundred U.S. sailors, and they offered the men from the base a splendid dance with a live band.[64] The social directors of the club were three "honorable" local, married women: Sra. Nieves Gorrate de Mirabent, Sra. Angelina Seisdedos de Menes, and Sra. Aminta Benítez de González, and these women selected and invited suitable local ladies.[65] The USO became an emblem of U.S. and Cuban social interaction. The Guantánamo *fuerzas vivas* wanted to elevate their social status, presenting Cuban women as acceptable partners for U.S. sailors. In the process, the Guantánamo bourgeoisie protected their privilege and claims to whiteness, for they did not want their daughters dancing with just any U.S. sailor. More pointedly, they did not want their daughters dancing with black U.S. sailors.

As a public venue, the USO crystallized how U.S. and Cuban racial prejudices could exist side by side. By all accounts, the USO did not invite Cuban women of color or allow African American sailors to socialize with the white Cuban *guantanameras*.[66] Cuban narrators often pointed to the USO as an example of U.S.-style Jim Crow segregation imposed on the Cuban landscape. For example, former base worker Juan Carlos Pulsara remembered that the USO did not permit black local women or black U.S. sailors from entering.[67] Walter Knight reiterated this incidence of discrimination with a bit more nuance. He pointed out that the black sailors had been allowed to enter the USO, but because it was a white organization, the white Cuban women had refused to dance with them. However, he too accused the United States of importing a more blunt form of racism: "In Holguín [home to UFC plantations], yes there was [racism], but here in Guantánamo, when I came, I did not see much racism. But then . . . the Americans came and influenced the rude people here," namely the club and bar owners. He explained that Guantánamo proprietors did not explicitly say, "You couldn't go there because you were black. They said, 'No, this is for friends.' " He admitted that "friends" by implication were only white Cubans, but Walter minimized this discrimination by describing it as a social or personal choice. "Here in Cuba there was no racism, no. It was a personal thing." While always recognizing that Guantánamo society maintained separate social circles for white and black Cubans, Walter Knight blamed the United States for "implanting" racial segregation.[68]

Walter Knight discussed Cuban social segregation and U.S. legal segregation as two separate systems: the first he appeared to accept, the second he did not. On the one hand, his testimony reflected an accurate reading of U.S. Jim Crow policies in the 1940s and 1950s. Yet, on the other hand, he provided equal evidence of Guantánamo's social prejudice, which excluded blacks and blackness through private social clubs and delineations of friendship. Walter's testimony articulated the overlapping layers of racism and racial hierarchies. Even in Cuba, a place designated in African American popular culture as an antiracist sanctuary, black sailors could not dance with white Cuban women.

In fact, in 1943 black U.S. sailors protested that they were not accepted at the USO, and they tried to organize an alternative club in town. Black messmen collected $325 to open a USO in Guantánamo for African American servicemen. Contrary to Juan Carlos Pulsara's memories, the U.S. intelligence officer recorded that black sailors *were* admitted into the USO. This acceptance came with the significant caveat that "the colored men would not dance and fraternize with" "the more respectable citizens' " daughters. Therefore, black enlisted men attended USO functions until they realized "they were being ostracized socially by the white girls attending."[69] In this account, the U.S. intelligence officer reversed the charge of U.S. racism and blamed the discrimination within USO on Guantánamo's social mores. In fact, both racial hierarchies worked to buttress each other to keep white and nonwhite communities apart.

In a particularly Guantánamo-specific solution, the West Indian Democratic Association offered its hall to U.S. black sailors. Perhaps this was to further curry favor with U.S. officers in the hope of gaining more jobs, or perhaps it was out of sympathy, solidarity, or identification with the rejected black sailors. In any case, this black West Indian society recognized itself as a possible alternative for the black *francos*. In a letter to the U.S. Navy, Jim Petinaud, a British World War I veteran, argued, "It has been said that the coloured service men are generally not given liberty owing to the lack of a suitable sanitary place for their entertainment. We are of the opinion that we have the place that will meet your approval. . . . We do not keep alcoholic beverages or strong drinks of any kind around so to be in keeping with army regulations."[70] Local racial- and national-based social clubs could now help enforce the separation of black men and white women, and this suited both the U.S. and Guantánamo authorities just fine.

The USO's public and social purpose became a flash point in memories related to race, class, and sex in Guantánamo society. U.S. officials blamed racial segregation in the USO on the Guantánamo leaders, and local *guantanameros* blamed the U.S. military for imposing Jim Crow.

Neither side admitted that the layers of social segregation reinforced racial discrimination within both a U.S. and a Cuban vocabulary. The two racial taxonomies were not incompatible, and both served to underpin white privilege and the neocolonial exchanges between U.S. men and local women.

MARRIAGE, STATISTICS, AND RACIAL CLASSIFICATION

U.S. sailors not only paid for sex and danced with Cuban women; dozens also married.[71] Unlike paid sexual encounters, which ended after an hour or an evening, marriage connoted social acceptability, along with a degree of racial, class, and national compatibility. For example, the *New York Times* published the wedding announcement of Rose de Quintana y Bustillos, a teacher in Santiago de Cuba who had studied at the University of Havana and the University of Minnesota, and John W. Hull, a journalist in the U.S. Navy, stationed at GTMO, and on his way to Yale University.[72] Rose de Quintana had already lived and studied in the United States, and the attractive accompanying photo announced her whiteness. Her class status, signified by her travel and educational achievement, suggested that Hull, a future Yale man, was not transgressing class or racial boundaries, and as the man, his U.S. masculinity was not compromised by taking on a Cuban wife. The *New York Times* society pages granted its approval of the match.

Still in Guantánamo and Caimanera, there was a level of anxiety that working-class and less respectable Cuban women were simply gold digging and attempting to parley sexual favors into marriage proposals. Lino Lemes cautioned, "They [the women] say that with the yankee *marinos* they could gain so much money. . . . [T]hey could marry the *marinos*, sons of millionaires. Yes sir, they said that they could meet a husband with the U.S. Armed Forces." He noted that many U.S. sailors did marry in Caimanera and Guantánamo, suggesting that "maybe this was one of the reasons" the secretary of the navy ended visits from *marinos* to "places of dubious morality."[73] The U.S. military was also concerned with the possibility that offshore romances could spark interracial marriages. Stemming from the U.S. military's World War II experience in Trinidad, the United States initiated a policy whereby U.S. servicemen needed to receive permission from a commanding officer before they could marry local women. The aim was to prevent white men from marrying local women of color.[74] With the Good Neighbor policy on the lips of commercial elites and naval officers, both were mum on whether Cuban women could make good wives for U.S. sailors and marines.

The Guantánamo civil registry recorded 101 marriages between U.S. men and Cuban women between 1921 and 1958 (see appendix).[75] Although it is quite possible that there were even more marriages—for example, men who married women in Santiago de Cuba, records that were miscataloged in the archive, and so on—this sample allows for a unique glimpse at U.S.-Cuban marriages. These unions occurred under the auspices of the Guantánamo municipality, a venue where U.S. men accepted the authority of Cuban law and sovereignty. Through the act of marriage, U.S. citizens acknowledged a Cuban legal system that operated apart from U.S. military control. In the 1930s and 1940s, the civil registry even recorded U.S. men's names in the Spanish style, including their mothers' surnames as well as their fathers' appellations. The record is silent about the motivations, manipulations, possible romances, and personal testimonies of the men and women involved. Instead, the legal documents reduce marriage to the statistical backgrounds of two people. In all of the marriages, the man was a U.S. citizen and the woman was living in Cuba. The number of marriages increased over time. Between 1940 and 1945 there were ten marriages; in 1946 alone there were ten marriages; and in 1957 thirteen marriages were recorded. The civil registry also recorded birthplace, parents' birthplaces, and sometimes the individual's race. This detailed information revealed a North American cohort that was neither homogenous, nor solely white. Rather, the U.S. military appeared multiracial and inflected by the legacies of North American imperialism. Individual men and women's choices and marriages displayed far more points of connection than the ideology behind the Good Neighbor policy might have suggested.

The majority of marriages cemented relationships between white U.S. men and younger white Cuban women. This underscored a U.S. paternalist model, which assumed a benevolent, white U.S. male and an immature Cuban female. However, there were important exceptions that disrupted this fantasy and revealed U.S. men marrying older Cuban women and U.S. men with their own Caribbean roots. True, many marriages did fit the above pattern. For example, Richard Martin, a twenty-three-year-old, white sergeant in the U.S. Marine Corps, married Pilar Lucia Hortensia de la Caridad Olivella Oduardo, a twenty-year-old, white Cuban.[76] On paper at least, this marriage, along with dozens of others, did nothing to dismantle the association of U.S. military power with whiteness or paternalism. At the same time, countering this image, in approximately 20 percent of the marriages in the civil registry, the Cuban woman was older than the U.S. man. For example, twenty-six-year-old Sylvia Bryan married twenty-year-old Herman Rogers, twenty-six-year-old Gloria Salvadora del Carmen Aranda married twenty-year-old Jack Monroe Leonard, and twenty-eight-year-old Josefina Gonzalez y Corses married the twenty-two-year-old U.S. sailor Norman Phillips.[77]

Many of the North American husbands also had family histories in Cuba, and several of the Cuban women could trace a parent to the U.S. mainland or Puerto Rico. For example, Claude William Abbot, a U.S. cable operator from Pennsylvania, married Aracelia Juana Boan y Pérez.[78] Abbot was a U.S. citizen, but his mother was from Santiago de Cuba, providing him with a cultural link to eastern Cuba. Or, in 1952 Raimundo Ortega, a U.S. citizen, married Olga Luz Rivero y Henriquez from Guantánamo. Ortega was born in New York, but his parents were both Cubans from Matanzas province just outside of Havana.[79] In another union, Eunice Ávila Gonzalez, a twenty-year-old Cuban woman married Jerry Owensby, a white, twenty-one-year-old sailor from South Carolina. Although meeting and marrying in Guantánamo, Gonzalez was from Havana, and her father was a U.S. citizen born in Key West.[80] These personal histories revealed transnational trajectories that defied a simple North American–Cuban binary.

In fact, 24 of the 101 couples involved partners of color; a U.S. man with Caribbean, Mexican, or Philippine connections; or a woman with ties to the United States or Puerto Rico.[81] A total of 9 U.S. men had a parent who was born in Cuba, Puerto Rico, or Mexico; and 5 of the women had parents who were born in Puerto Rico or the United States. Their lineages noted parallel migratory trends of Cubans, Puerto Ricans, and overlapping routes of U.S. colonial power—all which converged in Guantánamo. For example, this history of Caribbean migration and U.S. neocolonialism shaped Joe Ramos's background. Ramos's father was Cuban American, his mother was Puerto Rican, and Ramos himself was born in Florida. A sailor in the U.S. Navy, Ramos was stationed at GTMO in 1956, where he married Elisa María Hidalgo, a *blanca* (white) *cubana*.[82] Not only did Ramos marry a Cuban woman, but he also acted as a translator and witness when his shipmate, Marion Russell Guy, married Nancy Miriam Cardet Muñoz.[83] The child of a Cuban American and Puerto Rican couple, Ramos appeared comfortable in Spanish, and he took advantage of his bilingual skills in finding a spouse and helping his friends. Yet he still acted as a foot sailor in the U.S. Navy with its neocolonial presence in Guantánamo. In another instance, Felipe Muldez

Bagarez, a Filipino sailor in the U.S. Navy, married a Guantánamo woman in 1947. The local bureaucrat defined him, rightly or wrongly, as a U.S. citizen. The 1934 Tydings-McDuffie Act had classified Filipinos in the United States as aliens, and it was only through military service in World War II that Filipinos were able to naturalize and become U.S. citizens. The municipal authority noted Muldez's wife was *blanca,* but his own race was not identified.[84] As a Filipino, Muldez's neocolonial status was actually similar to that of his new spouse. Although it is impossible to judge or evaluate how Ramos or Muldez defined or understood their military experiences, their presence in the archival record testifies to a North American military population that itself was shaped by U.S. imperialism and neocolonialism.

In many cases, the marriage records also defined the couple's racial status, and North Americans of color were prominent. It is unclear whether the local administrative official asked for the individual's race, or if he made his own personal assessment.[85] What is clear is that, given the high proportion of people of color in Guantánamo, a disproportionate number of women were classified *blanca* in the civil registry. Only 9 women were *negra* or *mestiza* [mixed race] and 5 more had parents born in the West Indies, indicating that they also were very likely of color. This Cuban identification as *blanca* may, or may not, have been recognized in the United States. The municipal authority may have labeled the Cuban women *blanca* because white U.S. men accepted only white marriage partners. The official designation may have also been used to legally "make" these women white in an era when interracial marriages were prohibited in the U.S. South.

There is also ample evidence of black U.S. military men marrying local women, and they all appear to have married Cuban women of color. Although only 4 of the U.S. sailors' race was designated as *negra,* an additional 10 women were labeled *negra* or noted a West Indian parent. In addition, three records identified Cuban *mestiza* women marrying U.S. men of undefined race. Presumably these men were also of color, because it was highly unlikely for a white U.S. man to marry a woman legally designated as nonwhite. In total, the record suggests that at least 10 percent of all U.S.-Cuban marriages in Guantánamo included a black U.S. citizen. For example, in 1950 Horace Mays, a black sailor from Abbeville, South Carolina, married Veronica Valeria Claxton, a Cuban woman whose parents were born in St. Kitts.[86] In no instance did a black man marry a woman who was classified as white. Despite black sailors' U.S. citizenship and military service, their national position did not trump their race. Instead, local racial and social taboos against interracial marriage within Cuba, as well as U.S. laws, dictated that U.S. black men married only Cuban women of color. In the majority of these marriages, the Cuban woman was a West Indian descendant, and thus most likely spoke English, which could further facilitate the relationship.

In this vortex of neocolonialism, cultural overlap in U.S.-Cuban marriages was as striking as social divides. Rather than a simple importation of U.S.-style Jim Crow or a mythic Cuban social milieu that eschewed racial classification, U.S. and Cuban men and women navigated a spectrum of alternately competing and reinforcing racial, national, and gender hierarchies. These international marriages contradicted a simplistic notion that U.S. neocolonialism and paternalism operated seamlessly in personal relations. The U.S. military had its own diverse and bifurcated population, and its members could engage in liaisons that underscored the similarities between U.S. and Cuban communities. Far more nuanced than the U.S. Navy's official proclamations of goodwill and good neighborliness, the Guantánamo civil registry revealed interwoven histories of slavery, migration, and neocolonialism that were embedded in the marriages of U.S. men and Cuban women.

MOVIE THEATERS AND M-26-7: PRIVATE AND PUBLIC ENCOUNTERS ON THE BASE

Just as U.S. sailors and marines entered an unaccustomed social and racial milieu in Guantánamo, local workers on the base had to adapt to U.S. social norms and military culture on GTMO. Like most U.S. military installations around the world, GTMO emerged as a North "American oasis" in the heart of Cuba.[87] It was a hyper–North American environment and an exaggeration of U.S. suburbia.[88] In direct opposition to the U.S. sailors and marines who took "liberty" and ran free in Guantánamo, base workers' movements were regimented and controlled.

Workers' recollections of the physical and psychological confines of the base ranged from a sense of wonder to bitterness. Some workers marveled at GTMO's pristine setting and manicured façade, which stood in clear opposition to Guantánamo's unhygienic streets. For example, Rosa Johnson, a domestic worker, was struck by the physical difference: "I believe they [GTMO] had a person who came whenever a leaf fell, because you never saw a leaf or a piece of paper in the streets. Nothing."[89] However, other workers were less awed by the base's sterility and criticized the military order for constricting their mobility. They did not necessarily prefer the orderly, U.S.-imposed landscape. For example, Maria Boothe, also a domestic servant in the 1950s, explained, "No, I didn't like it [GTMO] very much, because everything was prohibited there. It was a military life, and it wasn't the same [as life in Guantánamo]. You could walk only in certain zones, you couldn't go here, you couldn't go there, and you couldn't buy things in the stores. Everything was different for me."[90] She added that she was never poorly treated and her English language skills gave her a certain status, "but it appeared to me that nobody liked to be there. . . . It was like another country." Another domestic worker, Priscilla Baxter, remembered that "Cuba was always much more fun, and there were many parties, the cinema, the weddings, the families, friend-ships. . . . But on the base, no, on the base you worked the entire week and you had your day off [only] to go to the movies."[91] In both of these configurations Guantánamo and GTMO were imagined in a distinct bi-nary, which minimized the cultural and social exchanges that occurred every day.

Like the USO in Guantánamo, public spaces on the base brought the entrenched divisions between U.S. military personnel and Cubans into relief. Many local workers lived on the base during the week: the men lived in the civilian barracks, and the women lived in the homes of their employers. As suited a military base, social clubs were organized by rank, officers separated from enlisted men, and local employees divided from U.S. personnel. The golf courses, clubs, and recreational halls were all off-limits to base workers. The base cinema was the only social space where U.S. sailors and marines regularly interacted with local workers.

Base workers were reluctant to discuss their experiences with U.S. racial discrimination, but when they did mention it, they all pointed to the same example: the segregated base cinema. Juan Carlos Pulsara re-called the layout and the "discipline" of the theater. There were desig-nated sections for the officers, the subofficers, the U.S. civilian workers, and finally the Cuban workers. He even remembered a special ceremony, whereby the movie would not begin until the base commander had en-tered the cinema.[92] Maria Boothe concurred that the Cubans sat on one side and the North Americans on the other.[93] And Walter Knight noted that the Cuban workers did not even get actual seats, but rather sat in bleachers or on the steps.[94]

In the Cuban revolution's 1964 account of GTMO, the writer pointed to the base cinema as the ultimate implantation of U.S. Jim Crow in Cuba. "The Cubans who worked there [GTMO] were the victims of this discriminating system. . . . And if they wanted to go to the cinema . . . they had to sit in the last rows. There was a line which separated the "white men" from the 'black men.' The Cubans sat in the rows together with those who suffered the same system of discrimination."[95] The phrases "white men" and "black men" were printed in English, emphasizing U.S. racial prejudice in an era when the Cuban revolution promoted itself as a champion of Third World liberation and people of color in the United States. In our conversations, former base workers disagreed over whether the base cinema was segregated by race, for example, white North Americans on one side with all people of color (Cuban and North American) on the other, or by nationality, for example, all North Americans on one side and all local workers on the other. Juan Carlos Pulsara recalled that local workers sat in the same section as black U.S. sailors, while Maria Boothe and Walter Knight remembered the divisions based on nationality. This slippage is worth investigating further, but it does not diminish the movie theater's symbolic value in Guantánamo public memory or the residue of frustration etched in its stratified seating arrangements. The base cinema was the one recreational venue workers and military personnel shared, and its separate lines and rows stigmatized local workers. In Guantánamo, base officers enjoyed the privileges of neighborliness in exclusive clubs and bars, but GTMO workers could relax on the base only in the shadow of U.S. chauvinism.

Despite this clear example of prejudice within the base, the male retirees I interviewed were disinclined to further criticize their U.S. employers. Base workers, many Cubans of color and West Indians, would have been familiar with racism within Cuba and on U.S. sugar plantations. Racial discrimination on the base may not have been a qualitatively new experience in their work lives. Through a U.S. neocolonial vocabulary, the base could even offer social proximity to white North Americans and formal solutions to discrimination. For example, Ramón Sánchez, a self-described white Cuban, insisted, "I never saw that [racial problems]. We were treated very well. I'm talking about myself. They treated me very, very well." Ramón fondly recalled invitations to his supervisor's home at the holidays and meeting his family.[96] Santiago Ruiz, a Cuban of color, concurred that there were no racial problems on the base. The U.S. military even offered the possibility of identifying and correcting racial bias, a mechanism not available in pre-revolutionary or post-revolutionary Cuba. Santiago distinctly remembered a pamphlet, outlining procedures one could follow in cases of racial discrimination. "There was a bulletin. . . . Inside of it, I remember and I will never forget this, that one time it said: To the Cuban civil service workers: If at some moment anyone . . . has problems with something from the racial point of view, or for a religious reason. That is if some Cuban worker had some problem with this [discrimination], they gave a place where one could go to report the problem."[97] The U.S. military might have brought a Jim Crow-like movie theater onto the base, but it also had a legal code that directly addressed racial prejudice. In Santiago's memories this pamphlet was at least as remarkable as the segregated movie theater. It provided a procedure to combat bigotry, in contrast to the Cuban denial of racial discrimination. Although I would suggest that Santiago's faith in the U.S. military's commitment to nondiscrimination in the 1950s was misplaced, the degree to which this administrative remedy impressed him is notable.

At least as much as frustrations with racism, workers resented jobs that offered only menial labor and inconsistent employment. Private contract jobs were the least desirable positions, for they were short-term, came with no benefits, and relied on capricious hiring practices. They were also more likely to force workers into subservient positions, (e.g., waiters, maids, and bartenders), and offered little opportunity for advancement. Some of these positions were with private companies, like the Frederick Snare or Drake Winkleman corporations, and others were in the U.S. Navy's social clubs. Waiters, cooks, and bartenders often worked in the U.S. Navy's recreational departments (e.g., Officers' Club, Enlisted Club, etc.), and these jobs were designated as nongovernment employment paid through nonappropriated funds. For example, Walter Knight disliked his first job on the base, where he had been a waiter in the Officers' Club. "They worked you like a slave. . . . I didn't like that work [in the Club]. Then on Saturdays and Sunday there was even more work; some people liked it, but I didn't."[98] Luckily after a short time, Walter found a civil service position in an office where he worked eight hours a day and earned a higher wage.

Whereas men worked as both U.S. civil servants and private contract employees, women were far more likely to work for individual families as cooks, nannies, maids, and housekeepers.[99] Unlike the men who worked in offices, construction sites, and canteens—all public spaces—most women worked in private homes. Living in officers' houses and working with their families, these female workers had more daily contact with U.S. military personnel and their families. And because they were privately hired, they had none of the protections of civil service employment. Their wages were significantly lower than those of their male counterparts, and they were often at the mercy of their "mistresses." Whereas U.S. officials may have felt at "home" in Guantánamo, local women actually worked in their homes and cared for their children.

The guide to *Living Conditions at the Naval Base* offered a portrait of GTMO as an outpost where U.S. women could oversee local maids who would be grateful for the work. Classic colonial language positioned these domestic workers as no better than children. For example, domestic servants earned fifteen to thirty-five dollars a month. The U.S. Navy cautioned officers' wives that although "this [wage] may seem ridiculously low to most Americans," it was important to refrain from "our natural tendency to spoil them with extra gratuities." It conditioned officers' wives to expect domestic servants to offer "efficient" housecleaning, washing, ironing, and child care. Even more importantly, they were advised to regulate and restrict their servants' movements: "It is well to remember that if you allow too much freedom to your maid, you do her a disservice as well as the next Navy wife who might hire her."[100] Unlike sailors on leave in Guantánamo, domestics were able to enjoy only limited mobility within the base. The condescending and patronizing language was the flip side of the U.S. Navy's gendered approach to local women. If women in Guantánamo were sexualized and commodified, on the base, local women were valued only for their domestic skills.

In contrast, men had far more opportunities to find secure government positions and achieve a white-collar standard of living. The base enabled many working-class men to aspire to middle-class status and gain relative financial comfort, both of which would have been unimaginable in Cuba's sugar mills. As the economic options in present-day Guantánamo are generally inadequate, many of my informants now view their base employment as an era of stability and prosperity. The frustration and anger evident in the archival documents has since faded away in the wake of unmet promises by the socialist revolution. Even if they were members of the Cuban Communist Party and self-described agents of the revolution, former base workers often expressed pride in their time at GTMO, or at worst, a neocolonial ambivalence. For U.S. government employees, the base offered a clear path to advancement, transparent performance reviews, and a steady salary. Civil service positions came with so many advantages that many workers remained in them for twenty, thirty, even forty years.

Ramón Sánchez worked on GTMO for sixteen years before leaving the base after the revolution. He was a proud *fidelista* and *cederista* (supporter of the Committee for the Defense of the Revolution); however, he had almost nothing but pride in his job on the base. Throughout our conversation, he fondly recalled his former bosses and condemned the U.S.

government all in one breath. GTMO had not only improved his standard of living, but he learned to speak English and was promoted from a manual laborer to an office clerk. He insisted I interview him in English and punctuated his sentences with 1950s North American slang: "When I worked on the base, I loved my job. . . . You know what the first job I had was . . . sell[ing] Coca Cola in a Coke Shack." Ramón struck up a friendship with a pilot, who came by the store and practiced English with him. During World War II the Navy Exchange would run out of goods, and so the pilot asked Ramón to hold special items for him. This quid pro quo turned out to be a stroke of luck for Ramón: "He became a good friend of mine, and he said one day, 'Ramón, would you like to work in an office?' 'Office, me? Oh please, I don't know.' 'Don't worry, would you like to work?' This wouldn't be good for him, because I wouldn't be able to save things for him anymore." Still, Ramón switched jobs and began working in an office. He showed me his Efficiency Ratings, which ranked him "very good" to "outstanding" in most categories. At the outset, Ramón earned $16.80 a week, but by the time he left he had become the supervisor of the shipping orders and earned several times his original salary. He refused to say anything negative about his work at GTMO. "No, I liked my job, any work you give me I like, because I like to work."[101]

Now more than forty years later, many former U.S. civilian service workers view their base employment with a degree of nostalgia. U.S. government jobs offered status, security, and opportunities for promotion. Their salaries and ability to advance were notable high points in their professional lives. However, much of this wistfulness appears to be the result of the capriciousness and scarcity in today's Cuban economy. At the time in the 1950s, base workers were not immune from the political movements and growing nationalist dissent throughout Cuba. They might have been loyal to the United States for their economic security, but many were also engaged in the struggle against Batista. For a short window of time, these two political identifications were not in opposition. Even years later, people like Ramón Sánchez could be proud of both their "outstanding" civil service ratings and their participation in the Cuban revolution.

Vincent Andrews, a former base worker and coordinator of the 26 of July Movement from within the base, best illustrates the contradiction of neocolonial nostalgia alongside political subversion. In our conversations, Vincent alternated between fond memories of Caimanera and GTMO and his nationalist activism. In his testimony, these two narratives could coexist; he was both a base worker and an active revolutionary.

Of Jamaican descent, Vincent Andrews grew up in Caimanera, and his grandfather, grandmother, and mother had all worked on the base. As a youth, he did not harbor hostility against the U.S. government, and his grandfather raised him in accordance with British and Christian morality. He began to work on the base as a teenager in the late 1940s. At first, he was "very grateful to have a job there," and he cleaned the Officers' Club. One day when he was tidying an office, he saw a typewriter, sat down, and began typing out a personal letter. An officer entered the room and surprised Vincent. Vincent felt embarrassed to be caught, but the officer told him to continue. Four or five days later, the officer offered him a promotion. "He said to me, 'Vincent, do you want to learn how to use the typewriter? . . . Would you like to work in an office?' And I said, 'Me, yes!' And he said, 'Good, look. . . . You come to me in the morning, clean the area, including my office. After lunch, change your clothes and you will work in the office. And I am going to give you a raise.' "[102]

Not only did Vincent's story parallel Ramón's almost verbatim, but Vincent also took the officer's patronage as a sign of generosity and compassion. His personal relations with the U.S. official fostered a warm sentiment toward the base, despite his later conclusion that GTMO represented an imperialist force. He also interpreted the officer's social gestures in a positive light:

> I didn't see any racist treatment by [the officer]. I never had a drink of rum before. . . . Then one night I was working in an office and he was there. . . . He called to the canteen and asked for a scotch and soda, and said, "Wait a minute, would you like to have one, Vincent?" and I said, "I don't know." [Laughs.] And then he said, "Try one." He invited me. I drank for the first time. That is to say there was a person, whom I suspected to be racist, but he accepted that I worked there, and I cleaned his office. . . . Thus, this racist treated me very well. Did I have a reason to complain of his treatment? No, no, no. On the contrary, I remember him with much respect and as a very caring person.

In this setting, Vincent Andrews reiterated the U.S. Navy's desire to be seen as a paternalistic and benevolent employer. He accepted the officer as his benefactor and took the offer of scotch as a sign of "good neighborliness." At face value, the hierarchies appeared in place, the white U.S. Navy officer acknowledging his black Cuban–West Indian clerk. Even today, Vincent's memories appear relatively poignant and appreciative of this token of respect. It is likely that white *guantanameros* in the Union Club or the Colonia Español would not have considered drinking with him.

After several years at GTMO, Vincent Andrews made his way to Havana. There he studied at the University of Havana. He became radicalized after Batista's coup and grab for power, and he began working actively to remove Batista. He remembered secretly running off flyers for Fidel Castro and going to protests on campus. However, Vincent ran out of money and returned to Guantánamo in 1955. Upon his return, he found employment yet again on the base. This time, politicized, he joined the 26 of July Movement in Guantánamo. With a little prompting, he began actively recruiting and organizing members within the base. His career as a revolutionary was about to begin.

GUERRILLAS AND GTMO

From 1952 through 1958, relationships between U.S. citizens and the local men and women in Guantánamo developed against a political backdrop of U.S. support for the Batista regime. After the *golpe del estado* in 1952, Batista alternately wooed U.S. sugar interests and opened Cuba's shores to U.S. casinos, tourists, and crime, all the while eschewing democratic elections, abolishing civil liberties, and strong-arming the press. The narrative of Batista's decline and Fidel Castro's unprecedented and unlikely rise to power is well known. Fidel Castro emerged as one of many leaders in the anti-Batista campaign, and his attack on Moncada, a Cuban army installation in Santiago de Cuba on July 26, 1953, became the inspiration for the 26 of July Movement. In response to the Moncada attacks, Batista imprisoned Fidel on the Island of Pines in 1953, only to change course and order a poorly calculated amnesty in 1955. Fidel then exiled himself to Mexico, where he met Ernesto "Che" Guevara, recruited anti-Batista exiles, and planned for an armed struggle. On board the *Granma*, Castro returned to Cuba in December 1956, and his crew immediately suffered the blows of Batista's Army. Only eighteen of Castro's eighty guerrillas reached the Sierra Maestra in Oriente province, while fifty-one were arrested and eleven were killed. As Castro led the guerrilla force in eastern Cuba and recruited more soldiers, M-26–7 gained widespread support throughout Cuban cities and the countryside, with students, workers, and local business interests contributing to the overthrow of Batista.[103]

As the military conflict between Castro's guerrillas and the Cuban Army intensified in Oriente province, GTMO found itself in the same geographic region as the rebels. The *New York Times* emphasized this shared geography and noted "Señor Castro's" landing near the U.S.

naval station and Santiago de Cuba.[104] The juxtaposition of the guerrillas and GTMO offered an intense contrast in military power. The base was fortified and static, while the Cuban guerrillas lived hand to mouth and moved through the villages and mountains.

Still, individuals could move "between" these two military worlds. Notably, three sons of GTMO officers escaped the base to volunteer with Castro's guerrillas in March 1957. Victor Buehlman, 17, Michael L. Garvey, 15, and Charles Edward Ryan, 21, admired the guerrillas' spirit and wanted to join in their struggle. In letters to the U.S. Embassy and on their return, the boys emphasized their antipathy for the Batista dictatorship. Garvey declared, "I learned that people who want to be free can take any hardships." U.S. policy had not yet demonized Fidel Castro, and these teenagers underscored an idyllic, though fleeting, international camaraderie where even GTMO youth could join arms with the rebels. Robert Taber, a journalist for CBS, profiled these three boys in his television special, "Rebels of the Sierra Maestra," complete with exclusive interviews in the Sierra Maestra and Fidel Castro's first U.S. television appearance. Staying away from their families for close to two months, these North American youths identified with the rebels and transgressed the base's military boundaries. The overall effect was to invert the politics of the Good Neighbor policy. The image of the children of U.S. military officials fighting with Castro emphasized GTMO's proximity to the guerrillas. While on maps, checkpoints, roads, and reports, GTMO was cordoned off as a separate U.S. military enclave, Buehlman, Ryan, and Garvey's adolescent adventure signaled the instability and contradictions of a U.S. military installation abutting a revolutionary armed movement.[105]

These teenagers were not the only individuals to take advantage of GTMO's proximity for their own objectives. By 1958 base workers became a critical source of information, material, and equipment for the anti-Batista movement. U.S. and Cuban historians have recognized the 26 of July Movement's activity within GTMO; it was a well-known, if not well-documented, source of the rebels' strength in Oriente. Historian Thomas Paterson noted in passing, "Anti-Batista workers on the base spied for the rebels, and M-26-7 followers stole equipment." Historian Julia Sweig provided evidence that the U.S. consul in Santiago de Cuba arranged for a rebel leader to escape Cuba through GTMO, so that he could procure arms in Mexico City and Miami. In exchange, the U.S. diplomat believed he had a guarantee that the M-26-7 cell within the base would stop smuggling weapons. Sweig concludes it was a fool's bargain. The workers did not abide by the agreement and kept up the steady supply of ammunition and supplies. Cuban historian Gladys Marel García Pérez has also pointed to the workers at GTMO as a source of firearms and dollars.[106] Base workers' actions in M-26–7 reveal the level of informal and clandestine exchange between Guantánamo and GTMO. Rather than halting the guerrillas, the U.S. naval base paradoxically helped them along.

In September 1955 Frank País, the leading M-26–7 organizer and visionary in Santiago de Cuba, traveled to Guantánamo and established the city's first M-26–7 cell. This cell had seven members, including one woman. Its primary goal was to educate the community, produce and distribute propaganda, raise money, and locate safe houses for militants who needed refuge. M-26–7 gained widespread support in Guantánamo, with workers in the railroad and sugar industries participating in political strikes to deflect the Cuban Army's attention from the 1956 landing of *Granma*. As the rebel movement gained momentum, U.S. journalists reported that more than 80 percent of Oriente province opposed the Batista government.[107] Guantánamo's M-26–7 also organized attacks against Batista's Rural Guard and participated in acts of sabotage. For example, on August 4, 1957, Gustavo Fraga Jacobino, a base worker, union leader, and Trotskyist, died in a dynamite explosion while preparing for an M-26–7 attack.[108] Still, most base workers were less directly involved in sabotage than Fraga and had no affiliations with any variant of communism. Nationalist, anti-Batista base workers took advantage of GTMO's ample materials, pilfering arms, munitions, and supplies for the revolutionary cause.[109]

Vincent Andrews was one of the principal organizers of the 26 of July Movement on the base. Already working on the base and attending M-26–7 meetings, he was asked to coordinate the operations within GTMO. Andrews remembered this responsibility with honor and awe. It gave him "a certain pride, a very private satisfaction that is very difficult to describe. . . . It was indescribable. . . . I had, in the naval base, to create or reconstruct a Movement." Each cell had five members, and there were committees for propaganda, supply, labor, and fund-raising. All of the activity was clandestine. Success depended on secrecy and compartmentalization, with each member knowing only what was necessary. Along with arms and supplies, Vincent emphasized the importance of selling bonds. He remembered being able to raise thousands of dollars from within the base.[110]

Although not a high-level coordinator, Juan Carlos Pulsara took great relish in relating his involvement in M-26–7. His code name was "Juan

Manuel," and he helped raise money and siphon off supplies. For example, he remembered holding "raffles," which offered a pocket watch as the first prize. However, the prize watch was a ruse, and the profits from the raffle went straight to M-26–7: "That is, we would say to the individual, 'Look, this is for the 26 of July Movement. You already know that there isn't a dance or a watch.' And the individual could give one or two pesos, or whatever he wanted, you understand." Juan Carlos also stated that he volunteered to be part of the armed struggle. The local military commander, Félix Peña, thought better of it, deciding Juan Carlos would be more valuable on the base. So, Juan Carlos took advantage of his status as a commuter. Between 1955 and 1956 the northeast gate opened, and it facilitated the first direct road from Guantánamo to GTMO. Base workers could now drive or take a bus, rather than rely on trains and ferries. During this era, Juan Carlos would drive his car onto the base and fill it with duty-free gasoline. After filling the tank, he would drive to nearby Boquerón and unload all the gas, leaving only enough in his vehicle to return to the base and repeat the operation. All of the gas went straight to the rebel guerrillas fighting in the nearby mountains.[111]

The extent to which the U.S. officials knew about this stream of arms flowing to the rebels or wished to halt it remains unclear. In the State Department archives, there is little or no documentation of the 26 of July Movement's gun (and gasoline) running from within the base. Considering the detailed attention normally given to petty theft of everything from soap to cigarettes, this lack of official record and subsequent punishments is notable. One report detailed in retrospect that during the "Cuban revolt," the Supply Depot lost small arms and field artillery. The equipment was not recovered, nor was anyone found negligent.[112] Moreover, there is no evidence of GTMO's M-26–7 smuggling operations in the Guantánamo press. The Batista regime implemented a policy of heavy censorship, which silenced the Castro rebels and M-26–7 from the papers and commercial radio. In contrast, the *New York Times* published a story about Robert Franklin Riggs, a U.S. sailor from Baltimore stationed at GTMO who was caught supplying arms and ammunition to the rebel troops.[113] Cuban historians also note that individual U.S. sailors and marines aided the rebel cause.[114] Former workers recalled that an active smuggling ring operated with the complicit approval of U.S. sailors, marines, and civil service employees in the lower ranks. Ramón Sánchez even remembered U.S. sailors and marines buying M-26–7 bonds.[115] Walter Knight recounted that "Many [U.S. sailors] supported it, but not the [U.S.] government. . . . But yes, many sympathized.

Of course . . . it was clandestine, officially no one knew, but there were big [U.S.] people who helped. One had a fat face . . ."[116] Again, these oral testimonies poke holes in a conception of a monolithic U.S. military force. Individual men and women contributed money, aided the rebels directly, or just looked the other way. From a diplomatic point of view, such low-level theft was not worth a showdown for the U.S. Navy.

Clearly not all workers participated in M-26–7 activities, but those who did allowed for the construction of an anti-imperialist, revolutionary mythology, which thumbed its nose at the U.S. occupation. The base employees who were M-26–7 members did not directly challenge the U.S. military's imperial presence in Guantánamo Bay. They continued to work on the base and cash a paycheck; however, they capitalized on their ability to travel with relative ease on and off the base. By stealing gasoline, supplies, and arms, workers enabled a new revolutionary narrative, whereby Cubans took advantage of the base, rather than GTMO taking advantage of Guantánamo. The testimonies of smuggling and subterfuge were critical in reimagining GTMO and Guantánamo relations, not just as a place where U.S. sailors and marines could act with impunity, but as a place where base workers could participate in revolutionary activity. Workers could redefine their base employment as part of a nationalist struggle, rather than as one of collaboration or compromise. In this manner, workers manipulated GTMO's military purpose for their own ends.

By 1958 the Cuban rebels were publicly criticizing U.S. support for the Batista regime, while the U.S. government insisted that it was neutral in the conflict. The U.S. State Department was revising its policies toward Cuba and actively searching for a third leader who could replace Batista and trump Castro.[117] Yet while this stagecraft occurred in Havana, GTMO officials and local elites continued the charade of good neighborliness, maintaining the same language and tropes it had depended on since 1934. Even as the military fighting and media jousting were escalating, the GTMO base commander reiterated his commitment to the Good Neighbor policy. On June 23, 1958, Admiral Robert Ellis invited a delegation of local journalists and Dr. Antonio Civit Jané, the USO president, to the base to woo the local elite and demonstrate how GTMO aided Guantánamo's local economy. The resulting newspaper articles were remarkable for the utter absence of contemporary political content. *La Voz del Pueblo* emphasized the number of local employees on the base: there were 2,176 *no americanos* in the U.S. civil service and 1,306 *no americanos* in private clubs, canteens, and domestic situations.

Not surprisingly, the press emphasized the importance of the *francos,* and proudly reported that the servicemen preferred Guantánamo, and its greater range of amusements, to Caimanera.[118] The language was striking in its adherence to the same phrases that had dominated the press in earlier decades. It cited the importance of cooperation between the base and local citizens, remarked on the "solidarity between Cuba and the United States," and flagged the "Positive Reality" of the "U.S. Authorities' Good Neighbor policy" in the headlines. GTMO officials, the U.S. government, and the Cuban government were not prepared for their new neighbors—Raúl Castro's Second Oriental Front.

By March 1958 the military conflict was escalating, and Raúl Castro, Fidel's brother, led a contingent of guerrillas into the hills surrounding Guantánamo. There, in close proximity to the U.S. naval base, he established the Second Oriental Front. The U.S. military reported that the fighting resulted in significant worker absenteeism and occasionally in "a complete lack of transportation, trains, bus[es], private vehicles, and boats to or from the base."[119] Batista's air force retaliated against the rebels by bombing the Guantánamo countryside. The U.S. had cut off military aid to Batista in 1958, but Raúl believed GTMO continued aiding the Cuban Air Force by surreptitiously refueling Batista's planes and supplying weapons to the Cuban military. In this volatile context, several base workers took advantage of their privileged employment and began shuttling information from GTMO to the Rebel Army.

In the most famous and controversial example, a base worker secretly snapped photos of a Cuban military plane being refueled at GTMO. Raúl identified the photo as a propaganda boon: "It is a nuclear bomb—we have to save it and use it at the opportune moment!"[120] The State Department claimed that the Cuban planes were on the base to replace defective weapons that Batista had ordered before the arms embargo. Although technically true, this distinction was irrelevant to Raúl Castro and the guerrillas.[121] The base workers' counter-intelligence operations had produced evidence to justify retaliation against North Americans. In June 1958 Raúl executed Military Order No. 30, Operación Antiaerea (Operation Anti-Aircraft) and set in motion a plan to kidnap U.S. citizens and use them as human shields to halt Batista's bomb raids, gain publicity, and leverage a pledge of neutrality from the U.S. government.[122]

On June 28, 1958, a busload of twenty-eight U.S. sailors and marines were on leave in Caimanera. As they returned to the base after a night of boozing and womanizing, Rebel Army Lieutenant José Q. Sandino lay in wait. He eyed the U.S. Navy bus and signaled it to stop. Sandino fired his gun into the air. The driver, Juan Alberto Tito, a Cuban base worker, wanted to continue to the base. Tito insisted his responsibility was to the U.S. Navy. Sandino threatened him and ordered the bus under his command. The *francos* were now hostages.

In his first conversations with the U.S. sailors, Sandino recalled the presence of Spanish-speaking *norteamericanos*. A U.S. officer confronted him with the help of a Puerto Rican marine. Sandino told the officer to remain calm, assuring him that nothing untoward would take place.[123] Sandino's testimony did not specifically attribute translation skills to the Puerto Rican, but it appears likely that he helped navigate this tense and unusual conversation. In fact, four of Raúl Castro's hostage sailors had Latino surnames: Carmelo de Jesús-Narváez of New York, Alfredo Hernández of California, Adelberto Márquez of Ohio, and Waldo Reyes of Florida. Joseph Anderson and Albert Matthews were African American servicemen from New York City.[124] The Castro rebels looked down on all of the marines as imperialists and added special contempt for the nonwhite members. One of the rebel leaders, Manuel Fajardo, disparaged them all as "[t]he most detestable men in the world. It isn't my opinion as a *Comandante* of the Rebel Army but my opinion as a man. Those men looked down on us Cubans as savages. . . . There were all kinds of people: Syrians, Puerto Ricans, Mexicans. A real foreign legion of men from everywhere but out of the same mold." In his opinion, the marines were uncouth and contemptible, and he reserved special hostility for a Mexican American who had tried to escape.[125]

Once in the rebel camp, the sailors joined more than a dozen North American civilians who had also been kidnapped. These hostages worked for the U.S.-owned Moa Bay Mining Corporation, the United Fruit Company, and the U.S. government–run Nícaro nickel plant. Raúl Castro had targeted the economic and military personnel of U.S. power in Cuba to make his political point. He had three demands: first, the U.S. publicly had to affirm its neutrality and stop selling arms to the Cuban government; second, Cuban planes could not refuel or receive arms at GTMO; and third, he wanted a U.S. observer to witness Batista's bombing campaigns.[126] Through this exploit, Raúl gained international publicity. He had gambled correctly that the U.S. hostages would stymie Batista's raids and give his soldiers a brief reprieve without triggering a U.S. invasion.

After a few tense weeks of official negotiations, the rebels released the hostages. The United States did not see any obstacle to meeting Raúl's primary demands. Officially, the U.S. government had already pledged neutrality and cut off weapons to Batista. The Eisenhower administration stifled calls for a military invasion, and the U.S. consul in Santiago de Cuba managed to defuse tensions. U.S. diplomatic officials and journalists traveled to the Guantánamo hillside, parleyed with the rebels, and succeeded in gaining the hostages' release. The civilians were allowed to leave first, followed by the military personnel.

On their return to GTMO, the sailors expressed a range of emotions. Naval Airman Thomas Mosness was the most effusive about his adventure. He practiced his "fast draw" with the rebels and declared he was "just like one of them."[127] Even though he lost twenty pounds, Private Anderson remarked, "Those rebels got a lot of heart. They are not fighting for money."[128] These men did not seem to imbibe the resentment felt by Fajardo. *Time* and *Life* offered romanticized accounts of the kidnappings, complete with dramatic photographs of the rebel camp and descriptions of barbeque feasts on the Fourth of July.[129] In contrast, Airman Alfredo Hernández, the Mexican American from California, fled the camp for twelve hours before being recaptured. Nor did Seaman Angelo Mpazicos glamorize his ordeal, "We had our own troubles up there."[130] The father of Albert Matthews, the kidnapped African American sailor from the Bronx, summed it up when he said, "I can't figure it out. He was in both World War II and the Korean conflict and was never wounded or captured before."[131] For his son at least, Cuba had suddenly become more perilous than two previous wars.

Raúl Castro's strategy of kidnapping U.S. citizens shattered U.S. sailors' comfort on Cuban soil. The experience transformed U.S. sailors and marines from *francos* on liberty into captives. Now, the rebels exerted control and dominated the local landscape. In Guantánamo, this incident was almost invisible in the heavily-censored, pro-Batista press. In contrast, Raúl gained significant publicity in the U.S. media, with the *New York Times, Newsweek, Life,* and *Time* all following the story. Yet Admiral Ellis changed his public language only slightly following the crisis. In response to the kidnappings, Ellis repeated the language of the Good Neighbor policy and now claimed that GTMO had "good relations" with the rebels.[132] Despite this assurance, the era of cocktail parties and Cuban-American Friendship days was coming to an end. The U.S. Navy halted liberty parties, and Guantánamo no longer seemed so neighborly.

Days later, the U.S. Navy broke decades of precedent and deployed U.S. marines in Cuban territory to safeguard GTMO's water supply at the Yateras River. Raúl Castro and the Second Oriental Front had been harassing the base by turning the water tap on and off. Batista responded by withdrawing government troops, arguing that the Cuban Army could protect the base water supply only if the United States contributed more arms or money to its defense. Many U.S. officials regarded this as a ploy by Batista to push the U.S. military into the conflict.[133] Crossing GTMO's boundary, U.S. marines warily entered Cuba on duty for the first time in decades. No longer "tourists," the marines were in the Guantánamo countryside in their military capacity. The *New York Times* predicted their presence would be "like a barb stuck in the flesh of every Cuban as long as they remain."[134] Vincent Andrews remembered that Commander Peña had been eager to attack the U.S. marines standing guard at the river. Vincent had counseled against it. In his opinion, any provocation would be "ridiculous." He told Peña that "the desire that you have is not stronger than mine to beat the imperialists and everything like that, but we have to be practical."[135] The U.S. Navy also wanted to de-escalate the situation. Within days it negotiated an agreement with the rebels who agreed to stop interfering with the base water supply.[136] The U.S. military retreated and the nearby rebel units did not further interrupt the water.

Over Christmas 1958, the rebel forces entered Caimanera and Guantánamo and declared victory. Within days Batista fled the island. After decades of the Good Neighbor policy, the United States was faced with a new, yet unknown, political neighbor.

CONCLUSION

The social, sexual, and racial encounters between U.S. military personnel and local *guantanameros,* which had caused so much social instability and flux, were about to end. After the Cuban revolution, U.S. military personnel would no longer enjoy liberty parties in Guantánamo, and fewer and fewer workers would commute onto the base. This zone of contact was about to become a zone of isolation. The era of unequal and asymmetrical relationships between Guantánamo and GTMO had demonstrated the ambiguities of neocolonialism.

Base workers expressed a great deal of ambivalence about their U.S. employers. Rosa Johnson's anger at her employer did not diminish her affection for U.S. culture. For U.S. government employees, the base offered stability, advancement, and occasionally even a glass of scotch offered in a moment of neocolonial benevolence. Elderly men and women overwhelmingly remembered their years on the base as good ones, complete with higher status and opportunity. Yet this sentiment could coexist with narratives of resistance and nationalism. This was the paradox of neocolonialism. Even those who participated in the nationalist 26 of July Movement remained complicit in the U.S. imperial project. Resistance and loyalty were not mutually exclusive, but rather intertwined and part of complex strategies. Accustomed to their status "in between," base workers saw no contradiction in their simultaneous loyalty to GTMO and their participation in M-26–7 activity. The triumph of the Cuban revolution and the abrupt rupture in U.S.-Cuban relations would soon force workers to choose.

4

A "Ticklish" Position
Revolution, Loyalty, and Crisis, 1959–1964

Victor Davis commuted between Guantánamo and the base for more than fifty years. His GTMO career began just after World War II, survived the Cuban revolution, and continued until his retirement in 2005. At several times during our conversation, he aptly used the term "ticklish" to describe workers' sensitive positions.[1] Victor was born in Banes, where his Jamaican parents worked in the environs of the United Fruit Company. When he was ten years old, his parents separated and he moved to Jamaica with his mother. At the outbreak of World War II, he volunteered for the British Army to see the world, not comprehending the full consequences of his actions. After experiencing six years of war in Europe, Victor was disappointed with the limited job opportunities and the lack of vocational training available to West Indian veterans after the Allied victory. After three years of unemployment in Jamaica, Victor returned to his father's home in Cuba and soon applied to work on the base. His first GTMO job was exciting; he was hired as a crash firefighter at the base airport. Unfortunately, he was laid off, because base officials wanted only "American people" to work at the airport. Victor remarked that there was nothing he could do. Luckily, within months, his fortune changed and he was selected for a job in the Supply Department. This was the position he maintained for decades.

Victor Davis spoke only obliquely about the Cuban revolution and the subsequent "ticklish" problems confronting base workers. After 1959, arbitrary changes, mass firings, and political surveillance reached new heights and injected an increased level of insecurity into workers' employment. Victor Davis witnessed GTMO's transformation from a base defined by debauchery to a military outpost defined by Cold War hostilities. Like the majority of base workers, he attempted to balance between these two poles, and he was more successful than most. Victor held onto his job, but now he had to placate the U.S. Navy *and* revolutionary officials.

From the initial triumph of the revolution in January 1959 through the massive layoffs of base workers in 1964, the politics of working on the base was fundamentally reshaped by the Cuban revolution. By prophetically declaring, "This time the revolution is for real," Fidel Castro consciously connected the 26 of July Movement's victory with the Cuban wars of independence, José Martí, and the 1933 struggle against Machado.[2] Revolution spoke to a nationalist, uncompromising *cubanismo* and a centuries-long battle against slavery, dictatorship, corruption, and foreign control.[3] Within months of consolidating power, Castro became a vigorous critic of U.S. capitalism and imperialism, defying decades of Cuban pandering to U.S. economic and political interests. Cuba's subsequent alliance with the Soviet Union, the following CIA-directed Bay of Pigs invasion, and the Missile Crisis became key turning points that punctuated and punctured U.S.-Cuban relations in the early 1960s. The resulting standoff fell into the tropes of the Cold War. However, the local manifestations of the Cuban revolution did not necessarily mirror the international conflict with the United States. Instead, the post-1959 narrative of Guantánamo politics decenters U.S.-Cuban relations from its well-known trajectory and, in the process, reveals the consequences of the Cuban revolution in base workers' daily lives.

What did it mean to be revolutionary in Guantánamo in 1959? Could a GTMO base worker be a good revolutionary? How did the Cuban government construct base workers as alternately counterrevolutionary and revolutionary? And to what extent did workers leverage their "loyalty" as a way to pressure the U.S. Navy to fulfill its neocolonial promises of economic security? How did the revolution play out in the military landscape between Guantánamo and GTMO?

The U.S. naval base in Guantánamo Bay remained a potent icon and physical reminder of U.S. imperialism. When President Eisenhower broke diplomatic relations with Cuba in 1961 as one of his last acts of

state, he emphatically did not include a U.S. withdrawal from Guantánamo Bay. U.S. Navy officials conceded that GTMO was "by far the
cheapest of our bases anywhere," and the rent of $3,386 per year was
"ridiculously" low.[4] Rear Admiral Edward J. O'Donnell's justification
for the U.S. presence was succinct: "We've got a pretty simple mission.
There's a pretty good treaty and by treaty we are going to stay here."[5]
By pointing to the 1903 and 1934 treaties and implying Cuban consent,
the U.S. Navy denied the Platt Amendment's coercive history and the imperial legacies of the base. The similarities between U.S. policies and European colonialism were not lost on others. Even in the United States,
several readers of the *New York Times* compared the U.S. occupation of
Guantánamo Bay to the French base in Bizerte, Tunisia, the Portuguese
colony of Goa in India, and Britain's claim to Gibraltar in Spain.[6] Still,
despite international solidarity with anti-imperial, decolonization movements, Fidel Castro recognized that ousting GTMO was not worth a direct military conflict with the United States. President Osvaldo Dorticós
Torrado brushed aside concerns of a Cuban assault against GTMO: "We
are audacious and valiant, but we are not stupid."[7] Instead, the Cuban
government would wait patiently for the day that the territory would be
returned to Cuban control. Over the past four decades, the Cuban government has refused to recognize the legitimacy of the lease agreements
or the base itself. As an act of symbolic protest, the U.S. check has remained uncashed since 1960.

In this context, GTMO base workers became volatile symbols of loyalty or betrayal with propaganda value on all sides. Between 1959 and
1964, approximately three thousand men and women continued to
commute to the base. Workers' neocolonial ambivalence, constrained
choices, and mixed loyalties underscored the risks and benefits associated with their "ticklish" positions. Base workers' "in-between" status
was not new, but Fidel Castro's victory and the Cuban revolution intensified workers' conundrum. Base workers experienced the rupture of
diplomatic relations in their pocketbooks and their daily commutes.
Their employment, wages, and pensions became points of contention,
which delineated the divide between Cuban sovereignty and U.S. neocolonialism.

For base workers in Guantánamo, the Cuban revolution would fundamentally reshape the political and economic valence of their employment. The era was rife with binaries: capitalism versus communism, revolutionaries versus counterrevolutionaries, and imperialists versus
anti-imperialists. Yet these stark divisions belied the far more nebulous

Figure 10. Campesino rejecting U.S. rent for the naval base. *Sierra Maestra*, July 17, 1964. Courtesy of the Elvira Cape Provincial Library, Santiago de Cuba.

ground that local workers traversed after the Cuban revolution. In fact, base workers' decisions and stories demonstrated just how unstable categories such as *revolutionary* and *loyal* could be.

THE TRIUMPH OF THE REVOLUTION IN GUANTÁNAMO AND CAIMANERA

In the days following the 26 of July Movement's victory, the local press in Guantánamo eschewed years of state censorship and launched into a full-blown critique of the Batista regime. The editor of *La Voz del Pueblo*, José Vázquez Pubillones, finally decried the injustices and the constant "terror of fear, torture, and death" under Batista. Vázquez singled out Guantánamo as a city that had suffered with stoicism and sacrifice, and he looked forward to the "hard work of rehabilitation," and rebuilding the local economy. Vázquez was optimistic the new era would bring "liberty and justice."[8]

La Voz del Pueblo also lashed out against the U.S. naval base's complicity with the Batista government. The previously conservative newspaper compared U.S. naval officials to Batista's "hit men" and "henchmen." On January 27, 1959, *La Voz del Pueblo* charged the new base commander, Admiral Frank W. Fenno, with "forget[ing] the old and cordial relations," that had reigned under the Good Neighbor policy. The paper also attacked naval intelligence officers for questioning base workers who had participated in revolutionary activities and equated these interrogations with "mental and physical tortures." On release, detained workers testified that they were given poor food, forced to sleep on the hard ground, repeatedly woken up to disrupt their sleep patterns, and beaten by the base guards. Vázquez's embrace of revolutionary language anticipated Castro's later denunciations of GTMO: "Cuba, with Fidel at the vanguard, has just won a revolution like none other in history. But an appendix remains in the center of the island that has been liberated from tyranny: The U.S. naval base in our bay of Guantánamo."[9] These confrontations transpired in the immediate wake of Castro's victory. Published in January 1959, the clash between base workers and U.S. officials, as well as the journalistic invective, predated overt U.S.-Cuban hostilities by many months. This exchange is remarkable for its early date and its discordance with the United States' purported policy of working with the revolutionary government. In Guantánamo, there was conflict from the start.[10]

The revolution brought Guantánamo's contradictory, neocolonial predicament to the forefront. Pent-up anti-Americanism and anger against the Batista regime coexisted with a desire to retain strong economic ties to the U.S. base. In response to the alleged abuse against base workers, the editor of *La Voz del Pueblo* appealed to the *New York Times* and made a case for base workers' civil liberties and rights. He alerted the *Times* to unlawful detentions and called for a U.S. commission to investigate activities on the base. To drive his point home, José Vázquez Pubillones returned to the language of good neighborliness: "It is not possible that two neighboring people, with such brotherly and unified social and economic orders, could be separated by military officials acting outside the limits of their positions."[11] The *New York Times* sent a sympathetic reply, but it did not publish any subsequent articles on GTMO or the base workers.[12] This exchange embodied the instability and possibility of the moment. Vázquez felt emboldened to publicly criticize the U.S. base and describe it as an "appendix," useless and potentially fatal; yet, he still saw the U.S. press and public as potential allies and "neighbors."

In Guantánamo, commercial elites debated the ramifications of this new revolution. Despite the joy of watching Batista flee and their growing admiration for Fidel, Guantánamo's business class could not imagine, and did not desire, a local economy independent from the base and the *francos*. Liberty parties had come to a standstill since the Rebel Army's victory. Admiral Fenno insisted they could not resume shore leaves without an invitation from the revolutionary government in Havana. Fearing anti-American sentiment and a lack of protection for U.S. *marinos*, he believed the "atmosphere was not yet ripe for liberty parties."[13] Merchants, shopkeepers, and bar owners were poised for the return of U.S. military personnel, and the local press continued to invoke "good neighborliness" in the early months of 1959. Still, the *francos* did not come back. As a result, the local press cried, "Economically, Caimanera is in agony."[14]

The U.S. consul in Santiago de Cuba noted the region's economic decline. He too hoped liberty parties would commence again, for they would improve the economy and renew social relations between Cuba and the United States. He also noted the propaganda value of the *francos*. Without them, "the American point of view does not get put across on an informal basis as it might be."[15] Throughout 1959, U.S.-Cuban diplomatic relations remained officially open and cordial, but the signs of rupture and growing isolation were already apparent.

Rather than concentrate on liberty parties or base workers, the new revolutionary government first championed fishermen in Guantánamo Bay as a way to assert economic independence and territorial, or in this case, marine control. Local fishermen did not depend on the same neocolonial exchanges as Guantánamo's other economic sectors. They traditionally occupied a small niche in Caimanera, but with the new revolutionary calculus, their needs and rights gained resonance and national publicity. In March 1959, fishermen, with the assistance of government officials, claimed that GTMO impeded their rights and conducted military exercises in the most desirable fishing waters.[16] *Revolución* and *Sierra Maestra*, M-26-7's newspapers in Havana and Santiago de Cuba, and *Hoy*, the Communist daily, represented the fishermen as potent, independent, working-class revolutionaries confronting the powerful naval base. Calling on the injustices of Caimanera's limited sovereignty, *Sierra*

Maestra asked, "How many times . . . have the fishermen of Guantánamo and Caimanera had to struggle in order to freely search for sustenance in the waters they have seen since birth?" *Revolución* demanded "Justice for Caimanera," where "the U.S. base authorities [have] condemned more than a hundred poor families to hunger" and "prohibited them from fishing in Cuban territorial waters." *La Voz del Pueblo* concluded its editorial with the refrain that the water was "Cuban."[17] But these cries fell on deaf ears. Admiral Fenno removed the fishermen from GTMO's environs.[18] Still, this wave of protest and attention to local fishermen indicated the changing tides of U.S.-Cuban relations. Government officials were quick to harness anti-American and anti-imperialist sentiments, searching for new ways to establish Guantánamo's economic independence and political sovereignty.

Another way to assert Guantánamo's local authority was for the revolutionary government to declare a new regimen for U.S. liberty parties that emphasized the rule of Cuban law. Cuban authorities did not ban U.S. *francos* outright. Instead, they insisted on a new policy that reversed the traditional "pass" system. Now, *marinos* would be classified as foreigners on Cuban soil. Guantánamo officials proposed the following: *francos* would have to wear civilian, not military, dress on shore leave; they would be subject to Cuban, not U.S., law while in Caimanera and Guantánamo; they would be issued "tourist" cards on leave; and U.S. armed patrols could not accompany them.[19] These regulations stripped U.S. sailors and marines of their military status on Cuban soil and reversed the neocolonial equation that had defined U.S. liberty visits for decades. Cuban authorities also proposed registering U.S. military personnel stationed on the base as foreigners in Cuba, just as it registered West Indian, Spanish, and other foreign nationals. The U.S. ambassador refused, arguing that, according to the lease agreement, "the jurisdiction of the Cuban Government would not extend to American personnel resident on the base."[20] Throughout the first half of 1959, optimistic U.S. diplomats desired a renewal of liberty parties, pointing to "good personal relations between Americans on the base and Cubans" as one of GTMO's key "favorable factors."[21] But these new requirements made liberty visits untenable. Most likely Cuban authorities were well aware that the U.S. Navy would not comply with their terms or return to Guantánamo's shores.

When GTMO officials were trying to settle a new liberty party accord, they had to negotiate with their former employee, Vincent Andrews. Former base worker and M-26-7 leader Vincent Andrews left the naval base to become Guantánamo's first revolutionary mayor, signaling the fundamental power inversion.[22] Vincent remembered his transition from base worker to government official. He noted that his previous conversations with naval officers had been as a waiter in the Officers' Club. Now, he was the mayor of Guantánamo: "One day the naval admiral called me [laughs]. . . . Now I'm reminded of this! Imagine, in 1959, the admiral from the base called me." The admiral invited Vincent to come to GTMO to discuss the return of liberty parties. Vincent took some delight in refusing the admiral's invitation: "I told him that I was very sorry, but that I had to decline the invitation, because I had other work to do. I didn't want to speak with any admiral!" Instead, he invited the admiral to Guantánamo, but this invitation was also declined. Vincent continued that the naval officers felt unsafe in revolutionary Cuba and wanted to bring patrol guards to protect the *marinos* on leave. This was unacceptable. "I knew that he wanted to discuss the 'liberty' [parties] and resume the *francos*. . . . But with arms and these things to protect them. . . . And I told him, 'But look, until the days before the Triumph, the base sent *francos* here on weekends and at the same time Batista was assassinating our youth. You came here without protection then. And now that we have eliminated that [Batista's violence], you are asking me if you can come with protection? I am very sorry but I can not accept that.'" Vincent laughed and concluded, "I didn't yet have any ideological preparation in any of this, I just thought it was simple logic. . . . They never came again, but that was my last act with the naval base in Guantánamo." Soon bored by the minutiae of local politics, Vincent Andrews joined the Agrarian Reform campaign and was later an official in the Ministry of Foreign Affairs.[23]

Vincent Andrews's pride in Guantánamo's newfound autonomy did not solve the city's economic problems. In the spring of 1959, the economic character of the revolution was still up for grabs. Liberal reformers and business interests remained identified with the 26 of July Movement, and Fidel Castro had not yet consolidated national authority or centralized the economy. In Guantánamo, questions about the revolution, anti-Americanism, and the economy were being publicly debated. There was a growing chasm between the business elites and spokespeople for the 26 of July Movement. The merchants and club proprietors could not imagine a functioning or thriving economy without the frequent visits of U.S. sailors and marines. In contrast, the M-26–7 leaders insisted on greater economic dignity and did not lament the loss of the *francos*.

There was only a brief moment when disagreements about the Cuban revolution's relationship to the U.S. naval base were permitted in the open. The debate in the press, particularly in *La Voz del Pueblo,* provides a unique window on how commercial elites and revolutionaries alternately defined "revolution" and "counterrevolution" in Guantánamo. Although *La Voz del Pueblo* criticized the U.S. Navy more openly than it had in the past, it did not look kindly on Communists who it blamed for blatant anti-Americanism. In these first months after Castro's victory, the revolutionary 26 of July Movement and the Communist Party were two separate entities, often competing rather than cooperating with each other. However, in Guantánamo, the Communist Party's anti-imperialism coincided with the new revolutionary functionaries' own aims to keep *marinos* out of the city.

In July 1959, *La Voz del Pueblo* published its most explicit exposé on the *francos* and Guantánamo's economic crisis. In an editorial column, José Vázquez Pubillones, of *La Voz del Pueblo,* expressed his alarm at the absence of *francos* and Caimanera's growing poverty. He thanked Fidel for contributing a hundred thousand pesos to the fishing industry, but remained worried about the "emerging inappropriate anti-Americanism" in Guantánamo. He chastised "our own officials" for stifling the return of U.S. liberty parties. In his opinion, this was not in the community's economic interests.

A week later, the "responsible" Joaquín Álvarez Torralba defended the revolutionary officials and utilized the new language of counterrevolution. To his mind, the Cuban-imposed restrictions on liberty parties were essential to safeguard Cuba's sovereignty. He dismissed Vázquez's descriptions of Caimanera's previous "happiness" and "prosperity" as nostalgic and inaccurate, pointing to the lack of fishing rights as a key example. Álvarez feared Vázquez's critique could be used by domestic and external counterrevolutionaries. Álvarez concluded he "trusted" Vázquez would recognize "these truths" with "revolutionary sincerity."

As the editor, Vázquez had the final word, at least in this brief exchange. He attributed the burgeoning anti-Americanism to Communists, who he believed were charging "yankee imperialism" at every opportunity: "They want to implant the brutal and inhuman laws of Russia on our island." In this moment of ideological flux in July 1959, Vázquez believed he could criticize local Communists, lobby for U.S. liberty parties, and still maintain his revolutionary credentials. He concluded confirming his faith in "the positive example" of "a true revolution."[24]

Vázquez and Álvarez's disagreement about the local economy, anti-Americanism, and communism reveals the era's fleeting openness and the internal struggle over the content of the Cuban revolution. In the public realm, they were defining and criticizing each other's definition of "revolution." In fact, both sides had merit. Vázquez was correct that Guantánamo's economy relied on U.S. dollars, and that the Cuban revolution had not offered an equivalent replacement. He also distinguished between the Communist Party and the Cuban revolution as two distinct entities as, at the time, they were. In turn, Álvarez gave voice to years of resentment against U.S. military arrogance and affronts to local authority. He warned against equating Caimanera's past dependence with wealth and prosperity. Álvarez also foreshadowed the more ominous possibilities of the Cuban revolution when he characterized Vázquez's editorials as possible fodder for counterrevolutionaries. Their exchange revealed the conflicts in this early revolutionary moment as well as the temporary lack of central authority. As with most independent papers, the summer of 1959 marked the last time *La Voz del Pueblo* questioned or criticized the 26 of July government in print or ran opposing editorials.

In the following year, Castro ousted liberal reformers from his cabinet, silenced the press, and consolidated power. Castro gave an institutional voice to years of resentment against U.S. economic and political arrogance in Cuba, and his charges against U.S. imperialism resonated with much of the Cuban public.[25] By the end of 1959, the 26 of July Movement also came to an accord with the Cuban Communist leadership and welcomed overtures from the Soviet Union.[26] The U.S.-Cuba Cold War showdown was well underway.

Throughout Oriente province, the Cuban revolution brought new educational opportunities, accessible health care, and redistribution of land and wealth, which disproportionately improved the lives of rural Cubans and Cubans of color. In Guantánamo, the community received five new medical facilities, much needed drainage systems, new roads, agrarian collectives, and houses.[27] But for Guantánamo's business elites and merchants, the end of the *francos* was the end of the local economy. The bars and brothels simply no longer had a customer base.

By 1960 the U.S. Navy confined liberty parties to GTMO's bars and baseball fields *inside* the base. These liberty parties now aimed to intimidate the Castro government and to flex U.S. military muscle. For example, in October 1960, the U.S. Navy announced that 1,450 marines were granted "shore leave" *within* GTMO to "make the U.S. presence felt" in Cuba. These marines had been conducting amphibious exercises in the Caribbean on the USS *Boxer*. The decision to authorize their shore leave on the U.S. base in Guantánamo Bay had been authorized by President Eisenhower. The Cuban government interpreted the increased number of U.S. military personnel on its soil as a direct threat to security. Dismissively, the *New York Times* ignored both Cuban fears and historic precedent, stating that the United States would not be "wicked or foolish enough to attempt an armed conquest of Cuba." Even so, the *Times* admitted, "it would have been more tactful to let them [the 1,450 marines] stretch their legs in Puerto Rico or Jamaica—or even in Florida."[28] This liberty party was an attempt to show U.S. military strength, but it paradoxically demonstrated the U.S. Navy's impotence. As *National Geographic* reported, "For some living within the confines of the seven-foot-high chain-link fence is like being in an idyllic prison camp."[29]

In fact, with the complete halt to liberty parties outside the base and the rejection of meetings between Guantánamo officials and U.S. naval officers, "the only persons traveling freely back and forth [to and from the base were] the Cuban employees."[30] Unlike the *francos,* the men and women who worked on the base continued to travel on and off the base. Base workers weathered the initial political transformations in 1959 and, even as tensions increased, neither the United States nor Cuba made a serious effort to sever this ongoing personal exchange. Base workers became the singular population balancing between the strictures of the base and the revolutionary government.

"DO YOU SELL YOUR DOLLARS?": U.S. DOLLARS, PESOS, AND THE BASE UNION

Base workers' anomalous position between Cuba and the naval base made them conduits for broader debates about U.S.-Cuban relations. With international attention focused on Cuba's turn toward the Soviet Union and socialism, base workers' negotiations resonated outside the environs of Guantánamo. In the atmosphere of heightened anti-Americanism, the revolutionary Cuban government was quick to respond to base workers' complaints. Labor leaders rekindled older debates about inequalities between U.S. and local workers, and they rewrote their protests with the language of revolution. However, the breakdown in U.S.-Cuban relations also reframed base workers in a potentially counterrevolutionary position. Given their close contact with the U.S. military and dependence on U.S. dollars, workers could be accused of being spies and *gusanos* (literally "worms"— the Cuban term for counterrevolutionary). The Cuban government avoided military confrontation with GTMO, but it also turned labor conflicts into a way to define revolutionary (and counterrevolutionary) behavior within the local population.

In the months following the Cuban revolution, the base workers' union was reinvigorated and reorganized. It renewed efforts to gain equal pay for equal work, retirement pensions, and a renegotiation of the treaty.[31] These complaints were not new. Workers had been protesting the discrepancy between local and U.S. pay scales since the 1940s. However, the fissure in U.S.-Cuban relations made base workers' demands potentially explosive, and their complaints even reached the U.S. media.[32] U.S. officials also witnessed "numerous placards" in Guantánamo, which called for a "Revision of the Treaty" and claimed the support of more than four thousand base workers. U.S. officials downplayed these protests; they believed the base workers "confused" the lease agreements with working conditions.[33] U.S. diplomats refused to register an actual critique of U.S. occupation or a new thrust of anti-imperial nationalism.

By October 1959, the official stance of the base union's new secretary general, Federico Figueras Larrazabal, clearly articulated an anti-imperialist position. Figueras had worked at GTMO as a machinist since 1952, and the base workers elected him as their new union representative in May 1959.[34] His election was part of a national wave of union elections after the revolution. The 26 of July Movement and the old guard Communist Party members competed with each other over the role of trade unionism, the right to strike, and the role of the CTC in the Cuban revolution. Hoping to bind the loyalty and institutional power of organized workers to the revolutionary government, the 26 of July Movement called for union elections in April and May 1959. M-26–7 members won 90 percent of the leadership positions and declared a six-month no-strike pledge. By the end of 1959, the CTC was fully reorganized to support the Cuban revolution's national goals at the expense of workers' economic interests and independent unionism.[35]

The new base workers' union reflected this turn to national and political objectives. Secretary General Figueras assailed the United States and organized the base workers under a revolutionary mantle. "That treaty which profoundly damages the national interests of our nation is anachronic [sic] and, from the revolutionary point of view, constitutes an iron link in the long chain which strangled the Cuban people until January 1, 1959. The chain has been broken by the effort of the people and of the revolutionary government, but that iron link remains embedded in our flesh and in our spirits.[36] Figueras blasted the 1903 Lease

Agreement and spoke far more bluntly about U.S. imperialism and violations of Cuban sovereignty than any previous base union leader. The revolutionary base union gained significant support and developed a functioning infrastructure. It had eighteen officers and at least fifty-five
delegates representing numerous divisions, including the Naval Exchange,
the Enlisted Men's Club, the hospital, and the mail room.[37] More overtly
political in nature than its early-fifties predecessor, it expressed broadly
shared critiques of the U.S. naval base, but also carried a far greater degree of risk for workers' own employment.

Because it was coupled with anti-imperialism, the base employees' decades-long campaign for equal pay for equal work found a national public platform. Unlike workers in the domestic sectors (e.g., sugar, tobacco,
and coffee) who were discouraged and prevented from striking in the
name of national unity, base workers who challenged their low wages
could be defined as revolutionary actors. They were standing up to the
U.S. imperialists and demanding respect and equitable compensation.
Through labor disputes the Cuban government could critique the U.S.
military base. As *Hoy* proclaimed, "It was not just a problem between a
worker and an employer, but between imperialism and the Cuban revolution."[38] At the national CTC Congress held in November 1959, the
leadership passed a resolution condemning the wage discrepancy between
Cuban and U.S. workers at GTMO. In addition, the CTC proclaimed its
nationalist credentials and withdrew from the AFL-CIO–sponsored,
inter-American labor alliance.[39]

On March 4, 1960, a French ship, the *Coubre,* exploded mysteriously
in Havana harbor and killed seventy-five dock workers. The fallout from
this incident had consequences not just for U.S.-Cuba relations, but also
for the base union in Guantánamo. The *Coubre* had been carrying
weapons for the Cuban government, and Castro suspected the United
States of foul play. He had no evidence, but he drew parallels between
the *Coubre*'s blast and the 1898 explosion of the *Maine.*[40] Through this
historical analogy, Castro used the event to flame fears of a U.S. attack;
the *Coubre* marked a new nadir in U.S.-Cuban relations. Federico
Figueras seized this moment to emphasize base workers' insider positions
and access to sensitive military information. He encouraged commuters
to monitor the base and be on watch for a possible U.S. assault: "Workers at the naval base have to be alert to unmask any maneuver of the
North American imperialists similar to that which they performed when
they blew up the *Maine.*" Admiral Fenno fired Figueras for this inflammatory speech, describing Figueras's words as "slanderous" and "un-

founded." Dismissed from his position at GTMO, Figueras resumed his verbal tirade in town.[41]

The Cuban Ministry of Foreign Relations lodged a formal protest with the United States against Federico Figueras's dismissal. U.S. diplomats did not consider this incident of "great importance," and they chose not to make any "special concessions" to "appease" the Cuban government.[42] In particular, they were not going to pressure GTMO to rehire Figueras. On the contrary, Figueras had "repeatedly made unfounded and slanderous public statements" with the intent to "incite" anger against the United States and the base. Reinstating him would "damage" rather than "improve" local relations. U.S. Ambassador Philip Bonsal also scoffed at Cuban concerns that the base had hired former members of the Batista Army. He admitted that eight new employees had been members of the Cuban Army before 1959, but none of these men had been charged with "crimes or counterrevolutionary" activities.[43] With this subtle concession, Bonsal admitted that GTMO should not actively recruit local employees who opposed Castro and the 26 of July Movement.

In the process, the Cuban government framed base workers as either revolutionaries, like Federico Figueras, or counterrevolutionaries, like the suspected former Batista Army regulars. Figueras became known as the exemplary base worker, who spoke against U.S. imperialism and was unjustly fired by the naval base. In a public meeting in Guantánamo, Figueras led the mass rally with chants of "Viva la Revolución! Viva Fidel! Down with Yankee Imperialism!"[44] Good neighborliness and inter-American friendship were thereby erased from public discourse. Revolutionary linguistic tropes redefined the U.S. naval base as the enemy and as a potential source of counterrevolutionary terror. The Cuban government also stopped cashing the U.S. government's annual payment stipulated by the lease agreement, in this way demonstrating its belief that the U.S. occupation of Guantánamo Bay was an illegitimate affront to Cuban sovereignty. For the workers who continued to commute to the base, this growing distrust soon extended to their earnings and access to U.S. dollars.

Over the course of nine months in 1960, the United States and Cuba gradually severed all economic ties. The United States eliminated Cuba's sugar quota and imposed an economic embargo, eliminating almost all U.S. trade with Cuba. In turn, Cuba progressively nationalized its economy, sought alternate trade partnerships with the Soviet Union, and charged the United States with economic aggression.[45] The Cuban economy became unsteady and volatile. In this context, U.S. dollars became economically and politically suspect.[46] Fearing that the peso would soon be worthless, middle- and upper-class Cubans sought to exchange their devaluating pesos for U.S. currency. As a result, an active black market in U.S. dollars emerged. The Cuban government outlawed this speculation and decried it as a "grave offense against Cuba's national monetary credit." The black market weakened the Cuban economy and identified its practitioners with U.S. imperialism.[47]

At this time, base workers were paid directly in U.S. dollars. In fact, the U.S. government repeatedly pointed to the seven million dollars GTMO contributed to Guantánamo's economy through base workers' salaries each year. Even Fidel Castro admitted that the base was a regrettable necessity for the community. The U.S. naval base provided a degree of economic security, which the revolution had not yet replaced. At first, base workers were expected to exchange their U.S. dollars into Cuban pesos on the honor system. But out of $150,000 paid each week to Cuban employees, workers deposited only $38,000 into the National Bank. In May 1960, the Cuban government made certain workers would no longer have a choice in the matter and built a small outpost of the National Bank just outside the gates of the base. On payday, Cuban soldiers would escort workers from the gates of the base to the National Bank and, in this manner, the government could mandate the currency exchange. Base workers were allowed to retain 10 percent of their earnings in U.S. dollars (to buy cigarettes, food, and drinks in the base canteens), but they had to change the remaining 90 percent at a rate of one dollar to one peso. Given the depreciation of the Cuban peso, base workers lost the value of their U.S. dollars in this transaction. To sweeten the incentive, Castro promised a thousand houses to those workers who deposited their money in the National Bank rather than sell their dollars on the black market.[48] Base workers who publicly followed the government directive could keep their jobs and still demonstrate their loyalty and identity with the Cuban revolution.

For workers, this new policy squarely confronted the contradiction of their long-standing ties to the U.S. military outpost on the one hand, and the demands of the new revolutionary nationalism on the other. As the *New York Times* quipped, the base workers were leading "double lives."[49] Many resented the Cuban government's interference with their livelihoods and hoped to keep as many U.S. dollars as possible. The U.S. Navy worked in tandem with the base workers, instituting new procedures to "eliminate some of the pressure." It stopped listing base workers' salaries, so that the Cuban government would not know how much

Figure 11. Cuban base workers receiving pay, February 1, 1960. Photo by Hank Walker. Courtesy of Time & Life Pictures and Getty Images.

each worker earned.[50] Other workers hoarded their dollars and traded them on the black market, colloquially termed the *molina,* or mill, because one could put U.S. dollars into it and grind out more Cuban pesos. In contrast, good revolutionary citizens would voluntarily and willingly exchange their U.S. dollars one to one for pesos. For example, Rosa Johnson remembered fulfilling the revolution's new standards of citizenship and loyalty:

> You have to take it [your salary] to the bank, because the bus don't leave you nowhere but the bank. And you have to get off the bus, and go into the bank. You can't change it nowhere else. [Laughs.] You cannot, what they say, you cannot put it in the mill. To increase it. No, no. You have to take it to the bank. And all the money, I take it to the bank. . . . Oooh, I bring out the American money, and I take it to the bank. And they change it for Cuban money. I did that. That is why today, Fidel is giving me, what you call it . . . a help. . . . He give me a help. Thank God for Fidel.

And without missing a beat, Rosa made the revolution's messianic message complete and broke into the Christian standard, *What a Friend We Have in Jesus.*[51]

Not all base workers exchanged their currency so dutifully. In 1960 *La Voz del Pueblo* reported ten base workers were jailed and fined for trafficking in foreign currency.[52] Not exchanging one's U.S. salary was seen as akin to treasonous behavior. Into this fray, the base workers' union reincarnated itself as a revolutionary, nationalist organ outside the base. Rather than agitating for workers' salaries *on* the base, this time it exhorted workers to change their dollars into pesos *off* the base. The base union invoked language of revolution, patriotism, and nationalism, indicating how reluctant base workers might have been to trade in their valuable dollars. For example, the union published an open letter to the base workers, which commenced with the language of morality, "We are going to talk, you and me, in silence, as if I was your conscience." The pamphlet then cut to the chase, "Answer me this yourself. Don't avoid it. Are you selling your dollars? Don't lie. Don't sell them." The pamphlet exhorted the worker to recognize his or her feelings of patriotism and national pride in the revolution. "Don't you tremble when you hear the national anthem? Don't you feel pride to be yourself today in the world at the vanguard of the oppressed peoples?" Now came the moment of shame, "Ahhh. But you sell your dollars. Don't you feel embarrassed . . . when you act like a delinquent, taking care that no one can see you hide as you cheat your country and receive your thirty U.S. dollars, like a Judas? Don't you feel the whip as it lashes your consciousness (because you do have consciousness). . . . You repent? Then you are Cuban. The generous *patria* [homeland] will pardon you."[53] This revolutionary entreaty called on base workers' *conciencia,* which depended on Cubans' voluntary labor and collective identity.[54] The base union and workers' salaries gained import in this moment when definitions of revolutionary and counterrevolutionary behavior were being constructed. A base worker could be "revolutionary," but only if he or she exchanged their salary into Cuban pesos.

Base workers who were fired for their political leanings could also be recast as revolutionary players. In the years immediately following the Cuban revolution, several base workers cast their lot with the nationalist project. For example, base workers Manuel Prieto Gómez and Rolando Quintero were dismissed from GTMO in 1961.[55] On January 5, 1961, the base police detained Prieto and accused him of being an agent for the Cuban government and stealing U.S. documents.[56] Prieto later claimed that intelligence officers beat him, threatened him with death, and hooked him up to a lie detector. He insisted that he supported the revolutionary government, but was not an agent for anyone. Then the base officials tried the opposite tack, offering Prieto good work, money, and access to the United States, if he would cooperate with them.

Prieto again insisted, "I have already chosen the place where I want to be, in Cuba, my country."[57] A month later, in February 1961, Quintero was also interrogated and placed under duress. He expressed particular scorn for the Puerto Rican translator, Maldonado, who participated in his interrogation. Quintero described Maldonado as "despicable" and a "traitor to his country." Quintero formally resigned from the base in protest during the April 1961 Bay of Pigs invasion.[58] The Cuban government constructed Prieto and Quintero as victims of U.S. imperial aggression. This image remains today. Rolando Quintero recounted his experience in perfect English for a British documentary in 1991, and in 2004 Cuba's official newspaper, *Granma,* profiled Manuel Prieto Gómez's experiences of detention and torture. The article concluded that Caimanera was an expression of the Cuban people's resistance against imperialism, and it would never suffer being a North American colony again.[59]

Not all fired base workers were lionized by the state, but this rhetoric allowed other workers to cast themselves in revolutionary colors as well. In 1961 Ramón Sánchez, a base employee, enrolled in an evening program in Communist ideology and studied Marx, Engels, and Lenin. He claimed that his neighbor reported his political activities to the naval intelligence authorities who then "grabbed him" and interrogated him. Ramón admitted his new political leanings to the base authorities. As a result, two marines took him to the fence and said, "Good-bye." He was dismissed on August 14, 1961, and the U.S. Navy provided an official notice stating that "your service and conduct indicates that you are unsuitable for further government employment." The navy provided him with severance pay covering 240 hours of annual leave. Ramón added that "three months after they pushed me out, they sent me a check . . . $2,399.01. Not bad. I changed it at that time. At that time, 1961, [it was] one dollar for one peso." He justified the poor exchange rate as a matter of patriotism and self-sacrifice. "My country needed that. I didn't get mad. I liked it, my country needs that. Okay, take it."[60] Ramón emphasized his decision to be part of the revolution and educate himself politically. However, unlike Vincent Andrews or Rolando Quintero, he had not left the base voluntarily or shunned base employment. Instead, he was "thrown out." Although he had not left on his own volition, Ramón's dismissal became a sign of honor, indicative of his revolutionary credentials. Ramón proudly showed me the document he received terminating his employment with the U.S. military.

For workers who continued commuting to the base, the early years of the Cuban revolution created a precarious environment for their economic well-being. Their employment with the U.S. Navy was now cast in a decidedly unfavorable light. Base workers had to accommodate to the Cuban government's nationalist rhetoric and objectives, without alienating their U.S. employers. As verbal barbs, economic ideologies, and military stockpiling ratcheted up U.S.-Cuban relations, the physical journeys between Guantánamo and GTMO reflected the growing rupture and isolation between the two countries and the two communities.

THE CACTUS CURTAIN, PATTY CANDELA, AND THE BRIGADA DE LA FRONTERA

In the early 1960s, anxiety, suspicion, and military aggression defined U.S.-Cuban relations, and these tensions manifested themselves along the border between the base and Guantánamo. Both governments increased the level of militarization and preparedness around the base. The U.S. and Cuban militaries reinforced barbed wire fences, initiated military patrols, erected twin watchtowers, and planted massive minefields. From 1960 to 1961, the U.S. military laid down a minefield that ringed the seventeen-mile border that separated U.S. and Cuban territory. More than fifty thousand U.S. antipersonnel and antitank landmines shielded GTMO from a full frontal attack. The U.S. Navy posted warning signs in Spanish and English, explaining that the landmines were to deter a Cuban offensive against the base. It maintained that the landmines were "precautions" and should not be considered "aggressive."[61] The Cuban military retaliated by planting a parallel minefield on its side of the boundary. From 1961 through 1965, the landmines resulted in at least ten U.S. and Cuban deaths, including victims from engineering accidents, revelers at a night swimming party that went awry, and a Cuban national hoping to escape onto the base.[62] The landmines created a violent barrier between the base and its adjoining Cuban territory.[63] Surveillance and isolation became key features entrenched in this desolate environment.

If they hoped to hold onto their economic security and base jobs at GTMO, base workers had to navigate this politically tense terrain, dubbed the "cactus curtain."[64] In 1961, Fidel Castro prevented any new hires from the local community, and all GTMO base workers had to receive special clearance from the Cuban government to continue working on the base.[65] Because the Cuban government feared a local incident could spark a U.S. invasion, Castro warned base workers to "refrain

Figure 12. East boundary fence of Guantánamo naval base, January 11, 1961. Photo by Dmitri Kessel. Courtesy of Time & Life Pictures and Getty Images.

from any action that would give the United States a pretext for attacking Cuba."[66] Base workers also faced an inverse of the World War II–era "pass" system. They now had to gain permission from the Cuban government to commute on and off the base. The appointed president, Osvaldo Dorticós Torrado, issued Law 927, which required base workers to apply for passes to safeguard Cuba's "territorial integrity." Workers who traveled to the base in private cars also had to register their vehicles.[67] Each day, local workers traveled to the northeast gate where they would be greeted by two signs: "Ground Defense Force: U.S. Naval Base

Guantánamo Bay, Cuba" and *"República de Cuba: Territorio Libre de América"* (Cuban Republic: Free Territory of America). The Cuban government used the bank where workers exchanged their salaries as a checkpoint. Cuban officials would frisk the workers and check their paperwork. Then, the workers would cross to the U.S. side where they were again searched. On the return trip, officials would again pat the workers down in an effort to prevent theft and espionage. Long lines formed on either side of the checkpoints, and some workers described the process as "humiliating and drastic."[68]

The U.S. media constructed base workers as potent symbols of U.S.-Cuban relations, and it romanticized their employment in a neocolonial idiom that artfully erased U.S. suspicion of the same workforce. *Life,* the *Saturday Evening Post,* and *National Geographic* swooped down to capture a glimpse of this U.S. military base on the edge of confrontation with Cuba.[69] These feature pieces depicted base workers as generally hostile to the Cuban revolution and ultimately loyal to the United States. For example, the *Saturday Evening Post* profiled the base and reported that "despite Castro's incessant anti-American propaganda over the radio, in the press, in pamphlets and schoolbooks, the relationship between the Americans and Cuban workers at the base is generally good." There had been no evidence of "sabotage, extreme absenteeism, or work stoppages."[70] As recorded in another feature article, a Cuban base worker told the journalist, " 'Ah . . . these are sad times.' Then in a lowered voice, so no one around us could hear, he added, 'But they will one day be gone, and we will be warm friends again.' "[71] The U.S. media also downplayed base workers' possible allegiance to the Cuban revolution and Cuban nationalism, even when it reported that sixty base workers had resigned to protest the U.S.-backed Bay of Pigs invasion. Instead, the *New York Times* mapped the language of loyalty onto the remaining base workers, reporting that they cheered the invasion, favored the anti-Castro fighters, and were teary-eyed on learning of their defeat.[72] This spate of articles presented idealized accounts of commuters, stressing their allegorical allegiance to the United States and conveniently overlooking the years of previous animosities.

In an alternate narrative, Rosa Johnson, a domestic worker, recalled with humor the increased vigilance at the U.S. checkpoint. Rosa explained that there was a white line on the base. Workers would stand in front of the white line and wait to be searched by the U.S. "policemen." "They search you, and then you go over to the Cuban [side], and they search you again. You understand me?" Rosa remembered a woman

Figure 13. Cuban base workers on the Guantánamo naval base, February 1, 1960. In this image, the Cuban worker observes the U.S. guard peering into his pocket. Photo by Hank Walker. Courtesy of Time & Life Pictures and Getty Images.

who was trying to smuggle U.S. consumer goods off the base: "Listen to me. One day a woman . . . you know what she did? She put a clock between her panty, and she, and she forgot to . . . put off the alarm. And when she reached the gate . . . wheeeee!"[73] The alarm rang and rang from between her legs right there at the front gate. Although Rosa narrated this story as a comedic sketch, the alarm clock exemplified a longer, less politicized tradition of petty theft. It also symbolized the new Cold War sirens between Cuba and the United States. This incident appears apocryphal, tying together domestic servants' claims to a moral economy and invoking the humiliation of the strip searches that were soon to follow. Despite the anecdote, increased monitoring meant that petty theft declined. Risking one's job or political status was no longer worth smuggling cigarettes, silver spoons, or alarm clocks. The revolution had finally solved the problem of theft for GTMO.

In September 1962, only a month before the Missile Crisis, the Cuban government rerouted workers' commutes, intensified its own vigilance, and required daily strip searches at the border. The Cuban militia bulldozed six tank roads, built a ten-foot-wide cactus wall, and constructed a guard post to better observe U.S. military activities.[74] The militia also stopped using the bank as a checkpoint and built new facilities just outside the U.S. guards' visibility. It constructed a walkway between the new checkpoint and the northeast gate. The path was approximately one mile long, enclosed by a chain link fence, and dubbed the "cattle chute." The Cuban government justified these fortifications as necessary given the threat of U.S. invasion. *Life* published a photo of this arid no-man's land, describing the new environment as punctured by "cruel, big-needle cactuses."[75] By drawing attention to the "cruel" cacti, the U.S. media diminished the far more dangerous minefields in the public imagination.

For workers, forced strip searches at the border were the most humiliating aspect of this increased militarization. Workers had two sets of clothes. On reaching the Cuban checkpoint, they had to undress, often walk naked across the inspection platform, and then don a separate outfit they would wear only to the base.[76] On their way home to Guantánamo, workers had to reverse the ritual, remove their base clothes, and return home in their original garments. Maria Boothe, a domestic worker, recalled that commuters had to completely undress. She added that there were female guards to check the women, and male guards to check the men. She left the base in the spring of 1959, so she never experienced this process herself.[77] U.S. accounts differ as to the extent and frequency of these strip searches, but the removal of clothing became a post-revolutionary component of base workers' commutes. *Time* reported that some workers had to strip completely as each item of clothing was inspected, whereas others removed their shirts and pants. Waiting for the inspection could take more than two hours in each direction.[78] In 1962 the U.S. Navy Depot commented on the strip searches, although it oddly minimized their effects on worker morale. "The Depot continued business as usual. Civilian employees who reside off the base reservation persistently came to work in spite of their being stripped of their clothes on many occasions, searched and subjected to abusive language by militiamen who stood guard at the frontier borders of the base. Throughout the Depot there was an inevitable feeling of the strange uncertainty of Cold War, but morale remained high and productivity continued undiminished."[79] The U.S. Navy Depot's naïve emphasis on workers' morale and productivity minimized their fragile positions. The nudity was ostensibly to prevent the workers from bringing anything from the base back into Cuba, but its effect was mortifying. The strip searches forced workers to cross the *frontera "desnudo"* (naked), magnifying workers' physical and psychological vulnerability.

Despite the repeated shaming, many commuters tenaciously held onto their base jobs. Their persistence and commitment to GTMO employment quietly rebuked the revolutionary government's promise of economic prosperity and plenty in Guantánamo. In the early 1960s, the revolutionary authorities were revamping Guantánamo's urban, commercial economy and replacing it with an agricultural base. They faced considerable resistance to this program, and revolutionary proponents decried Guantánamo as a bourgeois and "parasitic" region.[80] Many base workers may have benefited from the revolution's investment in health care and education, even supporting its nationalist zeal, but most were not willing to forfeit their access to U.S. employment and steady salaries. The sugar industry, with its reliance on manual labor and constant insecurity, did not offer an attractive alternative. Given the choice between work in revolutionary Cuba or the base, most endured the harassment and still wanted to commute. As a result, their revolutionary credentials were constantly under suspicion.

As diplomatic discourse between Cuba and the United States broke down, the Cuban Army mustered a new unit, the Brigada de la Frontera (Border Brigade), which came to symbolize unblinking resilience and preparedness against U.S. imperialism. At first, the local militia was relatively amateur, emerging out of the M-26–7 forces in Guantánamo and Santiago de Cuba. With no beds and little food, conditions were rough for the Cuba militia.[81] The U.S. marines who stood guard said these units were unprofessional and "didn't pay much attention to camouflage. They often came up to the fence and cursed the Yankees."[82] Throughout 1959 and 1960, the Cuban government believed GTMO was engaged in counterrevolutionary activities: recruiting base workers as spies, harboring exiles, and preparing to provoke the Cuban militia to justify a U.S. invasion.[83] In the wake of the United States' animosity and documented plots against the Castro government, these fears were not without merit.

In 1961 the Cuban Army professionalized the local militia and renamed it the Brigada de la Frontera, reconfiguring it as an elite unit. Guantánamo was dubbed the *primera trinchera de defensa* (first trench in the line of defense) against U.S. imperialism. The U.S. marines noted the improved military training, weapons, and camouflage of their Cuban counterparts, and attributed these advances to Soviet guidance and support.[84] Alberto Torres, the former base worker and early Communist Party member, became the commander of the new battalion. Alberto was from Caimanera and identified himself as a *guantanamero;* however, he noted that the brigade recruited soldiers from outside the region. "It would not have been suitable to have *guantanameros* there . . . because it would have been too easy for the Yankees to provoke them. But it's not as if we discriminated against the *guantanameros*."[85] Alberto Torres did not raise the other reason the Brigada de la Frontera did not recruit from Guantánamo. Its other function was to screen the base workers. In all likelihood, the Cuban military leadership did not trust the local population, so long identified with the U.S. base, and feared *guantanameros* might compromise security.[86]

The Cuban government's martial stance did not emerge in a vacuum, and its fears of a U.S. invasion materialized in Playa Girón (Bay of Pigs). In April 1961, President John F. Kennedy gave the green light to 1,200 Cuban exiles, funded and trained by the CIA, to attack Cuba and spark rebellion throughout the island. Kennedy, however, did not order the air power or the U.S. military assistance necessary for victory. In less than three days, the Cuban exiles dramatically failed to oust Castro and overturn the Cuban revolution. The vast majority surrendered, and this solidified Castro's control over the government.[87] As the event played out, GTMO was hundreds of miles away and at best a footnote to the invasion.[88] Even though the Bay of Pigs ended in disaster and a loss of face for the Kennedy administration, the Cuban government feared future attacks as well as dangers emanating from GTMO.

Just a few months later, in August 1961, the Cuban government's concerns seem to have been validated. It claimed GTMO was sheltering anti-Castro exiles and masterminding a multifaceted plot, code-named Patty Candela. In brief, Raúl Castro was scheduled to attend the annual 26 of July rally in Santiago de Cuba in 1961. The CIA, in conjunction with a small cohort of anti-Castro base employees and exiles, reportedly planned to smuggle arms off the base, station sharpshooters at the rally, and assassinate Raúl Castro during the celebrations. According to Cuban accounts, the goal was not only to murder Raúl and decapitate the revolutionary leadership, but to provoke a Cuban attack on nearby GTMO. If the Cuban Armed Forces threatened GTMO, the United States could then justify an invasion. Through counterintelligence operations, the Cuban Armed Forces learned of the plot and squashed it, killing several counterrevolutionary exiles in the process. The Cuban government also detained 159 individuals for conspiracy and confiscated a large number of arms, including two cannons, four bazookas, twenty-three Springfield rifles, three grenades, a box of mines, additional artillery, and ammunition. All the weapons were U.S.-made and thus indicted the base. Ernesto

"Che" Guevara denounced the U.S. aggressions at the hemispheric Punta del Este meeting in Uruguay in August 1961.[89] Cuban filmmaker Rogelio París commemorated the events in the 1976 film *Patty Candela*.[90]

The Patty Candela campaign disappeared from U.S. accounts and narratives, but it is an evocative example of how the base ignited fears of counterrevolutionary action, and how the Cuban government manipulated these fears. The national Cuban press paid particular attention to the participation of base workers in the poorly executed plot. It claimed that base workers cooperated with U.S. military officials and helped move the weapons off the base. Although the reports did not condemn all base workers, the counterrevolutionary activity of a select few cast suspicion on the group as a whole.[91]

Pointedly, *Hoy* utilized the U.S. press for its own ends. It republished a *National Geographic* photo essay that had emphasized U.S. military surveillance along GTMO's perimeter. *Hoy* quoted *National Geographic* and pirated its photographs demonstrating the U.S. military's vigilance and preparedness. Given the U.S. representations of tight security, barbed wire, and fortifications, the Cuban government claimed that counterrevolutionaries could not have transported U.S. weapons off the base without U.S. knowledge: "The complicity of the naval admirals cannot be in doubt. . . . It is impossible to take so many arms off the base without the chiefs knowing!"[92] By drawing attention to the U.S. media's own images, *Hoy* reinterpreted the U.S. representation of military strength in the Cold War. The Cuban press argued that U.S.-produced images of martial power "proved" that the U.S. Navy had monitored all the happenings on the base, including plots against the Cuban state.

The Patty Candela incident magnified the Castro government's anger and suspicions against GTMO. Still, Cuban officials' recognized their limited military options and the logic behind "Patty Candela." If the United States provoked the Brigada de la Frontera, it could use a minor confrontation as a pretext to invade the island. The Cuban government's main objective was to deter military conflict, even as insults, stones, and occasional gunshots were exchanged across the barbed wire fence. The Brigada de la Frontera was ordered to avoid direct confrontation with U.S. *marinos* at all costs. Ironically, the stand-off demonstrated how the United States' massive military strength could appear powerless. The Cuban press mocked the U.S. forces, "How impotent the Yankees must feel!" and lauded its own militia's perseverance and restraint, "Face to face the Cuban soldiers and the Yankees physically represent two worlds. On one side there is patience, work, and valor. On the other side, there

Figure 14. "Guard and Sentry Dog Patrol Border." *National Geographic,* March 1961. *Hoy* reprinted this image after the Patty Candela incident to "prove" U.S. knowledge of activities on GTMO's border. Courtesy of W. E. Garrett and National Geographic Image Collection.

are rocks, cowardly insults, and provocations. It reminds us of Berlin."[93] In this peripheral, Cold War outpost, military power had become omnipresent and yet oddly ineffective.

Not surprisingly, each side blamed the other for escalating the conflict. For example, in the weeks leading up to the Missile Crisis, the U.S. Navy recorded multiple incidents of Cubans aiming their rifles and throwing stones at U.S. marines on guard.[94] In turn, the Cubans claimed the United States repeatedly violated Cuban territory. In 1962 the Cubans counted 309 shots fired across the border, 4,912 violations of Cuban airspace (a record high), 236 objects thrown across the fence, 17 "offensive" acts, and 488 verbal attacks.[95] The revolutionary press lauded the *brigada* for remaining stoic and moderate even when goaded. It ridiculed the Yankees for being poor shots, jumpy with the trigger, and vulgar, saving particular venom for a Mexican American marine and his misplaced loyalties: "This badly born Latino is not interested in the theft of Mexican land. . . . He shouts more and insults more than the true North Americans."[96] In contrast, the Cuban men who stood guard on the *frontera* represented self-control, courage, and patriotism. In strained literary verse, two members of the brigade, Amaury Rodríguez and Miguel Fonseca, wrote a poem valorizing their position: "I am going to recover it! / And I will clean my land / Cuban, firm, and glorious / From imperial territory." These soldiers also reclaimed José Martí's beloved *palma,* memorialized in *Versos Sencillos* and later popularized in "Guantanamera": "This is why I am here / Defending my flag / Reclaiming this palm / the only one on the border. . . . Do you see this Cuban palm? It is my real palm!"[97] The Cuban press constructed these soldiers as true revolutionary heroes. They guarded the Cuban *patria* from attack and stood face-to-face against the U.S. military aggressors.

Although fences, launches, and guard posts had always separated the U.S. military zone from its Cuban environs, the intensified militarization of the early 1960s physically and symbolically severed the base from Cuban territory. And if the Brigada de la Frontera represented one ideal of revolutionary manhood, abused Cuban base workers represented another.

RUBÉN LÓPEZ SABARIEGO: THE FINAL BASE WORKER MARTYR

In October 1961, Rubén López Sabariego, a Cuban base worker, died along GTMO's border under particularly dubious circumstances.[98] Rubén López was forty-eight years old and lived in the nearby village of Boquerón with his wife, Georgina González, and his nine children. He had worked at GTMO since 1948 as a bus driver.[99] U.S. naval officials suspected López was a "Castro agent," but even so, they allowed him to keep his job.[100] On Saturday, September 30, 1961, López left his house at ten in the morning to go to work. His wife did not hear from him again.

In the national Cuban press, Georgina González became the main protagonist as she loyally and persistently inquired after the whereabouts of her husband. When López did not return from work, she made her way to the northeast gate and demanded information. López's coworkers led

González to believe he had been unlawfully detained on the base, and she wanted answers. In *Hoy*'s account, González confronted U.S. military officers three times. The first two times, the U.S. officials dismissed her concerns and criticized the Cuban revolution. They told her to look "in Cuba" because Castro's followers frequently kidnapped and murdered disloyal workers. But on her third and final visit, the base chaplain informed her that López's dead body had been found in a ditch within the base. Distraught, González entered the base and saw her husband's decomposing body. It was in horrific condition. The priest insisted that the public health risks were too great, and that López's remains had to be buried immediately within the confines of the base. González refused, insisting that López be buried in the *patria*.[101]

The act of "crossing" now confronted a cadaver that, in effect, needed a "pass." The U.S. Navy was reluctant to authorize the removal of López's corpse off the base. At one point, U.S. officials even told González there were no coffins available for the job. González initiated the painful and bureaucratic process of certifying her husband's death and gaining a public health clearance from GTMO's medical officers. After a great deal of hassle and intrigue, González succeeded in gaining the proper paperwork and transported López's body to Guantánamo. Once in Cuba, Guantánamo doctors conducted an autopsy and concluded López had been beaten and tortured with heavy weapons. They posited that he had been detained for two weeks, imprisoned in the base jail, and tortured to death.[102] In contrast, the U.S. Navy admitted that López's body had been found in a shallow grave inside the base, but said no more. The U.S. Navy pointed out that the matter was "under investigation," and the U.S. Marine Corps had "nothing further to add."[103] The U.S. military did not court-martial anyone involved in the incident.

The Cuban government spearheaded mass rallies and heralded Georgina González as a loyal and revolutionary wife and mother. Local chapters of the Federation of Cuban Women (FMC), the Committee for the Defense of the Revolution (CDR), and workers' organizations issued telegrams condemning López's murder.[104] Unlike local outcries surrounding the Kid Chicle or Salomón cases, this time protesters found a champion in the national government. In fact, the rallies were state-organized, and Raúl Castro led chants such as, "Yankee Assassins!" and "*Fuera la base Caimanera!*" (Out with the base!) The Cuban government recognized López's death as emblematic of the United States' disregard for base workers and proof of its capacity for violence. Moreover, the U.S. Navy now appeared accountable to no one. In this context, the base worker was no longer a potential agent of counter-revolution, but was rather reconstructed as the ultimate worker in the face of imperial aggression.

Georgina González became the public figure who personified grief and strength. Her presence allowed for the symbolic transference of López's contradictory and compromised base work onto the more revolutionary terrain of a widow's rage and sorrow. The first issue of *Mujeres,* a popular magazine that projected an ideal socialist femininity, profiled Georgina González. It defined Cuba's sorrow as González's sorrow: "*Mujeres,* echoing the palpitations of Cuban women, recognizes in its first issue, the popular clamor and energetic condemnation of this act by the imperialist government that brought pain and suffering to a Cuban family."[105] The Cuban government turned López into a martyr for the revolution.

This might have been the end of the account were it not for Lt. William A. Szili, a U.S. marine who demanded justice on his own terms. As in the Rodríguez and Salomón cases, the U.S. military refused to consider Cuban jurisdiction and sought to avoid the Cuban legal system. Lt. Szili, one of the main actors in López's death, came forward two years later. Ironically, he too protested the lack of due process. He accused the U.S. military of foregoing a court-martial to minimize the paper trail and publicity. Discharged, Szili had difficulty finding work and was denied government benefits. Audaciously, Szili turned to his U.S. Congressman, Representative Richard S. Schweiker, and requested a congressional investigation.[106]

Szili recalled that Rubén López had been a Castro agent who had a tendency to wander into unauthorized territory. One evening Szili and Captain Arthur J. Jackson, a winner of the Congressional Medal of Honor during World War II, shared a nightcap at the Officers' Club and drank "perhaps six martinis."[107] Later that night, Captain Jackson spotted López in an ammunition storage area. Jackson contacted the base police and was told to throw López off the base, which was "not an unusual procedure at Guantánamo."[108] Rather than escort López to the main gate, Captain Jackson and Lt. Szili brought him to a little-used gate on the periphery of the base, with the intention of sending him straight back to Cuban territory. The gate was rusted shut. Szili left to get a sledgehammer to break open the gate. In the interim, Captain Jackson forced the gate open, and López and Jackson both crossed over into Cuban territory. At this point, Jackson alleged that López tried to grab his pistol. Claiming self-defense, Jackson shot and killed López on Cuban territory. When Szili returned, "it was mass confusion."[109]

López's body either fell off a cliff because of the force of the shot, or Captain Jackson threw his body over the cliff to avoid detection. In either case, López's corpse landed on a rocky beach. Jackson and Szili left the body there overnight. The next day they returned to the scene of the crime and decided to hoist the body back onto the base. According to Szili, he and Jackson were spooked; it was too risky to leave the body exposed. In a tragicomedy of errors they first used a regular rope that broke under the body's weight, and then switched to a nylon cord. With the aid of three additional officers and six enlisted men, they succeeded in retrieving López's body and buried it in a shallow grave eight hundred feet inside of GTMO's boundary. Szili defended the decision to cover up the case as a necessary precaution. They had to avoid "international repercussions." He minimized López's death and noted Castro's adeptness with propaganda: "Castro has the ability of taking the story of a Boy Scout helping the old lady across the street and turning it into an attempted rape. I felt he could do the same thing with this incident."[110] Szili and Jackson's mediocre attempts at secrecy were unsuccessful, and rumors about the incident spread at a cocktail party. On October 15 base officials searched for and discovered the body. Jackson resigned from the Marine Corps, and Szili was discharged.

Szili's account did not corroborate Georgina González's nor Raúl Castro's earlier accusations of detention and torture, but nonetheless, it damned the United States and GTMO policies in its own right. Despite Szili's protestations, López's murder was far graver than "helping an old lady across the street" and did not need Castro's reinterpretation to foment anti-American sentiments. Szili and Jackson's violence and callousness tapped into years of anger against the U.S. military's occupation and license in Guantánamo. The U.S. Navy recognized the potential propaganda and diplomatic disaster of the situation and wanted the case closed without a paper trail. That was why it had rejected a court martial in the first place.[111] At first Representative Richard Schweiker advocated for Szili. He believed Szili was a "victim of circumstances," who had a right to "his day in court," that is, a U.S. court.[112] However, Szili's version of events placed the shooting in Cuban territory, outside GTMO's jurisdiction. With more publicity, the U.S. Navy feared Castro might insist on a trial—in a Cuban court. After a week or two of intensive press coverage, Szili conceded, "Maybe I should have kept my mouth shut."[113] The Cuban press picked up the story and proclaimed, "The imperialists confess to the crime of Rubén López Sabariego."[114] Jackson and Szili's cruelty and violent ineptitude were not official government policy; however, the cover-up was. The U.S. Navy's silence and studied obfuscation served to shore up the base, while avoiding direct confrontation with Cuba.

The story of Rubén López demonstrates just how much symbolic freight base workers' bodies could be asked to carry, and how select base workers could be elevated into the pantheon of revolutionary martyrs. The outrage following Rubén López's death paralleled earlier protests over Lino Rodríguez's death in 1940 and Lorenzo Salomón's detention in 1954. Intertwining the accusations and denials from the Rodríguez and Salomón cases, López's death fused together charges of murder and torture. In 1961 the revolutionary government orchestrated public rallies, which replaced previous grassroots demonstrations, and channeled long-standing grievances into revolutionary fervor. Still, the Cuban government was not prepared to escalate the conflict or go to war over the life of a base worker. The risks were simply too high. López's death signified the tangible threat and power of U.S. violence and its tragic consequences for Guantánamo. Rather than retaliating with military force, the Cuban government refashioned base workers as revolutionary agents.

Rubén López, thereby, joined the ranks of Federico Figueras and Manuel Prieto as workers unfairly fired, beaten or, in López's case, murdered by the U.S. Navy. López's death enabled the revolutionary government to articulate its critique of the base through a working-class idiom, by harnessing decades of base workers' protests of arbitrary U.S. power and grafting them onto the revolutionary project. This process preserved the binary of "revolutionary" and "counterrevolutionary" that discounted the more ambiguous position of the majority of base workers.

In the following month, Guantánamo officials renamed the former meeting hall of the Colonia Española (an elite, Spanish ancestry association) the Círculo Popular "Rubén López Sabariego."[115] To commemorate the anniversary of Rubén López's death, local Guantánamo officials also planned an event for October 19, 1962, to memorialize the "humble worker."[116] Unbeknownst to the event organizers, the ceremony would coincide with, and be trumped by, the Missile Crisis.

CRISIS: MISSILES, WOMEN, AND WORK

Unlike the accounts of Figueras, Prieto, and López, which skirt the fringes of the archives, the 1962 Missile Crisis is front and center in the grand narrative of twentieth-century international history. The USSR's bid to install nuclear missiles in Cuba and the Kennedy administration's response brought the two Cold War superpowers precipitously close to direct military confrontation and, fortunately for all, ended in diplomatic negotiation and concession rather than nuclear annihilation.[117] Recent scholarship has compellingly recentered Cuba as a central player in the crisis, rather than merely as the stage. Through declassified documents and "critical oral history," historians have demonstrated that Cuba's fear of a U.S. invasion, and not Soviet geopolitical strategy, was the central factor in Nikita Khrushchev's original decision to install nuclear weapons in Cuba.[118]

The Missile Crisis unintentionally demonstrated GTMO's limited military efficacy in an age of nuclear war. By the end of the crisis, the base's symbolic value outweighed its strategic purpose. GTMO's primary military operation during the Missile Crisis was not an attack on Cuba, but the evacuation of U.S. civilian employees, women, and children. This emphasis on domesticity and women monopolized the base's resources at the outset of the crisis. The departure of U.S. women also made visible the only female population remaining on the base—local domestic servants. And for base workers the Missile Crisis was yet another moment that tested workers' loyalty to the U.S. Navy, or at least their tenacity to their jobs. In this nexus of superpower stand-offs and nuclear brinkmanship, gender, evacuation, and work shaped GTMO's environment during the Missile Crisis.

The Missile Crisis raised the question of foreign military bases' utility in the Cold War. At the most basic level, the U.S. government refused to tolerate Soviet nuclear missiles in such close proximity to the continental United States. However, it was not lost on top officials that the United States had comparable bases near Soviet territory, namely in Turkey and Italy. In the first days of the Missile Crisis, the U.S. Mission to the United Nations, led by Adlai Stevenson, bluntly suggested a proposal to withdraw *all* military bases from Cuba, including GTMO, as one solution to the crisis. Stevenson succinctly pointed to GTMO's irrelevance: "If this proposal should be accepted and carried out, the Soviets would have lost an important military asset in Cuba, while we would have lost a base which is of little use to us. This would be a major victory, not a defeat." Through this line of reasoning, all of GTMO's military functions could be accomplished on U.S. bases in Puerto Rico and Florida, while the far more valuable U.S. missiles in Turkey and Italy could be sustained. As a strategic military outpost, GTMO was of "little real importance."[119]

The Kennedy administration did not follow this counsel, nor did it launch a preemptive attack as many military officials urged. Instead, it engaged in a high-stakes quarantine and prevented Soviet ships from delivering additional weapons to Cuba. Exceptionally tense days, nerve-wracking diplomacy, and the deployment of secret envoys ensued. Choosing to avoid nuclear conflict, Khrushchev agreed to remove Soviet missiles from Cuba under UN supervision, on the condition that the United States agreed not to invade Cuba. The United States also consented to remove its nuclear missiles from Turkey, but not as a public quid pro quo. Fidel Castro was not privy to these agreements, and he was outraged to have been sidelined. In turn, he issued his own demands, including the end to the U.S. economic embargo and the complete withdrawal of the U.S. naval base in Guantánamo Bay.

In a new position of strength, the United States was completely unwilling to discuss closing GTMO.[120] In a circular to U.S. embassies throughout the developing world, Secretary of State Dean Rusk insisted that the United States had acquired GTMO through a treaty that, in his words, was "no, repeat, no threat to Cuba." He emphasized that GTMO had "not even exerted influence on the Castro regime." Rusk added that the base could not be seen as a menace to Cuban sovereignty.[121] Through this strained logic, the secretary of state cited GTMO's very weakness and irrelevance in Cuba as the reason the United States needed to keep it. Diplomatic communiqués indicated that State Department officers had difficulty defending this stance in the developing world. The U.S. ambassador to Lebanon reported that Rusk's arguments were "not very impressive in this part of the world," and their successful dissemination would be a "formidable" task. Fortunately, he concluded, there was no great local interest in the topic.[122]

During the Missile Crisis, GTMO personnel shifted into high gear, and all of its resources were "devoted exclusively" to defense duties from October 22 through December 12, 1962.[123] The base monitored the quarantine and contributed to the Caribbean defense. GTMO tripled its forces, and the population spiked from its normal 3,150 to 9,087 military personnel.[124] Still, the United States was not emboldened to launch an attack directly from GTMO, and in a state of war with the U.S.S.R., GTMO would have been destroyed immediately. In this context, GTMO's one major exercise is notable for its civilian, rather than military nature.

The evacuation of U.S. women, children, and civilians was one of the first public signals of military crisis. On October 22, 1962, John F. Kennedy delivered a televised speech about the discovery of Soviet missiles in Cuba and the subsequent quarantine. In this address, he announced that GTMO dependents would be immediately evacuated. The removal of U.S. women, along with the closing of schools, scouting expeditions, and social affairs, signaled the readiness for war.[125] In the most practical sense, this was a precautionary measure to remove non-military personnel from the direct line of a nuclear confrontation. It also defined the departure of military wives and children as part of, and not separate from, a martial strategy. One marine claimed that the evacuation was "one of the best planned and executed military operations" he had ever observed.[126]

The Missile Crisis unfolded as the U.S. Navy was conducting its regular defense exercises at GTMO from October 21 to 22, and it soon became "obvious that someone was not going by the 'book.' "[127] Admiral Edward J. O'Donnell called his officer corps for a face-to-face meeting and prepared them for the evacuation. To avoid a television or radio announcement, he decided that an officer would personally deliver a handbill to each family. In retrospect, Admiral O'Donnell believed that the handbill had been the "masterstroke" that "minimized excitement and emotional reaction."[128] Owing to GTMO's volatile location, each family had a prepacked suitcase. The evacuees were instructed to "Please keep calm and carry out all directions given you." They were to leave their pets behind, carry a single suitcase, and wait in their yards for a bus to escort them to the ships. The handbill concluded by referring to the women's feminine accessories and the need for secrecy: "God bless you. We will all miss you. Put this in your purse. Do not leave it lying around the house or yard."[129] Admiral O'Donnell concluded that the women demonstrated "wonderful emotional strength" and "behaved just magnificently."[130] The men adjusted to the new environment: "No complaints were heard except that the commissary store sold out of TV dinners the day following evacuation."[131]

In total, the U.S. Navy evacuated 2,432 women and children from the naval base on four ships that brought them to U.S. naval bases in Norfolk and Little Creek, Virginia.[132] The U.S. media depicted these women as patriotic, loyal, and brave. For example, Mrs. Norman Le Mieux was quoted as saying, "I'd like to go back and be with my husband. . . . A lot of the women feel that way and wanted to stay. We are not afraid to go back."[133] Other women adopted the lexicon and language of exile, which would become so powerful for the concurrent generation of Cuban exiles. In one personal testimony, Joyce Hughes Matthews recounted being ripped from the teenage idyll of her "beloved GTMO." She had lived on the base for two years, and remembered how distraught she had been tying her dog to the front tree, packing her bag, and saying good-bye to her father. Despite the passage of time, Matthews held on to her memories and claimed GTMO as her "home." She lamented that her teenage years had been burdened by the weight of history. "There is no special place in my heart that can conjure up visions like those of GTMO. . . . I am still waiting for the day that I can return to my 'home' and one more time walk the beaches and stand on the soil that I have come to love. As coral dust filters through the air in GTMO, it still fil-ters down to my heart. I envy you who are there, and maybe, one day, I will return."[134] It is hard to ignore the neocolonial twang of a U.S. teenager waxing nostalgic for her GTMO "home" in the era of the Cuban revolution and Missile Crisis. Her paean to GTMO contained un-intended parallels to Cuban exiles' longings. She also voiced no con-sciousness or recognition that nearby Cubans had no rights or access to Guantánamo Bay's sands and corals.

Throughout the Missile Crisis, gender and a disruption of domesticity were the central realities at GTMO. The base was of course engaged in defensive exercises and prepared for attack, but in the memories, reports, and accounts of the crisis, the evacuation stands out and overshadows military stories.[135] The attention focused on the evacuation also served to ignore those who stayed: the local base employees, women as well as men.

For base workers, the Missile Crisis posed yet another hurdle signify-ing the abnormality of their work lives and a test to their divided loyal-ties. In September 1962, there were 2,194 local civil service employees, 590 nonappropriated fund employees, and 440 domestic servants on the base.[136] Although there was notable absenteeism immediately after the evacuation, most workers continued their daily commute in the upcom-ing days. The U.S. military noted that Cuban employees registered a "calm reaction to dependent evacuation," and inferred from their pres-ence that the Cuban government had not hardened its attitude.[137] U.S. of-ficers went one step further and praised base workers' valor: "It must be emphasized that these Cuban civilians came to work during this period of uncertainty at great personal risk and sacrifice to themselves."[138] Not only were base workers brave, they were also deemed loyal to the U.S. military. The Atlantic Command's official account reported, "At no time, did the commander indicate the slightest doubt about the loyalty or mo-tives of his Cuban labor force."[139] This report went on to describe the base workers' attitudes as excellent and included that 40 men volunteered to stand watch alongside base policemen. Some workers saw the Missile Crisis as the occasion to become "permanent base residents," effectively defecting.[140] In all, the U.S. Navy fired only 2 men as suspected infiltrators during the Missile Crisis. However, 13 workers resigned due to their revolutionary leanings.[141]

For domestic servants on the base, the evacuation of U.S. women opened up new professional opportunities. Many U.S. military wives had held office, clerical, and management positions on the base. Their departure hurt the base's efficiency and left several departments shorthanded. Given the need for labor, administrative offices turned to the only supply of female labor left on the base—local domestic servants. No longer needing maids to keep house, U.S. officers suddenly tapped English-speaking maids for their clerical skills.[142] From the military's perspective this was an effective way to replace wives' domestic and professional labor. "Speaking of maids, at the time of the evacuation most of the maids were automatically unemployed. Fortunately enough, jobs could be found to keep them gainfully employed at the naval base with the thought that they would ultimately be needed again as maids. The Public Works Center, Special Services, and the Naval Supply Depot hired a number of these maids as house cleaners, waitresses and key punch operator trainees, respectively. Some of these maids did so well that they are now permanent civil service employees."[143]

As a result, domestic servants identified the Missile Crisis with new opportunities and the possibility of having their intellectual and professional skills recognized by their U.S. employers. For example, Claire Winchester worked as a domestic and remembered the effect the Missile Crisis had on her own employment. She spoke English, and therefore was offered a job in an office. "Yes, there were a lot of domestics and servants that had education, that they could do that work. You understand? They made a test, I remember, we all went to the test. I and two friends of mine, and we passed our test." Claire kept her new job until the wives returned.[144] For Claire, the Missile Crisis meant a reprieve from domestic labor. These details appear at odds with the Missile Crisis's trajectory of high-level negotiation and barely averted nuclear war. For GTMO's base workers the Missile Crisis changed their daily patterns, inverting gender norms and redefining domestic work.

The return of the navy wives and children in December 1962 signaled that the diplomatic realm had resumed its stalemated normalcy and that the military threat had passed.[145] At this point, many local women returned to domestic service. That Christmas there were special celebrations, and many famous entertainers traveled to GTMO to play for the reunited families, including Ed Sullivan, Louis "Satchmo" Armstrong, Connie Francis, and Eddie Fisher.[146] Over the next year and a half, there were no major incidents that substantially disrupted GTMO's routine. U.S. naval officials continued to define base workers as loyal employees, distinct from the Communist soldiers who patrolled the border. To this end, the U.S. Navy expanded its religious counseling and "Cuban Adult Education Program," which offered English and math classes to base workers. In the Cold War mindset, the U.S. Navy described these limited programs as "vital[ly] important in developing future leaders for Cuba imbued with the ideals for liberty."[147] Such a program was a clear sign of the base officials' Cold War fantasies and limited grasp on Cuba's political reality. Unlike the U.S. government's influence in most of Latin America, GTMO-directed "Cold War activities" had a remarkably short radius. Base workers were the U.S. military's only direct audience for pro-American propaganda in Cuba, and these men and women were simply in no position to become Cuba's "future leaders."

Base workers often met harassment and suspicion as they carried on with their commute, but the Cuban government did not prohibit their employment. They continued to exchange their money, disrobe as they crossed the border, and submit to searches. This changed in February 1964, when a minor face off between Fidel Castro and Lyndon Johnson ended with Castro cutting the water supply to the base and the U.S. Navy laying off hundreds of local workers. One base worker could not remember the exact cause of the layoffs. "I don't remember what the problem was. . . . It was after, after the Crisis. Do you know about the Crisis? Yes, after the Crisis, then they had to reduce the number of people who were on the base. Then they were all fired. And the way in which they fired people wasn't right. They went and said, 'You, you, you, you, you, get your things,' but they didn't give any time to get anything . . . and they put them in a car and brought them to the border."[148] In his narrative, the language of the 1962 Missile Crisis merged with the massive layoffs in 1964. For workers, this rash of firings was far more traumatic than nuclear brinkmanship. It terminated their access to U.S. dollars and steady employment. This was their crisis.

THE 1964 WATER CRISIS: "CUBA OR THE BASE"

On February 1, 1964, the U.S. Coast Guard spotted four Cuban fishing trawlers near the Dry Tortugas Islands, a small archipelago seventy miles from Key West, Florida. The coast guard stopped the boats, inspected the vessels, and found thirty-eight Cuban fishermen and 5,500 pounds of fish. The boats were trespassing U.S. territorial waters, but there was nothing illegal on board. Rather than release the boats as was customary, the Coast Guard escorted them to Key West. There, the state of Florida claimed that the Cuban fishing boats violated the 1963 Florida Territorial Waters Act, which outlawed "alien Communists" from taking the state's "natural resources," in this case, fish. Florida officials jailed the fishermen and impounded the boats.[149] Florida state politics were already strongly influenced by the anti-Castro, Cuban exile community in Miami. The *New York Times* editorialized that it was a serious mistake to let Florida create U.S. foreign policy: "The sooner the matter is taken out of their [Florida's] hands and the fishermen sent back to Cuba the better."[150]

However, it was too late, and Fidel Castro retaliated. In response to the jailed fishermen, Castro cut off the water supply to the U.S. naval base in Guantánamo Bay. For decades, GTMO had relied on fresh water from Cuban territory outside the base's boundaries, and this dependence had always been a source of vulnerability and concern.[151] Castro described the water suspension as an act of Cuba's "free and sovereign will" against this "new imperialist insolence."[152] For Lyndon Johnson, Castro's manipulation of GTMO was unnerving, following all too closely on the heels of anti-American protests in Panama.[153] Running for president, Senator Barry Goldwater linked the two episodes, chastising Johnson on the campaign trail for his weakness in Latin America. Goldwater offered a direct threat to Castro, "Turn it [the water] on or the marines are going to turn it on for you and keep it on."[154] Johnson acted more cautiously and a plan emerged to make the base self-sufficient: ration water, build a desalinization plant, and fire the Cuban workers.[155]

The U.S. government's linkage of water and labor self-sufficiency was immediate. GTMO Admiral John Bulkeley was full of bluster and anti-communist vigor. A decorated World War II hero, Bulkeley had recruited the young John F. Kennedy to be a PT skipper in the Pacific. In the midst of the water conflict, Bulkeley reveled in his position of staring down Castro, and he was quick to respond to Castro's propaganda and provocations.[156] Water was the first order of business. Officials instituted an "austerity" plan, which rationed water consumption to a quarter of normal use and eliminated lawn watering and car washing. The U.S. Navy also signed a contract with a private company to build a massive desalinization plant that would purify 1.4 million gallons of seawater a day and promised to be operating in less than six months. In the interim, two tankers delivered 10 million gallons of water, likely making it the "most expensive water in the world" to date.[157]

For Cuban workers, the consequences were quick, harsh, and unexpected. The Johnson administration ordered GTMO officials to fire the majority of local hires. The U.S. Navy clung to a language of neocolonialism and continued to describe the base workers as overwhelmingly loyal, even as they fired the vast majority without cause. Admiral Bulkeley remarked that amazingly only a minuscule number of Cuban workers blamed the United States for the crisis: "All the rest blamed Castro and the Cold War."[158] Despite absolving the U.S. Navy of blame, GTMO officials offered workers a blunt choice—Cuba or the base. If workers chose "Cuba," they sacrificed their jobs, U.S. salaries, and government pensions. If they chose "the base," they had to cut all ties with Cuba and their families for the foreseeable future. Throughout 1964, the U.S. Navy initiated six waves of layoffs and put the question to 2,000 Cuban employees. Of those faced with "Cuba or the base," 448 chose "the base." Approximately 1,500 chose "Cuba." A final 750 workers retained their positions as commuters and remarkably did not have to choose.[159]

One long-term base worker, Ricardo Baylor, remembered this confrontation vividly. He had secured a position in the Ships Department in 1948 and worked there until 1964, the year when "they threw me out." Ricardo survived several of the layoffs, but a sympathetic supervisor pulled him aside and informed him that he would be let go in the next group. Ricardo had to decide whether to remain on the base or return home. His brother had already chosen to exile himself and stay on the base. Ricardo was at a loss, but he had a pregnant wife and knew he needed to go back. His brother cried as Ricardo left the base. In choosing to return to Guantánamo, Ricardo lost his claim to base retirement benefits. With particular venom, Ricardo blamed the U.S. government for taking his youth. Now that he is in his seventies, he is still waiting for a U.S. government pension for his 16 years of base employment.[160] Ricardo narrated his decision to cast his lot in Cuba as a personal story based on family ties, rather than an adherence to any particular political ideology. Like Ricardo, most workers chose their families in Cuba and never returned to the base.

Although the majority of workers chose Cuba, they were enraged that the United States had broken its commitment to workers' retirement. After years as good neocolonial subjects, the base workers had been discarded en masse and left without economic security. For example, Santiago Veranes worked in the plumbing department for fifteen years. In an interview with the Guantánamo press, he explained: "They [base officials] did not have any type of consideration for us. And not only me . . . I had an average of fifteen years. There were *compañeros* there who had worked for thirty-six years, and there wasn't any consideration for this. . . . They fired me in a cynical form, without explanation, without consideration, and without equanimity. We hoped there could have been a more moderate way, another policy for those of us who had dedicated so many years to the job."

These workers never returned to the base again, and the promise of U.S. benefits remained false and empty. Francisco Ardines, who had worked in the Cleaning Department, recounted:

> They called us in to sign our "liquidation" without giving us any explanation and without letting us ask for any claims for all the years that we had been working there. What were their motives for laying us off? And at the same time, they fired us. We also demanded the retirement that we had paid into for so many years, but they said that didn't go to people who were fired, and they said no. They gave us papers to sign and brought us to the police, and they had us until four-thirty in the afternoon. At that time they took us to the border.[161]

Published in *Venceremos,* the state-run Guantánamo newspaper after 1962, this feature is notable for its absence of top-down analysis. Although still an official organ, *Venceremos* published workers' narratives with relatively little mediation. Through these first-person testimonials, workers framed their stories as discarded employees and betrayed neocolonial subjects. Base workers emphasized the arbitrary nature of their dismissals, rather than narrate their travails through the rhetoric of nationalism and patriotism. Only in the final interview did a worker attest to his love for Cuban sovereignty, the ideals of José Martí, and the socialist revolution.[162] Other contemporary Cuban accounts in the local and national media defined this event through the language of anti-imperialism, but this singular article provided a fleeting example of workers' economic insecurity and anger without burdening it with revolutionary import.

In the following days, this would change, as the Cuban government defined workers' decisions into an uncompromising binary. Dignified workers remained in Cuba; traitors chose exile and sided with the imperialists. Entering the fray, Fidel Castro presented himself as the savior of these workers. With a turn of a phrase, the base workers were no longer suspect potential counterrevolutionaries; now they were victims of arbitrary U.S. imperial power.[163]

The Cuban government seized the opportunity to discredit the U.S. government's paternal promises and offer its own services in their place. In its coverage of the layoffs, *Venceremos* emphasized the two-tier pay scale that had consistently paid Cubans less than their U.S. counterparts. It also repeated accusations of U.S. discrimination against base workers as Cubans, Latinos, and people of color. The Cuban media and government no longer chastised the workers for their suspect employment or reliance on U.S. dollars. It erased the stigma that had defined base workers' commutes since the Cuban revolution. Fidel Castro announced, "We never interfered with the coming and going of the base workers." Instead, the Cuban state redefined them as "workers who had no other way of sustaining their families and for many years had to work for the monstrous imperialism."[164]

The government also recognized the symbolic, as well as material, importance of workers' pensions. Because base workers could no longer rely on the benevolence of the United States, the Cuban government could cast itself as their benefactor. The U.S. Navy decided to provide pensions only for the workers who remained on the base in exile. Workers who returned to Cuba would receive nothing. *Venceremos* lauded the men and women who resisted this financial temptation and chose to abandon the base. Recognizing the opportunity to rescue workers from U.S. duplicity, the Cuban government promised to come to the aid of base retirees and pay their pensions.[165]

The Cuban government invited international journalists to meet with former base workers and witness the ruptured aqueduct that had prompted the U.S. dismissal policy in the first place. In this setting, former base workers told their stories in a more political, defiant, and nationalist guise as they answered questions from the Soviet news agency TASS, Radio Rebelde, and Radio Moscow. Workers emphasized the racism on the base, pointing to the segregated officers' clubs and barracks. They also reiterated their individual nationalism and loyalty to Cuba. For example, Ramón Planas Montoya, a seventy-two-year-old worker, said that he had been thrown out because he talked back too much: "They threw me out on Tuesday, and they did not pay me my retirement." In this exchange, Planas explained his rapid firing as a result of his feistiness, rather than the water crisis that was beyond his control. María Luisa Deroucelet, who had been a domestic servant on the base for seven years, criticized her low pay and the high cost of travel. One of her sons was a member of the Rebel Army. She told her mistress that she preferred to stay in Cuba. Agustín Torres Rodríguez also stressed his nationalism. When he was asked if he wanted to stay and work on the base, he replied, "I am going to stay with my children, because before everything, I am Cuban."[166]

These workers became symbols of the revolutionary government's commitment to the working class, as well as testaments to the heartlessness of the U.S. government. In their testimonies for the national and international press corps, these workers self-consciously linked their situations to earlier examples of U.S. brutality. For example, *Hoy* also profiled Planas and, in this version, he denounced the United States for robbing him of his pension. He concluded, "With these same eyes of mine, many years ago, I saw a U.S. official kill a Santiago boxer, nicknamed Kid Chicle." Manuel Prieto also returned to the national stage and retold his travail of being detained and beaten in 1961.[167] Through these accounts, the Cuban government consolidated the years of U.S. abuses and created a teleological trajectory of memory from 1940 to 1964. Into this opening, Fidel denounced the layoffs as violations of workers' rights, calling them "arbitrary" and "inhuman."[168] This statement resonated because it invoked the years of mistreatment that base workers had experienced. Yet, it simultaneously erased workers' more ambiguous status since the Cuban revolution. In one fell swoop, the base workers had been reconstructed as full members of the Cuban revolution.

The Cuban government provided laid-off base workers with new jobs that aided the revolution and provided for their families. A Guantánamo government official declared, "The revolution will guarantee you work, the people take you into their breast."[169] In a public event, the National Bank began distributing funds to the displaced workers. Luis Díaz Iglesias received ninety-two pesos, which was the salary he received every two weeks on the base. He exclaimed, "We never doubted the word of the revolutionary government." Juan Davinson, another worker who benefited from the Cuban government's largesse, declared, "Only a socialist government is capable of humanism. Imperialism believes in tyranny, hunger, and misery, but the revolution does not abandon us, and we are profoundly grateful." In the first two weeks, the National Bank paid more than twenty-eight thousand dollars to displaced workers in Caimanera and Guantánamo.[170]

Laid-off base workers were given agricultural as well as bureaucratic positions, but their satisfaction was largely determined by their gender. In my conversations in Guantánamo, female employees benefited the most from this transformation. Former domestic servants began to work as English teachers, secretaries, and social workers. No longer limited to working for U.S. military families, they could gain skills and have jobs that served a greater social purpose. For example, after the Cuban revolution, Maria Boothe worked at an old-age home, which she greatly preferred to domestic service on the base. Working with the elderly, she felt that she was caring for those in need and contributing to the community.[171] Priscilla Baxter, also a former domestic servant, became a receptionist at the local university. She favored this position; it came with more status and professional responsibility. In this work, she had the opportunity to speak with people from throughout the island. In addition, she had far greater social freedom and was no longer confined to the strictures of the base during the week.[172] Moreover, domestic servants had been private hires, not U.S. government employees. They had never had claims to U.S. government pensions. In contrast, men, particularly those with U.S. civil service positions, did not welcome the denouement. For example, Ricardo Baylor had held a white collar position in the Ships Department. His U.S. supervisor had warned him that if he returned to Cuba, he would just be cutting cane. And Ricardo said that had been accurate: within weeks of being laid off he was in the sugar cane fields.[173] Thus, former base workers who had previously enjoyed a degree of security and professional status regretted their lost positions. They criticized the U.S. government for throwing away their years of service. In today's Cuba, with its shortages and economic hardships, a U.S. pension is golden, and many workers from this 1964 cohort have tried to access them.

From the U.S. Navy's perspective, GTMO was well on its way to being self-sufficient. After the layoffs, it went full speed ahead with the desalinization plant. The goal was to complete it by the July 26 holiday to counter Cuban propaganda efforts.[174] The careful "chess game" along the military border intensified. With Admiral Bulkeley at the helm, the United States ratcheted up sophomoric pranks and responses to Cuban harassment. For example, the Cuban *brigada* began to use floodlights to blind and harass marine sentries on patrol. To shine their own "light" on the matter, Bulkeley ordered the Seabees and Cuban base workers to construct the "largest Marine Corps emblem in the world" directly in the line of the spotlights. As a result, when the Cuban *brigada* directed its lights on the patrol, it would illuminate the emblem. Bulkeley explained with satisfaction, "There are no more floodlights."[175] However, the game of cat and mouse could also become violent. On June 10, 1964, Cuba charged the United States with shooting and wounding Private José Ramírez Reyes and Private Andrés Noel Larduet, and on July 20, nineteen-year-old Ramón López Peña was shot and died.[176]

Ramón López Peña was the first soldier in the Brigada de la Frontera to die, and his death transformed the image of the revolutionary hero from the dead, detained, or discarded base worker to the martyred soldier.

(Although they shared a surname, Ramón López Peña, the *brigada* soldier, was no relation to Rubén López Sabriego, the murdered base worker.) López Peña was born in Puerto Padre, a small town near Holguín. He had served in the Cuban Army for two years and ten months, the majority with the Brigada de la Frontera. He also belonged to the Unión Jóvenes de Comunistas (UJC), or the Young Communist League. *Venceremos* announced: "Today the city of Guantánamo is in pain. It is in pain because the people have lost one of their valiant sons."[177]

Once again the details surrounding the case were murky, and the U.S. Navy denied responsibility. Several Cuban guards reportedly had shot at the marine sentries on duty. In return, a U.S. sentry fired a single warning shot into the air and over their heads. Admiral Bulkeley said Castro had "staged a masterpiece," and claimed that the ensuing outrage over a felled Cuban soldier was all for show. U.S. marines believed that the stretchers carrying the Cuban "bodies" were empty. Admiral Bulkeley speculated that López Peña had died in circumstances unrelated to GTMO and that his cadaver had been used disingenuously.[178] The State Department reported that the Cuban government wanted to gain propaganda points to coincide with the July 26 celebrations and a regional meeting in Latin America.[179] Raúl Castro strongly and sarcastically refuted the U.S. case. He stated that a U.S. marine had killed Ramón López Peña, and U.S. denials of this fact were insupportable.[180] The Cuban government took its case to the United Nations and charged the United States with 1,181 provocative actions from October 1962 to April 1964, including the death of López Peña.[181]

Raúl Castro came to Guantánamo and consciously linked the 1961 death of base worker Rubén López Sabriego to the 1964 demise of soldier Ramón López Peña: "One more time we are going down this path. One more time we walk bitterly to the cemetery. One more time we bury in this heroic ground one of our valiant sons, killed by the enemy."[182] Ramón López Peña was added to the list of Cubans who had been "assassinated" along GTMO's border since the revolution. As in the case of López Sabriego, the protest was orchestrated from above, and the community's suffering took on a militant tenor: "Today we pledge that thousands of Yankees will die, if one day the Yankees invade us."[183] Another parallel was the prominence of a female survivor. López Peña's mother became the key spokesperson attesting to the valor of her deceased son, much like López Sabriego's wife had in 1961. Rather than bemoan her son's death, Eunomia Peña proclaimed, "If it is necessary to give our lives to defend the revolution, we will give them," and his father, Andrés

Figure 15. The Plaza of the Revolution in Guantánamo, April 2006. Honoring fallen members of the 26 of July Movement and the *Brigada de la Frontera*, this public movement includes Ramón López Peña's name as one of Guantánamo's revolutionary martyrs. Photo by Jana K. Lipman.

López, added, "I only wish that I was younger so that I could put on my son's uniform and take his place in the Batallón Fronterizo and defend my country like he always did."[184]

In this moment, Ramón López Peña, the revolutionary soldier, replaced Lino Rodríguez, Lorenzo Salomón, and Rubén López Sabriego, the base workers, as the ultimate martyr and symbol of U.S. brutality. The soldiers of the Brigada de la Frontera set the new standard for revolutionary heroes, eclipsing the base workers. In the 1964 July 26 celebration in Santiago de Cuba, there were special honors for five "Heroes of Labor," with special notice for agricultural and industrial workers. A base worker was not included in this year's ceremony. Instead, the worker who evoked the greatest crowd response was José Ramírez, a wounded soldier who patrolled the military border and belonged to the Brigada de la Frontera.[185] The mantle of *revolutionary* was thoroughly mounted on the soldiers along the border and disassociated from the base workers. With the majority of base workers fired in 1964, the remaining cohort of commuters was identified even more strongly with the base and thus sidelined from the revolutionary project.

The approximately seven hundred workers who continued to commute to the base held onto their tenuous, "ticklish" positions. Victor Davis was one of these men. They formed an anomalous cohort, which traversed the militarized and guarded ground between Guantánamo and GTMO, despite the rupture in diplomatic and economic ties. Because no new workers could be hired, their number only decreased over time. The Cuban revolution made these commuters an anachronism in their own community; however, they were not cast out, nor were they prevented from working on the base. They worked for the U.S. military and claimed benefits from the U.S. government, while remaining Cuban citizens and claiming benefits from the Cuban government. For the U.S. Navy, the loss of the majority of its Cuban workforce begged the question of labor as well as that of politics. Who would replace the local workers? The answer was to hark back to earlier waves of Caribbean migration, U.S. capital, and contract labor. After dismissing the Cuban labor force, the U.S. military began to hire Jamaicans.

5

Contract Workers, Exiles, and Commuters
Neocolonial and Postmodern Labor Arrangements

n the aftermath of the 1964 layoffs, the U.S. Navy hired 489 Jamaican contract workers.[1] Through this process, GTMO inadvertently developed a new military model, which uncoupled the base and its geography. The majority of base workers would soon be migrants from developing countries with neocolonial ties to the United States. They performed service-oriented tasks, such as tending to the military's mess halls, account books, and manicured lawns. Under this new labor regime, GTMO reflected postmodern global trends toward outsourcing labor, recruiting foreign migrants on a contract basis, and separating the workplace from the people who lived there.[2] The U.S. military also retained a diminishing number of Cuban commuters and exiles, but, over the years, their experiences became more and more anachronistic. Base workers continued to negotiate for rights and benefits, but their ability to do so was increasingly constricted. With new workers, GTMO entered a new phase. GTMO embraced the advantages of a postmodern and privatized workforce and, through it, gained unprecedented independence from Cuban politics and the Guantánamo community.

Importing a contract workforce did not erase the knowledge the working class had of the Cuban revolution, and some of the first Jamaican workers protested their living conditions and threatened to ally themselves with Fidel Castro. In 1964 the United States reported that 60 Jamaican contract workers attended an "inflammatory" meeting on the base. According to State Department records, approximately 16 men spoke at this public meeting. These new workers expressed anger and discontent and "threatened violence and subversive actions against the base." Garth E. Thomson, a boilermaker, Eric Ball, a gardener, and Lloyd Harvey, an auto mechanic, all volunteered to burn down GTMO's wooden buildings. Fredrick Murray proposed that the Jamaicans march on the base commander's quarters to demand their "rights." Michael A. Chavannes and Adrian A. Gayle offered to carry letters to Fidel Castro. And Steadman Bloomfield stuck a knife in the table and threatened "to get some 'white meat.'" The U.S. Navy immediately terminated and deported the eight Jamaican contract employees who allegedly led the meeting. The Jamaican labor minister and prime minister "congratulated" the U.S. officials for their swift action and agreed to enhance their security clearance procedures. The U.S. Navy's ability to bring foreign workers to the base at will and likewise to deport them, all without publicity or protest, opened a new era of migration to the base.[3]

When I found this incident in the U.S. archives, I first interpreted it as an example of how the Cuban revolution remained a potent touchstone for Jamaican contract workers at GTMO.[4] Despite the fact that the U.S. Navy had fired its local Cuban workforce, it could not entirely escape its political geography or the anti-imperial imagination the Cuban revolution had sparked throughout the developing world. In fact, Jamaican contract workers had threatened to leave the base and lodge their complaints directly with Castro. However, when I recounted this event to Ricardo Baylor, a former Cuban base worker who had been laid off in 1964, he offered his own analysis. He agreed with the U.S. Navy's actions; the contract workers were "troublemakers." More to the point, the Cuban workers had never been so difficult. He believed the U.S. Navy had thrown out its best workers and so was forced to cope with under-skilled and ungrateful employees. In Ricardo's view, the Jamaican contract workers were replacement workers, akin to scabs, who had taken his job and his financial security. Although most of his bitterness was directed at the U.S. government, he felt no sympathy for the Jamaicans.[5]

The divisions in GTMO's post-1964 workforce represented competing generations, nationalities, political perspectives, and, as in Ricardo Baylor's case, degrees of luck. Three groups of workers coexisted on the base: overseas contract workers, Cuban permanent base residents, and Cuban commuters. The Jamaican contract labor program underscored the overlapping legacies of U.S. imperialism and Caribbean migration to Guantánamo. U.S. sugar interests had successfully recruited West Indian migrants to eastern Cuba in the early twentieth century, and in the late twentieth century, the U.S. military's labor needs brought Jamaican workers straight to GTMO. A small contingent of Cuban commuters and exiles worked alongside these Jamaican contract workers, but the U.S. military base in Guantánamo Bay was well on its way to reinventing its civilian workforce into an all-contract, migrant population. This model de-emphasized GTMO's location within Cuba, even as the U.S. Navy romanticized the presence of the elderly, long-standing Cuban workers. The remaining Cubans and the Jamaican contract workers represented two generations of the U.S. Navy's labor strategies. U.S. officials preserved elements from their 1940s and 1950s neocolonial practices, while they simultaneously restructured the base as a postmodern, deterritorialized workplace.

Animosity between Cuba and the United States remained palpable throughout the mid-1960s, and in 1966 a U.S. sentry shot and killed Luis Ramírez López, a member of the Cuban Brigada de la Frontera.[6] The U.S. claimed that Luis Ramírez López had infiltrated the base and was shot on the U.S. side of the border, while the Cuban government claimed he was shot without provocation on the Cuban side. This tragedy triggered another round of political bluster with the Cubans heralding him as a martyr.[7] Yet despite the public acrimony, by 1967 even Cuban accounts reported that provocations, including gunshots, verbal harassment, territorial violations, and injured soldiers decreased in severity and ebbed to a low-grade hum. For example, the Cuban government recorded seventy-nine shots fired into Cuban territory in 1966, but only two in 1967.[8] With the U.S. military's focus on the Vietnam War, GTMO was out of the strategic spotlight and was one of the safer places at which a U.S. marine or sailor could serve. The base gained a reputation as a "28,000 acre amusement park," and "a good place to become an alcoholic," albeit, a paradise without available heterosexual gratification.[9]

Despite GTMO's limited military function, it remained under U.S. control even after the United States had relinquished its claims to the Chaguaramas base in Trinidad and the Panama Canal, for the simple reason that the base was in Cuba. The United States did not want to provide a symbolic victory to Fidel Castro or the Soviet Union.[10] In many ways, the base became an anachronism, with minimal strategic use. Yet in other ways, the base developed a new purpose, one closely tied to its increasing isolation from Cuba.

JAMAICAN CONTRACT WORKERS

After 1964, when the U.S. Navy began its search for new workers to replace its reliance on Cuban commuters, it found that the costs and challenges were daunting. U.S. civilian employees typically earned three times the average local salary. Moreover, because of GTMO's isolation, the U.S. Navy had difficulty recruiting suitable civilian workers from the United States. GTMO attracted only below-average U.S. applicants and people with "drinking and other emotional and/or escapist type problems."[11] Outside employees also required substantially more infrastructure. The Cuban commuters had required "practically no logistic[al] support," but replacements from the United States or a third country would "impose tremendous new requirements" on "housing, messing, transportation, and every conceivable form of physical and moral support."[12] The U.S. Navy added that Cuban domestic workers had freed military wives from their household responsibilities and, as a result, 160 U.S. women had joined GTMO's civilian workforce. Base officials estimated that with the termination of local maids, U.S. women would no longer be able to hold these base jobs. To fill the openings on the base, GTMO would have to recruit outside workers, ideally at low wages. The U.S. Navy calculated it saved five million dollars by hiring Jamaican contract workers rather than U.S. civilians.[13]

By 1967 the U.S. Navy employed more than 1,200 Jamaican contract workers.[14] They were hired on four-month, renewable contracts as cooks, drivers, janitors, construction workers, cashiers, and employees in the Public Works Department. Jamaicans faced many hardships, including overcrowded living facilities, marked by leaking roofs, noise, filth, poor sanitation, and an acute lack of privacy.[15] They also lived far from home and without the support of a family unit. Even though base wages were pegged to the prevailing Kingston economy, psychological and material difficulties were not included in their monetary compensation. As a result, it was difficult for the base to retain skilled workers for any extended period of time.

The U.S. Navy and the Jamaican government developed a relationship that reinforced Jamaica's neocolonial and Cold War position vis-à-vis the United States. Jamaica had gained its independence from Great Britain in 1962, and Alexander Bustamante, the first prime minister of Jamaica, firmly positioned himself as a staunch U.S. ally and an unwavering anti-communist.[16] There was a verbal agreement that the Jamaican Ministry of Labor would recruit workers, conduct security checks, and provide physical examinations of all potential GTMO hires. This arrangement accentuated the Jamaican government's Cold War stance against Communist incursions in the Caribbean and its desire to foster closer economic ties with the United States. It also illustrated Jamaica's dependent position on the United States; it did not even have the power to demand an official labor agreement with the U.S. Navy. Instead, the Jamaican overseas contract program operated on an informal basis and without a written agreement throughout the 1960s.[17]

The Jamaican contract worker program was indicative of a new era of U.S. influence and power in the Caribbean. The United States demanded an ideological commitment to anti-communism, while taking advantage of high unemployment and economic distress in Jamaica. This neocolonial relationship intertwined many elements of traditional colonialism, such as unequal economic power and paternalistic disdain, along with the U.S. neocolonial need to celebrate formal independence and national sovereignty.

On a day-to-day basis, the U.S. Navy, in a decidedly colonial manner, criticized the Jamaican government and disparaged Jamaican contract workers as uncooperative and under-skilled. For example, U.S. officials were frustrated by the lackadaisical attitude of Jamaican officials and poor communication with the Jamaican Ministry of Labor. It took approximately 4.2 months to recruit an unskilled employee from Jamaica, a lag that GTMO officials believed was excessive. The U.S. Navy also claimed that Jamaican contract workers were less qualified than their Cuban counterparts. In a base-wide survey, officials concluded that 21.3 percent of the Jamaican workers did not possess the requisite skill level for their current positions. U.S. officials also complained that training Jamaicans was counterproductive. Once workers acquired new skills, they often chose to find better jobs in Kingston rather than renew their base contracts.[18]

These objections also reflected the cultural legacies of British rule and U.S. attitudes toward young, black male employees in the late 1960s. Colonial and racist attitudes dominated managers' critiques of Jamaican workers. For example, the 1967 Workforce Study suggested that the Jamaican workers' "morale problems" were based on their general immaturity, inability to plan for the future, and "their fundamental and unsophisticated attitudes toward sex." U.S. supervisors openly criticized the Jamaicans' "lack of native industry," "color," "language," and "body odor," and then "branded most Jamaicans as worthless." The report concluded that these "deprecatory" and "demeaning" attitudes reinforced new employees' lack of motivation and general discontent.[19] While recognizing that U.S. disrespect created a negative work environment, U.S. officials had no qualms about taking advantage of this cheap labor source or reinforcing the military's hierarchy. For example, in 1973 a group of enlisted U.S. sailors organized a recreational center, but they did not want to clean or maintain it. According to an *Esquire* profile, Chief Ray Schrepple solved their problem: "I told 'em go ahead and hire yourself a Jamaican at a dollar an hour. So now the place is spotless and the boys don't have to clean it up."[20] Even an enlisted man could hire a Jamaican contract worker to do the dirty work for him.

The overseas Jamaican contract program overlapped with an older generation of West Indians who had traditionally been the most privileged workers on the base. In the 1940s and 1950s, GTMO had hired West Indian migrants and their descendants in disproportionate numbers, and these English-speaking men and women still represented a significant percentage of the remaining Cuban commuters and permanent base residents.[21] These two West Indian populations—the older Cubans of West Indian descent and the newer Jamaican contract workers—occupied two sides of GTMO's labor policies and neocolonial stereotypes. On the one hand, the Cuban–West Indian commuters and permanent residents were valued as loyal, well-behaved, and highly skilled employees, and they themselves often reinforced this sentiment. On the other hand, the U.S. officials and the older workers looked down on the new wave of Jamaican contract workers as disorderly, rude, and unskilled.

The elderly Cubans of West Indian descent were quick to distinguish themselves from the Jamaicans. For example, Derek Stedman worked on the base from 1945 through 1991. Both of his parents were Jamaican migrants, and in Guantánamo he belonged to a Masonic Lodge for West Indian descendants. However, when I asked him about the Jamaican contract workers, he did not identify himself with the Jamaicans. He commented: "There were many differences [between the Jamaicans and the Cubans], because several of them did not want to work. They were good-for-nothing, they didn't want to work. And then you gave them work and they didn't [work]. . . . Many of them were thrown out and sent back to Jamaica."[22] Victor Davis, another long-term base commuter, also reflected this division. In Cuba, Victor identified quite strongly with the West Indian community. Not only had he lived in Jamaica as an adolescent, but he was also an active member of the British West Indian Welfare Centre and played cricket each Sunday. However, when he spoke about the Jamaicans and the Cubans on the base, he aligned himself with the Cubans. In his opinion, many of the Jamaican contract workers "were a bit rough" and would try and steal things off the base and break the law. He did not report these incidents, because he did not want to be a "stoolie or something like that," but he added that "we, the Cubans, we don't do like that. If it's against the law, we don't do that."[23] GTMO officials also noted that the Cuban base residents did not welcome the Jamaican contract employees in their living quarters, considering them "noisy" and "undisciplined."[24]

The testimonies of these two men reflect the precarious position of the Cuban–West Indian commuters and their generational position. Both Derek Stedman and Victor Davis belonged to West Indian associations in Guantánamo, yet this affiliation did not forge a bond of solidarity with post-1964 Jamaican contract laborers. In fact, it was quite the reverse. The elderly commuters were firmly situated in their Cuban political economy, and their ties were to an older West Indian community *within* Cuba. And Victor was wrong that Cubans did not steal. They had done so repeatedly in the past. It was the new risk to their employment and the economic differential between base employment and work in revolutionary Cuba that made commuting workers so cautious and well-behaved, not their nationality.

The Jamaican contract workers represented a new phase in GTMO's labor history. Despite supervisors' complaints and the resentment of older workers, this labor model came with many benefits for the base that the pre-revolutionary commuter system did not deliver. The U.S. Navy did not have to negotiate with a local municipality. It could also conduct the vast majority of labor relations out of the public spotlight. Although the Jamaican contract labor program was not secret, it received very little public attention in Cuba, Jamaica, or the United States. There was no Jamaican equivalent of *La Voz del Pueblo* or *El Vigilante* publicizing base workers' concerns to a broader community. And although the U.S. Navy had to maintain amicable relations with the Jamaican Ministry of Labor, it was not occupying Jamaican territory or violating Jamaican sovereignty. As a result, it did not have to make many concessions to a foreign national government. The United States could also easily eliminate any worker opposition by not renewing an individual's contract. Workers' complaints were managed through a designated, base-sanctioned Jamaican-Cuban Civic and Recreation Council. The possibility of an independent union had disappeared.

The one time a Jamaican contract worker entered the public spotlight was when Trevor Berbick, the man Mike Tyson later defeated in his first title match, became a heavyweight champion in the early 1980s. Berbick had learned to box when he was a contract employee at GTMO. Hired as a clerk and machine operator, he later worked in the U.S. Marine Corps' nightclub. He was supposed to keep order in the club, and he sometimes needed to throw a punch rather than "swat them [marines] with menus or a sommelier's key." Berbick began taking boxing lessons and honed his craft on the base. "After that I never had any trouble. They're supposed to be toughies, but once I established myself as champion of the base, they gave me respect. The best way to be friends with a marine is to beat him up."[25]

Berbick's "friendship" with the marines might have been established through a corporeal punch, but the U.S. Navy used a far more staid and official set of symbols. In the 1960s GTMO established an elaborate annual Jamaican Independence Day celebration. It was accompanied by reggae music, displays of U.S. and Jamaican flags, and "traditional Jamaican foods," such as curried goat, and saltfish and ackee. In these ceremonies, U.S. officials and Jamaican ministers made speeches attesting to the mutually beneficial relationship between the United States and Jamaica. For example, in 1969 Rear Admiral Hildreth compared the Jamaicans to the mission-essential, back-up crews in the Apollo space expedition. "Without the Jamaicans, life at Guantánamo Bay would not be the same."[26] The 1982 edition of the *History of Guantánamo Bay* trumpeted the importance of GTMO's Jamaican Independence Day celebrations as a sign of the base's harmonious relations with the Jamaican workers.[27] Many U.S. and Jamaican officials visited the base for this public festivity, including L. G. Newland, the Jamaican minister of labor and national insurance, and W. T. M. Beale, the U.S. ambassador to Jamaica.[28] In 1973 the mayor of Kingston even opted to celebrate Jamaican Independence Day on GTMO rather than in Jamaica.[29] The Jamaican government continues the overseas worker program to this day as a government-to-government initiative. It places men and women predominantly in the hotel and agricultural industries in the United States and Canada. The remittances add more than 1.2 billion dollars annually to the Jamaican economy, and they aid the development of a Jamaican middle class.[30] The GTMO contract labor program is a small component of this much larger overseas employment project, but it persists nonetheless. The Jamaican government recruits skilled workers in information technology and accounting, as well as barbers, cooks, and store clerks for the base.[31] As recently as 2005, the *Guantánamo Gazette* dedicated a full-page photospread, "Jamaican Independence Day: GTMO Style," which appropriated Bob Marley's "Redemption Song" in its celebration. Jamaica's postmaster general attended the festivities, and Jam Rock entertainment provided reggae music.[32] In this public display, U.S. neocolonialism was projected in its most positive light, providing work and economic opportunity with the approval of an independent, yet less powerful, island nation.

This celebration marked the *neo* side of U.S. neocolonialism. The U.S. government hired Jamaicans on short-term contracts because it had failed to accept Cuba's political independence. The United States could recognize Jamaican independence only because the Jamaican government remained such a junior partner to U.S. military and economic power. This created the paradox of celebrating Jamaican independence, even as the military occupied Cuban territory. The U.S. Navy set about reconstructing the earlier language of good neighborliness that had been common in the 1940s and 1950s, but now the Jamaicans replaced the Cubans as the neocolonial subjects. By 2000 many of the base workers were also Filipinos and, in a telling performance, the U.S. Navy now celebrates Philippine Independence Day on the U.S. naval base in Guantánamo Bay.[33] Thus, without irony, the U.S. Navy publicly and proudly proclaims its ability to provide work for contract laborers, while ignoring the legacies of 1898 and military occupation in the Caribbean and Pacific.

PERMANENT BASE RESIDENTS, EXILES, AND REFUGEES

When confronted with the choice, "Cuba or the base" in 1964, hundreds of workers chose to stay on the base in exile or had already defected.[34] The U.S. naval base dubbed them "permanent base residents," and this community embodied two reinforcing possibilities. First, the workers who remained on the base constituted a relatively inexpensive and exceptionally loyal population. Their continued dedication not only to the United States, but to GTMO in particular, justified and exemplified the United States' neocolonial benevolence and uninterrupted occupation. Second, their permanent status was a potent reminder of the possibility of exile *within* Cuba. Since the Cuban revolution, hundreds of men and women have attempted to leave Cuba by jumping over the fence and swimming across Guantánamo Bay. This avenue of escape and knowledge of U.S. protection transformed GTMO into a beacon of freedom for disenchanted Cubans, just as the U.S. military had hoped. But GTMO's liminal status as a place governed by the United States, but not of the United States, resulted in dystopian possibilities as well. The base could be a sanctuary or it could be a prison for these exiles and refugees.

The U.S. military allowed Cuban base workers to stay within the confines of GTMO as long as they continued working, but many wanted to relocate their families to the United States. In 1965 there were 642 permanent base residents; in 1966 the number decreased to 511; and in 1967 there were 377 Cubans living on the base.[35] Base residents were able to participate in the 1965 Varadero Family Claim Program, or "Freedom Flights," which facilitated Cuban migration to the United States. This program created a legal channel and enabled émigrés to sponsor their families in Cuba. The U.S. and Cuban governments authorized two flights a day between Varadero, Cuba, and Miami, Florida, from 1965 through 1971.[36] Erasing the distinction between U.S. territory and the U.S. naval base, "permanent base residents" were granted the same rights as Cuban residents in the United States to participate in the Varadero program.[37] With this decree, the U.S. government signaled the base workers' unique status. Although the base workers did not live *in* the United States, they too could sponsor their families and resettle in the United States. Once family members left Cuba, many base workers joined their relatives and did not return to GTMO.

The U.S. Navy's attitude toward this population was mixed. Ideologically, it remained committed to the Cuban permanent residents as "valuable" anti-communists and "some of its [the base's] finest worker talent." They were also comparatively "inexpensive" employees. In the short run, permanent base residents were highly desirable workers, for they possessed relatively high skills at a low pay grade. For example, the 1967 Workforce Study cited Rudolfo Núñez, a permanent base resident, as a known quantity, more reliable and less expensive than a U.S. civilian or Jamaican contract worker. Replacing him would cost at least three times the U.S. Navy's current expenditures. Still, the U.S. government feared encroaching expenses if it sheltered the permanent base residents indefinitely. Cuban residents were similar to the Jamaican contract workers in that they required additional housing, dining, and support services. In fact, the U.S. Navy prevented most permanent base residents from bringing their spouses and families to GTMO, because it feared fostering an old-age home within the base. As symbols of neocolonial loyalty, the U.S. Navy could not just eject the long-term base workers once they had aged. When permanent base residents were no longer productive workers, the U.S. Navy felt compelled to provide medical care and burial services for them. It allowed permanent base residents to be buried in the base cemetery as "destitute wards of the United States" and designated this "charity" as a "Cold War activity."[38]

The U.S. Navy predicted that by 1970 there would be less than 100 permanent base residents, including a few families, 20–25 elderly retirees, and a dozen single women who could do only "light domestic work."[39] While the population did decline, a steady number remained fixtures on the base. In 1976 there were approximately 370 full-time Cuban residents, in 1984 there were still 188, and in 2006 only 12 elderly Cuban men and women continued to live on the base.[40] These men and women made GTMO, and not the United States or Guantánamo, Cuba, their home. This small cohort opted to stay on their native soil, but in the managed, safe, and highly structured confines of a U.S. military community.

With the worst of the U.S.-Cuba confrontations behind them, the U.S. Navy sponsored the first post-revolutionary Cuban-American Friendship Day on December 10, 1969. Much like Jamaican Independence Day had celebrated Jamaican culture, this day boasted Cuban music, roast pork, and awards for long-term Cuban employees.[41] The holiday commemorated the sixty-sixth anniversary of the 1903 Lease Agreement. The date was clearly meant to imply a mutually beneficial military agreement and ignore the decades-long Cuban critique of the base treaty as well as contemporary hostilities with the Cuban government. In 1970 GTMO's rear admiral applauded the Cuban base workers' tenacity and endurance: "You represent the permanent members of the base. Most of us are transients, we come and we go. But the Cuban community is permanent. I feel your contributions are the greatest."[42] Base officials later moved Cuban-American Friendship Day to the birthday of José Martí, the father of modern Cuba's independence and nationalist movements.[43] By 2006 the U.S. Navy celebrated Cuban-American Friendship Day with a group run from the base camp to the northeast gate, led by U.S. marines bearing U.S. and Cuban flags. The 2006 GTMO commander echoed the 1970 rear admiral's praise of Cuban workers' longevity and commitment: "They [the Cuban workers] are our corporate memory, our naval station elders, and our true host nation support."[44] With only twelve permanent residents remaining and three elderly Cuban commuters, this ceremony illustrated how the base projected itself as an exemplary, paternalist employer. From the U.S. Navy's perspective, the permanent base workers' continued decision to make their homes on GTMO symbolically justified more than one hundred years of U.S. military occupation.

Permanent base residents also embodied the tragedy of divided Cuban families since the revolution. As thousands of Cubans have resettled in the United States, they have often been kept from visiting their families by financial constraints and legal impediments, while others have stayed away because of their own political antipathy to the revolutionary government. However, in Guantánamo, families were not divided between Havana and Miami, but within their own country. For years, men and women who chose "the base" could not communicate frequently or openly with their relatives who chose "Cuba." In one emotional example, a 1991 British television program profiled two brothers. One, Patrick Duffus, had defected onto the base and remained there as a permanent base resident, while the other, his brother Granville Duffus, remained a commuter from Guantánamo. The two brothers did not speak to each other on a regular basis. Patrick feared getting his brother in trouble and did not even feel comfortable inviting him to his home for lunch. He did not want his brother to risk losing his Cuban pass. These interviews were poignant as both men justified and came to terms with their choices. Granville appreciated the healthcare and education his children and grandchildren had received from the Cuban revolution. He expressed no regrets about remaining in Cuba. "I regard it as a good life—at least I am living in my country. This is where I was born, and this is my country. So I prefer to go to work and come back every evening with my family. He's satisfied with his life over there, and I'm satisfied with my life over here." His brother Patrick was more pensive. "I am a U.S. citizen, and I'm living free. I bought my house in Clearwater, Florida, and I'll do about two years more and then go to Clearwater, Florida. . . . I just want to enjoy life. That's one thing I'd like to go visit [Guantánamo]–just to visit the place where I used to run around barefooted. I would take off my shoes and run up and down and look for my old friends, if they are still alive. I would love that. That's one thing always on my mind. I would love to go and visit my hometown where I was born and grown up."[45] This family separation and sense of exile increased in intensity, because the geographic proximity was so negligible. Base residents were exiles, even though they remained in Cuba.

The permanent base residents also marked GTMO as a place of refuge where Cuban dissidents could seek escape. Beginning in 1959, thousands of opponents of the Cuban revolution traveled to the United States as "tourists" or with visa waivers. The United States classified Cuban émigrés as political refugees rather than immigrants, because they were fleeing a Socialist, and soon Communist, dictatorship. In the language of the

Cold War, Cuban refugees represented Castro's oppression and the United States' promise of freedom. To aid these anti-communist refugees, the United States eased their travel from Cuba to Miami and bypassed immigration restrictions.[46] GTMO could also be a point of departure and, in January 1961, U.S. citizens and their dependents living in eastern Cuba were admitted onto the base and flown to the United States. The *New York Times* noted that the men and women who flocked to the base were only "technically Americans." These "Cuban Yankees" or "Yankee Cubans" "had Cuban spouses, spoke Spanish, and had built bombs for Fidel Castro. Now, they wanted to leave."[47] For this brief moment, men and women who could demonstrate claims to U.S. citizenship were allowed to enter the base legally and fly to Miami. Proof of U.S. citizenship, which had once enabled workers to leverage jobs, was now a final ticket onto the base and out of Cuba. But these were not the only men and women to seek an exit through GTMO. In fact, future refugees would not have to "prove" any Americanness, technical or otherwise. Instead, hostility and opposition to the Castro government would be enough.

Men and women without access to airline flights or U.S. relatives turned to GTMO. They began jumping over the fence and swimming across the bay as early as 1960. The 1903 Lease Agreement explicitly prevented the base from being a sanctuary for individuals fleeing Cuban law, and it included language governing the United States to deliver "fugitives from justice" back to Cuban authorities.[48] In violation of the 1903 treaty, GTMO operated a quiet policy of sheltering refugees from revolutionary Cuba and ferrying them to U.S. shores.

From 1964 until 1969, the number of Cubans who braved the minefields, scaled the base fences, and swam across the bay increased each year. In 1965 there were 72 "fence jumpers," and the number climbed to 138 in 1966, and to 515 in 1967.[49] In 1968 it doubled to more than 1,000.[50] The Brigada de la Frontera's objective changed from protecting Cuba against U.S. aggression to preventing Cuban refugees from making their escape. Despite its vigilance, dozens of Cubans reached the base in the 1960s, placing a significant burden on GTMO's "very meager refugee facilities." GTMO officials added, "It was absolutely necessary at all times to cover the program with complete secrecy, yet at the same time, house, clothe, feed, interrogate, and as quickly as possible evacuate the large numbers to Miami by air."[51] The least discreet incident occurred in 1969, when at least 150 Cubans reportedly rammed a bus across GTMO's fence. A gunfight between the refugees and the Brigada de la Frontera ensued, and 88 Cubans reached the base. The remaining men and women were either shot or captured by the Cuban military.[52] The U.S. Navy sent the surviving refugees to Miami where they were processed alongside the Varadero arrivals who had U.S. sponsors.[53] On arrival in Florida, reporters became more skeptical of the refugees' stories. For example, how had no one been injured by the landmines, and how had 88 people scaled the barbed-wire fence without anyone being wounded? *Newsweek* suggested that the U.S. guards had helped facilitate the incident, but then denied it because of the 1903 Lease Agreement's provisions against aiding fugitives.[54] Regardless, Cubans recognized the U.S. naval base as a potential exit route. As one refugee explained, "If the road to Guantánamo was open, the base would sink under the sea from the number of Cubans who would go there to get away."[55]

This conception of Guantánamo as a safe haven, a beacon, and a U.S. refuge began appearing in Cuban exile literature. Jorge Oliva, a poet born in Guantánamo, fled Cuba by swimming across Guantánamo Bay. He then came to the United States, where he lived in New York until his death in 1986. His poetry invoked the proximity of Caimanera and GTMO, and it shed light on his fateful swim. Now rather than *francos* and liberty parties, the Beach Boys and their electric guitars radiated music and ideas of "America" into Cuba:

> The night spread out over the bay
>
> It is the time of hot and salty wind,
> the rumor of the sea,
> of the cruel singing of the crickets
> of the sleepless lights of Caimanera
> and its everlasting, bristly wakefulness
> in the apparent stillness of the summer.
>
> Not far,
> where the sea opens and breaks into the bay,
> the "beach boys" violently tear up the night,
> trample,
>   yell
> with their brilliant electric guitars
> from the "U.S. American Forces Radio Guantánamo Bay."[56]

Oliva's poem did not invoke the decadence and debauchery of the U.S. culture that invaded Caimanera and Guantánamo in the 1940s and 1950s, but rather an energy and possibility vibrating from the base and a break from the "cruel singing crickets" and "sleepless lights of Caimanera."

Cuban writer Reinaldo Arenas memorialized Oliva's swim across Guantánamo Bay as a vision of possibility in his memoir and critique of revolutionary Cuba, *Before Night Falls.* He recounted, "Even to own a diving mask and flippers was a privilege in Cuba. . . . Jorge Oliva trained with them many, many times, until one day he was able to swim to the Guantánamo Bay naval base, and freedom."[57] In his book, Arenas celebrated Oliva's arrival in New York and included an anecdote where Oliva mocked the revolutionary establishment. According to exile lore, Oliva sent a telegram to Nicolas Guillén, the revolutionary and nationalist poet: "Didn't you call me a *pargo* [Cuba: red snapper/gay]? Well, I swam away."[58] Later Arenas traveled to Guantánamo himself, a town he described as "horrendous," "flatter and more provincial even than Holguín," in hopes of replicating Oliva's swim. But despite attempts to evade the Cuban soldiers, he failed to reach the base.[59] Instead, Arenas left Cuba with the Mariel Boatlift in 1980.

These representations of the base as a sanctuary existed alongside equally strong dystopian tendencies embedded in GTMO. For when Arenas fled with the Mariel Boatlift, the United States did not welcome this second generation of Cuban refugees with the same enthusiasm it had for earlier exiles. In 1980 the Cuban government opened the Mariel port to any Cuban who wished to leave. More than 120,000 congregated at the docks and piled into a small fleet of boats captained by Cuban Americans who risked their lives to transport these men and women to Florida. The Castro government used this as an opportunity to expel problematic individuals from the island, including criminals, the mentally ill, dissidents, and homosexuals. As a result, the Mariel generation was characterized as delinquent, and even deviant. Although the convicted criminals constituted a relatively small percentage of the overall population, they dominated the press coverage and public representation of the Mariel Boatlift.[60]

In fact, several U.S. politicians openly suggested sending these undesirable refugees back to Cuba, specifically through the U.S. naval base in Guantánamo Bay. They recognized GTMO's ambiguous position as a stateless space, within Cuba, but not of it. For example, West Virginian Senator Robert Byrd argued that Cuban refugees who had been rioting at U.S. Fort Chaffee, Arkansas, (a refugee relocation camp) should be "identified, arrested, and deported." If Cuba would not accept them, the United States should send them to GTMO, "open the gates and just push them through."[61] A year later, a thousand Cubans remained at Fort Chaffee without U.S. homes, and many of them were designated as mentally ill, homosexual, disabled, or elderly. The Reagan administration considered transporting these individuals to GTMO. Presidential spokesperson David Gergen emphasized that such a move would not technically be deportation, because the United States did not "consider the base to be Cuban territory."[62] And in even stronger language, New York Mayor Ed Koch recommended, "We should ship them all back to Guantánamo Bay, build a prison on the edge of the base and then move the fence back to the other side, so the prison would be on Cuban property. A judge can stop you from taking territory, but not from giving it back."[63]

In the end, the Mariel Boatlift refugees were not sent to GTMO. Yet, in an eerie actualization of Gergen and Koch's 1980 suggestions, the U.S. naval base became a detention center for undesirable Haitian and Cuban refugees in the 1990s. Haitians first arrived on the base via rafts and small boats as early as 1977.[64] The Haitians were escaping a brutal dictatorship, but because it was not a Communist dictatorship, the U.S. did not grant them refugee status. In 1991 a military coup toppled Haitian President Jean Bertrand Aristide's government, resulting in an exodus of Haitians who sought asylum in the United States. Rather than offering protection, the United States intercepted more than twenty thousand Haitians at sea and dispatched the vast majority to GTMO. The United States claimed that Haitians held at GTMO were not protected by the U.S. Constitution. It then executed a legal strategy to repatriate them without legal counsel. The Clinton administration euphemistically deemed GTMO a "safe haven." Haitians could either remain in the camps indefinitely or return to Haiti, but they would not be allowed entrance into the United States. With the reinstatement of Aristide, the majority returned to Haiti. Despite its stated goals to represent liberty and U.S. values, GTMO did not act as a symbol of hope for the Haitian community.[65]

Cubans who were accustomed to preferential treatment in U.S. immigration policy were shocked when they too were detained at GTMO. In 1994 the Cuban government announced that those who wanted to leave the island on their own initiative would not be stopped. Given the economic hardships of the post-Soviet Special Period, thousands of Cubans pieced together hand-made rafts, which they hoped would carry them to the United States. This mode of transportation gave them their name, the *balseros,* or raft people. These men and women fully expected to be allowed entry like previous generations of Cuban refugees. However, not wanting to encourage a mass exodus, the Clinton administration intercepted the *balseros* and redirected more than twenty-five thousand Cubans to GTMO. Forced to live in holding camps, the Cuban refugees lacked adequate housing and daily necessities. Unrest, protest, and boredom characterized the camps, as the *balseros* waited for a change of policy and safe passage to the United States. Cuban Americans in Miami were outraged that their compatriots were denied access to the United States. To them, it seemed a betrayal and capitulation to the Castro government.

In the end, Cold War logic overcame broader human rights principles; Cubans would be admitted to the United States, and Haitians would be sent back to Haiti. In the aftermath of this *balsero* crisis, the U.S. and Cuban governments negotiated the "wet foot, dry foot policy" to deter future immigration. This policy allowed the *balseros* on GTMO to enter the United States, but all future *balseros* found at sea would be returned to Cuba. Only those who reached land would be granted refugee status and allowed to stay. The policy also provided a mechanism for more Cubans to solicit visas legally through the U.S. Interest Section.[66]

Except for the remaining elderly permanent base residents, GTMO's utopian promise as a refuge within Cuba had vanished. GTMO's proximity became a cruel paradox, which offered the temptation of U.S. residence, but the living conditions of a jail. Cubans and Haitians now associated GTMO with harsh surroundings, prison-like camps, and lengthy delays. Throughout the crisis, the United States established a precedent whereby GTMO did not have to extend U.S. legal guarantees to all its inhabitants.

THE COMMUTERS

And through all the political changes and hostilities, a small cohort of base workers continued to live in revolutionary Cuba and commute daily to the base. After the massive layoffs in 1964, the U.S. Navy retained approximately 750 local commuters. By 1967 this number had dropped to 450.[67] These commuters, a predominantly male, skilled, and long-serving group, straddled the worlds of socialist Guantánamo and the anti-communist naval base. As one long-term commuter noted, "We live in two systems . . . but we are used to it."[68] Derek Stedman, another worker, remembered, "There was a time when it was a little, a little, I'm going to say it was a little dangerous to cross the border. We had to cross every morning, going and coming, but we all got used to it."[69] Often these workers described themselves as "loners" who kept out of politics.[70] In one manner, these last commuters had chosen to throw their lots in with the Cuban revolutionary project; they had more than ample opportunities to defect and resettle in the United States. But in another manner, the commuters became the symbolic link to an older era of U.S.-Cuban and GTMO-Guantánamo relations when base employment and exchange had been the norm. The commuters' increasingly anachronistic presence highlighted both the lack of economic opportunities in revolutionary Guantánamo and workers' attachment to their country and their homes.

Between 1964 and 1968, vigilance and fear remained palpable along the *frontera*. The Cuban government continued to keep close tabs on the remaining commuters. Just as in the 1940s, the journey was arduous, time-consuming, and psychologically challenging. A Cuban government bus fetched commuters at 4:00 A.M. in Guantánamo. It would drive them to the checkpoint at the northeast gate, where workers would change into their base clothes and pass through the Cuban inspections. The commuters would then walk over a mile through the "cattle chute" to the U.S. side, where they would again be inspected. Once over the U.S. border, they entered a second bus, which delivered them to their various posts within the base. In the evenings, the process reversed itself. It took approximately two hours each way. Despite the political hostilities, for most commuters the economic compensation remained worth the time, difficulties, and surveillance.

With regular gunshots fired across the fence, ten Cuban casualties, and the fear of CIA-engineered invasion plans, the GTMO border was a volatile Cold War flash point in the mid-1960s.[71] The commuters were the only population permitted to travel between Guantánamo and GTMO. Their access made both the U.S. and Cuban governments suspect them as prospective spies and conduits of information. The U.S. Navy's Investigative Service stated that the commuters could, even without "malicious intent," share detailed accounts about the base with their friends and family and, in this way, inadvertently "divulge a great deal of information" to the Cuban government.[72] U.S. officials believed that the Cuban government planted spies within the commuter population, who reported on workers who cheated on exchanging their take-home pay for pesos, appeared to be working for base intelligence, and made anti-Castro statements. The U.S. Navy also noted that Cuban security forces recruited yet more workers, labeled "unwilling informants," who collected information to keep their passes.[73] The report concluded, "It was quite evident that there was a concentrated effort on the part of the Government of Cuba to be continually aware of base activities, and an equally concentrated effort on the part of the naval counter-intelligence support activity was needed to combat it."[74] In this litany of intelligence reports, GTMO officers unwittingly opened and answered a few sensitive questions.[75] Why would the United States allow workers they suspected of spying to remain on the base? How many commuters *were* working for U.S. base intelligence? Why did either government permit Cuban employees to travel across the militarized border? Although this report did not directly refer to the CIA, the Cuban government's fears do not appear entirely unfounded. But the revolutionary authorities also never issued an outright ban on base employment. Along with the U.S. Navy, the Cuban government could also gain valuable intelligence from the base workers. Allowing a select group to commute, the U.S. and Cuban governments presumably believed that there was knowledge and access to be gained from this working-class exchange that outweighed the risks of sabotage or subversion.

By 1968–69, active provocations and violations of Cuban airspace and territory decreased, and the U.S. marines and Cuban soldiers stared across the fence with a studied vigilance that was soon characterized by boredom and monotony.[76] With the Vietnam War escalating in Southeast Asia, Cuba was no longer a dominant Cold War theater, and the military personnel stationed at GTMO complained of endless days and lack of purpose. No new Cuban hires were allowed, and in 1967 the U.S. Navy anticipated that the aging commuters would cease to be an integral part of the workforce by 1969, and by 1972, they would be "nonexistent."[77] However, rather than fading away or retreating to Guantánamo, the remaining Cuban commuters held doggedly to their jobs and continued traveling from Guantánamo to the base.

With the elimination of local commerce between Guantánamo and GTMO, Guantánamo faced an economic crisis after the Cuban revolution. Its identification with the U.S. naval base continued to shadow its representation within Cuba, and the revolutionary government sought to replace Guantánamo's dependence on commerce, mainly with agriculture. A 1967 economic study conducted by an academic team from the University of Havana criticized Guantánamo's lack of productive development. The great successes of the Cuban revolution had not had the same repercussions in Guantánamo as they had in the rest of the island.[78] Over the next decades, the revolutionary government aimed to reorient the local economy to salt mines, local construction, and sugar, coffee, cocoa, and citrus cultivation.[79] In 1977 the Cuban government divided Oriente into five separate provinces to decentralize regional administration. Guantánamo became an independent province, with the city of Guantánamo as its capital.[80] For most men and women, GTMO's economic influence was only a memory; however, its cultural power persisted. In Guantánamo, men and women remember that throughout the 1980s GTMO's radio and television channels often went unblocked, allowing them secret, but privileged, access to Solid Gold, Soul Train, and the Oprah Winfrey show. They embraced this clandestine North American pop culture, but it came with no material benefits. In fact, Guantánamo remained marginal and among Cuba's poorest regions. In 2004, it had the highest infant mortality rate in Cuba.[81]

In the face of food shortages and economic hardships, base commuters maintained a privileged position in Guantánamo. Even when they had to change their U.S. dollars into pesos, they had access to U.S. goods and medicines. Many workers even brought prescriptions from their relatives and filled them at the base dispensary. The U.S. Navy permitted this medical aid as part of its "humanitarian relationships with the civilian community."[82] The decline of the Cold War elevated these anomalous base workers to an even more advantaged class in the Guantánamo community. In the wake of a détente between the United States and Cuba during the Carter administration, the 1979 base commander advocated for commuters to receive U.S. government pensions. (Because of the U.S. economic embargo, an earlier generation of workers had to defect in order to receive their pensions.) This new provision covered those still working in 1979. After 1979, a commuter could retire, receive a U.S. government pension, and stay in Cuba. If he died before his spouse, his widow could collect the pension for the duration of her lifetime. This change in U.S. policy opened a direct route to economic security and relative wealth for the remaining commuters and their families.

The Cuban economy suffered enormously after the collapse of the Soviet Union and the termination of Soviet aid and preferential trading agreements. Fidel Castro euphemistically dubbed the early 1990s the "Special Period." Food shortages, gas shortages (which resulted in mass hitchhiking), and the absence of everything from cooking oil to soap defined the Special Period. These economic hardships hit eastern Cuba particularly hard, and many *orientales* moved to Havana without official residence papers, and crowded in with relatives. Men and women in Havana derided these eastern provincials as *los palestinos,* a snide reference to their unofficial status and desperate state. With the acute need to generate capital, the revolutionary government opened its doors to tourism in 1993 and authorized the circulation of the U.S. dollar for the first time.

This created a two-tiered economy in Cuba, whereby men and women who had access to U.S. dollars lived in relative comfort, while those who depended on Cuban pesos had extremely limited purchasing power. The final cohort of base commuters fell into the first category. For the first time since 1960, they no longer had to exchange their U.S. salaries for Cuban pesos. Instead, they could keep their U.S. dollars.

Each month the remaining commuters carry several thousand U.S. dollars across the *frontera* to distribute to the surviving pensioners and widows. The Cuban government takes a minimal fee from each pensioner, but there is no income tax. The retirees have an account book that lists each individual entitled to a pension, and they ensure that the money is properly distributed. As the average monthly salary in Cuba is equivalent to ten dollars, a base worker's pension of several hundred dollars a month is a fortune.[83]

The distribution of these pensions made the post-1979 commuters and retirees some of Guantánamo's wealthiest citizens. In contrast, workers who had been fired in 1964, or retired between 1964 and 1979, had limited access to this neocolonial privilege and hard currency. The result was a great deal of anger and hostility within the community. A small cottage industry of bureaucratic lobbying emerged whereby former base employees compiled their work histories and petitioned the U.S. Office of Personnel Management for their pensions. Still, even when a worker could document his or her employment and retirement contributions, the U.S. government refused to remit this money directly to Cuba. It argued the U.S. embargo prohibited U.S. dollars from entering the Cuban economy. As Walter Knight succinctly noted, "The retirement only covers people from 1979 until now. . . . They [the U.S. government] say that they are thinking to see if it can go to a third country, but the problem is they don't want to resolve it."[84] Most former base workers echoed the same complaint they had in 1964; they had been callously and heartlessly dismissed after contributing to the U.S. military's strength.

A few workers have managed to negotiate and arrange for a person to accept the pension in a third country, such as Spain. These intermediaries often take a significant cut, in the range of fifty percent, and then wire the difference to the elderly retiree in Cuba.[85] However, the vast majority are left with nothing but resentment. In my conversations with former GTMO employees, desperation and desire for their lost U.S. pensions was a constant refrain. In one meeting, three men agreed to speak with me, largely because they wanted to present their case for pensions to a broader audience. One had worked through the 1990s and received a U.S. pension. A second had worked in the Officers' Club until the mid-1970s, but this was a "non-appropriated" position and did not guarantee a pension. The third had been laid off in 1964. He had petitioned the U.S. government and provided documentation of his twenty-three years of service, but he had been repeatedly denied a pension. Throughout our conversation, these men insisted, "We are not political. We were workers, and we had nothing to do with politics. We only worked and worked and worked, without getting involved in any type of political situation with either country."[86] Because of the years of hostility, these men defined "political" narrowly, and they did not want to acknowledge that their employment had any political ramifications nor, in their old age, did they want to antagonize either government. International relations in this case meant the daunting task of lobbying the U.S. government for direct benefits from *within* Cuba.

Those who are lucky enough to receive their pensions are quite worried about their fates once the final three commuters end their daily trek to the base. These workers are already well past retirement age, but they are the crucial link between the base and Guantánamo. Because of the U.S. embargo, the direct courier and cash system is the only arrangement that has brought pensioners' U.S. dollars to Guantánamo. It is safeguarded only by the remaining commuters. The pensioners are hoping to negotiate an agreement with the U.S. Interest Section, so they can continue to receive their annuities when the final worker retires. The U.S. embargo and the lack of diplomatic relations stand in the way. Victor Davis believed base retirees were unfairly inconvenienced because they had chosen to live in Cuba. He explained with notable understatement, "We are living in Cuba, and due to some technicalities . . . we're considered a 'blocked country.'" He concluded somewhat optimistically, "What's the difference now, you know what I mean. . . . What's to really stop it [the pensions] from coming. . . . Yes, we are working on that."[87] Derek Stedman, another pensioner, was less hopeful, "The only thing we think about is what will happen when the last . . . [commuters] stay here [Guantánamo]. We have to see where we are going to get our pensions from."[88] And Walter Knight commented, "I believe that when no one continues commuting, we are going to have to resolve this problem one way or another."[89] In the mid-1990s, the U.S. Navy and U.S. Interest Section discussed several methods by which to facilitate the distribution of the pensions. However, as of this date, there is no agreement or plan in place.

Most of the workers today are not U.S. civilian service employees, and they do not have rights to U.S. pensions. Instead, private companies have followed in the footsteps of the Frederick Snare and Drake Winkleman corporations, and contract workers have become the norm. In 2007 two major firms with GTMO contracts are Burns and Roe, which operates GTMO's electrical and water utilities, and the Pentad Corporation, which provides food services. Burns and Roe's tenure on the base began during the 1964 water crisis; it was the engineering firm that built the desalinization plant. Since the 1990s, its scope has expanded to include sewage treatment, airfield and security lighting, facility repairs, and engineering support. It also oversees GTMO's port operations, including managing its tugboats, ferries, and watercraft services, and its air traffic control. In 2006, it won a ten-year utility contract valued at more than sixty million dollars, and an operating services contract worth 128 million dollars.[90] The company employs many Filipino contract workers. During GTMO's 2007 Philippine Independence Day celebration, the organizing committee explicitly thanked Burns and Roe for excusing Filipinos from work to attend dance rehearsals and the celebration. A Filipina employee for Burns and Roe was also crowned Miss Philippine Independence Day Celebration.[91] The Pentad Corporation, a Las Vegas–based firm, which supplies GTMO's dining halls, also recruits Filipino laborers.[92]

Many of the older commuters remarked on the difference between their government positions and the status of the new overseas contract workers. For example, Derek Stedman emphasized the emergence of private companies on the base: "Then the companies came and they took the work from the government . . . and then the thing changed, no? . . . Then the government isn't responsible. . . . The company was the one that had the work."[93] Walter Knight seconded this as a significant change, "They bring people here from India, from places where there are low wages. Filipinos. They pay them very little, but for them it is enough money. . . . Now there are all Jamaicans and Filipinos. Because now it is all contract—understand?" Working side by side contract employees, these elderly commuters recognize that the U.S. government no longer takes responsibility or offers comparable benefits to the new employees. Instead, workers have become less expensive and more expendable. When the final three Cuban commuters retire, the United States will be able to close the book on this loyal, but disproportionately expensive, workforce. It has found a new way to meet its labor needs independent from the Cuban community.

Finally, these last commuters who have stayed in Cuba have a sense of their historical importance. Many of the people I interviewed in

Guantánamo asked me where my video camera was, because the other interviews they had given were with journalists and TV crews. The remaining commuters had experienced Guantánamo's neocolonial heyday, the excesses of North American culture and consumption, the revolutionary movement against Batista, and the subsequent socialist government. Through it all, the base had defined their lives. Walter Knight offered an almost throw-away line at the end of our conversation, "*Yo eché mi vida a la base,*" an idiomatic phrase meaning "I threw my life in with the base." The ambivalence, compromises, and acceptance in his sentiment struck me as indicative of base workers' troubled positions and pragmatic choices. Walter continued: "You know that in life there are good parts and bad parts, and I am grateful because I have always earned . . . my salary. . . . It has helped me enough. Much of the treatment has changed—this is true—they treat me well. It has changed enough. . . . And you know, we are like relics, we Cubans who stay here [Cuba]. Ah . . . the whole world wants to know us. All the world wants to interview us, because they say that we are historical."[94]

Walter Knight and other base workers valued their U.S. government salaries, but they knew that neither the United States nor the Cuban government's promises were guaranteed. Thus, workers made choices and then had to live with them. Their narratives sketch a history of U.S.-Cuban relations that elude binaries and complicate easy analyses of U.S. imperialism or the Cuban revolution. Instead, the intricacies and daily negotiations between base workers and the U.S. naval base demonstrate a working-class history of foreign relations. As the U.S. military turns away from local employment strategies in its basing network, one recognizes that these men and women posed constraints and forced the United States to negotiate with local communities. Now, the U.S. naval base has found new workers from Jamaica and the Philippines who do not have any particular attachment to Cuba or Guantánamo. The legacies of 1898 have reinvented themselves in a decidedly twenty-first century idiom.

Epilogue
Post 9/11: Empire and Labor Redux

n 2004, Angelo de la Cruz, a forty-six-year-old Filipino worker, made
his living as a truck driver in Iraq. De la Cruz's journey to Iraq followed
the well-traveled path of many overseas workers. He had eight children, but he was unable to support his family in the Philippines. Seeking
opportunity and a high salary, de la Cruz traveled to Saudi Arabia where
he became an employee for the Saudi Arabian Trading and Construction
Company. On July 7, 2004, de la Cruz was transporting fuel from Saudi
Arabia to Iraq. En route, a contingent of insurgents identifying themselves with the Islamic Army of Iraq kidnapped de la Cruz. They demanded that the Philippines withdraw all of its military personnel from
Iraq by July 20, 2004, a month earlier than scheduled. If the Philippine
government did not comply, the kidnappers threatened to behead de la
Cruz.[1]

Under the leadership of President Gloria Arroyo, the Philippines had
joined President Bush's Coalition of the Willing and stationed fifty-one
"humanitarian" soldiers in Iraq. Strategically insignificant, this contingent demonstrated the Philippine government's public support for the
U.S. mission. However, the vast majority of Filipinos in Iraq did not belong to this military contingent. Rather, most worked as private contract
employees, as truck drivers, office workers, and maintenance staff in the

military's subcontracted support services. In fact, more than seven million Filipinos work throughout the globe on short-term contracts in the United States, Europe, Asia, the Gulf states or, as in de la Cruz's case, Iraq. Their remittances add billions of dollars a year to the Philippine economy. Given the large number of overseas Filipino workers, de la Cruz became a sympathetic national figure. The press dubbed him the "Filipino Everyman," and his plight embodied the hopes and fears of Filipinos at home and abroad. Popular pressure mounted for President Arroyo to send Philippine forces home and save de la Cruz. The U.S. and Iraqi governments vehemently urged the opposite path. An early withdrawal would be a direct capitulation to the kidnappers and send "the wrong signal to terrorists."[2]

President Arroyo listened to her Filipino constituency and made her decision.[3] She pulled out the Filipino troops. Having successfully forced the hand of diplomats, the kidnappers released de la Cruz. He arrived in his home village of Buenavista, forty miles north of Manila, feted by his family and the national government. He wore a T-shirt proclaiming, "I am a Filipino."[4] In the wake of his rescue, the Philippine government issued a ban against overseas employment in Iraq to protect its citizens from further violence and chaos.

In kidnapping a Filipino worker, the Iraqi militants recognized the intersection of diplomacy and labor. On its face, the incident is remarkable in that a civilian worker's fate swayed foreign affairs and eroded the U.S. alliance. On closer inspection, de la Cruz's suffering also drew attention to the complications of a civilian overseas workforce in a war zone. With only a few dozen Filipino troops stationed in Iraq, militants kidnapped an accessible contractor rather than a commissioned Filipino soldier, erasing the line between government actors and private civilian employees. In fact, there are 30,000 to 35,000 foreign nationals who work for private contractors in Iraq, and their numbers easily dwarf the 23,000 foreign military personnel in the Coalition of the Willing.[5] And despite the Philippines' prohibition of employment in Iraq, the promise of high salaries continued to entice Filipino workers. De la Cruz may have been saved, but four other Filipinos were killed in Iraq in 2005. In 2006 approximately 3,000 to 6,000 undocumented Filipinos worked on U.S. bases in Iraq in defiance of the ban.[6]

De la Cruz belongs to the same cohort as Lino "Kid Chicle" Rodríguez, Lorenzo Salomón, and Ruben López, all civilian workers who became symbols of diplomatic disputes and local anxieties. Base employment was central to Guantánamo's economy, but when a worker's well-being or life was at stake, it invoked not just a personal loss, but the political pulse of the era. Economic competition, Cold War myopia, and the Cuban revolution's inversion of Guantánamo's political geography came to life in the stories of these individual men. Likewise, the kidnapping of de la Cruz revealed a new, vulnerable overseas contract labor population. His plight did not generate sympathy within Iraq or the United States, but rather became a cause célèbre in the Philippines. De la Cruz is part of a new generation of workers who buttress the power of the U.S. military. Their experiences and protests are part of a longer tradition of foreign civilian workers who simultaneously supported and set limits to U.S. military power.

GTMO base workers' stories foreshadow and inform the U.S. military's transformation in the years leading up to the millennium and in the aftermath of 9/11. In the 1940s and 1950s, it was the base workers who stood up and voiced their dissatisfaction with the U.S. military's hypocritical legal standards. As early as 1940, José Fernández and Pedro Salgado wrote to Franklin Roosevelt that the privately controlled Frederick Snare Corporation "mocked the laws" of both the United States and Cuba.[7] The leaders of the base workers' union also condemned the U.S. military for its anti-democratic and extra-legal practices after the detention of Lorenzo Salomón. By the late 1950s, base workers who identified with the 26 of July Movement took advantage of GTMO's supplies and arsenals for their own military ends. These midcentury, working-class critiques unsettle our contemporary sensibility that the controversies surrounding the U.S. naval base in Guantánamo Bay, including the allegations of torture and absence of law, are completely new. Voices from the Guantánamo archives attest to the fact that base workers recognized GTMO's strained relationship to the law long before the U.S. military turned the base into an indefinite prison for alleged Al Qaeda detainees.

"CLOSE GUANTÁNAMO"

In global discourse, GTMO has morphed into the ultimate symbol of U.S. imperialism and unchecked power. The ongoing confinement of alleged enemy combatants has perverted U.S. principles of due process. Even former Secretary of State Colin Powell belatedly called on the U.S. government to "close Guantánamo." "Every morning, I pick up a paper and some authoritarian figure, some person somewhere, is using Guantánamo to hide their own misdeeds. . . . And so essentially, we have shaken the belief that the world had in America's justice system by keep-ing a place like Guantánamo open and creating things like the military commission. . . . We don't need it, and it's causing us far more damage than any good we get for it."[8]

I add my voice to the chorus of those who believe the U.S. government should "close Guantánamo." Unfortunately, as of this writing, the United States has no intention of closing Guantánamo. The chairman of the Joint Chiefs of Staff, Admiral Mike Mullen, can publicly declare that he would "like to see it [GTMO] shut down," even as the U.S. military is busy constructing a new "refugee camp" on the base that can hold up to ten thousand people.[9]

The detention camps are not "Guantánamo," nor are they even all of GTMO. I would urge the United States to close the detention camps *and* to close GTMO for good. Returning the territory surrounding Guantá-namo Bay to Cuba would finally bury the legally contorted Platt Amend-ment and its nineteenth-century imperialist foundation. Far from capit-ulating to the revolutionary government or communism, neither of which pose a threat to the United States, this would affirm the rule of law and begin the process of accepting Cuban sovereignty. The return of ter-ritory may seem unlikely, but the existence of GTMO ensures that it will be even more difficult to reestablish the United States' public commit-ment to human rights. GTMO's disturbing practices have already cre-ated a precedent. Patterns of legal evasion and all-but-sanctioned torture have proliferated outside of GTMO and onto other U.S. military instal-lations.

With contemporary interest focused on the detainees, I argue that we also need to keep our eyes on the treatment of workers. The labor his-tory of the naval base in Guantánamo Bay signals changes in the mili-tary regarding the proliferation of isolated bases and the growth of pri-vatization. Far from being secondary influences, base workers were actors, and their experiences anticipated and directed these changes.

GTMO'S LESSONS IN GEOGRAPHY: LILY PADS, BUBBLES, AND BLACK SITES

GTMO was not only ahead of its time regarding privatization and for-eign contract labor, but it was also the first military base to establish a tortured relationship with geography. Before 1959, Guantánamo, com-plete with its economic dependence, political compromises, and reputa-tion for sexual excess, was similar to communities abutting U.S. military bases throughout the world. Although local specificities differed, base workers in Japan, South Korea, and western Germany faced many of the same constraints, benefits, and contradictions as the men and women in Guantánamo. Ironically, the Cuban revolution and the consequent isolation created the conditions the U.S. government now finds so valuable. The base remained in Cuba to stand strong against Castro and communism, but it had as little to do with Cubans as possible.

As the U.S. military readies itself for new challenges in the twenty-first century, GTMO appears to be at the forefront of the military's strategic thinking. Since the end of the Cold War, the U.S. military has questioned the utility of large, post–World War II overseas bases and their accompanying neocolonial complications. In 2006 the United States commanded 766 military facilities throughout the globe. This number does not include "temporary" sites in Iraq and Afghanistan, nor does it include the growing number of small sites that are less than ten acres or valued at under one million dollars.[10] For the U.S. military, these large post-war installations came with many strategic advantages, and collectively they shaped its Cold War defenses. With foreign nations, the U.S military negotiated Status of Forces Agreements (SOFAs), which governed jurisdiction, financial arrangements, and the limits of U.S. power. Although SOFAs were almost always written to favor the United States, the bases relied on continual social exchanges and amicable host country relations. In the wake of political changes and individual assaults, the U.S. military had to adapt to local and national politics as well as latent nationalism. For example, in the wake of the Marcos era, the Philippine Congress voted against renewing leasing agreements for the Subic Bay naval base and the Clark air base in the Philippines. The U.S. Navy had to comply and close its installations. Or, in 1995, two U.S. marines and a U.S. sailor raped a twelve-year-old girl in Okinawa. This event spurred massive protests in the region, after which the U.S. government had to relent and allow that the U.S. servicemen be tried under Japanese law. The three men were convicted, and each served six to seven years in Japanese prison.[11] Overseas bases require a great deal of public political management, and the Defense Department has proposed downsizing some of these older and larger installations for smaller basing arrangements, which are arguably more like GTMO.

In 2004 the Defense Department issued its new global posture initiative, emphasizing the importance of agility and flexibility.[12] It aimed to avoid the constraints foreign nations place over U.S. bases, such as complex legal agreements and the need for a host country's approval for military maneuvers.[13] To protect itself from these political complications, the U.S. military plans to build smaller cooperative security locations or "lily pads," rather than larger bases that must develop a symbiotic relationship with a host country. These military installations are being proposed in locations as diverse as Aruba and Senegal.[14] The Defense Department wants to station U.S. forces only where they are "wanted and welcomed by the host government and populace."[15] While this may sound like an admirable goal, the Defense Department's ultimate objective is to act with as much autonomy and impunity as possible. It recognizes that each "welcome" may be temporary. Investing in multiple small bases enables the military to hedge its bets in case of shifting alliances and changes in governments.[16] Proposed seabases are perhaps the greatest manifestation of this new strategy. They are predicated on the belief that sovereign nations may refuse to host U.S. bases, and so they reject the very need for territorial control.[17] In short, they solve the problem by eliminating the host nation.

For now, nations are still agreeing to host U.S. military installations. The U.S. has new arrangements with countries in the former Soviet bloc, such as Bulgaria and Romania.[18] Along with smaller bases, the U.S. government has also been searching for locations for isolated secret prisons. In 2004 the *Washington Post* reported that the CIA was holding unnamed suspected high-level terrorists in "black sites." Reportedly Afghanistan, unnamed Eastern European countries, and Thailand had green lighted prisons where "alternative interrogation methods" would be condoned. These prisons relied on complete discretion and the ignorance of all but a handful of individuals. The CIA initiated these black sites after capturing several alleged terrorists. At first, they sent them to GTMO, but as GTMO detainees' cases weaved their way through the U.S. court system, the CIA sought to evade judicial review. Reportedly at one point, the CIA considered prison ships in international waters, and it even looked for a deserted island. An island in Zambia's Lake Kariba was suggested, but the CIA rejected the proposal because it did not trust the Zambians. Instead, the CIA opted for using former Soviet prisons in Eastern Europe.[19] In 2007 the *New Yorker* reported that elaborate dummy flight plans were engineered to erase any evidence that the CIA flew prisoners into Poland. The Polish government denies it hosted such a black site, but journalists and investigators continue to collect evidence refuting this claim.[20] From the disturbing irony of occupying former Soviet prisons to the establishment of new alliances in the post-Cold War era, the secret prisons' physical locations remain crucial. The host countries offer invisibility and protection from domestic and international law. To date, it is unknown what they received in return, although one can imagine financial rewards and the goodwill of the U.S. administration.

Just as eerily, the Green Zone in Iraq offers striking parallels to how GTMO was after the Cuban revolution. The United States established the Green Zone, Saddam Hussein's former compound, to insulate U.S. officials from the violence of Baghdad. Razor wire, multiple checkpoints, and concrete blast walls isolate U.S. personnel in what is colloquially called "the bubble." Contact with Iraqis is limited. Iraqis who wish to enter the Green Zone must wait in long lines and subject themselves to multiple identity checks and body searches.[21] In an account that might sound familiar to a retired base worker who remembers stripping at the Cuban checkpoint, one journalist remarked, "During the course of a recent day of meetings in the Green Zone, I was sniffed by dogs six times, sent my bags through four metal detectors, was photographed once by a body scanner that can see through my clothes and was patted down too many times to count."[22] With another nod to post-1964 GTMO, the United States has ensured its water and electricity supplies are "independent" of Iraq. Since the U.S. occupation, Iraq's utilities have been disastrously unreliable, and so the United States is financing separate water, electricity, and sewage systems for its sole use. The U.S. embassy will be completely "self-sufficient" from Baghdad.[23]

Unlike the proposed low-impact lily pad bases, the U.S. government is building the largest U.S. military installations in more than a generation in Iraq. This is a contradictory project. Publicly the U.S. government denies any intention of "permanent" bases in Iraq, but it has invested millions of dollars in base construction along with a heavily fortified U.S. embassy.[24] Although this project may be an exception, a return to hulking facilities in an age of lily pads, these bases are also emblematic of newer military initiatives, namely privatization and isolation. These bases imprint U.S. military power into the landscape, even as they are imagined as operating independently from Iraqi communities. To be sure, Iraqi insurgents are far more destructive than any Castro agent ever was, but the United States' solution to the violence and upheaval in Iraq has mirrored its response to the post-revolutionary 1964 GTMO water crisis: cut off ties with the local population and import workers from far away.

PRIVATIZATION AND THIRD COUNTRY NATIONALS

Privatization in the military has become de rigueur, and outsourcing permeates almost all aspects of the military's work, from dishwashing and truck driving to interrogations and tactical surveillance. Civilians perform many "traditional military functions," and public attention has focused on how these "civilian contractors," "mercenaries," or "privatized military firms" challenge traditional notions of government oversight, military order, and the law.[25] In 2007 there were approximately 125,000 private contractors stationed in Iraq, and of those, nearly 20,000 bore weapons.[26] Private firms lure U.S. civilians to Iraq with promises of high wages, ranging from $70,000–$100,000 a year, to compensate for the extreme risks and hardships. These rates surpass both comparable blue-collar jobs in the United States and the U.S. Army's own salaries.

Blackwater, a U.S.-based firm, has been at the cutting edge of privatizing security and military operations, while KBR (formerly Kellogg, Brown, and Root) manages the vast majority of the military's service needs. In total, KBR holds approximately twenty billion dollars in government contracts in Iraq, ranging from supplying the U.S. military's cafeterias to managing the Iraqi oil industry's reconstruction.[27] KBR, in turn, subcontracts many of its projects to secondary and tertiary companies, such as First Kuwaiti, Prime Projects International (PPI), Gulf Catering, and Saudi Trading and Construction Company.[28] In this milieu, GTMO's history of private contractors provides a useful foil. Although of a different magnitude and an earlier generation, companies like the Frederick Snare Corporation and the Drake Winkleman Corporation set the stage for private contractors on U.S. military bases.

During World War II and the Korean War, the Snare and Winkleman corporations relied on Cuban labor to expand GTMO's military facilities. In contrast, on the recently built U.S. bases in Iraq, KBR and its subcontractors largely shun Iraqi workers. The U.S. military and private contractors fear that insurgents could use base employment as an entrée onto the base and attack U.S. military facilities. Iraqis have worked in the U.S.-controlled Green Zone as janitors and gardeners, but fear pervades their employment. For example, according to journalist Rajiv Chandrasekaran, the United States would not allow them to work in the cafeterias, because they worried that Iraqis would poison their food.[29] As a result, the workers building the massive $592 million U.S. embassy in the Green Zone are almost all foreign workers. Recognizing the need for more jobs in Iraq, the U.S. Senate has suggested that the contracting company hire more Iraqis "if they can be properly screened."[30] On at least one base, security has even been cited as one of the reasons for separate latrine facilities for U.S. citizens and Iraqi translators. On Forward Operating Base Warhorse outside of Baqouba, there was one bathroom for

U.S. citizens and a separate bathroom for Iraqis and foreign nationals. U.S. officials have justified this practice for both security and cultural reasons, but Ahmed Mohammed, an Iraqi translator, bluntly called the policy "racist."[31] Iraqis also live in fear that their association with the United States will cost them their lives. One woman did the laundry for a British firm within the Green Zone for several months. Even when she no longer worked for the company, she continued to squat in the Green Zone. She was too terrified to leave. Because her job indirectly aided the occupation, militants have left messages on her cell phone threatening, "Your blood will wash all over your body."[32]

To meet the U.S. military's labor needs, Middle Eastern subcontracting firms have recruited workers from the Philippines, Pakistan, Sri Lanka, Nepal, and India. These contract workers are labeled Third Country Nationals (TCNs), and for decades TCNs have traveled to the Gulf region to work in the oil industry and the service sector. Since the onset of the Iraq war, thousands of TCNs have also provided crucial labor for the U.S. military in Iraq. First and foremost, private companies hire TCNs because they accept low wages and because they are not Iraqis. GTMO's post-1964 labor history gains traction in this context. Just as Jamaican contract workers were less expensive and ultimately less demanding than their Cuban counterparts, TCNs offer similar benefits to the U.S. military in Iraq. Subcontractors peg salaries to workers' home countries, for example, India or the Philippines, and so TCNs earn between $200 and $1000 a month, often less than 10 percent of a comparable U.S. civilian's wages. Private contractors also skimp on security measures for TCNs. For example, South Korean engineers and Indian laborers have complained that they were not issued helmets or flak jackets. In addition, the companies transported TCNs in buses without the expensive, but necessary, armed escorts.[33]

Third Country Nationals in Iraq have also found themselves employed by low-level subcontractors. There is no single entity, and certainly not the U.S. military or the U.S. State Department, who takes responsibility for their well-being. Workers generally pay a fee to a recruitment company in their home country, which then places them with a private firm in the Middle East. Their job may be subcontracted yet again once they are in Iraq, creating a multilayered system that distances the TCNs from the U.S. companies and the U.S. government. As a result, TCNs face abuse, and private contractors can operate essentially outside the law. For example, John Owen, a former employee for First Kuwaiti, which holds a contract with KBR, reported that managers regularly beat workers. In addition, there are no safety standards and medical neglect is rampant. In one instance an Egyptian construction worker fell and broke his back and "no one ever heard from him again."[34] Workers often have little knowledge of their immediate employer, and the lack of transparency allows a collective avoidance of responsibility for foreign workers.[35] Most TCNs in Iraq are resigned to the lack of oversight. As one Indian employee lamented, "We can blame neither the Americans nor the Iraqis. . . . It's the company which cheated us."[36]

TCNs' journeys or "commutes" to Iraq also raise considerable concerns about the U.S. government's complicity with human trafficking. GTMO base workers' commutes were long, physically taxing, and often psychologically stressful two-hour affairs, but they were always voluntarily. It was difficult to obtain a pass, but GTMO and the Snare Corporation actively recruited local labor. Since 1964, Cuban commuters, Jamaicans, and Filipinos have worked on GTMO by choice. In contrast, subcontractors have difficulty convincing TCNs to travel to Iraq, and they have utilized manipulative, coercive, and bluntly illegal practices to meet their work needs. For example, a U.S. civilian contractor, Rory Mayberry, explained that he had been on an airplane from Kuwait with dozens of Filipino workers contracted by First Kuwaiti. The Filipinos thought the airplane was bound for Dubai, but instead they were going to Iraq: "When the plane took off and the captain announced we were headed for Baghdad, all you-know-what broke loose. People started shouting. It wasn't until a security guy working for First Kuwaiti waved an MP5 [sub-machine gun] in the air that people settled down. They realized they had no choice."[37]

In another case publicized by the *Chicago Tribune,* a group of Nepalese men signed papers with Moon Light, a private labor brokering company in Nepal. Many of these men believed they had accepted jobs at a luxury hotel in Jordan. Once in Jordan, the Moon Light workers were handed over to Bisharat and Partners, a Jordanian labor firm, which was subcontracted by Daoud and Partners, a subcontractor of KBR. Bisharat and Partners had slated the workers for Iraq. Heavily in debt and without return plane tickets, the workers had no choice. They boarded buses headed for the Al Asad air base north of Fallujah. Traveling in an unarmed caravan along the Amman-Baghdad highway, twelve Nepalese were kidnapped by insurgents. Weeks later, the militants executed them.[38]

Other workers also recount stories of bait and switch practices, where they agreed to a job in Kuwait or Jordan, only to then find themselves in

Iraq. Once in Iraq, private contractors often confiscated TCNs' passports to prevent workers from leaving the country or seeking other employment.[39] Sri Lankan national Tapan Oh Prayti complained, "They took our passports so we wouldn't flee anywhere."[40] TCNs bereft of their passports and return airfare were essentially captives in Iraq and working against their will. The situation has been so dire that the U.S. military intervened and ordered subcontractors to stop violating international human trafficking law and to return employees' passports on request.[41] Unfortunately, it is unclear how well these standards are being enforced. A U.S. State Department inspector general investigated some of the allegations against First Kuwaiti and found no evidence of wrongdoing; however, he also admitted his review was "limited in scope" and the company had "three months notice" to prepare for his visit.[42] In addition, there are still reports of subcontracting firms and private employers holding TCNs' passports in Iraq.[43]

Worker activism in Iraq is thinly documented, and the accounts that have surfaced beg for more details. For example, on May 11, 2004, there was a mortar attack on Camp Anaconda and 600 TCNs quit en masse, rather than risk dying in a future attack. Filipino workers have escaped their work sites and relied on truck drivers to smuggle them back across the border to Kuwait. Hundreds of Pakistani workers building the future U.S. Embassy went on strike. In response, the subcontractor returned 375 workers to Pakistan. Filipinos have held strikes and "sick outs" against KBR and PPI because of poor working conditions and lack of overtime pay, and they were then joined by their Indian, Sri Lankan, and Nepalese counterparts. In this instance the Philippine government intervened to protect its citizens and offered free flights home to disgruntled workers. In another instance, a group of Indian workers credibly threatened to leave the U.S. military base where they worked unless their living conditions improved. The company acquiesced, and their drinking water and rations became more tolerable. On arriving back in India, the workers filed complaints against the employment agency that had hired them. And like the Philippine government, the Indian government has banned its citizens from working in Iraq.[44] Although poorly enforced, these bans demonstrate state-level attempts to protect workers from exploitation and abuse.

Uprooted from their home countries and existing in a war zone, foreign workers struggle with concerns that do not register with the Iraqi government or communities. Iraq has no loyalty or connection to these workers, and instead many see them as collaborators with the U.S. occupation.

TCNs can not call on nationalism, nor can their own national governments offer much protection other than outlawing recruitment to Iraq. In a far more dangerous setting, TCNs are the heirs to the Snare and Winkleman employees and the Filipino and Jamaican contract workers on GTMO. The U.S. occupation in Iraq is buttressed by workers from throughout Southeast and South Asia who are particularly vulnerable and geographically displaced. This complements the U.S. military's embrace of installations that, like GTMO, gain their power from secrecy and seclusion.

CONCLUSION

Today, the international map of imperial power is far more circuitous than the social milieu of Guantánamo. Angelo de la Cruz was only one of thousands of Filipinos hoping to earn higher-than-average wages in the War on Terror. And so perhaps it is not shocking that in 2002, Filipinos built the prisons that first held the alleged Al Qaeda detainees on GTMO. They worked for a subcontracting firm with ties to KBR, and their grueling work schedule entailed twelve-hour days, seven days a week. They earned approximately nine hundred dollars a month, plus access to specially imported foods, such as tilapia, ginger, and fish sauce. Filipinos built the high-tech prisons, but they were also confined to isolated quarters. One worker, Jojo, vented, "Aside from the good food and pay, we lived like prisoners—we had our own guards and could not leave our compound." On completion, the Filipino workers flew from GTMO to Jamaica to Miami to San Francisco, where they were constantly under surveillance, not even able to visit the restroom alone. One frustrated worker asked, "Why are you doing this to us, keeping us like prisoners? You should treat us better. We were the ones who built the prisons of your enemy."[45] More than one hundred years after the 1898 U.S. invasions of Cuba and the Philippines, these Filipino workers found themselves utilized as low-cost labor in the War on Terror. Thousands of miles from their home country, Filipinos on the U.S. naval base in Guantánamo Bay lay bare the unanticipated consequences of U.S. militarism in the nineteenth and twenty-first centuries.

The history of base workers in Guantánamo demonstrates what happens when a foreign military base is isolated from its geography and kept separate from local people. In essence, when military bases attempt to operate in hermeneutically sealed compounds and with no social ties to nearby communities, GTMO is created—GTMO circa 2002, complete with orange jumpsuits and cages. Pre-revolutionary Cuba or North American neocolonialism should not be romanticized, but that period shows that Guantánamo and its workers mattered. For most of the twentieth century, workers placed checks on the base, compelling the U.S. military to acknowledge GTMO's Cuban politics and economic and social expectations. Men and women in Guantánamo developed complex relationships with the *imperio* in their midst. Many were grateful for their jobs, but resentment of discriminatory and paternalist practices existed. Base workers gained status because of their steady jobs and affiliation with North Americans, but they also regularly stole goods from their employers to enhance their salaries and, later, to forment revolution. And even after the Cuban revolution, some elderly commuters and former workers petitioned the U.S. government to meet its obligations. They insisted on their right to U.S. government pensions and their right to live in Cuba.

As the U.S. military adapts to the War on Terror, it is worth asking who does the dishes, serves the beers, and "waxes the floor" of empire. Whether they are in GTMO or Iraq, Afghanistan, Guam, Diego Garcia, or Dakar, base workers with ambivalent loyalties delineate the boundaries of political control, and their stories speak to the lived experiences of empire.

Guantánamo Civil Registry, 1921–1958

	Husband[1]				Wife[2]			
Year	Birthplace	Parents' Birthplace	Race[3]	Age	Birthplace	Parents' Birthplace	Race[3]	Age
1921	Alabama	Puerto Rico and U.S.		21	Santiago	Cuba		19
1922	Arkansas	U.S.		23	Guantánamo	Cuba		16
1924	Pennsylvania	U.S.		27	Puerto Rico	Cuba		23
1924	New York	U.S.	Blanca	22	Caimanera	Cuba	Blanca	36
1927	U.S. Virgin Islands	U.S.	Negra	22	St. Kitts	Cuba and Spain	Negra	19
1930	Tennessee	U.S.		26		Cuba	Blanca	21
1930	Vermont	U.S.		32		Cuba	Blanca	15
1932	Pennsylvania	Italy	Blanca	52		Cuba	Blanca	46
1935	Pennsylvania	U.S.	Blanca	30	Guantánamo	Canary Islands	Blanca	20
1935	North Carolina	U.S.		25	Guantánamo	Spain	Blanca	17
1936	Puerto Rico	Puerto Rico		47	Guantánamo	Cuba	Blanca	26
1940	Massachusetts	U.S.	Blanca	26	Caimanera	Cuba	Blanca	25
1940	New York	U.S.		31		Cuba		19
1940	New Jersey	Cuba and U.S.	Blanca	23	Caimanera	Cuba	Blanca	21
1941	Pennsylvania	U.S.	Blanca	22		Cuba		18
1941	Georgia	Cuba and U.S.	Blanca	44	Caimanera	Cuba	Blanca	29
1941	New York	Cuba	Blanca	30		Puerto Rico	Blanca	24
1944	Florida	U.S.		18		Cuba		17
1944	Florida	U.S.		21	Havana	Cuba	Blanca	23
1944	Florida	U.S.		21	Caimanera	Cuba	Blanca	19
1945	North Carolina	U.S.	Blanca	23	Caimanera	Cuba	Blanca	19
1946	Texas	U.S.	Blanca	27		Cuba and Sweden		16
1946	North Carolina	U.S.		20	Guantánamo	Cuba	Blanca	26
1946	Florida	U.S.		22	Guantánamo	Cuba	Blanca	26
1946	New York	U.S.		22		Spain	Blanca	20

1946	Pennsylvania	Italy		24	Guantánamo	Spain	Blanca	17
1946	Missouri	U.S.	Blanca	22	Oriente	Spain	Blanca	22
1946	Pennsylvania	U.S.		22	Guantánamo	Cuba		17
1946	Louisiana	U.S.		28	Guantánamo	Cuba		20
1946	Georgia	U.S.	Blanca	27	Oriente	Cuba	Blanca	18
1946	Connecticut	U.S.		22		Cuba	Blanca	28
1947	Kentucky	U.S.	Blanca	20		Cuba	Blanca	27
1947	New York	U.S.		33	Guantánamo	Spain		29
1947	Florida	U.S.		23	Camagüey	Cuba	Blanca	15
1947	Delaware	U.S.	Blanca	30	Santiago	Cuba and U.S.	Blanca	20
1947	Philippines	Philippines		21	Guantánamo	Cuba	Blanca	25
1947	Pennsylvania	U.S.	Negra	21		Cuba and Jamaica	Mestiza	21
1948	Illinois	U.S.		21		Cuba		18
1948	Florida	U.S.	Blanca	25	Banes	Cuba and Jamaica	Negra	27
1948	Texas	U.S.	Blanca	23		Cuba and Spain	Blanca	20
1949	Texas	Mexico		22		Cuba	Blanca	14
1949	Alabama	U.S.	Blanca	21	Caimanera	Cuba	Blanca	21
1949	Alabama	U.S.	Negra	29		Cuba	Mestiza	21
1950	Texas	U.S.	Blanca	34	Guantánamo	Cuba	Blanca	32
1950	South Carolina	U.S.	Negra	24	Oriente	St. Kitts	Negra	18
1951	Carolina	U.S.	Blanca	27		Cuba	Blanca	31
1951	Pennsylvania	U.S.	Blanca	22		Spain	Blanca	28
1952	Mississippi	U.S.	Blanca	24		Cuba	Blanca	28
1952	New York	Cuba		21	Guantánamo	Puerto Rico	Blanca	15
1953	Wisconsin	U.S.		22	Caimanera	Cuba		14
1953	Pennsylvania	U.S.		22		Cuba		20
1954	Georgia	U.S.		33		Cuba and Spain		
1954	New York	U.S.	Blanca	25	Guantánamo	Jamaica	Mestiza	19
1954	New York	Canada and U.S.		29	Guantánamo	Cuba	Blanca	19
1954	Texas	U.S.		21		Cuba and Spain		21

(continued)

(continued)

Year	Husband Birthplace	Husband Parents' Birthplace	Husband Race[3]	Husband Age	Wife Birthplace	Wife Parents' Birthplace	Wife Race[3]	Wife Age
1954	New York	U.S.		21	Havana	Cuba		21
1954	Ohio	U.S.		21		Cuba and Spain		21
1954	Connecticut	U.S.		28		Cuba	Blanca	30
1954	New York	U.S.	Blanca	21	Guantánamo	Cuba	Blanca	18
1954	Washington DC	U.S.		23	Guantánamo	Cuba	Blanca	16
1955	West Virginia	U.S.		23	Caimanera	Cuba	Mestiza	18
1955	New Jersey	U.S.	Blanca	22		Cuba	Blanca	22
1956	New York	U.S.	Blanca	26		Cuba	Blanca	24
1956	Florida	Cuba and Puerto Rico	Blanca	27		Cuba	Blanca	20
1956	New Hampshire	U.S.		22		Cuba and Dominican Republic		15
1956	Pennsylvania	U.S.		25		Cuba	Blanca	20
1956	Michigan	U.S.		22	Caimanera	Cuba		23
1956	Texas	U.S.		21		Cuba		
1956	North Carolina	U.S.		31		Cuba		27
1956	Massachusetts	U.S.		33		Cuba		25
1956	Massachusetts	U.S.		21		Cuba		19
1956	Massachusetts	U.S.		35		Cuba		25
1956	Ohio	U.S.		33		Cuba and Spain		21
1956	South Carolina	U.S.		21	Havana	Cuba and U.S.		20
1956	Nebraska	U.S.		31	Caimanera	Cuba and Puerto Rico		19
1957	Florida	U.S.		32		Cuba		30
1957	Ohio	U.S.		21		Cuba		18

1957	Ohio	U.S.	Caimanera	Cuba		22	23
1957	Pennsylvania	U.S.		Cuba		31	25
1957		U.S.		Cuba	Mestiza	27	24
1957	Texas	U.S.	Jamaica	Jamaica		69	45
1957	Indiana	U.S.		Cuba		21	23
1957	Texas	U.S.		Cuba		29	26
1957	New York	U.S.		Cuba		23	20
1957	Pennsylvania	U.S.		Cuba		22	18
1957	North Carolina	U.S.		Cuba and Jamaica		21	20
1957	New Hampshire	U.S.		Cuba	Blanca	22	21
1957	Colorado	Italy		Cuba		54	41
1958	Connecticut	U.S.	Havana	Cuba		21	16
1958	Alabama	U.S.		Cuba		22	22
1958	Washington	U.S.	Caimanera	Cuba		21	22
1958	North Carolina	U.S.		Cuba		21	21
1958	Pennsylvania	U.S.		Cuba		21	19
1958	Indiana	U.S.		Cuba		21	17
1958	Georgia	U.S.	Jamaica	Cuba	Negra	32	29
1958	New Jersey	U.S.		Jamaica		22	26
1958	Pennsylvania	Cuba and U.S.	Guantánamo	Cuba and Jamaica		21	25
1958	Pennsylvania	U.S.	Guantánamo	Cuba		23	22
1958	Connecticut	U.S.		Cuba		21	20
1958	West Virginia	U.S.		Guadelupe		20	26

SOURCE: Guantánamo Civil Registry, Guantánamo Provincial Archive.

[1] In all cases, the husband was identified as a U.S. citizen.

[2] In all but two cases, the wife was identified as a Cuban citizen. In two instances, the wife was identified as a British West Indian subject or a Jamaican.

[3] Race is indicated in the Spanish feminine form, as it was in the original record, to agree with *raza*. If race is not indicated for the husband or wife, it is because it was not identified in the civil registry.

Notes

INTRODUCTION

1. Jana K. Lipman, "Between Guantánamo and Montego Bay: Cuba, Jamaica, Migration and the Cold War, 1959–62," *Immigrants and Minorities* 21 (November 2002): 31. Robert Duncan (pseud.), personal interviews, Havana, Cuba, July 20, 2001 and August 1, 2001. (Interviews conducted in English.)

2. For a sampling, see Jane Mayer, "The Experiment: A Reporter at Large," *New Yorker,* July 11, 2005; Jane Mayer, "Outsourcing Torture," *New Yorker,* February 14, 2005; Jeffery Toobin, "Inside the Wire," *New Yorker,* February 9, 2004; Seymour Hirsch, "Torture at Abu Ghraib," *New Yorker,* May 10, 2004; Michael Ratner and Ellen Ray, *Guantánamo: What the World Should Know* (White River Junction, VT: Chelsea Green, 2004); Erik Saar and Viveca Novak, *Inside the War: A Military Soldier's Eyewitness Account of Life at Guantánamo* (New York: Penguin, 2005); Victoria Brittain and Gillian Slovo, *Guantánamo: Honor Bound to Defend Freedom* (London: Oberon Books, 2004); Joseph Margulies, *Guantánamo and the Abuse of Presidential Power* (New York: Simon and Schuster, 2006); David Rose, *Guantánamo: The War on Human Rights* (New York: New Press, 2004); and Magnus Fiskesjo, *The Thanksgiving Turkey Pardon, the Death of Teddy's Bear, and the Sovereign Exception of Guantánamo* (Chicago: Prickly Paradigm, 2003).

3. Daniel Schorr, "Guantánamo: Not a Gulag, but Surely a Stain," *Christian Science Monitor,* June 10, 2005, http://www.csmonitor.com/2005/0610/p09s02-cods.html (accessed August 19, 2006); "Annan Backs UN Guantánamo Demand," *bbcnews.com,* February 6, 2006, http://news.bbc.co.uk/1/hi/world/

americas/4722534.stm (accessed August 19, 2006); "Carter Urges Closing of Guantánamo Prison," *Washington Post,* June 8, 2005, http://www.washingtonpost.com/wp-dyn/content/article/2005/06/07/AR2005060701631.html (accessed August 19, 2006); "Colin Powell Says Guantánamo Should Be Closed," June 10, 2007, http://www.reuters.com/article/topNews/idUSN1043646920070610?feedType=RSS (accessed June 11, 2007); and Thom Shanker and David Sanger, "New to Job, Gates Argued for Closing Guantánamo," *New York Times,* March 23, 2007.

4. Amy Kaplan, "Where Is Guantánamo?" *American Quarterly* 57 (September 2005): 854. See also Amy Kaplan, "Homeland Insecurities: Reflections on Language and Space," *Radical History Review* 85 (Winter 2003): 82–92; Giorgio Agamben, *State of Exception,* trans. Kevin Attel (Chicago: University of Chicago Press, 2005); Gerald L. Neuman, "Anomalous Zones," *Stanford Law Review* 48 (May 1996): 1197–1234; and Judith Butler, *Precarious Life: The Powers of Mourning and Violence* (London: Verso, 2004).

5. David Thelen, "The Nation and Beyond: Transnational Perspectives on United States History," *Journal of American History* 86 (December 1999): 965–75; and Micol Seigel, "Beyond Compare: Comparative Method after the Transnational Turn," *Radical History Review* 91 (Winter 2005): 62–90.

6. Formative articles on this theme include Seigel, "Beyond Compare"; Thelen, "The Nation and Beyond"; Robin Kelley, " 'But a Local Phase of a World Problem': Black History's Global Vision, 1883–1950," *Journal of American History* 86 (December 1999): 1045–77; Ian Tyrell, "Making Nations/Making States: American Historians in the Context of Empire," *Journal of American History* 86 (December 1999): 1015–44; Ian Tyrrell, "American Exceptionalism in an Age of International History," *American Historical Review* 96 (October 1991): 1031–55; Shelley Fisher Fishkin, "Crossroads of Cultures: The Transnational Turn in American Studies; Presidential Address at the American Studies Association, November 12, 2004," *American Quarterly* 57, no. 1 (2005): 17–57; and C. A. Bayly and others, "AHR Conversation: On Transnational History," *American Historical Review* 111 (December 2006): 1440–64.

7. For a sampling of this work, see Gloria Anzaldúa, *Borderlands/La Frontera* (San Francisco: Aunt Lute Books, 1999); Seth Fein, "New Empire into Old: Making Mexican Newsreels the Cold War Way," *Diplomatic History* 28 (November 2004): 703–48; Paul Gilroy, *The Black Atlantic: Modernity and Double Consciousness* (Cambridge, MA: Harvard University Press, 2007); Penny Von Eschen, *Satchmo Blows Up the World: Jazz Ambassadors Play the Cold War* (Cambridge, MA: Harvard University Press, 2006); Theresa Rundstetler, " 'Journeymen': Boxing, Race, and the Transnational World of Jack Johnson" (PhD diss., Yale University, 2007); Michelle A. Stephens, "Black Transnationalism and the Politics of National Identity: West Indian Intellectuals in Harlem in the Age of War and Revolution," *American Quarterly* 50, no. 3 (1998): 592–608; Peggy Levitt, *Transnational Villagers* (Berkeley: University of California Press, 2001); and Nina Glick Schiller, Linda Basch, and Cristina Blanc-Szanton, *Towards a Transnational Perspective on Migration: Race, Class, Ethnicity, and Nationalism Reconsidered* (New York: Annals of the New York Academy of Sciences, 1992).

8. Bayly, "AHR Conversation," 1446.

9. Marion Emerson Murphy, *The History of Guantánamo Bay,* 1953 ed. (U.S. Naval Base, Guantánamo Bay: District Publications and Printing Office Tenth Naval District, 1953), 31–36. Written by Admiral Murphy in 1953, this in-depth account of the base is technically an "unofficial" history. However, it appears on the U.S. Naval Station in Guantánamo Bay's "official" website, albeit with a disclaimer, http://www.nsgtmo.navy.mil/htmpgs/gtmohistorymurphy .htm (accessed June 13, 2006). It has been updated twice, first in 1964 and again in 1982.

10. Bryce Wood, *The Making of the Good Neighbor Policy* (New York: Columbia University Press, 1961); Randall Bennett Woods, *The Roosevelt Foreign-Policy Establishment and the "Good Neighbor" The United States and Argentina, 1941–1945* (Lawrence: Regents Press of Kansas, 1979); Irwin Gellman, *Roosevelt and Batista: Good Neighbor Diplomacy in Cuba, 1933–1945* (Albuquerque: University of New Mexico Press, 1973); Eric Paul Roorda, *The Dictator Next Door: The Good Neighbor Policy and the Trujillo Regime in the Dominican Republic, 1930–1945* (Durham, NC: Duke University Press, 1998); Max Paul Friedman, *Nazis and Good Neighbors: The United States Campaign against the Germans of Latin America in World War II* (Cambridge: Cambridge University Press, 2003); and Greg Grandin, "Your Americanism and Mine: Americanism and Anti-Americanism in the Americas," *American Historical Review* 111 (October 2006): 1042–66.

11. Thomas G. Paterson, *Contesting Castro: The United Status and the Triumph of the Cuban Revolution* (New York: Oxford University Press, 1994); James G. Blight, Bruce J. Allyn, and David A. Welch, *Cuba on the Brink: Castro, the Missile Crisis, and the Soviet Collapse* (New York: Pantheon Books, 1993); and Aleksander Fursenko and Timothy Naftali, *"One Hell of a Gamble": The Secret History of the Cuban Missile Crisis, Khrushchev, Castro, and Kennedy, 1958–1964* (New York: W. W. Norton, 1997). The following works are groundbreaking in their analyses of the Cold War in "peripheral" or "marginal" regions: Piero Gleijeses, *Conflicting Missions: Havana, Washington, and Africa, 1959–1976* (Chapel Hill: University of North Carolina Press, 2002); and Stephen G. Rabe, *U.S. Intervention in British Guiana: A Cold War Story* (Chapel Hill: University of North Carolina Press, 2005).

12. For an informative account of the linguistic and political histories of *neocolonial* and *postcolonial,* see Robert J. C. Young, *Postcolonialism: An Historical Introduction* (Oxford: Blackwell, 2001).

13. Amy Kaplan and Donald E. Pease, eds., *Cultures of United States Imperialism* (Durham, NC: Duke University Press, 1993). Mary Louise Pratt coined the term *contact zone* as a "space of colonial encounters" (6–7). Given the U.S. military incursion and its relations with the surrounding Cuban communities, this framework provides a helpful lens onto the conflicts and negotiations between U.S. sailors and marines and Cuban base workers. Mary Louise Pratt, *Imperial Eyes: Travel Writing and Transculturation* (London: Routledge, 1992). In this vein, see Richard White, *The Middle Ground: Indians, Empires, and Republics in the Great Lakes Region, 1650–1815* (Cambridge: Cambridge University Press, 1991); Gilbert Joseph, Catherine LeGrand, and Ricardo D. Salvatore,

eds., *Close Encounters of Empire: Writing the Cultural History of U.S.–Latin American Relations* (Durham, NC: Duke University Press, 1998); Ann Laura Stoler, "Tense and Tender Ties: The Politics in North American History and (Post) Colonial Studies," *Journal of American History* 88 (December 2001): 829–65; Neil Smith, *American Empire: Roosevelt's Geographer and the Prelude to Globalization* (Berkeley: University of California Press, 2003); and Ann Laura Stoler, ed., *Haunted by Empire: Geographies of Intimacy in North American History* (Durham, NC: Duke University Press, 2006).

14. Michael Hunt, *Ideology and U.S. Foreign Policy* (New Haven, CT: Yale University Press, 1987); Gail Bederman, *Manliness and Civilization: A Cultural History of Gender and Race in the United States, 1880–1917* (Chicago: University of Chicago Press, 1995); Kristin Hoganson, *Fighting for American Manhood: How Gender Politics Provoked the Spanish-American and Philippine-American Wars* (New Haven, CT: Yale University Press, 1998); Emily Rosenberg, *Financial Missionaries to the World: The Politics and Culture of Dollar Diplomacy, 1900–1930* (Cambridge: Harvard University Press, 1999); Laura Wexler, *Tender Violence: Domestic Visions in an Age of U.S. Imperialism* (Chapel Hill: University of North Carolina Press, 2000); Mary Renda, *Taking Haiti: Military Occupation and the Culture of U.S. Imperialism, 1915–1940* (Chapel Hill: University of North Carolina Press, 2001); Stoler, "Tense and Tender Ties"; Melani McAlister, *Epic Encounters: Culture, Media, and U.S. Interests in the Middle East, 1945–2000* (Berkeley: University of California Press, 2001); Amy Kaplan, *The Anarchy of Empire in the Making of U.S. Culture* (Cambridge, MA: Harvard University Press, 2002); and Christina Klein, *Cold War Orientalism: Asia in the Middlebrow Imagination, 1945–1961* (Berkeley: University of California, 2003).

15. Mark Philip Bradley, *Imagining Vietnam and America: The Making of Postcolonial Vietnam, 1919–1950* (Chapel Hill: University of North Carolina Press, 2000); and Seth Jacobs, *America's Miracle Man in Vietnam: Ngo Dinh Diem, Religion, Race, and U.S. Intervention in Southeast Asia 1950–1957* (Durham, NC: Duke University Press, 2005).

16. Julie Greene makes a similar argument in her review essay, "The Labor of Empire: Recent Scholarship on U.S. History and Imperialism," *Labor: Studies in Working Class History of the Americas* 1 (Summer 2004): 113–29. Robert Vitalis also emphasizes the role of workers and foreign policy in the Middle East. See *America's Kingdom: Mythmaking on the Saudi Oil Frontier* (Stanford, CA: Stanford University Press, 2006).

17. Robert E. Harkavy, "Thinking about Basing," *Naval War College Review* 58 (Summer 2005): 12–42. For a critique of U.S. military bases, see Chalmers Johnson, *The Sorrows of Empire: Militarism, Secrecy, and the End of the Republic* (New York: Henry Holt, 2004); and Johnson, *Nemesis: The Last Days of the American Republic* (New York: Henry Holt, 2006).

18. Cynthia Enloe, *Bases, Beaches, and Bananas: Making Feminist Sense of International Politics* (Berkeley: University of California Press, 1989); Joseph Gerson and Bruce Birchard, eds., *The Sun Never Sets: Confronting the Network of Foreign U.S. Military Bases* (Boston: South End, 1991); Katherine T. McCaffrey, *Military Power and Popular Protest: The U.S. Navy in Vieques, Puerto Rico*

(New Brunswick, NJ: Rutgers University Press, 2002); Katherine H. S. Moon, *Sex Among Allies: Military Prostitution in U.S.-Korean Relations* (New York: Columbia University Press, 1997); Harvey Neptune, *Caliban and the Yankees: Trinidad and the United States Occupation* (Chapel Hill: University of North Carolina Press, 2007); Catherine Lutz, *Homefront: A Military City and the American 20th Century* (Boston: Beacon, 2001); Mark L. Gillem, *America Town: Building the Outposts of Empire* (Minneapolis: University of Minnesota Press, 2007). For Guantánamo, Cuba, see Louis A. Pérez Jr., *On Becoming Cuban: Identity, Nationality, and Culture* (New York: Harper Collins, 1999), 238–42.

19. John Major, *Prize Possession: The United States and the Panama Canal, 1903–1979* (Cambridge: Cambridge University Press, 1993); John Lindsay-Poland, *Emperors in the Jungle: The Hidden History of the U.S. in Panama* (Durham, NC: Duke University Press, 2003); Eileen Suárez Findlay, *Imposing Decency: The Politics of Sexuality and Race in Puerto Rico, 1870–1920* (Durham: Duke University Press, 2000); and Laura Briggs, *Reproducing Empire: Race, Sex, Science, and U.S. Imperialism in Puerto Rico* (Berkeley: University of California Press, 2002).

20. Jim Garamone, "Rumsfeld, Myers Discuss Military Global Posture," American Forces Press Service, September 23, 2004, http://www.defenselink.mil/news/Sep2004/n09232004_2004092311.html (accessed June 20, 2006). Also see Kurt M. Campbell and Celeste Johnson Ward, "New Battle Stations?" *Foreign Affairs*, September–October 2003, http://www.foreignaffairs.org/20030901faessay82507/kurt-m<->campbell-celeste-johnson-ward/new-battle-stations.html (accessed June 20, 2006); Ryan Henry, "Transforming the U.S. Global Defense Posture," *Naval War College Review* 59 (Spring 2006): 13–28; Joseph Gerson, "U.S. Foreign Military Bases and Military Colonialism: Personal and Analytical Perspectives," American Friends Service Committee, http://www.afsc.org/newengland/pesp/Bases-Chapter.htm (accessed June 13, 2007); and Harkavy, "Thinking about Basing."

21. For a historical critique of the Magna Carta, see Peter Linebaugh, "The Secret History of the Magna Carta," *Boston Review*, Summer 2003, http://bostonreview.net/BR28.3/linebaugh.html (accessed July 11, 2007).

22. "Welcome to Guantánamo," *La Revista Oriental*, September 1955.

23. José Vázquez Pubillones, "Sobre los marinos americanos y nuestra ciudad," *La Voz del Pueblo*, May 13, 1946; and Lino Lemes García, "Volverán los marinos a Caimanera," *La Voz del Pueblo*, May 16, 1950.

24. "400 jornaleros de la base naval serán declarados excedentes," *La Voz del Pueblo*, July 15, 1946; and "El Sec. Gral. de la Federación Americana del Trabajo estará en Gtmo. próximamente," *La Voz del Pueblo*, October 18, 1950.

25. "El comercio del poblado de Caimanera no recibe las visitas de los marinos francos," *La Voz del Pueblo*, March 27, 1939; Lino Lemes García, "Impresiones de mí visita al poblado de Caimanera," *La Voz del Pueblo*, March 31, 1939; and Juan Quintero Ávila, "Se aprestan las fuerzas vivas del poblado, a dar batalla por sus mejoras" *La Voz del Pueblo*, January 18, 1947.

26. Although its history is tied to the naval base, there are relatively few texts on Caimanera alone. One of the few is Ana Celia Pérez Rubio and others,

"Historia local de Caimanera" (unpublished manuscript, Guantánamo Provincial Archive, February 22, 1995).

27. Fifteen News Questions, *New York Times,* February 15, 1948, p. E2; and Fifteen News Questions, *New York Times,* March 13, 1949, p. E2.

28. Jules B. Billard, "Guantánamo: Keystone in the Caribbean," *National Geographic,* March 1961, 420–36; Hanson Baldwin, "Guantánamo: Ours or Castro's?" *Saturday Evening Post,* September 24, 1960, 19+; and Hanson Baldwin, "Clouds over Guantánamo," *New York Times Magazine,* August 21, 1960, 20+.

29. Sección de Historia del PCC de la Provincia Guantánamo, *Guantánamo: Apuntes para una cronología histórica* (Santiago de Cuba: Editorial Oriente, 1985).

30. Iraida Sánchez Oliva and Santiago Moreaux Jardines, *La Guantanamera* (Havana: Editorial José Martí, 1999).

31. Idilio Isaac Rodríguez, "Opinión editorial," *Venceremos,* November 19, 1962.

32. In many of my sources, the writer drops the accent from "Guantánamo." This occurs in a range of documents from Cuban newspaper headlines to U.S. diplomatic papers. As a matter of consistency, I include the accent in the text even when it does not appear in the original source.

33. I conducted my interviews in 2004–2005. I always began the interview in Spanish, but occasionally my informant would switch to English. The men and women who preferred English included West Indian descendants and those who had learned English on the base and were eager to refresh their language skills. I use pseudonyms for my informants. Given the personal nature of the interviews and the small community of Guantánamo, I believe this level of privacy is appropriate. In the first reference to each speaker, I will note the language in which the interview was conducted.

My work has been strongly influenced by anthropologists and historians who use oral testimonies along with archival sources to demonstrate the intersection of local, national, and international narratives. See Michel Rolph-Trouillot, *Silencing the Past: Power and the Production of History* (Boston: Beacon, 1997); Denise Brennan, *What's Love Got To Do With It? Transnational Desires and Sex Tourism in the Dominican Republic* (Durham, NC: Duke University Press, 2004); Ann Farnsworth-Alvear, *Dulcinea in the Factory: Myths, Morals, Men and Women in Colombia's Industrial Experiment, 1905–1960* (Durham, NC: Duke University Press, 2000); Patricia Pessar, *From Fanatics to Folk: Brazilian Millenarianism and Popular Culture* (Durham, NC: Duke University Press, 2004); and Ann Laura Stoler, *Carnal Knowledge and Imperial Power: Race and the Intimate in Colonial Rule* (Berkeley: University of California Press, 2002).

34. Rosa Johnson (pseud.), personal interview, Guantánamo, Cuba, November 9, 2004. (Interview conducted in English and Spanish.)

35. When I returned to Guantánamo in April 2006, I learned that one of my informants and final commuters had passed away in the beginning of 2006.

36. Stoler, *Haunted by Empire,* 4.

PROLOGUE

1. Commander of Naval Base to Chief of Naval Operations, Re: Labor relations at the naval base, October 29, 1952, U.S. National Archives and Records Administration (NARA), College Park, MD, RG 181, Records of Naval Districts and Shore Establishments, Commander U.S. Naval Station, Guantánamo Bay, Cuba, Weekly Intelligence Summaries and Correspondence Files, 1949–55, Box 2. In future citations I refer to this collection as RG 181, GTMO, Weekly Intelligence Files, 1949–55.

2. CCP en Guantánamo, Sección de Historia del Comité Provincial del Partido en Guantánamo, *Reseña histórica de Guantánamo*, (Santiago de Cuba: Editorial Oriente, 1985), 10; Diego Bosch Ferrer and José Sánchez Guerra, *Rebeldía y apalencamiento: Jurisdicciones de Guantánamo y Baracoa* (Guantánamo: Centro Provincial de Patrimonio Cultural, 2003), 20–21.

3. Juan Pérez de la Riva, "Una isla con dos historias," in *El Barracón: Esclavitud y capitalismo en Cuba* (Barcelona: Editorial Crítica, 1978). Essay originally published in *Cuba Internacional,* October 1968, 32–37. For a more contemporary account of Cuban regional history, see Hernán Venegas Delgado, *La región en Cuba: Un ensayo de interpretación historiográfica* (Santiago de Cuba: Editorial Oriente, 2001).

4. Pioneering scholarship on Cuba has investigated the Cuban construction of race. See Rebecca Scott, *Slave Emancipation in Cuba: The Transition to Free Labor, 1850–1899* (Princeton, NJ: Princeton University Press, 1985); Aline Helg, *Our Rightful Share: The Afro-Cuban Struggle for Equality, 1886–1912* (Chapel Hill: University of North Carolina Press, 1995); Alejandro de la Fuente, *A Nation for All: Race, Inequality, and Politics in Twentieth-Century Cuba* (Chapel Hill: University of North Carolina Press, 2001); Ada Ferrer, *Insurgent Cuba: Race, Nation, and Revolution, 1868–1898* (Chapel Hill: University of North Carolina Press, 1999); Alejandra Bronfman, *Measures of Equality: Social Science, Citizenship, and Race in Cuba, 1902–1940* (Chapel Hill: University of North Carolina, 2004); Lillian Guerra, *The Myth of José Martí: Conflicting Nationalisms in Early Twentieth-Century Cuba* (Chapel Hill: University of North Carolina Press, 2005); and Joanna Beth Swanger, "Land Rebellion: Oriente and Escambray Encountering Cuban State Formation, 1934–1974" (PhD diss., University of Texas, Austin, 1999).

5. William B. Blocker to Col. T. N. Gimperling, NARA, Havana, April 21, 1936, RG 84, Foreign Service Posts of the State Department, Santiago de Cuba Consulate, General Records, 1936, vol. 7, 811–851.51, Box 5. (Future references to this collection will refer to it as RG 84, STGO, Gen.)

6. Ferrer, *Insurgent Cuba,* 54–55.

7. For works on the Cuban War of Independence in Guantánamo, see David Carlson, "The Cuban War of Independence in Guantánamo, 1895–1898: A Regional Study of Insurgency and Intervention" (master's thesis, University of North Carolina, 2001); José Sánchez Guerra and Wilfredo Campos Cremé, *La batalla de Guantánamo, 1898* (Havana: Ediciones Verde Olivo, 2000); José Sánchez Guerra, *Mambisas guantanameras* (Guantánamo: Editorial el Mar y la Montaña, 2000).

8. Ferrer, *Insurgent Cuba;* and Swanger, "Land Rebellion: Oriente and Escambray."

9. The historiography of the Spanish-American War or the War of 1898 reveals the debate among historians about the United States' role as an imperial power. Among Cuban historians there is no debate. William Appleman Williams, *The Tragedy of American Diplomacy,* new ed. (W. W. Norton, 1988); Ernest May, *Imperial Democracy: The Emergence of America as a World Power* (Chicago: Imprint, 1961); *Walter LaFeber, The New Empire: An Interpretation of American Expansion, 1860–1898,* 35th anniv. ed. (Ithaca, NY: Cornell University Press, 1998); Philip S. Foner, *The Spanish-Cuban-American War and the Birth of American Imperialism* (New York: Monthly Review, 1972); Louis A. Pérez Jr., *The War of 1898: The United States and Cuba in History and Historiography* (Chapel Hill: University of North Carolina Press, 1998); Herminio Portel Vilá, *Historia de la guerra de Cuba y los Estados Unidos contra España* (Havana: Publicaciones de la Oficina del Historiador de la Ciudad, 1949); Emilio Roig de Leuchsenring, *Cuba no debe su independencia a los Estados Unidos* (Buenos Aires: Hemisferio, 1965); and Oscar Luis Abdala Pupo, *La intervención militar norteamericana en la contienda independentista cubana, 1898* (Santiago de Cuba: Editorial Oriente, 1998).

10. "Our Flag Flies at Guantánamo," *New York Times,* June 12, 1898, p. 1.

11. "With the Fleet Off Santiago," *New York Times,* June 14, 1898, p. 1.

12. "Guantanamo as a Naval Base: Officers of the North Atlantic Squadron Favor the Retention of the Bay," *New York Times,* August 18, 1898, p. 3.

13. Louis A. Pérez Jr. forcefully makes this argument in his essay, "The Construction of the Cuban Absence," *War of 1898,* 81–107.

14. "Troops in No Danger," *New York Times,* June 15, 1898, p. 1; "Sharp Fighting at Guantanamo," *New York Times,* June 16, 1898, p. 1; "Caimanera Fort Demolished," *New York Times,* June 17, 1898, p. 1; and "Valor of the Marines," *New York Times,* June 27, 1898, p. 3.

15. "Guantanamo as a Naval Base," *New York Times,* August 18, 1898, p. 3.

16. See Eric T. Love, *Race over Empire: Racism and U.S. Imperialism, 1865–1900* (Chapel Hill: University of North Carolina Press, 2004), 200. Love argues that U.S. imperial aspirations were sharply restricted by the fear of acquiring territory in tropical climates populated by non–Anglo Saxons. Love cites Panama as a place where the United States wanted territory for a canal, but without responsibility for Panamanians. On U.S. attitudes toward Cuba's racial composition, also see de la Fuente, *A Nation for All;* Ferrer, *Insurgent Cuba;* and Amy Kaplan, "Black and Blue on San Juan Hill," in *Cultures of United States Imperialism* (Durham, NC: Duke University Press, 1993), 219–36.

17. "The Platt Amendment," in *The Cuba Reader: History, Culture, and Politics,* ed. Aviva Chomsky, Barry Carr, and Pamela Maria Smorkaloff (Durham, NC: Duke University Press, 2003), 147–49.

18. Bradley Reynolds, "Guantánamo Bay, Cuba: The History of an American Naval Base and Its Relationship to the Formulation of U.S. Foreign Policy and Military Strategy toward the Caribbean, 1895–1910" (PhD diss., University of Southern California, 1982), 218.

19. For synthetic accounts of the U.S. occupation and politics of the Platt Amendment, see Hugh Thomas, *Cuba; or, The Pursuit of Freedom* (London: Eyre and Spottiswoode, 1971); Louis A. Pérez Jr., *Cuba: Between Reform and Revolution* (New York: Oxford University Press, 1995), 185–87; Louis A. Pérez Jr., *Cuba between Empires, 1878–1902* (Pittsburgh, PA: University of Pittsburgh Press, 1983); Louis A. Pérez Jr., *Cuba under the Platt Amendment, 1902–1934* (Pittsburgh: University of Pittsburgh Press, 1986); and Louis A. Pérez Jr., *Cuba and the United States: Ties of Singular Intimacy* (Athens: University of Georgia Press, 1990). For a Cuban historian's analysis of the U.S. naval base, see Olga Miranda Bravo, *Vecinos indeseables: La base yanqui de Guantánamo* (Havana: Editorial Ciencias Sociales, 1998).

20. Mary Ellene Chenevey McCoy, "Guantánamo Bay: The United States Naval Base and Its Relationship to Cuba" (PhD diss., University of Akron, 1995), 50–51.

21. Richard Challener, *Admirals, Generals, and American Foreign Policy, 1898–1914* (Princeton, NJ: Princeton University Press, 1973); and McCoy, "Guantánamo Bay," 50.

22. Ibid., 95–96.

23. Lease of Lands for Coaling and Naval Stations, February 23, 1903, U.S.-Cuba, art. 3, *T. S.* no. 418, quoted in Murphy, *History of Guantánamo Bay, 1953 ed.*, 66.

24. "Cuba Offers Naval Station," *New York Times*, November 8, 1903, p. 4; and McCoy, "Guantánamo Bay," 53.

25. José Vázquez Pubillones, Índice, *La Voz del Pueblo*, June 2, 1959.

26. Wayne Ellwood, "Yankees in the Midst," *The New Internationalist*, no. 301 (May 1998).

27. PCC de Guantánamo, *Guantánamo: Apuntes para una cronología histórica*.

28. Commander Naval Base to Chief of Naval Operations, Re: Budocks proposal for inclusion of requirements that contractors must comply with Cuban labor laws with regard to the use of Cuban nationals, October 20, 1952, RG 181, GTMO, Weekly Intelligence Files, 1949–55, Box 2.

29. Helg, *Our Rightful Share*; de la Fuente, *A Nation for All*; and de la Fuente, "Myths of Racial Democracy: Cuba, 1900–1912," *Latin American Research Review* 34, no. 3 (Fall 1999): 39–73.

30. "No Mercy to Be Shown Rebels," *New York Times*, May 29, 1912, p. 6.

31. Helg, *Our Rightful Share*, 219.

32. "Warships to Cuba after Marines Land," *New York Times*, June 6, 1912, p. 1.

33. Helg, *Our Rightful Share*, 225; and de la Fuente, *A Nation for All*, 71–78.

34. César J. Ayala, *American Sugar Kingdom: The Plantation Economy of the Spanish Caribbean, 1898–1934* (Chapel Hill: University of North Carolina Press, 1999), 202; Oscar Zanetti and Alejandro García, *United Fruit Company: Un caso del dominio imperialista en Cuba* (Havana: Editorial Ciencias Sociales, 1976); Louis Pérez, *On Becoming Cuban*, 220–38.

35. Louis Pérez, *On Becoming Cuban,* 220–37; and Catherine LeGrand, "Living in Macondo: Economy and Culture in a United Fruit Company Banana Enclave in Columbia," in *Close Encounters of Empire,* 333–68.

36. Juan Pérez de la Riva, "Cuba y la Migración Antillana, 1900–1931," in *La república neocolonial: Anuario de estudios cubanos,* vol. 2 (Havana: Editorial Ciencias Sociales, 1979); Aviva Chomsky and Aldo Lauria-Santiago, eds. *Identity and Struggle at the Margins of the Nation-State: The Laboring Peoples of Central America and the Hispanic Caribbean* (Durham, NC: Duke University Press, 1998); Franklin W. Knight, "Jamaican Migrants and the Cuban Sugar Industry, 1900–1934," in *Between Slavery and Free Labor: The Spanish-Speaking Caribbean in the Nineteenth Century,* ed. Manuel Moreno Fraginals, Frank Moya Pons, and Stanley L. Engerman (Baltimore: Johns Hopkins University Press, 1985), 94–116; Barry Carr, "Identity, Class, and Nation: Black Immigrant Workers, Cuban Communism, and the Sugar Insurgency, 1925–1934," *Hispanic American Historical Review* 78 (February 1998): 83–116; Marc McLeod, "Undesirable Aliens: Race, Ethnicity, and Nationalism in the Comparison of Haitian and British Subjects," *Journal of Social History* 21 (Spring 1998): 599–623; Marc McLeod, "Undesirable Aliens: Haitians and British West Indian Immigrant Workers in Cuba, 1898 to 1940" (PhD diss., University of Texas, Austin, 2000); Graciela Chailloux Laffita, Roberto Claxton, and Robert Whitney, "I Am the Caribbean: A West Indian Melting Pot in Cuba," in *Intra-Caribbean Migration: The Cuban Connection, 1898–Present* (publication of the proceedings, University of the West Indies, Mona, Jamaica, June 14–16, 2001); Graciela Chailloux Laffita, "La contribución antillana a la identidad cubana," *Debates Americanos* 12 (January–December 2002): 54–62; Jorge Giovannetti, "The Elusive Organization of 'Identity': Race, Religion, and Empire among Caribbean Migrants in Cuba," *Small Axe* 10 (2006):1–27; Jorge Giovannetti, "Black British Subjects in Cuba: Race, Ethnicity, Nation, and Identity in the Migratory Experience, 1898–1938" (PhD diss., University of North London, 2001); José Sánchez Guerra, *Los anglo-caribeños en Guantánamo, 1902–1950* (Guantánamo: Editorial el Mar y la Montaña, 2004); Jorge Ibarra, "La inmigración antillana" (paper presented at IV Encuentro de Historiadores Latinoamericanos y del Caribe, 1983); and Andrea Queeley, "A Dream Derailed? The English-Speaking Caribbean Diaspora in Revolutionary Cuba" (PhD diss., City University of New York, 2007). Jamaicans composed the majority of West Indian migrants, but many others came from Barbados, Trinidad and Tobago, and the Eastern Caribbean. "West Indian" also generally designated an individual from the British colonies. Although Haitian migrants are also from the West Indies, they were generally termed "Haitians" and not "West Indians." Few Haitians worked on the base. Despite the fact that all Caribbean people are arguably West Indians, I follow the standard practice of using West Indian to refer to men and women from the English-speaking islands.

37. de la Fuente, *A Nation for All,* 45–53, 100–5.

38. Chailloux, Claxton, and Whitney, "I Am the Caribbean."

39. Robert Whitney, *State and Revolution in Cuba: Mass Mobilization and Political Change, 1920–1940* (Chapel Hill: University of North Carolina, 2001); Frank Argote-Freyre, *Fulgencio Batista: From Revolutionary to Strongman* (New

Brunswick, NJ: Rutgers University Press, 2006); Louis A. Pérez, *Cuba: Between Reform and Revolution*, 229–75; and Thomas, *Cuba*, 615–88.

40. "New Cuban Treaty," *New York Times*, May 31, 1934, p. 18.

41. "La supresión de la Enmienda Platt suscita un júbilo indescriptible en toda Cuba," *Adelante*, May 30, 1934; Rodolfo Ibarra, "¡Ha muerto la Enmienda Platt!" *Adelante*, May 31, 1934; and "El nuevo tratado entre Cuba y EEUU comenzará a regir en la fecha en que se efectúe el cambio de ratificaciones," *Diario de la Marina*, May 30, 1934, p. 1.

42. "Las autoridades americanas confían en la eficacia de la policía de nuestro país," *Diario de la Marina*, May 30, 1934, p. 3.

43. *La Voz del Pueblo*, May 30 and May 31, 1934.

44. Treaty between the United States of America and Cuba, May 29, 1934, U.S.-Cuba, art. 3, 48, stat. 1682, *T. S.* no. 866, quoted in Murphy, *History of Guantánamo Bay*, 1953 ed., 67–68.

45. Murphy, *History of Guantánamo Bay*, 1953 ed., 7.

1. THE CASE OF KID CHICLE

1. "La víctima de Guantánamo," *Hoy*, December 22, 1940; "La madre de crianza de Lino Rodríguez tiene fe en nuestros tribunales," *Diario de Cuba*, December 22, 1940; Rolando E. Quintero Mena, "El caso Chicle: Un crimen del imperialismo yanqui que quedó impune," *El Managui, Sección de Investigaciones Históricas del Comité Provincial del PCC, Guantánamo* 4, no. 9 (1989): 3–12; McCoy, "Guantánamo Bay," 129–35; and George Weyler to Harry Story, November 27, 1941, RG 84, STGO, Gen., 1941, vol. 5, 812–886.7, Box 27. On fashion, working-class politics, and World War II, see Robin Kelley, "The Riddle of the Zoot Suit: Malcolm Little and Black Cultural Politics during World War II," in *Race Rebels: Culture, Politics, and the Black Working Class* (New York: Free Press, 1994), 161–81.

2. James Forestal to Liaison Office, January 6, 1941, NARA, RG 59/811.34537/286 PS/FF, State Department Decimal File, Box 3784. (All Record Group (RG) 59 State Department documents are located at NARA in College Park, MD. Future citations will include the decimal number and box number.)

3. James Forestal to Liaison Office, January 6, 1941, RG 59/811.34537/286 PS/FF, Box 3784.

4. Víctor Alonso, "Golpean brutalmente y lanzan al mar a un trabajador cubano en Caimanera," *Diario de Cuba*, December 18, 1940; and "El Cabo de Marina," *La Voz del Pueblo*, December 19, 1940.

5. Víctor Alonso, "Piden que sea juzgado en Cuba el Teniente West," *Diario de Cuba*, December 20, 1940; "La madre de crianza de Lino Rodríguez tiene fe en nuestros tribunales," *Diario de Cuba*, December 22, 1940; "Designado juez especial," *Hoy*, December 21, 1940; and "Demuestra la autopsia que fue asesinado el obrero cubano," *Información*, December 20, 1940. (*Información* clipping in RG 59/811.34537/284 PS/FF, Box 3784.)

6. Víctor Alonso, "Comprueba la autopsia o. Lino Rodríguez fue muerto a golpes antes de ser arrojado al mar," *Diario de Cuba*, December 19, 1940; "El cabo de la Marina Constitucional Hilberto Hidalgo fue recibido por el jefe de la

base naval aérea," *La Voz del Pueblo,* December 19, 1940; "Un testigo presencial de nuevos detalles sobre el crimen de Caimanera," *Hoy,* December 24, 1940; and "Memorando relacionado con el homicidio de Lino Rodríguez Grenot," December 26, 1940, Cuban National Archives, Secretaría de la Presidencia, Ministerio de Justicia, Caja 45, Número 2. (In future references, the Cuban National Archive will be noted as CNA.)

7. Cordell Hull to Frank Knox, Secretary of the Navy, May 1, 1941, RG 59/811.34537/284, Box 3784.

8. James Forestal to Liaison Office, January 6, 1941, RG 59/811.34537/286 PS/FF, Box 3784.

9. "Memorando relacionado con el homicidio de Lino Rodríguez Grenot," December 26, 1940, CNA, Secretaría de la Presidencia, Ministerio de Justicia, Caja 45, Número 2.

10. "Excerpt of Letter Addressed to Mr. Bonsal," March 19, 1941, RG 59/811.34537, Box 3784.

11. James Forestal to the Secretary of State, June 18, 1941, RG 59/811.34537, Box 3784.

12. "Report of the Board to Investigate and Report upon the Need, for Purposes of National Defense for the Establishment of Additional Submarine, Destroyer, Mine, and Naval Air Bases on the Coasts of the United States, Its Territories, and Possessions," December 1, 1938, RG 59/811.345/137, Box 5017.

13. "Fleet Will Shift to Atlantic in '39," *New York Times,* May 27, 1938, p. 11; "Navy to Build Up Atlantic Squadron," *New York Times,* October 20, 1938, p. 8; "Navy Board Urges 41 Defense Bases for Entire Nation," *New York Times,* January 4, 1939, p. 1; and "Congress to Vote Navy Equal to Any Other," *New York Times,* March 19, 1939, p. 28.

14. "Strategy in the Caribbean," *New York Times,* May 31, 1939, p. 22.

15. Rear Admiral Yates Stirling Jr., "Bases 'Vital Need' of American Navy," *New York Times,* August 23, 1940, p. 4. Daniel Yergin also argues that World War II was defined as a contest over oil. Daniel Yergin, *The Prize: The Epic Quest for Oil, Money, and Power* (New York: Simon and Schuster, 1991), 303–88.

16. "Roosevelt Plans South Atlantic Cruise to Watch the Fleet in Spring War Games," *New York Times,* January 11, 1939, p. 8; "2000 Mile Front Occupied by Fleet," *New York Times,* January 30, 1939, p. 3; "Midnight Starts Navy's 'Warfare,' " *New York Times,* February 13, 1939, p. 9; and "Roosevelt Leads War Games Survey," *New York Times,* February 28, 1939, p. 4.

17. Alonso de Armas, "Guantanameras," *Diario de Cuba,* March 19, 1939, p. 10.

18. U.S. Bureau of Yards and Docks, *Building the Navy's Bases in World War II: History of the Bureau of Yards and Docks and the Civil Engineer Corps,* vol. 1 (Washington DC: U.S. Government Printing Office, 1947), 25–33.

19. Thomas, *Cuba,* 724–36; "U.S. Will Give Up Cuban War Bases," *New York Times,* April 2, 1946, p. 1; and McCoy, "Guantánamo Bay," 105–15.

20. Gaylord T. M. Kelshall, *The U-Boat War in the Caribbean* (Annapolis, MD: Naval Institute Press, 1994), xiii–xvi; and Roland T. Carr, *To Sea in Haste* (Washington DC: Acropolis Books, 1975).

21. John R. Henry, "With the U.S. Marines, Guantánamo Bay," April 18, 1943, NARA, RG 181, Records of Naval District and Shore Establishment, U.S. Naval Station, Guantánamo Bay, Cuba, World War II Files, Box 3. (From this point onward, this collection will be referred to as RG 181, GTMO, World War II Files.)

22. "This Training Might Come in Handy: U.S. Marines Stationed at Guantánamo Bay, Cuba, Diving from a Forty-Six-Foot Cliff," *New York Times,* June 28, 1943, p. 6, photo.

23. Lino Lemes García, Guantánamo al día, *La Voz del Pueblo,* September 11, 1940; "Por la zona turística," *La Voz del Pueblo,* April 10, 1941; José Vázquez Pubillones, "Caimanera está disfrutando la edad de oro de su vida," *La Voz del Pueblo,* July 13, 1943; and Juan Quintero Ávila, "Se aprestan las fuerzas vivas del poblado a dar batalla por sus mejoras," *La Voz del Pueblo,* January 18, 1947.

24. "William G. Osment, Official of Cuban Railroad, 71, Dies in Hospital in Miami," *New York Times,* January 6, 1946, p. 40.

25. *Guía práctica y datos de la ciudad y término de Guantánamo* (Guantánamo: Recaredo Crespo, 1939). (Located in Guantánamo Provincial Archive in the archivist's private collection.)

26. de la Fuente, *A Nation for All,* 161–71; and Alberto Soler Zunzarren, *Guantánamo historia: Guía general* (1947). (Located in Guantánamo Provincial Archive in the archivist's private collection.)

27. Chailloux, "La contribución antillana"; West Indian Democratic Association (Sociedad de Antillanos Amantes de la Democracia), Caimanera, Guantánamo, Santiago de Cuba Provincial Archive, Fondos del Gobierno Provincial, Caimanera, 1943–48, Legajo 197, Número 1; and *Guía práctica de Guantánamo.*

28. Zunzarren, *Guantánamo historia,* 39–54.

29. Pérez, *On Becoming Cuban,* 220–37.

30. I would like to thank Dain Borges for this insight. Also see LeGrand, "Living in Macondo."

31. Informe del equipo de la Escuela de Historia, Universidad de la Habana, "Guantánamo: Esquema de la historia de una ciudad," unpublished report, José Martí National Library, Havana, Cuba, May 1967.

32. McCoy, "Guantánamo Bay," 146–84.

33. U.S. Bureau of Yards and Docks, *Building the Navy's Bases,* 78.

34. Ibid., 77–85; John Morton Blum, *V Was for Victory: Politics and American Culture during World War II* (San Diego: Harcourt Brace, 1976), 117–46; Steven Fraser, *Labor Will Rule: Sidney Hillman and the Rise of American Labor* (Ithaca, NY: Cornell University Press, 1991), 441–538; Doris Kearns Goodwin, *No Ordinary Time, Franklin and Eleanor Roosevelt: The Home Front in World War II* (New York: Simon and Schuster, 1994), 57–60, 156–60.

35. Murphy, *History of Guantánamo Bay,* 1953 ed., 31.

36. Rosalie Schwartz, *Pleasure Island: Tourism and Temptation in Cuba* (Lincoln: University of Nebraska Press, 1997), 48; Julie Wells, "Trip Brings Piano Tuner in Tune with Past," *Boston Globe,* February 15, 1998, http://www.stanwoodpiano.com/globecub.htm (accessed July 1, 2006); and "Snare Jubilee," *Time,* February 17, 1936.

37. George S. Messersmith, Ambassador's Memorandum, August 31, 1940, RG 59/811.34537/271, Box 3784.

38. Murphy, *History of Guantánamo Bay*, 1953 ed., 31–32.

39. Lino Lemes García, Guantánamo al día, *La Voz del Pueblo*, October 14, 1940.

40. *Hoy*, September 3, 1940. (*Hoy* clipping in RG 59/811.34537, Box 3784.)

41. Captain George Weyler to U.S. Ambassador, January 14, 1943, RG 181, GTMO, World War II Files, Box 3.

42. Ellis O. Briggs to Captain George Weyler, May 6, 1942, RG 181, GTMO, World War II Files, Box 3.

43. Lino Lemes García, "Situación difícil para todos," *La Voz del Pueblo*, July 26, 1940.

44. Lino Lemes García, Guantánamo al día, *El Vigilante*, August 10, 1940; and "Oficina de la Frederick Snare Corporation," *La Voz del Pueblo*, January 9, 1941.

45. Santiago Ruiz (pseud.), personal interview, Guantánamo, Cuba, November 18, 2004. (Interview conducted in Spanish.)

46. Ricardo Baylor (pseud.), personal interview, Guantánamo, Cuba, November 21, 2004. (Interview conducted in Spanish.)

47. In Spanish, *marino* means "sailor," but in Guantánamo, it connoted both U.S. sailors and marines.

48. Alberto Torres (pseud.), personal interview, Havana, Cuba, December 5, 2004. (Interview conducted in Spanish.)

49. Lino Lemes García, Guantánamo al día, *El Vigilante*, November 15, 1940; and "El caso Pomares-Ochoa," *La Voz del Pueblo*, November 18, 1940.

50. Guantánamo Municipal Museum, Guantánamo, Cuba, October 6, 2004.

51. Juan Carlos Pulsara (pseud.), personal interview, Guantánamo, Cuba, March 15, 2004 (Interview conducted in Spanish.); Pedro A. López Jardo, *Guantánamo y "Gitmo": Detalles y eventos históricos relacionados con Guantánamo, la ciudad del Guaso, y la base naval de los EEUU. Narrado por un guantanamero, extrabajador de la base naval* (Miami: Ediciones Universal, 2000), 67; Amitava Kumar, *Passport Photos* (Berkeley: University of California Press, 2000).

52. Base Public Works Officer to the Commander, Re: Complaint of Lemes Garcia to the FBI concerning wage scales at the naval operating base, Tabulation of average wages paid to Cuban employees, November 20, 1944, RG 181, GTMO, World War II, Box 3.

53. Lino Lemes García, "Evite una desgracia," *El Vigilante*, November 16, 1940; and Lino Lemes García, Guantánamo al día, *El Vigilante*, May 10, 1941.

54. "Cerca de Boquerón un yate hundió una lancha-motor en la que viajaban 25–30 hombres," *La Voz del Pueblo*, July 22, 1943.

55. Walter Knight (pseud.), personal interview, Guantánamo, Cuba, November 22, 2004. (Interview conducted in Spanish.)

56. Maria Boothe (pseud.), personal interview, Guantánamo, Cuba, November 23, 2004. (Interview conducted in Spanish.)

57. "¿Qué hubo de la carretera a Caimanera?" *La Voz del Pueblo,* August 22, 1945.

58. McCoy also makes this point and adds that until 1940, there were no phone connections between Guantánamo and the base. McCoy, "Guantánamo Bay," 115–16.

59. McLeod, "Undesirable Aliens: Haitians and West Indians," 3–7.

60. de la Fuente, *A Nation for All,* 100–105; and McLeod, "Undesirable Aliens: Haitians and West Indians," 87–91.

61. McLeod, "Undesirable Aliens: Haitians and British West Indians"; and Giovannetti, "Black British Subjects in Cuba."

62. José Clemente to FDR, May 22, 1941, RG 59/811.34537/324, Box 3784.

63. Milton Patterson Thompson to Captain W. R. Carter, August 5, 1938; Commandant W. R. Carter to Milton Patterson Thompson, August 9, 1938; and Milton Patterson Thompson to Dr. Angel Pérez, August 13, 1938. All located in RG 84, STGO, Gen., 1938, vol. 7, 811.3–841.5, Box 16 (emphasis added).

64. "Pide el alcalde municipal se utilicen obreros de Guantánamo en las obras de la base naval," *La Voz del Pueblo,* July 31, 1940.

65. Lino Lemes García, Guantánamo al día, *La Voz del Pueblo,* May 19, 1941.

66. Lino Lemes García, "Alerta obreros nativos," *El Vigilante,* June 13, 1940.

67. Lino Lemes García, "Un solo contratista obtiene contratos," *El Vigilante,* July 18, 1940.

68. Milton Patterson Thompson to George Messersmith, October 18, 1940, and Complaint against Guantánamo naval station by Sr. Lino Lemes García," October 7, 1940, RG 84, STGO, Gen., 1940, vol. 5, 830–886.7, Box 24; and "Persons Whose Entry into the U.S. Might Be Contrary to the Public Interest," September 27, 1940, NARA, RG 84, Foreign Service Posts of the State Department, Santiago de Cuba Consulate, Confidential Records, 1938–40, Box 3. (All future citations from this collection will be RG 84, STGO, Conf.)

69. Giovannetti, "The Elusive Organization of 'Identity'"; Giovannetti, "Black British Subjects in Cuba," 111–40, 176; McLeod, "Undesirable Aliens: Haitian and British West Indian Immigrant Workers," 127–65, 87–126; Tomás Fernández Robaina, "Marcus Garvey in Cuba: Urrutia, Cubans, and Black Nationalism," in *Between Race and Empire: African-Americans and Cubans before the Cuban Revolution,* ed. Lisa Brock and Digna Castañeda Fuertes (Philadelphia, PA: Temple University Press, 1998), 120–28; Jorge Ibarra, "La inmigración antillana"; and Carr, "Identity, Class, and Nation."

70. West Indian Democratic Association (Sociedad de Antillanos Amantes de la Democracia) Caimanera, Guantánamo, 1943, Santiago de Cuba Provincial Archive; Fondos del Gobierno Provincial, Materia Caimanera, 1943–48, Legajo 197, Número 1.

71. Lino Lemes García, "Alerta obreros nativos," *El Vigilante,* June 13, 1940.

72. Alien Registration on the Naval Base, October 8, 1943, RG 181, GTMO, World War II Files, Box 3.

73. "En una composición de cerveza, leche condensada y nuez moscada, un jamaiquino envenena a su familia," *La Voz del Pueblo,* April 27, 1942; "Ocupado el sobre que contenía la estricnina que utilizó el jamaiquino Anderson," *La Voz del Pueblo,* April 28, 1942; and "Ayer de tarde fue apuñaleado un jamaiquino vendedor de billetes y boletos," *La Voz del Pueblo,* October 2, 1942.

74. Giovannetti, "Black British Subjects in Cuba," 7–8. Although *jamaiquino* is grammatically correct, it was still seen as an insult. The press and local community collectively referred to all West Indians as "Jamaicans," disregarding the backgrounds of a significant proportion of the community.

75. For example, when Lino Lemes reported on Jamaicans in the press, he exclusively used the term *jamaiquino.* See Lino Lemes García, "Qué pasó en la estación naval?" *El Vigilante,* February 3, 1940; Lino Lemes García, "El puesto naval de Caimanera necesita más personal," *El Vigilante,* August 10, 1945; and Lino Lemes García, "Hay que acabar con los malcriados que molestan a los marinos que nos visitan," *La Voz del Pueblo,* December 21, 1945.

76. Lino Lemes García, "Un solo contratista obtiene contratos," July 18, 1940. There is also evidence in the local press of a small Chinese community on the base. Chinese workers worked almost exclusively in the service industries on the base, such as laundries and restaurants. See Lino Lemes García, "Protesta," *El Vigilante,* June 10, 1942; Lino Lemes García, "Barberos cubanos trabajan en la base americana de operaciones," *El Vigilante,* August 9, 1944; and Ana Daelé Valdés Millán, "Presencia china en la ciudad de Guantánamo 1906–1960" (master's thesis, Universidad de Oriente, Cuba, 2003).

77. José Octavio Muñoz, "Información obrera," *Oriente,* October 12–13, 1939. (Clipping located in RG 84, STGO, Gen., 1939, vols. 5–6, 621.1–832, Box 20.)

78. Juan Carlos Pulsara, personal interview, Guantánamo, Cuba, October 9, 2004.

79. For an analysis of Trinidadian workers caught between U.S. and British imperialism, see Neptune, *Caliban and the Yankees.*

80. Giovannetti, "Black British Subjects in Cuba."

81. In fact, the Panama Canal Zone executive secretary, C. A. McIlvaine, wrote to Santiago de Cuba for comparison of pay rates/pay scale, for "native employees, most of whom are colored West Indians." C. A. McIlvaine to Santiago de Cuba Consulate, June 15, 1939, RG 84, STGO, Gen., 1939, vols. 7–8, 833–886.3, Box 21. For scholarship on the Panama Canal and labor, see Julie Greene, "Spaniards on the Silver Roll: Labor Troubles and Liminality in the Panama Canal Zone, 1904–1914," *International Labor and Working-Class History* 66 (Fall 2004): 78–98; John Major, *Prize Possession,* 78–96; Michael Conniff, *Black Labor on a White Canal: Panama 1904–1981* (Pittsburgh, PA: University of Pittsburgh Press, 1985); and Rhonda D. Frederick, *"Colón Man a Come" Mythographies of Panamá Canal Migration* (Lanham, MD: Lexington Books, 2005). Two other important works on U.S. empire and the Panama Canal are Walter LaFeber, *The Panama Canal: The Crisis in Historical Perspective* (New York: Oxford University Press, 1978); and John Lindsay-Poland, *Emperors in the Jungle: The Hidden History of the U.S. in Panama* (Durham, NC: Duke University Press, 2003).

82. Christina Duffy Burnett and Burke Marshall, eds., *Foreign in a Domestic Sense: Puerto Rico, American Expansion and the Constitution* (Durham, NC: Duke University Press, 2001).

83. Gordon Burke to Juan Almodóvar Sánchez, November 15–18, 1943, RG 84, STGO, Gen., 1942, vols. 6–7, 811.1–891, Box 32.

84. Gordon Burke to the Secretary of State, January 5, 1944, RG 84, STGO, Gen., 1944, vols. 8–9, 822–892.3, Box 35.

85. Eddy Pagán Auffant to U.S. Consulate, February 20, 1939, RG 84, STGO, Gen., 1939, vol. 3, 131–562.2, Box 19.

86. Juan Martínez Lugo to Harry W. Story, September 9, 1940, RG 84, STGO, Gen., 1940, vols. 3–4, 310-M, Box 23.

87. Harry Story to Juan Martínez Lugo, September 11, 1940, RG 84, STGO, Gen., 1940, vols. 3–4, 310-M, Box 23.

88. Santos Lugo to U.S. Consulate, August 8, 1939, RG 84, STGO, Gen., 1939, vol. 3, 131–562.2, Box 19.

89. Pedro Salgado and José Fernández to FDR, September 3, 1940, RG 59/811.34537/278, Box 3784.

90. Pedro Salgado and José Fernández to FDR, September 3, 1940, RG 59/811.34537/278, Box 3784.

91. Confidential Memorandum, Re: Germans "hunting for butterflies," June 12, 1940, RG 84, STGO, Conf., 1938–40, All Numbers, Box 3; and "Father and Son Are Detained as Spying Suspects," *Havana Post,* June 18, 1940 (clipping), RG 84, STGO, Conf., 1938–40, All Numbers, Box 3. For the best work on Axis sympathizers in Latin America, see Friedman, *Nazis and Good Neighbors.*

92. Weyler to U.S. Ambassador, January 14, 1943, RG 181, GTMO, World War II Files, Box 3.

93. F. Mendoza, "Impresiones," *La Voz del Pueblo,* April 11, 1942; José Vázquez Pubillones, "Pepito Álvarez," *La Voz del Pueblo,* April 5, 1943; Harry Story to Harold S. Tewell, January 10, 1942, and Harold S. Tewell to Captain George L. Weyler, April 9, 1942, RG 84, STGO, Conf., 1941–42, All Numbers, Box 4.

94. James K. McGhie on Disturbances in Guantánamo Bay Area, June 15, 1945, RG 181, GTMO, World War II Files, Box 3.

95. Franklin Hawley to Dr. Manuel G. Miranda, January 4, 1945, RG 84, STGO, Conf., 1945, 832, Box 6.

96. Luis Pavón Tamayo, "La base militar yanqui," *Venceremos,* March 6, 1964; and permanent exhibition, Guantánamo Municipal Museum, Guantánamo, Cuba.

97. Lino Lemes García, "Una viril protesta por el bárbaro hecho de Caimanera," *El Vigilante,* December 18, 1940.

98. Víctor Alonso, "Golpean brutalmente y lanzan al mar a un trabajador cubano en Caimanera," *Diario de Cuba,* December 18, 1940, p. 1.

99. Lino Lemes García, Guantánamo al día, *El Vigilante,* December 23, 1940.

100. James Forestal to Department of State, January 6, 1941, RG 59/811.34537/286 PS/FF, Box 3784.

101. "En Caimanera se ha producido un suceso que ha suscitado viva protesta," *La Voz del Pueblo*, December 18, 1940.

102. Lino Lemes García, "Una viril protesta por el bárbaro hecho de Caimanera," *El Vigilante*, December 18, 1940.

103. Víctor Alonso, "Piden que sea juzgado en Cuba el teniente West, autor material del trágico suceso de Caimanera," *Diario de Cuba*, December 20, 1940, p. 1.

104. "Detenido el oficial americano que mató a un obrero cubano," *Diario de la Marina*, December 22, 1940.

105. "Pídese justicia en el caso del obrero asesinado por un teniente de los Estados Unidos," *Hoy*, December 19, 1940, p. 1.

106. Editorial, "Opiniones de *Hoy*," *Hoy*, December 19, 1940.

107. " 'Pequeña' cosa," *Hoy*, December 21, 1940.

108. "Expediente que contiene las protestas de diferentes instituciones del país por la muerte de Lino Rodríguez Grenot," December 18, 1940–January 3, 1941, CNA, Secretaría de la Presidencia, Caja 45, Número 2.

109. "Three U.S. Navy Men Held in Cuban Death: Officer Said to Have Hit Native Who Drowned at Guantánamo," *New York Times*, December 20, 1940, p. 4.

110. "Kid Chicle, Cuban Boxer, Slain by U.S. Naval Officer in Labor Dispute," *Chicago Defender*, December 28, 1940, p. 22.

111. Orme Wilson to the Director, Central Division, Navy Department, December 30, 1940, RG 59/811.34537/284A, Box 3784.

112. Captain George L. Weyler to Harry Story, July 3, 1941, RG 84, STGO, Gen., 1941, vol. 5, 812–886.7, Box 27.

113. Excerpt of Letter Addressed to Mr. Bonsal, March 19, 1941, RG 59/811.34537, Box 3784.

114. Maria Isabel Rodríguez Grenot and Clemencia Grenot to U.S. Consulate, September 8, 1941; Harry Story to Captain George L. Weyler, September 17, 1941; George Weyler to Harry Story, September 22, 1941; George Weyler to Harry Story, November 27, 1941; and Harry Story to George Weyler, December 2, 1941, all located in RG 84, STGO, Gen., 1941, vol. 5, 812–886.7, Box 27; and McCoy, "Guantánamo Bay," 129–35.

115. Harry Story to Harold S. Tewell, May 22, 1942, RG 84, STGO, Conf., 1941–42, All Numbers, Box 4.

116. Luis Pavón Tamayo, "La base militar yanqui," *Venceremos*, March 6, 1964.

117. Rigoberto Cruz Díaz, *Guantánamo Bay* (Santiago de Cuba: Editorial Oriente, 1977), 52–57.

118. Lino Lemes García, "El lamentable suceso de ayer en la estación naval," *El Vigilante*, November 26, 1940; and Lino Lemes García, "Falleció el obrero santiaguero Agustín Álvarez que sufrió un accidente en la base naval," *El Vigilante*, November 29, 1940.

119. Lino Lemes García, "Otro obrero muere en la base yankee," *El Vigilante*, February 15, 1941 (clipping); Lino Lemes García to President Roosevelt, February 16, 1941; and U.S. Department of State to Santiago de Cuba Consulate, March 27, 1941, RG 84, STGO, Gen., 1941, vol. 5, 812–886.7, Box 27.

120. Lino Lemes García, "La muerte misteriosa de un trabajador de la Snare Coporation," *El Vigilante,* May 14, 1941.

121. George Weyler to U.S. vice consul, October 31, 1941, RG 84, STGO, Gen., 1941, vol. 5, 812–886.7, Box 27.

122. "Estaba ebrio el marino de EU que mató al dependiente de la base naval de Caimanera," *Hoy,* October 31, 1941. There was no press coverage of this incident in the Guantánamo press.

123. Harry Story to Captain George Weyler, November 15, 1941, RG 84, STGO, Gen., 1941, vol. 5, 812–886.7, Box 27.

124. Captain George Weyler to Harry Story, November 26, 1941, RG 84, STGO, Gen., 1941, vol. 5, 812–886.7, Box 27.

125. Harry Story to Captain George Weyler, November 3, 1941, RG 84, STGO, Gen., 1941, vol. 5, 812–886.7, Box 27.

2. "WE ARE REAL DEMOCRATS"

1. Cristóbal A. Zamora, "Afirma el obrero cubano Lorenzo Salomón que fue maltratado en la base naval de EU en Caimanera," *Avance,* October 15, 1954; "Roba un obrero cubano la suma de $1543.26 en la base naval," *La Voz del Pueblo,* October 2, 1954; "Interesante carta sobre el caso Salomón del Sr. A. Berguelich," *La Voz del Pueblo,* October 25, 1954; and Joaquín Toirac Adames, "Apuntes sobre el movimiento obrero en la base naval norteamericana," *El Managui: Sección de Investigaciones Históricas del Comité Provincial del PCC Guantánamo* (1988): 3–8.

2. Cristóbal A. Zamora, "Denuncia el obrero L. Salomón al juzgado los atropellos de que afirma fue víctima en Camianera," *Avance,* October 18, 1954. Similar language also appeared in the base workers' bulletin, see Translation of Editorial Published in the Union of Base Workers and Employees Bulletin No. 9, September 1954, RG 59/711.56337/10–2254, Box 3180.

3. Cristóbal A. Zamora, "Afirma el obrero cubano Lorenzo Salomón que fue maltratado en la base naval de EU en Caimanera," *Avance,* October 15, 1954; and Translation of Editorial Published in the Union of Base Workers and Employees Bulletin No. 9, September 1954, RG 59/711.56337/10–2254, Box 3180.

4. Translation of Editorial Published in the Union of Base Workers and Employees Bulletin No. 9, September 1954, RG 59/711.56337/10–2254, Box 3180.

5. Conference with Mr. John Fishbrune, Latin American Labor Advisor, Re: To discuss labor relations at the naval base, November 18, 1954, RG 181, GTMO, Weekly Intelligence Files, 1949–55, Box 3.

6. Robert Whitney and Frank Argote-Freyre provide a cautionary and historical perspective on the pitfalls of viewing all of pre-1959 Cuban history as a precursor to the Cuban revolution. Whitney, *State and Revolution in Cuba,* 10–13; and Frank Argote-Freyre, "In Search of Fulgencio Batista: An Examination of Pre-revolutionary Cuban Scholarship," *Revista Mexicana del Caribe* 11 (2001): 193–227.

7. Toirac Adames, "Apuntes sobre el movimiento obrero en la base naval norteamericana."

8. On anti-Americanism, see Alan McPherson, *Yankee No! Anti-Americanism in U.S–Latin American Relations* (Cambridge, MA: Harvard University Press, 2003); and Grandin, "Your Americanism and Mine."

9. U.S. Bureau of Yards and Docks, *Building the Navy's Bases in World War II,* vol. 2.

10. Walter LaFeber, *America, Russia, and the Cold War, 1945–1992* (New York: McGraw Hill, 1993); and Smith, *American Empire.*

11. Harold Hinton, "Nimitz Sees Navy as Atomic Shield," *New York Times,* February 15, 1946, p. 1.

12. Murphy, *History of Guantánamo Bay,* 1953 ed., 48.

13. Operation Plan, Caribbean Command, June 15, 1949, RG 181, GTMO, Weekly Intelligence Files 1949–55, Box 1.

14. Command Structure of the Defense of the Caribbean (Prepared by Commander Caribbean Sea Frontier), May 21, 1948, RG 181, GTMO, Weekly Intelligence Files, 1949–55, Box 1.

15. Thomas Hagan, "Fleet Off Today for Record Games; Atomic Bombings to be Simulated," *New York Times,* February 21, 1949, p. 4; "Navy Armada Sails for War Exercises, Greatest in Peacetime, in Caribbean Sea, *New York Times,* February 22, 1949, p. 2; Hanson Baldwin, "Vieques 'Atom Test' Alters Navy Plans," *New York Times,* March 4, 1949, p. 7; and Hanson Baldwin, "Sea and Air 'War' Rages on Atlantic," *New York Times,* March 4, 1950, p. 8.

16. Hanson Baldwin, "Caribbean Bases Quiet," *New York Times,* March 8, 1949, p. 4.

17. Roorda, *The Dictator Next Door;* Walter LaFeber, *Inevitable Revolutions: The United States in Central America* (New York: W. W. Norton, 1983); and Greg Grandin, *The Last Colonial Massacre* (Chicago: University of Chicago Press, 2004).

18. Robert Whitney, "The Architect of the Cuban State: Fulgencio Batista and Populism in Cuba, 1937–1940," *Journal of Latin American Studies* 32 (2000): 435–59; Whitney, *State and Revolution in Cuba;* Argote-Freyre, "In Search of Fulgencio Batista"; Argote-Freyre, *Fulgencio Batista;* Samuel Farber, *Revolution and Reaction in Cuba, 1933–1960: A Political Sociology from Machado to Castro* (Middletown, CT: Wesleyan University Press, 1976); Morris H. Morley, "The U.S. Imperial State in Cuba, 1952–1958," *Journal of Latin American Studies* 14, no. 1 (May 1982): 143–70; de la Fuente, *A Nation for All,* 175–255; Thomas, *Cuba,* 691–788; and Pérez, *Between Reform and Revolution,* 276–95. Hugh Thomas uses the phrase "puppet presidents" in "Batista and the Puppet Presidents," *Cuba,* chap. 59.

19. The *Unión Revolucionaria Comunista* (URC) changed its name in 1944 to the *Partido Socialista Popular* (PSP). Despite this change, as a point of clarity, I will refer to both parties as the Communist Party.

20. Farber, *Revolution and Reaction,* 137–44.

21. Pérez, *Between Reform and Revolution,* 278; de la Fuente, *A Nation for All,* 222–35; Jon V. Kofas, *The Struggle for Legitimacy: Latin American Labor and the United States, 1930–1960* (Tempe: Arizona State University Press, 1992), 122–26; and Farber, *Revolution and Reaction.*

22. U.S. Ambassador to Philip Bonsal, Department of State, August 31, 1940, RG 59/811.34537/271, Box 3784; and George S. Messersmith to U.S. Department of State, Re: Attempt to create labor trouble at the base, September 5, 1940, RG 59/811.34537/270, Box 3784.

23. Kofas, *Struggle for Legitimacy,* 125.

24. Thomas, *Cuba,* 737–58.

25. Readiness of Plans for Prompt Action, June 26, 1948, RG 181, GTMO, Weekly Intelligence Files, 1949–55, Box 1; and Readiness of Plans for Prompt Action, October 15, 1948, RG 181, GTMO, Weekly Intelligence Files, 1949–55, Box 1.

26. Alberto Torres, personal interview, Havana, Cuba, December 5, 2004.

27. Confidential message from CNO to COMNOB, GTMO, OIR, January 1951, RG 181, GTMO, Weekly Intelligence Files, 1949–55, Box 3.

28. Commander of Naval Base to Chief of Naval Operations, Re: Budocks proposal for inclusion of requirements that contractors must comply with Cuban labor laws with regard to the use of Cuban nationals, October 20, 1952, RG 181, GTMO, Weekly Intelligence Files, 1949–55, Box 2.

29. Serafino Romualdi and Mr. Topping, Re: Labor difficulties at Guantánamo naval base, April 14, 1952, RG 59 711.56337/4–1452 CS/W, 1950–54, Box 3180; and Serafino Romauldi to Edward G. Miller, April 9, 1952, RG 59/711.56337/4–952 CS/W, Box 3180.

30. Industrial Relations Officer to the Base Commander, Re: Maternity benefits under Cuban law, November 20, 1952, RG 181, GTMO, Weekly Intelligence Files, 1949–55, Box 2.

31. Lino Lemes García, "El representante liberal, Dr. González Parra sigue realizando gestiones a favor de los obreros cubanos en los trabajos que se realizan en la base naval," *El Vigilante,* August 28, 1940; Lino Lemes García, Guantánamo al día, *El Vigilante,* May 31, 1940; Lino Lemes García, "Mujal y la Frederick Snare Corporation; Muchas obras en la estación naval yanqui," *El Vigilante,* March 25, 1950; and Lino Lemes García, "Fácil de comprobar," *El Vigilante,* May 31, 1940.

32. In all my research in Cuba and the United States, Lino Lemes's correspondence is by far the most prolific. I saw evidence of his letters in Washington DC, Havana, and Santiago de Cuba, as well as his almost daily editorials in *La Voz del Pueblo* and *El Vigilante.*

33. Lino Lemes to the President, February 16, 1941, RG 59/811.34537/301 PS/FF, Box 3784; and Lino Lemes to the President, February 12, 1941, RG 59/811.34537/304 PS/FF, Box 3784.

34. Lino Lemes García, "Ratifican los obreros," *El Vigilante,* October 2, 1940.

35. Lino Lemes García, "El Comodoro Mahoney realiza gestiones a favor de miles de obreros y empleados de la estación naval americana," *La Voz del Pueblo,* September 25, 1945.

36. Juan Quintero Ávila, "Un 20 por ciento de aumento piden los obreros en la e. naval," *La Voz del Pueblo,* April 8, 1947.

37. Translation of a letter to Vicente Tovar, February 6, 1945, RG 59/811.34537/5–545, Box 4674.

38. Angel Calzado to U.S. Secretary of State, Re: Complaint as to working conditions in the U.S. naval operating base at Guantánamo Bay, May 5, 1945, RG 59/811.34537/5-545, Box 4674.

39. Serafino Romualdi, *Presidents and Peons: Recollections of a Labor Ambassador in Latin America* (New York: Funk and Wagnalls, 1967); Kofas, *The Struggle for Legitimacy*, 16-18, 126-38; Pérez, *Between Reform and Revolution*, 287-88; and Thomas, Cuba, 736-58.

40. Paterson, *Contesting Castro*, 26.

41. Juan Quintero Ávila, "Demandará Caimanera Atención del Ministro de o. públicas," *La Voz del Pueblo*, January 14, 1948; "Caimanera demanda urgente atención para sus necesidades," *La Voz del Pueblo*, March 4, 1949; "Los estudiantes ocuparon el Instituto y la J. De Educación," *La Voz del Pueblo*, January 27, 1948; and "Apoyados los estudiantes por todos los sectores de la ciudadanía," *La Voz del Pueblo*, January 28, 1948.

42. R. Hart Phillips, "Grau Losing Grip on Cuban Public," *New York Times*, January 19, 1947, p. 31; "General Strike Creates a 'Dead' City in Cuba," *New York Times*, February 20, 1947, p. 14; and "The Want of a High School Causes a Riot in Cuba," *New York Times*, February 12, 1948, p. 20.

43. Thomas, *Cuba*, 777-86. Fidel Castro was also a member of the Ortodoxo Party in the early 1950s.

44. Harold Dana Sims, "Collapse of the House of Labor: Ideological Divisions in the Cuban Labor Movement and the U.S. Role, 1944-1949," *Cuban Studies* 21 (1991): 123-47.

45. Kofas, *The Struggle for Legitimacy*, 140; Thomas, *Cuba*, 775-86; and Pérez, *Between Reform and Revolution*, 276-95.

46. Ángel Ferrand Latoisón, "Mujal nos visita," *La Voz del Pueblo*, November 25, 1949.

47. Walter Knight, personal interview, Guantánamo, Cuba, November 22, 2004.

48. Robert Waters and Gordon Daniels, "The World's Longest General Strike: The AFL-CIO, the CIA, and British Guiana," *Diplomatic History* 29 (April 2005): 279-308; Rabe, *U.S. Intervention in British Guiana*; Ronald Radosh, *American Labor and United States Foreign Policy* (New York: Random House, 1969); and Hobart A. Spalding Jr., "U.S. and Latin American Labor: The Dynamics of Imperialist Control," *Latin American Perspectives* 3 (Winter 1976): 45-69. Robert Alexander's recent account is sympathetic to the AFL's anticommunist objectives, and Alexander himself worked closely with Serafino Romualdi and Jay Lovestone. Robert J. Alexander, *A History of Organized Labor in Cuba* (Westport, CT: Praeger, 2002).

49. Romualdi, *Presidents and Peons*.

50. See Waters and Daniels, "The World's Longest General Strike"; Rabe, *U.S. Intervention in British Guiana*; and Philip Agee, *Inside the Company: CIA Diary* (New York: Stonehill, 1975).

51. "Construirá la CTC una clínica obrera para Guantánamo y Yateras," *La Voz del Pueblo*, May 16, 1950; Lino Lemes García, "Las dos cartas del líder Mujal," *El Vigilante*, April 18, 1950; "Firmó E. Mujal la escritura que constituye el patronato para la administración y construcción de la clínica obrera,"

La Voz del Pueblo, July 15, 1950; and "El Senador Eusebio Mujal y el Dr. Gómez Martínez estarán mañana en Gtmo. Vienen a tratar con los obreros de la base naval americana, sobre problemas del sector," *La Voz del Pueblo,* July 22, 1950.

52. "Declaraciones del Secretario Gral. de la CTC en torno al problema de los trabajadores de la base naval americana de Caimanera," *La Voz del Pueblo,* October 3, 1950; and "Sindicato para la base de Caimanera: Lo pide la AFL al Departamento de Marina," *El Vigilante,* September 27, 1950.

53. "Hoy será entrevistado el líder obrero Romualdi en la CMKH," *La Voz del Pueblo,* October 20, 1950; and "En la Federación Obrera de Guantánamo y Yateras," *La Voz del Pueblo,* October 23, 1950.

54. Lino Lemes García, "Sindicalización, mejor jornal y otras mejoras al personal de la base, es un golpe mortal al comunismo," *El Vigilante,* October 4, 1950.

55. Murphy, *History of Guantánamo Bay,* 1953 ed., 51.

56. "U.S. Flag Presented to Union," *The Indian,* January 12, 1952.

57. *Your Navy Job: Information for Civil Service Employees,* GTMO U.S. Naval Station, Industrial Relations Office, 1953 (emphasis added). I would like to thank a former base worker for sharing this material from his personal collection.

58. Murphy, *History of Guantánamo Bay,* 1953 ed., 51; Serafino Romualdi to Edward Miller, Assistant Secretary of State, April 9, 1952, RG 59/711.56337/4–952 CS/W, Box 3180; and Naval Base Commander to Chief of Naval Operations, Re: Labor relations at the naval base, Guantánamo, Cuba, October 29, 1952, RG 181, GTMO, Weekly Intelligence Files, 1949–55, Box 2.

59. Serafino Romualdi to Edward Miller, Assistant Secretary of State, April 9, 1952, RG 59/711.56337/4–952 CS/W, Box 3180.

60. Commander Naval Operating Base to Commander Destroyer Forces, February 4, 1952, RG 181, GTMO, Weekly Intelligence Files, 1949–55, Box 2.

61. "Quedó constituido el Comité de Trabajadores de la b. naval," *La Voz del Pueblo,* October 30, 1950.

62. According to Harold Sims, in the mid-1950s during the Batista years, a majority of all workers, approximately one million people, belonged to over 1,600 unions. Harold Dana Sims, "Cuba," in *Latin America between the Second World War and the Cold War, 1944–1948* (New York: Cambridge University Press, 1992), 240.

63. Walter Knight, personal interview, Guantánamo, Cuba, November 22, 2004.

64. Juan Carlos Pulsara, personal interview, Guantánamo, Cuba, October 9, 2004.

65. Santiago Ruiz, personal interview, Guantánamo, Cuba, November 18, 2004.

66. Again, this parallels patterns in Panama. Julie Greene delineates the creation of gold and silver pay scales in the Canal Zone. Workers on the gold roll earned high wages and good benefits, while silver workers earned far less in a discriminatory and segregated workspace. See Greene, "Spaniards on the Silver Roll." Robert Vitalis also emphasizes the disparate pay scales and "Jim Crow"

regulations that separated U.S. and Saudi workers. See Vitalis, *America's Kingdom*.

67. Commander Naval Operating Base to Commander Destroyer Forces, February 4, 1952, RG 181, GTMO, Weekly Intelligence Files, 1949–55, Box 2.

68. U.S. Embassy to U.S. State Department, Re: Guantánamo naval base workers union broadcasts protests against reduction in forces, October 2, 1953, RG 59/711.56337/10–253, Box 3180.

69. Commander to Chief of Naval Operations, Re: Radio broadcasts by Union of Base Workers and Employees, January 29, 1954, RG 181, GTMO, Weekly Intelligence Files, 1949–55, Box 3.

70. Ramón Sánchez (pseud.), personal interview, Guantánamo, Cuba, October 4, 2004. (Interview conducted in English.)

71. U.S. Ambassador to Philip Bonsal, Department of State, August 31, 1940, RG 59 811.34537/271, Box 3784.

72. Pedro Salgado and José Fernández to Franklin Roosevelt, September 3, 1940, RG 59/811.34537/278, Box 3784.

73. Demand for certain benefits by Cuban laborers employed by civilian contractor doing work at Guantanamo naval base under lump sum contract, September 26, 1952, RG 59/711.56337/9–2652, Box 3180; Budocks Telegram, August 19, 1952, RG 59/711.56337/8–2252, Box 3180; Viggo Bertelsen to Harvey Wellman, August 22, 1952, RG 59/711.56337/8–2252, Box 3180; and Telegram to the White House, September 23, 1952, RG 59/711.56337/9–2352, Box 3180.

74. Lino Lemes García, "Los contratistas de la zona americana y la CTC," *El Vigilante,* July 27, 1951; Lino Lemes García, "Compañía americana quiere hacer obras en Guantánamo," *El Vigilante,* October 26, 1951; Lino Lemes García, "Carta sindical," *El Vigilante,* June 28, 1952; and Lino Lemes García, "Aumento a obreros de la b. yanqui," *El Vigilante,* September 4, 1953.

75. Lino Lemes García, "Nuevo sindicato en la base naval," *El Vigilante,* June 21, 1952; and Lino Lemes García, Guantánamo al día, *El Vigilante,* February 5, 1952.

76. "Someterá Cuba al gobierno de los EU el problema de los obreros de la base naval," *La Voz del Pueblo,* September 23, 1952.

77. U.S. Embassy to U.S. State Department, Re: Guantánamo naval base workers union broadcasts protests against reduction in forces, October 2, 1953, RG 59/711.56337/10–253, Box 3180.

78. Demand for certain benefits by Cuban laborers employed by civilian contractor doing work at Guantanamo naval base under lump sum contract, September 26, 1952, RG 59/711.56337/9–2652, Box 3180.

79. Serafino Romualdi to Edward Miller, Assistant Secretary of State, April 9, 1952, RG 59/711.56337/4–952 CS/W, Box 3180.

80. Base Commander to Industrial Relations Office of the U.S. Navy, Re: Labor relations information, April 1, 1952, RG 181, GTMO, Weekly Intelligence Files, 1949–55, Box 2.

81. Lino Lemes García, "Un solo contratista obtiene contratos," *El Vigilante,* July 18, 1940.

82. Lino Lemes García, "Mujal y el comercio exportador de Caimanera," *El Vigilante,* February 5, 1952.

83. Department of State to U.S. Embassy, Havana, November 9, 1953, RG 59/711.56337/11-953, Box 3180.

84. They were quite successful in this endeavor, and there is no mention of the fiftieth anniversary in *La Voz del Pueblo* or *El Vigilante* during the week of December 10, 1953.

85. Duany, "Importante asamblea en el sindicato de obreros y empleados de la base," *La Voz del Pueblo*, March 29, 1954.

86. U.S. Embassy to Department of State, Re: Guantánamo naval base workers union broadcasts, October 2, 1953, RG 59/711.56337/10-253, Box 3180.

87. Conference with Mr. John Fishburn, Latin American Labor Advisor, Department of State, Re: To discuss labor relations, November 18, 1954; and Chief of industrial relations to assistant secretary of the navy, November, 1954, RG 181, GTMO, Weekly Intelligence Files, 1949-55, Box 3.

88. U.S. Embassy to State Department, Re: Guantánamo naval base workers union broadcasts protests against reduction in forces, October 2, 1953, RG 59/711.56337/10-253, Box 3180.

89. James C. Scott, *Weapons of the Weak: Everyday Forms of Peasant Resistance* (New Haven: Yale University Press, 1985). Several historians have explored these concepts in working-class lives: see Tera W. Hunter, *To 'Joy My Freedom: Southern Black Women's Lives and Labors after the Civil War* (Cambridge, MA: Harvard University Press, 1997); Kelley, *Race Rebels;* and Neptune, *Caliban and the Yankees.*

90. Lease of Lands for Coaling and Naval Stations, February 23, 1903, U.S.-Cuba, art. 3, *T. S.* no. 418, quoted in Murphy, *History of Guantánamo Bay,* 1953 ed., 66.

91. Ricardo Baylor, personal interview, Guantánamo, Cuba, November 21, 2004.

92. Juan Carlos Pulsara, personal interview, Guantánamo, Cuba, October 9, 2004.

93. Victor Davis (pseud.), personal interview, Guantánamo, Cuba, October 8, 2004. (Interview conducted in English.)

94. Rosa Johnson, personal interview, Guantánamo, Cuba, November 9, 2004.

95. Franklin Hawley to J. J. Mahoney, Re: Documents relating to thefts on the base, March 21, 1945, RG 84, STGO, Conf., 1945, All Numbers, Box 6; "Roba un estibador cinco bulbos de penicilina sódica en la estación naval," *La Voz del Pueblo*, March 1, 1947; "Detenido un sujeto que vendió tres bicicletas hurtadas en la e. naval," *La Voz del Pueblo,* April 19, 1947; and "Ocupan en una casa objetos que robaron en la estación naval," *La Voz del Pueblo,* June 24, 1947.

96. "La policía descubre un importante robo realizado en la estación naval," *La Voz del Pueblo,* July 30, 1946; and "Atrapado por la policía otro de los que robaron en la estación naval," *La Voz del Pueblo,* August 1, 1946.

97. Chief Staff Officer to Base Provost Marshal, Re: Results of an investigation in Caimanera involving Fernández, Supply Department Employee #40293, and Juan Pérez (Pérez), Municipal Judge of Caimanera, December 2, 1944; and J. J. Mahoney to U.S. consul, October 12, 1945, both located in RG 84, STGO, Conf., 1945, All Numbers, Box 6.

98. Franklin Hawley to J. J. Mahoney, March 21, 1945, RG 84, STGO, Conf., 1945, All Numbers, Box 6.

99. Memorandum of Telephone Conversation, Re: Request from Base Command to assume jurisdiction for crimes committed within base area, September 17, 1952, RG 59/711.56337/9–1752, Box 3180; and September 26, 1952, RG 59/711.56337/9–1252, Box 3180.

100. Memorandum of Telephone Conversation, Re: Request from Base Command for authorization to try a Cuban civilian employee," July 28, 1952, RG 59/711.56337/7–2852, Box 3180.

101. Legal Advisor, State Department, to John L. Topping, July 29, 1952, RG 59/711.56337/7–2952, Box 3180.

102. Willard L. Beaulac, Re: U.S. naval base at Guantánamo: Disposition of Cuban criminal offenders, September 12, 1952, RG 59/711.56337/9–1252, Box 3180.

103. Memorandum of Conversation, Re: Guantánamo naval base, Base Command requests authorization to assume jurisdiction over Cuban employees for crimes committed on the base, September 26, 1952, RG 59/ 711.56337/9–1252, Box 3180.

104. Conversation with Commander Murphy, Re: Disposition of Cuban criminal offenders, October 23, 1952, RG 59/711.56337/10–2352, Box 3180.

105. Telegram, March 5, 1953, RG 59/711.56337/3–553, Box 3180.

106. Translator's Summary of Communication, Federación Estudiantil de GTMO, March 4, 1953, RG 59/711.56337/3–553, Box 3180.

107. Rear Admiral C. L. C. Atkenson to Luis Cardet, March 24, 1953, RG 59/711.56337/4–253, Box 3180.

108. U.S. Ambassador Willard Beaulac to Admiral Atkenson, Re: Disposition of Cuban criminal offenders, April 2, 1953, RG 59/711.56337/4–253, Box 3180; and Jurisdiction of Cuban courts in cases involving crimes committed on the U.S. naval operating base at Guantánamo Bay, May 12, 1953, RG 59/ 711.56337/5–1253, Box 3180.

109. Translation of Editorial Published in the Union of Base Workers and Employees Bulletin, No. 9, September 1954, RG 59/711.56337/10–2254, Box 3180.

110. Letter to the U.S. Embassy from the Sindicato de Obreros y Empleados de la base naval de operaciones de los EU, October 2, 1954, RG 59/711 .56337/10–2254, Box 3180; and Translation of editorial published in the Union of Base Workers and Employees Bulletin, No. 9, September 1954, RG 59/ 711.56337/10–2254, Box 3180.

111. Chief of Industrial Relations to Assistant Secretary of the Navy, Re: Labor relations, November 1954, RG 181, GTMO, Weekly Intelligence Files, 1949–55, Box 3.

112. Synopsis of Meeting with Representatives of the CTC and the AFL, concerning NAVBASE Guantánamo Bay, November 19, 1954, RG 181, GTMO, Weekly Intelligence Files, 1949–55, Box 3.

113. "Habrá una formula para el problema obrero de la base naval," *La Voz del Pueblo,* November 20, 1954; and "Promete: El Almirante J. H. Taylor gestiones de conciliación," *La Voz del Pueblo,* December 4, 1954.

114. Conference with Mr. John Fishburn, Latin American Labor Advisor, November 18, 1954, RG 181, GTMO, Weekly Intelligence Files, 1949–55, Box 3.

115. Toirac Adames, "Apuntes sobre el movimiento obrero en la base naval."

116. Commander to Base Industrial Relations Officer, Re: Information obtained from José Perera Carbonell, November 22, 1955, RG 181, GTMO, Weekly Intelligence Files, 1949–55, Box 3.

117. Vinton Chapin, Re: Guantánamo naval base union development, Embassy Dispatch 226, November 10, 1955, RG 181, GTMO, Weekly Intelligence Summaries, Box 3; and "Huelga de hambre," *El Vigilante,* August 31, 1955.

118. Translation of Handbill Distributed in Guantánamo City, Cuba, August 4, 1955 (Trans. IRO, Naval Station), RG 181, GTMO, Weekly Intelligence Files, 1949–55, Box 3.

119. Labor Relations Information, January 9, 1956; and Labor Relations Information, June 22, 1956. Both located in RG 181, GTMO, Weekly Intelligence Files, 1949–55, Box 3.

120. Walter Knight, personal interview, Guantánamo, Cuba, November 22, 2004.

121. "Pronunciamiento del sindicato de la base naval en el caso de Lorenzo Salomón," *La Voz del Pueblo,* October 13, 1954.

122. Juan Carlos Pulsara, personal interview, Guantánamo, Cuba, October 9, 2004.

123. Luis Pavón Tamayo, "La base militar yanqui," *Venceremos,* March 6, 1964.

124. Ramón Sánchez, personal interview, Guantánamo, Cuba, October 4, 2004.

125. Miguel Gómez (pseud.), personal interview, Guantánamo, Cuba, October 10, 2004. (Interview conducted in Spanish.)

126. Santiago Ruiz, personal interview, Guantánamo, Cuba, November 19, 2004.

127. Derek Stedman (pseud.), personal interview, Guantánamo, Cuba, October 15, 2004. (Interview conducted in Spanish.)

128. Juan González (pseud.), personal interview, Guantánamo, Cuba, October 10, 2004. (Interview conducted in Spanish.)

129. Juan Carlos Pulsara, personal interview, Guantánamo, Cuba, October 9, 2004.

130. Conversation with Graciela Chailloux, Havana, Cuba, February 2005. My informants ranged in age from their mid-seventies to ninety-three.

131. Lillian Guerra, "*Seremos como Martí?* Workers and Contradiction in the Cuban Revolution," unpublished working paper, April 2005.

3. GOOD NEIGHBORS, GOOD REVOLUTIONARIES

1. Rosa Johnson (pseud.), personal interview, Guantánamo, Cuba, November 9, 2004.

2. *Living Conditions at the U.S. Naval Base Guantánamo Bay, Cuba,* 1956, U.S. Naval Historical Center, Navy Yards, Washington DC, Vertical Files, "Guantánamo."

3. Rosa Johnson (pseud.), personal interview, Guantánamo, Cuba, November 9, 2004.

4. This work builds on Ann Laura Stoler's directive to explore "the ambivalences of those caught on the margins of empire" and the presumption that "colonial regimes were uneven and imperfect" in their rule. Stoler, *Carnal Knowledge and Imperial Power*, 10, 206. It also concurs with Eileen J. Suárez Findlay who demonstrates that an analysis of sexuality allows for an interpretation that "pushes us beyond another simple binary opposition that haunts Puerto Rican historiography—that of resistance and accommodation." Suárez Findlay, *Imposing Decency*, 4.

5. Wood, *The Making of the Good Neighbor Policy*; Gellman, *Roosevelt and Batista*; Roorda, *The Dictator Next Door*; and Friedman, *Nazis and Good Neighbors*. Roorda and Friedman offer the newest scholarly approaches to the Good Neighbor policy. Roorda includes a cultural analysis of military power in the Dominican Republic. Friedman's study on the deportation and imprisonment of Latin American Germans also examines the consequences of "neighborly relations" on a specific population.

6. "Solemnemente fue inaugurado en la fecha de la independencia EEUU el nuevo edificio de los veteranos," *La Voz del Pueblo*, July 5, 1949.

7. The local press praised Admiral Murphy for his social overtures and lauded him on his departure. See "Declarado huésped de honor de la ciudad, el Almirante E. Murphy," *La Voz del Pueblo*, July 7, 1951; "Solemne fue el acto de Confraternidad Cubana-Americana," *La Voz del Pueblo*, July 9, 1951; "Expresiva carta de congratulación del Almirante Murphy," *La Voz del Pueblo*, July 17, 1951; Lino Lemes García, "Se va un buen amigo de Cuba," *La Voz del Pueblo*, November 19, 1952; and Ángel Ferrand Latoisón, "Se le impondrá la gran Cruz Roja cubana al Almirante M. Murphy," *La Voz del Pueblo*, December 2, 1952. In addition, Admiral Murphy wrote *The History of Guantánamo Bay*, where he paid significant attention to local relations with Guantánamo.

8. "Declarado huésped de honor de la ciudad," *La Voz del Pueblo*, July 7, 1951.

9. "Textos del discurso pronunciado ayer por el Coronel Coruthers," *La Voz del Pueblo*, May 21, 1954.

10. Murphy, *History of Guantánamo Bay*, 1953 ed., 51; McCoy, "Guantánamo Bay," 142–43; "Pavoroso incendio en Caimanera," *La Voz del Pueblo*, July 1, 1946; Alfredo Oslé, "El formidable incendio de Caimanera," *La Voz del Pueblo*, October 15, 1947; and "El incendio de Caimanera," *La Voz del Pueblo*, March 11, 1948.

11. "Importantes donaciones hace la jefatura de la base naval a instituciones," *La Voz del Pueblo*, March 18, 1953; Índice, *La Voz del Pueblo*, January 12, 1954; and "Los carnavales en la base naval y todos sus premios," *La Voz del Pueblo*, March 2, 1954.

12. José Vázquez Pubillones, "Sobre los marinos americanos y nuestra ciudad," *La Voz del Pueblo*, May 13, 1946; "Nada se dice de los francos," *La Voz del Pueblo*, May 14, 1946; and Ángel Ferrand Latoisón, "Luchemos en 'pro' de Caimanera," *La Voz del Pueblo*, March 7, 1949.

13. Marilis de Dios Noris, "Efectos de la presencia de los marines yanquis en la ciudad de Guantánamo 1903–1952" (master's thesis, Universidad de Oriente, Cuba, May 2004), 67–86. Also see Pérez, *On Becoming Cuban*, 238–42.

14. "Visita al General Batista y al Embajador de EU una comisión de Caimanera cumpliendo moción de nuestro director, Gestionará el retorno de la Política del Buen Vecino con la base naval," *La Voz del Pueblo*, November 26, 1955.

15. Juan González García, letter to the editor, *La Voz del Pueblo*, September 7, 1957.

16. Ángel Ferrand Latoisón, "Fanfreluches: Un noble sentido de convivencia puede ser ayuda para Caimanera," *La Voz del Pueblo*, June 7, 1957.

17. On tourism to Cuba, see Pérez, *On Becoming Cuban*, 166–97, 469–71; and Schwartz, *Pleasure Island*.

18. Lino Lemes García, "El turismo local y Batista como en Trinidad," *La Voz del Pueblo*, July 15, 1954.

19. For just a a sampling of these references to "Guantánamo as a natural zone of tourism," see Lino Lemes García, Guantánamo al día, *El Vigilante*, February 26, 1946; Lino Lemes García, " 'Tiempo en Cuba' y Caimanera," *La Voz del Pueblo*, August 8, 1947; and Lino Lemes García, Guantánamo al día, *La Voz del Pueblo*, June 4, 1948.

20. Lino Lemes García, Guantánamo al día, *La Voz del Pueblo*, May 15, 1948 and June 4, 1948.

21. "Envío a Guantánamo," *La Revista Oriental*, May 1955.

22. Ángel Ferrand Latoisón, "Guantánamo y Caimanera son las dos ciudades más sucias del mundo," *La Voz del Pueblo*, July 6, 1949.

23. Oscar Brand, "Guantánamo Bay," *Every Inch a Sailor* (Collectors' Choice Music, Elektra Entertainment Group, 2006).

24. Lino Lemes García, Guantánamo al día, *El Vigilante*, February 26, 1946.

25. Federación de Mujeres Cubanas, "La prostitución: Una enfermedad social curable, una experiencia importante de la Revolución Cubana," unpublished report, Federación de Mujeres Cubanas, Havana, Cuba, 1988.

26. Lino Lemes García, Guantánamo al día, *La Voz del Pueblo*, January 16, 1947; and Lino Lemes García, "Volverán los marinos, pero . . ." *El Vigilante*, August 6, 1946.

27. "Fuerte escándalo en la extinguida zona," *La Voz del Pueblo*, July 9, 1943.

28. Cruz Díaz, *Guantánamo Bay*, 94.

29. Nicolás Dorr, "Confesión en el Barrio Chino," in *La Chacota* (Havana: Editorial Letras Cubanas, 1989), 171–238.

30. The FMC conducted thorough reeducation campaigns in the early 1960s and retrained prostitutes after the Cuban revolution. Although there is presumably a great deal of data, most of these records remain unavailable, because of the general difficulty in working with Cuban documents in the post-1959 era and because of concerns regarding confidentiality and the need to protect former prostitutes' privacy.

31. For key theoretical works and case studies, see Enloe, *Bananas, Beaches, and Bases;* Stoler, *Carnal Knowledge;* Stoler, *Race and the Education of Desire:*

Foucault's History of Sexuality *and the Colonial Order of Things* (Durham, NC: Duke University Press, 1995); Stoler, ed., *Haunted By Empire;* Ann McClintock, *Imperial Leather: Race, Gender, and Sexuality in the Colonial Contest* (New York: Routledge, 1995); Sandra Pollock Sturdevant and Brenda Stoltzfus, *Let the Good Times Roll: Prostitution and the U.S. Military in Asia* (New York: New Press, 1992); Suárez Findlay, *Imposing Decency;* Brennan, *What's Love Got to Do With It?;* and Moon, *Sex among Allies.*

32. This information comes from sixteen U.S. Navy venereal disease reports from March 1946. Medical Department, U.S. Navy, Venereal Disease Contact Report, March 1946, RG 84, STGO, Gen., 1946, 820–842.6, Box 41.

33. "Medical Department, U.S. Navy Venereal Disease Contact Report, March 1946, RG 84, STGO, Gen., 1946, 820–842.6, Box 41.

34. For works on prostitution, venereal disease, and the military, see Allan M. Brandt, *No Magic Bullet: A Social History of Venereal Disease in the United States since 1880* (New York: Oxford University Press, 1987); Paul A. Kramer, "The Darkness That Enters the Home: The Politics of Prostitution during the Philippine-American War," in *Haunted by Empire,* ed. Ann Laura Stoler (Durham, NC: Duke University Press), 366–404; Sturdevant and Stoltzfus, *Let the Good Times Roll;* and Moon, *Sex among Allies.* Harvey Neptune also explores "color blindness" and racial confusion of white American military personnel in Trinidad. Neptune, *Caliban and the Yankees,* 166–67.

35. Louis Pérez notes that even Ripley's *Believe It or Not* awarded Caimanera the distinction of being one of the world's dirtiest towns. Pérez, *Becoming Cuban,* 240.

36. Captain Roland W. Faulk, CHC, USN, interview by John T. Mason Jr., November 1974, U.S. Naval Institute's Oral History Collection, U.S. Naval Historical Center, Navy Yards, Washington DC, 58–61 and 244–48.

37. Cruz Díaz, *Guantánamo Bay;* Juan Carlos Pulsara, personal interview, Guantánamo, Cuba, October 9, 2004; and Alberto Torres, personal interview, Havana, Cuba, December 5, 2004.

38. Lino Lemes García, "Ocurrió en Santiago de Cuba: Un aviso a las madrecitas," *El Vigilante,* April 18, 1946; and Lino Lemes García, "Esta ciudad y Caimanera necesitan dispensarios anti-venéreos," *El Vigilante,* August 15, 1953 (emphasis added).

39. "Fuerte escándalo en la extinguida zona," *La Voz del Pueblo,* July 9, 1943; Lino Lemes García, "Ocurrió en Santiago de Cuba: Un aviso a las madrecitas," *El Vigilante,* April 18, 1946; and Lino Lemes García, "Diversiones sanas para los marinos piden las madres americanas; un millón de pesos invertidos en lupanares," *El Vigilante,* August 1, 1946.

40. Lino Lemes García, "Sugerencia del Profesor Oteiza Setién en la mesa redonda de la prostitución," *El Vigilante,* October 21, 1951; and Schwartz, *Pleasure Island,* 30–34.

41. "Carta dirigida al presidente de la república por Lino Lemes García, periodista de Guantánamo, acompañada de un artículo en el que expone las necesidades de frenar el auge de los vicios, las drogas, y el juego prohibido en esa localidad," November, 1940, CNA, Secretaría de la Presidencia, Caja 44, Número 75.

42. Lino Lemes García, Guantánamo al día, *El Vigilante*, February 26, 1946; Lino Lemes García, "Diversiones sanas para los marinos piden las madres americanas; un millón de pesos invertidos en lupanares," *El Vigilante*, August 1, 1946; Lino Lemes García, "Grau y la prostitución en Guantánamo," *El Vigilante*, March 13, 1946 (emphasis added); and Lino Lemes García, "Ocurrió en Santiago de Cuba: Un aviso a las madrecitas," *El Vigilante*, April 18, 1946.

43. Lino Lemes García, "Diversiones sanas para los marinos piden las madres americanas; un millón de pesos invertidos en lupanares," *El Vigilante*, August 1, 1946.

44. Walter Knight, personal interview, Guantánamo, Cuba, November 22, 2004.

45. Ramón Sánchez, personal interview, Guantánamo, Cuba, October 4, 2004.

46. Bernard Gotlieb to Spruile Braden, January 2, 1943, and "Turistas perjudiciales," *Libertad*, December 29, 1942, RG 84, STGO, Conf., 1943–44, All Numbers, Box 5, 832.

47. Harry Story to U.S. Ambassador R. Henry Norweb, March 1, 1946, RG 84, STGO, Conf., 1946–49, All Numbers, Box 7.

48. Lino Lemes García, Guantánamo al día, *La Voz del Pueblo*, January 28, 1948; and Lino Lemes García, "El turismo local y Batista como en Trinidad," *La Voz del Pueblo*, July 15, 1954.

49. Alberto Torres, personal interview, Havana, Cuba, December 5, 2004.

50. Juan Carlos Pulsara, personal interview, Guantánamo, Cuba, October 9, 2004.

51. In a collection of oral histories of African American messmen in the U.S. Navy, George E. Grimstead noted, "There weren't any [brothels] that would close their doors to you [in Hawaii, but] that *was* the case in the Caribbean [emphasis in original]. There, instead of having one big brothel in the red-light district, they'd just have all these women in their little houses or hovels along the street. We'd walk up to them . . . and they might say, "No, no, no, no." Well you knew right away what they meant: They did not want to have sex with a black. This was in Panama." Richard E. Miller, *The Messmen Chronicles: African Americans in the U.S. Navy, 1932–1943* (Annapolis, MD: Naval Institute Press, 2004).

52. de la Fuente, *A Nation for All;* Helg, *Our Rightful Share;* Guerra, *The Myth of José Martí;* and Ferrer, *Insurgent Cuba.*

53. I would like to thank Melina Pappademos for her comments and insights into Oriente's racial formation.

54. Soler Zunzarren, *Guantánamo historia.*

55. de la Fuente, *A Nation for All,* 161–71.

56. Lisa Brock and Digna Castañeda Fuertes, eds. *Between Race and Empire: African-Americans and Cubans before the Cuban Revolution* (Philadelphia, PA: Temple University Press, 1998).

57. de la Fuente, *A Nation for All,* 58–59.

58. William B. Blocker, Fortnightly Political Report, Santiago de Cuba, June 13, 1936, RG 84, STGO, Gen., 1936, vol. 6, 800–811.11M, Box 4.

59. U.S. Consulate, Santiago de Cuba, Re: William H. De Lung and William F. Collins, April 7, 1948, RG 84, STGO, Gen., 1948, 121–892.43, Box 46.

60. Willard B. Gatewood Jr., *"Smoked Yankees" and the Struggle for Empire, 1898–1902* (Urbana: University of Illinois Press, 1971); Mary Pat Kelly, *Proudly We Served, The Men of the USS Mason* (Annapolis, MD: Naval Institute Press, 1995); Miller, *The Messman Chronicles;* Yen Le Espiritu, *Home Bound: Filipino American Lives across Cultures, Communities, and Countries* (Berkeley: University of California Press, 2003), 98–126; and Jesse Quinsaat, ed., *Letters in Exile: An Introductory Reader on the History of Pilipinos in America* (Los Angeles, CA: UCLA Asian American Studies Center, 1976), 90–111.

61. Naval Intelligence Branch, GTMO, to District Intelligence Officer, Re: Racial problems: enlisted personnel, GTMO, August 19, 1943, RG 181, GTMO, World War II Files, Box 3.

62. Naval Intelligence Branch, GTMO, to District Intelligence Officer, Re: Racial problems: enlisted personnel, GTMO, August 19, 1943, RG 181, GTMO, World War II Files, Box 3.

63. Meghan Kate Winchell, "Good Food, Good Fun, and Good Girls: USO Hostesses and World War II" (PhD diss., University of Arizona, 2003).

64. Duany, "La inauguración del gran centro 'ASO' [sic]," *El Vigilante,* March 25, 1943.

65. Soler Zunzarren, *Guantánamo historia.*

66. de la Fuente, *A Nation for All,* 157–60.

67. Juan Carlos Pulsara, personal interview, Guantánamo, Cuba, October 9, 2004.

68. Walter Knight, personal interview, Guantánamo, Cuba, November 22, 2004.

69. Naval Intelligence Branch, GTMO, to District Intelligence Officer, Re: Racial problems: enlisted personnel, GTMO, August 19, 1943, RG 181, GTMO, World War II Files, Box 3. Throughout World War II, the United Service Organization often sponsored segregated USO clubs for black servicemen. See photographs in Sherie Mershon and Steven Schlossman, *Foxholes and Color Lines: Desegregating the U.S. Armed Forces* (Baltimore, MD: Johns Hopkins University Press, 1998); and Neptune, *Caliban and the Yankees.*

70. Jim Petinaud and P. W. Garage to George Wheeler, February 16, 1944, RG 181, GTMO, World War II Files, Box 2.

71. For examples in South Korea and the Dominican Republic, see Ji-Yeon Yuh, *Beyond the Shadow of Camptown: Korean Military Brides in America* (New York: New York University Press, 2002); and Brennan, *What's Love Got to Do With It?*

72. "Rose de Quintana Is a Future Bride: Teacher in Santiago de Cuba, Cuba, Engaged to John Hull Jr., Journalist in Navy," *New York Times,* July 21, 1954, p. 31.

73. Lino Lemes García, "Volverán los marinos, pero . . ." *El Vigilante,* August 6, 1946.

74. Neptune, *Caliban and the Yankees,* 172–73.

75. The Guantánamo Provincial Archive catalogued many of their marriage records by citizenship, allowing me to examine all the records the archivists had noted involving a U.S. citizen. These included marriages with Puerto Ricans and individuals from the U.S. Virgin Islands. There may have been other records of

U.S.-Cuban marriages that were not indexed. The records from the Guantánamo Civil Registry are summarized in a chart in the appendix.

76. Guantánamo Civil Registry, Guantánamo Provincial Archive, Expediente (Exp.) 9220, Legajo (Leg.) 338.

77. Guantánamo Civil Registry, Exp. 10023, Leg. 365; Guantánamo Civil Registry, Exp. 4828, Leg. 190; Guantánamo Civil Registry, Exp. 5934, Leg. 225.

78. Guantánamo Civil Registry, Exp. 4650, Leg. 184.

79. Guantánamo Civil Registry, Exp. 8718, Leg. 321.

80. Guantánamo Civil Registry, Exp. 10190, Leg. 370.

81. In this number, I am including women the Guantánamo Civil Registry identified as having a Jamaican parent. Although not all Jamaicans were people of African descent, in the Guantánamo context the vast majority identified as "Jamaicans" were people of color.

82. Guantánamo Civil Registry, Exp. 9303, Leg. 341.

83. Guantánamo Civil Registry, Exp. 9525, Leg. 347.

84. Guantánamo Civil Registry, Exp. 5364, Leg. 207. Until 1934, U.S. control over the Philippines made Filipinos "American nationals," but not citizens. There were also legal challenges to Filipinos' rights to marry white women. In the 1930s, the California legislature passed two bills to include Filipinos in its antimiscegenation statutes. Sucheng Chan, *Asian Americans: An Interpretative History* (London: Twayne, 1991), 60–61; Ronald Takaki, *Strangers from a Different Shore: A History of Asian Americans* (New York: Penguin Books, 1989), 330–32 and 358–63; and Mae M. Ngai, *Impossible Subjects: Illegal Aliens and the Making of Modern America* (Princeton, NJ: Princeton University Press, 2004), 119–20.

85. In the Guantánamo Civil Registry, race was not noted regularly after 1956. It is unclear whether this was due to local or national law. Also, race was sometimes, but sometimes not, included in earlier years. It is easier to ascertain how the Cuban woman's race was defined, because the documents often included a birth certificate which declared the infant's race at birth. For an analysis of the challenges of decoding Cuban racial identities in the archival records, see Rebecca J. Scott, "The Provincial Archive as a Place of Memory: The Role of Former Slaves in the Cuban War of Independence (1895–98)," *History Workshop Journal* 58 (Autumn 2004): 149–66. For a study on the politics of racial designations in government documents in the United States and the Caribbean, see Martha Hodes, "Fractions and Fictions in the United States Census, 1890," in *Haunted by Empire*, ed. Ann Laura Stoler (Durham, NC: Duke University Press, 2006), 240–70; and Hodes, "The Mercurial Nature and Abiding Power of Race: A Transnational Family Story," *American Historical Review* 108 (February 2003).

86. Guantánamo Civil Registry, Exp. 5734, Leg. 218.

87. R. Henry Norweb to U.S. Secretary of State, October 24, 1945, Re: Visit to Nicaro and Guantánamo naval base, RG 59 811.34537/10-2445, Box 4674.

88. See Enloe, *Bases, Beaches, and Bananas;* and Lutz, *Homefront.* Louis A. Pérez also provides a portrait of U.S. sugar mills in Cuba, which act as an informative counterpoint to the U.S. military base in Guantánamo Bay. Pérez, *On Becoming Cuban,* 220–38.

89. Rosa Johnson, personal interview, Guantánamo, Cuba, November 9, 2004.

90. Maria Boothe, personal interview, Guantánamo, Cuba, November 23, 2004.

91. Priscilla Baxter (pseud.), personal interivew, Guantánamo, Cuba, November 24, 2004. (Interview conducted in Spanish.)

92. Juan Carlos Pulsara, personal interview, Guantánamo, Cuba, October 9, 2004.

93. Maria Boothe, personal interview, Guantánamo, Cuba, November 23, 2004.

94. Walter Knight, personal interview, Guantánamo, Cuba, November 22, 2004.

95. Luis Pavón Tamayo, "La base militar yanqui," *Venceremos*, March 6, 1964.

96. Ramón Sánchez, personal interview, Guantánamo, Cuba, October 4, 2004.

97. Santiago Ruiz, personal interview, Guantánamo, Cuba, November 18, 2004.

98. Walter Knight, personal interview, Guantánamo, Cuba, November 22, 2004.

99. For literature on women's domestic labor, see Hunter, *To 'Joy My Freedom;* and Stoler, *Carnal Knowledge and Imperial Power.* For discussions on contemporary trends, see Grace Chang, *Disposable Domestics: Immigrant Women Workers in the Global Economy* (Cambridge, MA: South End, 2000); Rhacel Salazar Parreñas, *Servants of Globalization: Women, Migration, and Domestic Work* (Stanford, CA: Stanford University Press, 2001); and Barbara Ehrenreich and Alice Russell Hochschild, *Global Women: Nannies, Maids, and Sex Workers in the New Economy* (New York: Henry Holt, 2002).

100. *Living Conditions at the U.S. Naval Base, Guantánamo Bay, Cuba,* 1956, U.S. Naval Historical Center, Navy Yards, Washington DC, Vertical Files, "Guantánamo."

101. Ramón Sánchez, personal interview, Guantánamo, Cuba, October 4, 2004.

102. Vincent Andrews (pseud.), personal interview, Havana, Cuba, December 3 and December 7, 2004. (Interview conducted in Spanish.)

103. Paterson, *Contesting Castro;* Pérez, *Between Reform and Revolution,* 276–312; and Julia E. Sweig, *Inside the Cuban Revolution: Fidel Castro and the Urban Underground* (Cambridge, MA: Harvard University Press, 2002).

104. "Rebels in Havana Charge Betrayal," *New York Times,* April 22, 1957, p. 6.

105. Van Gosse, *Where the Boys Are: Cuba, Cold War America and the Making of a New Left* (London: Verso, 1993), 67–81; Paterson, *Contesting Castro,* 81–85; "3 Youths Missing," *New York Times,* March 8, 1957, p. 5; "Renewed Violence Reported in Cuba," *New York Times,* March 12, 1957, p. 12; "U.S. Studying Case of 3 Youths in Cuba," *New York Times,* March 28, 1957, p. 8; "Batista Says Foes Have Quit Hide-Out," *New York Times,* March 31, 1957, p. 5; "Cuba Says Castro Has Stopped Fight," *New York Times,* April 13, 1957, p. 12; "Rebels in Havana Charge Betrayal," *New York Times,* April 22, 1957, p. 6; and "2 U.S. Boys in Cuba Leave the Rebels," *New York Times,* May 10, 1957, p. 5.

106. Paterson, *Contesting Castro*, 62–64 and 105–6; McCoy, "Guantánamo Bay," 202–3; Sweig, *Inside the Cuban Revolution*, 60, 207; and Gladys Marel García-Pérez, *Insurrection and Revolution: Armed Struggle in Cuba 1952–1959*, trans. Juan Ortega (Boulder, CO: Lynne Rienner, 1998), 74.

107. Vicente Isla, ed., *Guantánamo: Primera trinchera anti-imperialista de Cuba* (Havana: Editorial José Martí, 1988), 39; García-Pérez, *Insurrection and Revolution*, 84; "U.S. Opens Parley with Cuba Rebels," *New York Times*, July 2, 1958, p. 12; and "Cuba Area's 'Truce' Is Expected to End, *New York Times*, July 21, 1958, p. 1.

108. Of an older generation, Fraga had gained experience with explosives in the campaigns against the Machado dictatorship in the 1930s. He later settled in Guantánamo and applied for a job on GTMO. Knowing that his militant past and Trotskyist affiliation would raise flags for U.S. officials, he changed his name from "Gustavo" to "Modesto" to elude the base intelligence officers' background checks. Fraga also appears in U.S. documents as an active base union leader. Although he does not appear to have been dismissed, U.S. officials did identify him as a "Trotskyite." Fraga was just one of many base workers who were active in the M-26-7 campaign to oust Batista. Bernardo Betancourt Molina, "Apuntes biográficos: 'Gustavo Fraga Jacomino,'" unpublished manuscript, Guantánamo Provincial Archives; and Vinton Chapin, Re: Guantánamo naval base union development, Embassy Dispatch 226, November 10, 1955, RG 181, GTMO, Weekly Intelligence Summaries, Box 3.

109. For an analysis of plantation workers in an anticolonial struggle, see Ann Laura Stoler, "Working the Revolution: Plantation Laborers and the People's Militia in North Sumatra," *The Journal of Asian Studies* 47 (May 1988): 227–47.

110. Vincent Andrews, personal interview, Havana, Cuba, December 3 and December 7, 2004.

111. Juan Carlos Pulsara, personal interview, Guantánamo, Cuba, October 9, 2004. Vincent Andrews also reiterated this strategy of buying gasoline for low prices on the base and carrying it to the rebels in Boquerón.

112. Resume of Supply Activities from 1950–58, Naval Supply Depot, U.S. Navy Operational Archives (USNOA), U.S. Naval Historical Center, Navy Yards, Washington DC, Post-1946 Command File, Shore Estab. Guantánamo Naval Station, Box 1246. (The USNOA houses GTMO's Command Histories (CH) after 1964. These files were labeled "Shore Estab. Guantánamo Naval Station." From this point, I refer to this collection as USNOA, Post-1946 Command File, GTMO.)

113. Efigenio Ameijeiras Delgado, *Más allá de nosotros: Columna 6 "Juan Manuel Ameijeiras" II Frente Oriental "Frank País"* (Santiago de Cuba: Editorial Oriente, 1984), 249–52.

114. "Cubans Seize American," *New York Times*, November 27, 1957, p. 6; "U.S. Sailor Faces Trial," *New York Times*, November 29, 1957, p. 16; and Van Gosse, *Where the Boys Are*, 88–93.

115. Ramón Sánchez, personal interview, Guantánamo, Cuba, October 4, 2004.

116. Walter Knight, personal interview, Guantánamo, Cuba, November 22, 2004.

117. Paterson, *Contesting Castro*; and Pérez, *Between Reform and Revolution*.

118. "Se estrechan más las relaciones entre la base naval de Guantánamo y Cuba," *La Voz del Pueblo*, June 23, 1958; "Serán mejorados los sistemas de agua y potencia eléctrica en la base naval, *La Voz del Pueblo*, June 24, 1958; and "En igualdad de condiciones," *La Voz del Pueblo*, June 25, 1958.

119. Resume of Supply Activities from 1950–58, Naval Supply Depot, USNOA, Post-1946 Command file, GTMO, Box 1246.

120. Columna 20 "Gustavo Fraga" Segundo Frente Oriental "Frank País," *En la línea de fuego* (Santiago de Cuba: Editorial Oriente, 1998), 80–81.

121. Mario Llerena, *The Unsuspected Revolution: The Birth and Rise of Castroism* (Ithaca, NY: Cornell University Press, 1978), 242–46; and Paterson, *Contesting Castro*, 125–73.

122. Paterson, *Contesting Castro*, 160–72; Van Gosse, *Where the Boys Are*, 81–94; McCoy, "Guantánamo Bay," 185–98; Ameijeiras Delgado, *Más allá de nosotros*; Columna 20, *En la línea de fuego*; Columna 18 "Antonio López Fernández" Segundo Frente Oriental "Frank País," *Hijos de su tiempo: Segundo Frente Oriental "Frank País"* (Havana: Ediciones Verde Olivo, 1998); and Miranda Bravo, *Vecinos indeseables*, 122–23.

123. Ameijeiras, *Más allá de nosotros*, 87–91.

124. "Servicemen Held in Cuba," *New York Times*, June 30, 1958, p. 3. On African American servicemen, see Van Gosse, "The African American Press Greets the Cuban Revolution," in *Between Race and Empire*, 266–80. Kidnapped black servicemen were also profiled in the *Amsterdam News*. "Lost 20 Pounds: Marine Reveals How Cubans Kidnapped Him," *Amsterdam News*, August 2, 1958; and "Bronx Seabee Tells of Capture in Cuba," *Amsterdam News*, August 9, 1958.

125. Carlos Franqui, *The Twelve*, trans. Albert B. Teichner (New York: Lyle Stuart, 1968), 104–5. Also see *Hijos de su tiempo*, 123–24.

126. Peter Kihss, "Cuban Rebels Free U.S. Sailor; Admiral Assails Raúl Castro," *New York Times*, July 11, 1958, p. 1; and Paterson, *Contesting Castro*, 160–72.

127. "Caught in a War," *Time*, July 14, 1958, p. 29.

128. "Marine Reveals How Cubans Kidnapped Him," *Amsterdam News*, August 2, 1958.

129. In *Where the Boys Are*, Van Gosse argues that the U.S. media had a romantic fascination with the Castro guerrillas and their performance of masculinity and heroic militarism. Also see "Caught in a War," *Time*, July 14, 1958, p. 29; and Lee Hall, "Cuba with Raúl Castro," *Life*, July 21, 1958, p. 29+.

130. Peter Kihss, "Cuba Rebels Free 7 U.S. Servicemen," *New York Times*, July 16, 1958, p. 20; and Peter Kihss, "Four Americans Freed in Cuba; Rebels Will Release Four a Day," *New York Times*, July 17, 1958, p. 15.

131. "Bronx Seabee Tells of Capture in Cuba," *Amsterdam News*, August 9, 1958, p. 3.

132. "U.S. Opens Parley with Cuba Rebels," *New York Times*, July 2, 1958, p. 12.

133. Paterson, *Contesting Castro*, 203–4; and McCoy, "Guantánamo Bay."
134. "Marines in Cuba," *New York Times*, July 30, 1958, p. 28.
135. Vincent Andrews, personal interview, Havana, Cuba, December 3 and December 7, 2004.
136. "U.S. Troops Land in Cuba for Duty," *New York Times*, July 29, 1958, p. 12; R. Hart Phillips, "Castro Protests Roles of Marines in Cuba," *New York Times*, July 31, 1958, p. 1; and "The Marines in Cuba," *New York Times*, August 3, 1958, p. E8.

4. A "TICKLISH" POSITION

1. Victor Davis, personal interview, Guantánamo, Cuba, October 8, 2004. Slavoj Žižek uses similar language, albeit to different ends, in *The Ticklish Subject: An Essay in Political Ontology* (New York: Verso, 1999).
2. Fidel Castro's January 1, 1959, speech in Santiago de Cuba, as cited in Marifeli Pérez-Stable, *The Cuban Revolution: Origins, Course, and Legacy* (New York: Oxford University Press, 1999), 3, 61.
3. Thomas, *Cuba*, 1037–90; Pérez, *Between Reform and Revolution*, 313–406; de la Fuente, *A Nation for All*, 259–316; Pérez-Stable, *The Cuban Revolution*; and Samuel Farber, *The Origins of the Cuban Revolution Reconsidered* (Chapel Hill: University of North Carolina Press, 2006). Focusing on an earlier era, Guerra, *The Myth of José Martí*.
4. Jack Raymond, "Pentagon Warns Cuba on Base; Says Rights Are Not Revocable," *New York Times*, October 28, 1959, p. 4; and "Mansfield Asks Harmony," *New York Times*, October 25, 1959. In 2007 the United States paid $4,085 a year.
5. Quotation of the Day, *New York Times*, January 6, 1961.
6. George Kirk, "Supports France on Tunisia," letter to the editor, *New York Times*, July 31, 1961, p. 18; M. H. Shagam, "Bases in Hostile Countries," letter to the editor, *New York Times*, August 9, 1961, p. 32; Sam Goldman, "Status of Guantánamo," letter to the editor, *New York Times*, August 26, 1961, p. 16; and Joao Da Silva, "Parallels to Goa Cited," letter to the editor, *New York Times*, December 18, 1961, p. 34.
7. "Dorticós Voices Claim" *New York Times*, February 8, 1964, p. 3; and "Castro Bars Haste over Guantánamo," *New York Times*, February 25, 1964, p. 1.
8. José Vázquez Pubillones, Índice, *La Voz del Pueblo*, January 7, 1959.
9. "Por cuestiones políticas son maltratados obreros cubanos en la b. naval americana," *La Voz del Pueblo*, January 27, 1959; and José Vázquez Pubillones, Índice, *La Voz del Pueblo*, January 27, 1959.
10. Paterson, *Contesting Castro*, 231–37.
11. José Vázquez Pubillones, Índice, *La Voz del Pueblo*, February 26, 1959; and José Vázquez Pubillones, Índice, *La Voz del Pueblo*, January 31, 1959.
12. In the months immediately following the Cuban revolution, the *New York Times* did not publish any articles that addressed the relations between Guantánamo, Cuba, and the U.S. naval base. The only related article was a small blurb on former President Ramón Grau San Martín's call for the U.S. withdrawal

from Guantánamo Bay. "U.S. Urged to Yield Base," *New York Times*, March 6, 1959, p. 7.

13. Liberty Situation and Other Problems at Guantánamo Naval Base, March 24, 1959, RG 59/711.56337/3–2459, Box 2886; and Matters Discussed during Admiral Fenno's Call on Ambassador, March 18, 1959, RG 59/711.56337/3–1859, Box 2886.

14. Lino Lemes García, "La economía local y la e. naval americana," *La Voz del Pueblo*, January 13, 1959; Lino Lemes García, "La rehabilitación del puerto," *La Voz del Pueblo*, January 9, 1959; Lino Lemes García, *El Vigilante*, April 3, 1959; Lino Lemes García, Guantánamo al día, *El Vigilante*, April 4, 1959; and José Vázquez Pubillones, Índice, *La Voz del Pueblo*, March 5, 1959.

15. Fishing Problems of Guantánamo Naval Base, March 30, 1959, RG 59/711.56337/3–2359, Box 2886; and Annual Review of U.S. Overseas Military Base System: Local Political Factors Affecting Guantánamo Naval Base, June 2, 1959, RG 59/711.56337/6–259, Box 2886.

16. Fishing Problems of Guantánamo Naval Base, March 30, 1959, RG 59/711.56337/3–2359, Box 2886.

17. Fishing Problems of Guantánamo Naval Base, March 30, 1959 (includes clipping, "Columna invasora," *Sierra Maestra*, March 20, 1959), RG 59/711.56337/3–2359, Box 2886; and Communist Daily *Hoy*'s Attack on Guantánamo Bay; Parallel Action by *Revolución* Organ of July 26 Movement, April 8, 1959, (includes clipping, "Justicia para Caimanera," *Revolución*, March 25, 1959), RG 59/711.56337/4–859, Box 2886. Also see José Vázquez Pubillones, Índice, *La Voz del Pueblo*, March 21, 1959.

18. Matters Discussed during Admiral Fenno's Call on the Ambassador, March 18, 1959, RG 59/711.56337/3–1859, Box 2886.

19. Liberty Situation and Other Problems at Guantánamo Naval Base, March 24, 1959, RG 59/711.56337/3–2459, Box 2886; José Vázquez Pubillones, Índice, *La Voz del Pueblo*, May 21, 1959; "Responde el responsable Joaquín Álvarez Torralba a 'Índice' de nuestro director con relación a las visitas de marinos," *La Voz del Pueblo*, July 7, 1959; Vázquez Pubillones, Índice, *La Voz del Pueblo*," July 9, 1959; Tad Szulc, "U.S. Navy Base Gets Along," *New York Times*, November 26, 1959, p. 20; and Vincent Andrews, personal interview, Havana, December 3 and 7, 2004.

20. Ambassador Bonsal to Secretary of State, August 18, 1959, RG 59/711.56337/7–1859, Box 2886; and Cuban Request to Register Americans on Guantánamo Naval Base, August 24, 1959, RG 59/711.56337/8–2459, Box 2886.

21. Annual Review of U.S. Overseas Military Base System: Local Political Factors Affecting Guantánamo Naval Base, June 2, 1959, RG 59/711.56337/6–259, Box 2886.

22. Vincent Andrews, personal interview, Havana, December 3 and 7, 2004; Matters Discussed during Admiral Fenno's Call on Ambassador, March 18, 1959, RG 59/711.56337/3–1859, Box 2886.

23. Vincent Andrews, personal interview, Havana, December 3 and 7, 2004.

24. José Vázquez Pubillones, Índice, *La Voz del Pueblo*, April 27, 1959; José Vázquez Pubillones, Índice, *La Voz del Pueblo*, July 2, 1959; Joaquín Álvarez

Torralba, "Responde el responsable Joaquín Álvarez Torralba a 'Índice' de nuestro director con relación a las visitas de marinos," *La Voz del Pueblo*, July 7, 1959; and José Vázquez Pubillones, Índice, *La Voz del Pueblo*, July 9, 1959.

25. Thomas, *Cuba*, 1234–99 and Pérez-Stable, *The Cuban Revolution*, 61–97.

26. Thomas, *Cuba*, 1250–51; and Farber, *Origins of the Cuban Revolution*, 147–49.

27. Swanger, "Lands of Rebellion," 327–74; "Más obras del municipio," *Sierra Maestra*, February 24, 1960; "Reforma agraria en Guantánamo y Yateras," *Sierra Maestra*, May 17, 1960; and "30 casas en Guantánamo," *Sierra Maestra*, May 20, 1960.

28. Jack Raymond, "President Backs Cuba Shore Leave," *New York Times*, October 30, 1960, p. 6; "Marines Won't See Towns," *New York Times*, October 30, 1960, p. 4; and "Cuba and Ourselves," *New York Times*, October 30, 1960, p. E10.

29. Jules B. Billard, "Guantánamo: Keystone in the Caribbean," *National Geographic*, March 1961, p. 420–36.

30. Liberty Situation and Other Problems at Guantánamo Naval Base, March 24, 1959, RG 59/711.56337/3–2359, Box 2886.

31. "Debe establecerse el comercio libre con la estación naval americana," *El Vigilante*, April 10, 1959.

32. "Cuban Labor Cuts Inter-America Tie," *New York Times*, November 23, 1959, p. 1; and Tad Szulc, "U.S. Navy Base Gets Along," *New York Times*, November 26, 1959, p. 20.

33. Liberty Situation and Other Problems at Guantánamo Naval Base, March 24, 1959, RG 59/711.56337/3–2359, Box 2886; Lino Lemes García, "Carta sindical sobre la base naval americana," *El Vigilante*, August 13, 1959; Pérez-Stable, *The Cuban Revolution*, 67+.

34. "Datos generales del despido del Secretario General de los trabajadores de la base de Guantánamo," *Dictámenes periciales de las FAR: El pueblo de Cuba demanda al gobierno de EU por daños humanos* (Havana: Ediciones Verde Olivo, 1999), 22–24. (Located in the Guantánamo Provincial Archive.)

35. Pérez-Stable, *The Cuban Revolution*, 70–73.

36. Possibility That Cuban Government May Request Revision of Status of U.S. Naval Base in Guantánamo Bay, October 16, 1959, RG 59/711.56337/10–1659, Box 2886.

37. Papers related to 1959 GTMO base workers' union, personal collection of José Sánchez Guerra in Guantánamo, Cuba.

38. "Ofrece trabajo obras públicas al obrero expulsado de la base naval yanqui por denunciar espionaje," *Hoy*, March 24, 1960.

39. "Cuban Labor Cuts Inter-America Tie," *New York Times*, November 23, 1959: p. 1; Joaquín Álvarez Torralba, Índice, *La Voz del Pueblo*, February 16, 1960; and Thomas, *Cuba*, 1249–51.

40. Thomas, *Cuba*, 1265–71.

41. R. Hart Phillips, "Admiral Defends Ouster of Cuban," *New York Times*, March 31, 1960, p. 3; "Pro-Reds Battle with Foes in Cuba," *New York Times*, March 26, 1960, p. 1; "Cuba vs. the U.S.," *New York Times*, March 27, 1960, p. E2; "Stakes at the Base," *Time*, March 28, 1960, p. 38; Manuel Ferrer Pérez,

"Provocación yankee a trabajadores de la base naval vigilan los obreros para evitar las autoridades hagan un sabotaje y se repita el caso del *Maine*: Entrevista con el Secretario del sindicato de la base," *Sierra Maestra*, March 10, 1960; and "Amenazan las autoridades yanquis con expulsión de la base al Secretario del Sindicato por la denuncia de *Sierra Maestra*," *Sierra Maestra*, March 17, 1960.

42. Tad Szulc, "U.S. Notes to Cuba Link Castro Rule to Rising Tension," *New York Times*, April 12, 1960, p. 1.

43. "Texts of Replies by U.S. to Three Protest Notes from Cuba," *New York Times*, April 12, 1960.

44. "Extraordinariamente nutridísima la concentración ayer en Caimanera," *La Voz del Pueblo*, May 14, 1960.

45. Thomas, *Cuba*, 1272–99; and Pérez, *Between Reform and Revolution*, 326.

46. Louis Pérez notes that Cuban employees for U.S. businesses were the first to leave Cuba. Pérez, *On Becoming Cuban*, 497–98.

47. Tad Szulc, "Cubans Sell Pesos on Black Market," *New York Times*, April 5, 1960, p. 17.

48. "Castro Cautions U.S. Base Workers" *New York Times*, November 17, 1960, p. 17; Tad Szulc, "Cubans Sell Pesos on Black Market," *New York Times*, April 5, 1960, p. 17; E. W. Kenworthy, "Havana to Impose Curb at U.S. Base: Acts to 'Capture' Dollars Earned by Cuban Aides at Guantánamo Bay," *New York Times*, May 25, 1960, p. 6; "Status of Base at Guantánamo Is Not Expected to Be Altered," *New York Times*, January 4, 1961, p. 3; Max Frankel, "Cuba Shows No Sign of Intent to Harass U.S. Naval Station," *New York Times*, January 8, 1961, p. 14; Max Frankel, "Havana Freezes Jobs at U.S. Base," *New York Times*, April 9, 1961, p. 4; and López Jardo, *Guantánamo y Gitmo*, 73–74.

49. Max Frankel, "Cuba Shows No Sign of Intent to Harass U.S. Naval Station," *New York Times*, January 8, 1961, p. 14.

50. Resume of Supply Activities, 1962, Naval Supply Depot, USNOA, Post-1946 Command File, Box 1246.

51. Rosa Johnson, personal interview, Guantánamo, Cuba, November 9, 2004.

52. "Trabajadores de la base naval a la cárcel," *La Voz del Pueblo*, August 19, 1960.

53. Letter from the Sindicato de la Base, January 9, 1961, Guantánamo Municipal Museum exhibit.

54 Pérez-Stable, *The Cuban Revolution*, 82–83, 94–96.

55. Cruz Díaz, *Guantánamo Bay*, 141–51.

56. "Torturan a un obrero cubano: estuvo secuestrado seis días y le obligaron a ingerir unas extrañas pastillas," *La Voz del Pueblo*, January 13, 1961; "Navy Denies Harming Cuban," *New York Times*, January 14, 1961, p. 3; and R. Hart Phillips, "Castro 'Waiting' to Get U.S. Base," *New York Times*, January 14, 1961, p. 3.

57. Cruz Díaz, *Guantánamo Bay*, 149.

58. *Gitmo: Cold War Cuba*, dir. Ian Stuttard, prod. Judith Weymant (Yorkshire Television Productions for ITV, 1991). I would like to thank Rafael Hernández for generously loaning me a copy of this documentary.

59. Jorge Luis Merencio, "Caimanera, resistencia cubana contra el imperio," *Granma,* November 6, 2004, p. 3.

60. Ramón Sánchez, personal interview and papers, Guantánamo, Cuba, October 4, 2004.

61. "U.S. Mines Land Near Base," *New York Times,* November 3, 1960, p. 15.

62. "Five Seamen Killed on U.S. Mine Field within Guantánamo," *New York Times,* May 5, 1964, p. 19; and Murphy, *Guantánamo Bay,* 1982 ed., http://www.nsgtmo.navy.mil/history/gtmohistoryvol2dedication.htm (accessed August 4, 2006). In total, at least twenty-four people have been killed in the landmines since 1961. Landmine Monitor Report, Cuba, 2004, http://www.icbl.org/lm/2004/cuba (accessed March 16, 2008).

63. The United States deactivated its minefield in the late 1990s, while the Cuban minefield remains active. Landmine Monitor Report, Cuba, 2004, http://www.icbl.org/lm/2004/cuba (accessed July 14, 2007).

64. The term "cactus curtain," an obvious riff on "iron curtain," was used in the U.S. media to characterize the separation between Cuba and GTMO, at least beginning in 1962; see "Congressmen Begin Guantánamo Study," *New York Times,* March 17, 1962, p. 13; and "Patrol along a Cactus Curtain," *Life,* April 27, 1962, p. 2–3. Also see Theodore K. Mason, *Across the Cactus Curtain: The Story of Guantánamo Bay* (New York: Dodd, Mead, 1984).

65. "A los trabajadores de la base naval americana," *La Voz del Pueblo,* January 21, 1961; and Max Frankel, "Havana Freezes Jobs at U.S. Base," *New York Times,* April 9, 1961, p. 4.

66. "Castro Cautions U.S. Base Workers," *New York Times,* November 17, 1960.

67. "A los trabajadores de la base naval americana," *La Voz del Pueblo,* January 21, 1961; and "Aviso: Aduana de Guantánamo–Caimanera," *La Voz del Pueblo,* December 19, 1960.

68. López Jardo, *Guantánamo y Gitmo,* 75–76; and Mason, *Across the Cactus Curtain,* 92–94.

69. "A Big U.S. Base Under Fire," *U.S. News and World Report,* December 14, 1959, p. 64; R. Hart Philips, "Island on an Island," *The New York Times Magazine,* January 10, 1960, p. 9; and Hanson W. Baldwin, "Guantánamo: Ours or Castro's?" *Saturday Evening Post,* September 24, 1960, p. 19.

70. Hanson W. Baldwin, "Guantánamo: Ours or Castro's?" *Saturday Evening Post,* September 24, 1960, p. 19.

71. Jules B. Billard, "Guantánamo: Keystone in the Caribbean," *National Geographic,* March 1961, p. 420–36.

72. "U.S. Base to Lose Cubans for a Day," *New York Times,* April 27, 1961, p. 3; "Naval Base Gets Landing Report," *New York Times,* April 20, 1961, p. 10; "Havana Rejoices Fires Guns in the Air," *New York Times,* April 21, 1961, p. 3; and Max Frankel, "Castro Youth Patrols Help Police Prevent Uprising," *New York Times,* April 20, 1961, p. 1.

73. Rosa Johnson, personal interview, Guantánamo, Cuba, November 9, 2004.

74. "Congressmen Begin Guantánamo Study," *New York Times,* March 17, 1962, p. 13.

75. "Patrol along a Cactus Curtain," *Life*, April 27, 1962.

76. Mason, *Across the Cactus Curtain*, 93–94.

77. Maria Boothe, personal interview, Guantánamo, Cuba, November 23, 2004. In my conversations with former workers in Guantánamo, most were reluctant to discuss the strip searches with me. No one voluntarily discussed this surveillance. When I asked how the commute had changed after the revolution, my informants were vague. As I was forty-five years younger than my youngest informant, I decided not to press on this question of nudity and embarrassment.

78. "Cuba: Containment Shuffleboard," *Time*, September 28, 1962, p. 32.

79. Resume of Supply Activities, 1962, Naval Supply Depot, USNOA, Post-1946 Command File, GTMO, Box 1246.

80. Informe del equipo del Escuela de Historia, "Guantánamo: Esquema de la historia de una ciudad."

81. Concepción Martínez Incháustegui, Felipa Suárez Ramos, and Sonia Maldonado González, *Punta de vanguardia: Historia de la Brigada de la Frontera* (Santiago de Cuba: Editorial Oriente, 1986), 53.

82. Philip Ben, "A Visit to Guantánamo," *The New Republic*, December 8, 1962, p. 10–11.

83. Martínez, Suárez, and Maldonado, *Punta de vanguardia*, 42–45; and Felipa Suárez and Pilar Quesada, *A escasos metros del enemigo: Historia de la Brigada de la Frontera* (Havana: Ediciones Verde Olivo, 1996), 38, 47.

84. Philip Ben, "A Visit to Guantánamo," *New Republic*, December 8, 1962, p. 10–11.

85. Alberto Torres, personal interview, Havana, December 5, 2004.

86. López, *Guantánamo y Gitmo*, 75–76.

87. Thomas, *Cuba*, 1300–11 and 1355–71; Fursenko and Naftali, *"One Hell of a Gamble,"* 56–100; Peter Wyden, *Bay of Pigs: The Untold Story* (New York: Simon and Schuster, 1979); and James G. Blight and Peter Kornbluh, *Politics of Illusion: The Bay of Pigs Invasion Reexamined* (Boulder, CO: Lynne Rienner, 1998).

88. Warren Hinckle and William W. Turner, *The Fish Is Red: The Story of the Secret War against Castro* (New York: Harper and Row, 1981), 80–88; and Blight and Kornbluh, *Politics of Illusion*, 89. There is limited evidence about a diversionary exile force in Eastern Cuba. The CIA appears to have hoped a contingent would land near Guantánamo and engineer a fake "attack" on GTMO. The aim was to blame Castro for aggressions against the base, which would in turn have justified a full U.S. military response. As things turned out, however, the anti-Castro contingent failed to land and nothing happened. Although further classified documents may remain, to this point, I have found no evidence detailing GTMO's role in the Bay of Pigs.

89. "Dan informe sobre el atentado a Raúl Castro," *Hoy*, August 12, 1961; "Detalles del frustrado plan de autoagresión en Caimanera," *Prensa Libre*, August 13, 1961; Richard Eder, "U.S. Base Aided Plot Cuba Says," *New York Times*, August 13, 1961, p. 19; and Hinckle and Turner, *The Fish Is Red*, 104–6. Hinckle and Turner's account of nefarious CIA plots against Castro is both sensationalized and scantily footnoted. However, given the dearth of declassified CIA documents on this point, I believe its parallels with the Cuban press are no-

table. For a critique of *The Fish Is Red*, see John Leonard, Review: Books of the Times, *New York Times*, September 24, 1981.

90. *Patty Candela*, dir. Rogelio París (Havana: Instituto Cubano del Arte e Industria Cinematográficos, 1976).

91. "Dan informe sobre el atentado a Raúl Castro," *Hoy*, August 12, 1961; and "Detalles del frustrado plan de autoagresión en Caimanera," *Prensa Libre*, August 13, 1961.

92. "Dan informe sobre el atentado a Raúl Castro," *Hoy*, August 12, 1961.

93. "U.S. Naval Base," *Hoy*, February 11, 1964.

94. Summary of Items of Significant Interest, Period 110070 1–120700, Rock Throwing Incident at Guantánamo, August 12, 1962, Digital National Security Archive (DNSA), Cuban Missile Crisis, CC00273; Summary of Items of Significant Interest, 090701–100700, October 1962, DNSA, Cuban Missile Crisis, CC00571; and Summary of Items of Significant Interest, Period 120701–130700, October 1962, DNSA, Cuban Missile Crisis, CC 00596. These documents are accessible through the Digital National Security Archive, a joint project between ProQuest and the National Security Archive at George Washington University.

95. Rafael Hernández, *La seguridad nacional de Cuba y la cuestión de la base naval de Guantánamo* (Havana: Centro de Estudios sobre América, 1988).

96. "U.S. Naval Base," *Hoy*, February 11, 1964.

97. Suárez and Quesada, *A escasos metros del enemigo*, 146–47.

98. McCoy, "Guantánamo Bay," 261–67.

99. "Asesinado un obrero cubano en la base naval," *Hoy*, October 20, 1961.

100. "Cuban 'Spy' Death Embroils Marines," *New York Times*, April 27, 1963, p. 1+; and "Ex-Marine Tells How He Helped Bury Cuban's Body," *New York Times*, April 28, 1963, p. 1+.

101. "Perdimos un compañero; pero ganamos una bandera de combate," *Hoy*, October 21, 1961; and "La viuda de Rubén López y tres de sus hijos mayores," *Hoy*, October 27, 1961.

102. "El sepelio del obrero Rubén López, el más extraordinario que recuerda Guantánamo," *La Voz del Pueblo*, October 21, 1961; "Fue asesinado el obrero Rubén López S. así lo han declarado su viuda Georgina González y su hija Angélica en entrevistas con ellas celebradas," *La Voz del Pueblo*, October 21, 1961; and "Perdimos un compañero; pero ganamos una bandera de combate," *Hoy*, October 21, 1961.

Gloria González had to procure her husband's body from U.S. officials and carry it across an international border between Guantánamo and GTMO. This event predated two of Cuba's iconic films about bureaucracy, socialism, and death. Tomás Gutiérrez Alea's famous early critique, *Death of a Bureaucrat*, was released in 1966. Almost thirty years later, he returned to similar themes in *Guantanamera*, his 1995 film about escorting a cadaver from Guantánamo to Havana. See *La muerte de un burócrata* (*The Death of a Bureaucrat*), dir. Tomás Gutiérrez Alea (Havana: ICAIC, 1966); and *Guantanamera*, dir. Tómas Gutiérrez Alea (Havana: ICAIC, 1995).

103. "Cuban's Body Found on Bay," *New York Times*, October 18, 1961, p. 28; "U.S. Gets Cuba Message," *New York Times*, October 24, 1961, p. 32;

and "U.S. Still Studies Guantánamo Death," *New York Times,* November 16, 1961, p. 17.

104. "Condenan los trabajadores cubanos el crimen de la base naval de Caimanera," *Hoy,* October 25, 1961.

105. "Nuevas victimas del imperialismo" *Mujeres,* November 15, 1961.

106. Political columnist Jack Anderson broke the story in the *Washington Post.* See Jack Anderson, "Guantánamo Story Hushed Up," *Washington Post,* April 26, 1963, p. D13; "Cuban 'Spy' Death Embroils Marines," *New York Times,* April 27, 1963, p. 1+; "Ex-Marine Tells How He Helped Bury Cuban's Body," *New York Times,* April 28, 1963, p. 1+.; Tom Wicker, "Ex-Marine to Go to White House," *New York Times,* April 30, 1963, p. 7; "Inquiry in Slaying of Cuban Dropped," *New York Times,* May 4, 1963, p. 2; "Ex-Marine Avoids White House Fete," *New York Times,* May 2, 1963, p. 14; "Congressman Drops Bid for Inquiry in Szili Case," *New York Times,* May 10, 1963, p. 19; "The Hero and the Hush Up," *Time,* May 10, 1963, p. 17; "Occurrence at Guantánamo," *The Nation,* May 11, 1963, p. 386; and "Marine Justice," *The New Republic,* June 1, 1963, p. 7.

107. The Hero and the Hush Up," *Time,* May 10, 1963, p. 17.

108. "Ex-Marine Tells How He Helped Bury Cuban's Body," *New York Times,* April 28, 1963, p. 1+.

109. Ibid.

110. Ibid.

111. When historian Mary Ellene McCoy visited the base in 1991, she asked naval officials about the case. They refused to speak with her about it. McCoy, "Guantánamo Bay," 263.

112. "Ex-Marine Tells How He Helped Bury Cuban's Body," *New York Times,* April 28, 1963, p. 1+.

113. "The Hero and the Hush Up," *Time,* May 10, 1963, p. 17.

114. "Confiesa el imperialismo el crimen de Rubén López Sabariego," *Venceremos,* May 5, 1963.

115. "Anuncio," *La Voz del Pueblo,* November 4, 1961; and "Tuvo brillante verificativo en la mañana de ayer en el Círculo Popular 'Rubén López Sabariego,' " *La Voz del Pueblo,* November 6, 1961.

116. "Aniversario de un crimen," *Venceremos,* October 15, 1962.

117. The Missile Crisis is alternately referred to as the Cuban Missile Crisis in the United States, the October Crisis in Cuba, and the Caribbean Crisis in Russia. For a sampling of memoir, older scholarship, newer interpretations, and document collections, see Robert F. Kennedy, *Thirteen Days: A Memoir of the Cuban Missile Crisis* (New York: W. W. Norton, 1968); Thomas, *Cuba,* 1372–1419; Blight, Allyn, and Welch, *Cuba on the Brink;* Fursenko and Naftali, *"One Hell of a Gamble";* Laurence Chang and Peter Kornbluh, eds., *The Cuban Missile Crisis, 1962: A National Security Archive Document Reader* (New York: New Press, 1998); Daniela Spenser, ed., *Espejos de la guerra fría: México, América Central, y el Caribe* (Mexico City: Centro de Investigaciones y Estudios Superiores, 2004); Adolfo Gilly, "A la luz relámpago: Cuba en octubre"; and Daniela Spenser, "La crisis del Caribe: Catalizador de la proyección soviética en América Latina," in *Espejos de la guerra fría,* 215–45, 281–317.

118. Jorge Domínguez, foreword to *Cuba on the Brink;* and Blight, Allyn, and Welch, *Cuba on the Brink.*

119. Tactics in the UN Security Council, October 20, 1962, DNSA, Cuban Missile Crisis, CC 00707; Political Program to Be Announced by the President, October 20, 1962, DNSA, Cuban Missile Crisis, CC00723; and Why the Political Program Should Be Kept in the Speech, October 21, 1962, DNSA, Cuban Missile Crisis, CC00759.

120. Briefing Paper for the President's November 20, 1962 Press Conference on Castro's Five Points Including Demand We Leave Guantánamo, November 19, 1962, DNSA, Cuban Missile Crisis, CC02433.

121. Argument against Any Comparison of Soviet Missile Bases, November 10, 1962, DNSA, Cuban Missile Crisis, CC02217.

122. U.S. Retention of Cuba Base is Difficult to Sell, November 14, 1962, DNSA, Cuban Missile Crisis, CC02318.

123. Command History, Fleet Training Group for the period 1 January 1962 to 31 December 1962, March 21, 1963, USNOA, Post-1946 Command File, GTMO, Box 1244.

124. Cuba Fact Sheet, October 27, 1962, DNSA, Cuban Missile Crisis, CC01477; and Annual Historical Report of the Commander in Chief Atlantic for Calendar Year 1962, April 29, 1963, DNSA, Cuban Missile Crisis, CC03086.

125. See Enloe, *Bananas, Beaches, and Bases;* and Lutz, *Homefront.*

126. Robert G. Neal to Edward J. O'Donnell, March 18, 1969, Edward J. O'Donnell Papers, Hoover Institution Archives, Folder 74077–10.V. (The Hoover Institution Archives are located at Stanford University, Palo Alto, California.)

127. Business as Usual II, Resume of Supply Activities, 1962, Naval Supply Depot, USNOA, Post-1946 Command File, GTMO, Box 1246; and Command History, 1 January 1962–31 December 1962, March 21, 1963, USNOA, Post-1946 Command File, GTMO, Box 1244.

128. Edward O'Donnell to Robert G. Neal, April 17, 1969, Hoover Institution Archives, Edward J. O'Donnell Collection, Folder 74077–10.V.

129. 1962 Handbill, Hoover Institution Archives, Edward J. O'Donnell Collection, Folder 74077–10.V.

130. Edward O'Donnell to Robert G. Neal, April 17, 1969, Hoover Institution Archives, Edward J. O'Donnell Collection, Folder 74077–10.V.

131. U.S. Naval Air Station, OPNAV Report for 1959, USNOA, Post-1946 Command File, GTMO, Box 1242.

132. "Information on Ships Arriving with Dependents from GTMO," October 24, 1962, DNSA, Cuban Missile Crisis, CC01129.

133. "Guantánamo Families, En Route Home, Tell of Tearful, Hasty Evacuation," *New York Times,* October 24, 1962, p. 22; and Thomas Buckley, "2,432 Guantánamo Evacuees Are Greeted at Norfolk Base," *New York Times,* October 26, 1962, p. 18.

134. Joyce Hughes Matthews, "The Rock," www.nsgtmo.navy.mil/gazette/History_98–64/Hisadd4.html (accessed June 29, 2004). This article has since been removed from the U.S. Navy's GTMO website.

135. Murphy, *Guantánamo Bay*, 1982 ed., http://www.nsgtmo.navy.mil/history/gtmohistorymurphyvol1ch19.htm (accessed August 4, 2006).

136. Cuban Workforce Employed at Naval Base, Guantánamo, September 6, 1962, DNSA, Cuban Missile Crisis, CC00364.

137. Summary of Significant Messages Regarding the Cuban Situation 220701–230700, October 23, 1962, DNSA, Cuban Missile Crisis, CC00949; Summary of Items of Significant Interest, Period 240701–250700, October 25, 1962, Cuban Missile Crisis, CC01327; and Summary of Items of Significant Interest, Period 20700, October 27, 1962, DNSA, Cuban Missile Crisis, CC001528.

138. Business as Usual II, Resume of Supply Activities, 1962, Naval Supply Depot, USNOA, Post-1946 Command File, GTMO, Box 1246.

139. CINCLANT Historical Account of Cuban Crisis, April 29, 1963, DNSA, Cuban Missile Crisis, CC03087.

140. Resume of Supply Activities, 1962, Naval Supply Depot, USNOA, Post-1946 Command File, GTMO, Box 1246.

141. CINCLANT Historical Account of Cuban Missile Crisis, April 29, 1963, DNSA, Cuban Crisis, CC03087.

142. Resume of Supply Activities, 1962, Naval Supply Depot, USNOA, Post-1946 Command File, GTMO, Box 1246.

143. Business as Usual II, Resume of Supply Activities, 1962, Naval Supply Depot, USNOA, Post-1946 Command File, GTMO, Box 1246.

144. Claire Winchester (pseud.), personal interview, Guantánamo, Cuba, October 15, 2004. (Interview conducted in English.)

145. Business as Usual II, Resume of Supply Activities, 1962, Naval Supply Depot, USNOA, Post-1946 Command File, GTMO, Box 1246.

146. U.S. Naval Air Station, OPNAV Report for 1959, USNOA Post-1946 Command File, GTMO, Box 1242; and Murphy, *Guantánamo Bay*, 1982 ed., http://www.nsgtmo.navy.mil/history/gtmohistorymurphyvol1ch19.htm (accessed August 4, 2006).

147. GTMO Annual Cold War Activity Report, July 8, 1964, USNOA, Post-1946 Command File, GTMO, Box 1243.

148. Derek Stedman, personal interview, Guantánamo, Cuba, October 15, 2004.

149. "The Caribbean: Troubled Waters," *Newsweek*, February 17, 1964, p. 13–14; and "Rusk's Statement on Seizure of Four Cuban Vessels," *New York Times*, February 8, 1964, p. 3.

150. "Those Cuban Fishermen," *New York Times*, February 9, 1964, p. 22; "Fishing for Guantánamo," *New York Times*, February 9, 1964, p. E10; and "Water for Guantánamo," *New York Times*, February 7, 1964, p. 30.

151. McCoy, "Guantánamo Bay," 146–84.

152. "Text of the Cuban Note," *New York Times*, February 7, 1964, p. 14; and "Nota al gobierno de EEUU advirtiendo la suspensión de agua a la base yanqui," *Hoy*, February 7, 1964.

153. Alan McPherson, "Courts of World Opinion: Trying the Panama Flag Riots of 1964," *Diplomatic History* 28 (January 2004): 83–112.

154. Charles Mohr, "Send in Marines, Goldwater Says," *New York Times*, February 7, 1964.

155. McCoy, "Guantánamo Bay," 276–311; Murphy, *Guantánamo Bay*, 1982 ed., https://www.cnic.navy.mil/Guantanamo/AboutGTMO/gtmohistgeneral/gtmohistmurphy/gtmohistmurphyvol2/gtmohistmurphyvol2ch1/CNIC_047247 (accessed March 16, 2008); and William B. Breuer, *Sea Wolf: A Biography of John D. Bulkeley* (Novato, CA: Presidio, 1989).

156. Breuer, *Sea Wolf*; and Joan Bulkeley Stade, *Twelve Handkerchiefs: The Global Journey of Alice Wood Bulkeley through World War II and the Twentieth Century with an American Navy Hero* (Tucson, AZ: Patrice, 2001).

157. "Base Goes 'Austere,'" *New York Times*, February 7, 1964, p. 15; "Emergency Steps Described," *New York Times*, February 7, 1964, p. 15; "Salt-Water Conversion Studied," *New York Times*, February 8, 1964, p. 4; "Water Project Advanced," *New York Times*, February 14, 1964; and "Use of Cuban Water Charged," *New York Times*, February 17, 1964.

158. "Cubans Reported Blaming Castro," *New York Times*, February 16, 1964.

159. 1967 Work Force Study, August 15, 1967, USNOA, Post-1946 Command Files, GTMO, Box 1243.

160. Ricardo Baylor, personal interview, Guantánamo, Cuba, November 21, 2004.

161. "Hablan obreros desplazados de la base naval yanqui," *Venceremos*, February 21, 1964.

162. Ibid.

163. "Responde Fidel al despido en masa de obreros de la base," *Hoy*, February 14, 1964.

164. "Fidel: 'Nunca hemos interferido la entrada y salida de los trabajadores de la base,'" *Venceremos*, February 13, 1964.

165. Gabriel, "Paga la revolución pensión a los obreros jubilados de la base naval de Caimanera; se negó EU a pagarles," *Venceremos*, February 13, 1964; and "Fidel: 'Nunca hemos interferido la entrada y salida de los trabajadores de la base," *Venceremos*, February 13, 1964.

166. "Visitan a Guantánamo periodistas extranjeros," *Venceremos*, February 21, 1964.

167. Norberto Fuentes, "¡Donde la revolución nos sitúe, allí estaremos! 437 desplazados en la base naval de Guantánamo," *Hoy*, February 16, 1964.

168. "Responde Fidel al despido en masa de obreros de la base," *Hoy*, February 14, 1964.

169. "Reunión del PURS de Guantánamo con los obreros desplazados de la base naval yanqui," *Venceremos*, February 28, 1964.

170. "Reunión del PURS de Guantánamo con los obreros desplazados de la base naval yanqui," *Venceremos*, February 28, 1964; "Iniciado el pago a los obreros desplazados de la base naval yanqui," *Venceremos*, February 28, 1964; and "300 mil pesos, situados para pagar de inmediato a desplazados en la base," *Hoy*, February 15, 1964.

171. Maria Boothe, personal interview, Guantánamo, Cuba, November 23, 2004.

172. Priscilla Baxter, personal interview, Guantánamo, Cuba, November 24, 2004.

173. Ricardo Baylor, personal interview, Guantánamo, Cuba, November 21, 2004.

174. "Guantánamo Plant Spurred," *New York Times*, July 8, 1964.

175. "Guantánamo Outplays Cubans' Harassment," *New York Times*, July 12, 1964; Breuer, *Sea Wolf*, 221–30; and McCoy, "Guantánamo Bay," 296–98.

176. "Cuba Says Guard at Base Was Shot by Marine," *New York Times*, June 11, 1964, p. 3; "Cuba Says Guard at Base Was Shot," *New York Times*, July 21, 1964, p. 10; and "¡Monstruoso crimen!" *Venceremos*, July 20, 1964.

177. "¡Monstruoso crimen!" *Venceremos*, July 20, 1964.

178. Breuer, *Sea Wolf*, 229–30.

179. "U.S. Denies Charge," *New York Times*, July 21, 1964, p. 10; and Thomas J. Hamilton, "Guantánamo Admiral Rebuts Castro Accusation," *New York Times*, July 30, 1964, p. 7.

180. "Que viva la paz, pero con los fusiles, cañones y tanques bien engrasados, que tenemos nosotros—Raúl," *Venceremos*, July 24, 1964; and "Lucharemos medio siglo más si es necesario—Raúl Castro," *Hoy*, July 21, 1964.

181. "Advierte Cuba a la ONU sobre los peligros de las provocaciones de los militares yanquis de la base," *Hoy*, July 23, 1964.

182. "Que viva la paz, pero con los fusiles cañones y tanques bien engrasados, que tenemos nosotros—Raúl," *Venceremos*, July 24, 1964.

183. "Llamamiento del PURSC regional," *Venceremos*, July 20, 1964.

184. "El BON Fronterizo encarna la ideología de Martí con la bravura de Maceo, reforzada con el Marxismo-Leninismo, expresó el Ministro de las FAR, Raúl Castro," *Venceremos*, July 24, 1964.

185. Thomas J. Hamilton, "Castro Leads Cubans in a Rally For His 26th of July Anniversary," *New York Times*, July 26, 1964, p. 16.

5. CONTRACT WORKERS, EXILES, AND COMMUTERS

1. 1967 Workforce Study, August 15, 1967, USNOA, Post-1946 Command File, GTMO, Box 1243.

2. In using the term "postmodern," I define it in a labor framework, rather than as a method of cultural critique. "Postmodern" signifies the global economy's turn to information- and service-oriented sectors, often disassociating the corporation, the place of work, and the home nation of workers and consumers. See Michael Hardt and Antonio Negri, *Empire* (Cambridge, MA: Harvard University Press, 2000), 280–300. Migrant and contract labor programs have developed in conjunction with these trends, often creating populations that fill critical labor niches, but that are deprived of rights, protections, and social integration. For case studies on South Asian and Filipino migrants, see Myron Weiner, "International Migration and Development: Indians in the Persian Gulf," *Population Development Review* 8 (March 1982): 1–36; and Salazar Parreñas, *Servants of Globalization*.

3. U.S. Embassy in Kingston to U.S. State Department, EMBTEL 108, October 12, 1964; U.S. Embassy in Kingston to Secretary of State, Re: Jamaican security risks at GTMO, October 12, 1964; U.S. Embassy in Kingston to State De-

partment, EMBTEL 108, 109, October 13, 1964; U.S. Embassy in Kingston to Secretary of State, Re: Jamaican security risks at GTMO, October 14, 1964; and U.S. Embassy in Kingston to U.S. State Department, Re: Jamaican security risks at GTMO, October 16, 1964. All documents located in NARA, Central Foreign Policy Files 1964–66, Defense, Def IT-Def 1 Japan 1/1/64, File JAM Def 15, Box 1647.
According to the U.S. diplomatic reports, two short articles appeared in the *Jamaican Star*. The first quoted Michael Chavannes on the poor conditions at GTMO. However, the U.S. diplomats in Kingston spoke with the paper's editors to minimize any controversy. The next editorial emphasized the need for better security procedures in Jamaica to prevent "trouble makers" from participating in the contract labor program. No report of this incident appeared in the U.S. or Cuban media.

4. Lipman, "Between Guantánamo and Montego Bay."

5. Ricardo Baylor, personal interview, Guantánamo, Cuba, November 21, 2004.

6. 1966 Command History Narrative, USNOA, Post-1946 Command File, GTMO, Box 1242; "Cubans Accuse U.S. in Sentry's Death," *New York Times*, May 23, 1966; Richard Eder, "Killing of Cuban Confirmed by U.S.," *New York Times*, May 25, 1966; and Suárez and Quesada, *A escasos metros del enemigo*, 112–18.

7. Max Frankel, "U.S. Warns Cuba on Guantánamo," *New York Times*, May 29, 1966.

8. Hernández, *La seguridad nacional de Cuba*.

9. Tom Miller, "The Sun Sometimes Sets on the American Empire," *Esquire*, September 1973, p. 97+.

10. "Is There a Plan to Give Up Guantánamo?" *U.S. News and World Reports*, March 30, 1964, p. 6; and "Castro: 'Yankee Go Home,'—U.S.: 'We're Here to Stay,'" *U.S. News and World Reports*, August 27, 1973, p. 56. For a Cold War analysis of GTMO's political importance as a bulwark against the Soviets, see Martin J. Scheina, "The U.S. Presence in Guantánamo," *Strategic Review* 4 (Spring 1976): 81–88. For an opposing view doubting GTMO's strategic utility, see Wayne Smith, "The Base from the U.S. Perspective," in *Subject to Solution: Problems in Cuban-U.S. Relations*, eds. Wayne A. Smith and Esteban Morales Domínguez (Boulder, CO: Lynne Rienner, 1988), 97–101.

11. 1967 Workforce Study, August 15, 1967, USNOA, Post-1946 Command File, GTMO, Box 1243.

12. Ibid.

13. Ibid.

14. 1967 Command History Chronology and Narrative, February 9, 1968, USNOA, Post-1946, Command File, GTMO, Box 1243.

15. 1967 Workforce Study, August 15, 1967, USNOA, Post-1946 Command File, GTMO, Box 1243.

16. "Out of Many, One People: An Interview with Premier Alexander Bustamante on the Eve of Jamaican Independence," *National Catholic Review*, August 11, 1962, p. 592–93.

17. 1967 Workforce Study, August 15, 1967, USNOA, Post-1946 Command File, GTMO, Box 1243.

18. Ibid.

19. Ibid.

20. Tom Miller, "The Sun Sometimes Sets on the American Empire," *Esquire*, September 1973, pp. 97+.

21. All children born in Cuba had the right to claim Cuban citizenship after 1940. At the age of eighteen, a West Indian descendant would have to choose between Cuban citizenship or status as a British subject. After the Cuban revolution, the Cuban government enabled all West Indians who wanted Cuban citizenship to acquire it. Although some elderly men and women continue to claim a British identity, the vast majority of the second, third, and fourth generations identify themselves as Cuban or as both Cuban and West Indian. Graciela Chailloux Laffita, Roberto Claxton, and Robert Whitney, "I Am the Caribbean: A West Indian Melting Pot in Cuba," in *Intra-Caribbean Migration: The Cuban Connection, 1898–Present* (publication of the proceedings, University of the West Indies, Mona, Jamaica, June 14–16, 2001).

22. Derek Stedman, personal interview, Guantánamo, Cuba, October 15, 2004.

23. Victor Davis, personal interview, Guantánamo, Cuba, October 8, 2004.

24. 1967 Workforce Study, August 15, 1967, USNOA, Post-1946 Command File, GTMO, Box 1243.

25. George Vecsey, "Berbick's Ring Poise Came the Hard Way," *New York Times*, April 11, 1981, p. 21; and Michael Katz, "It's Boxing Hoopla Time Again," *New York Times*, February 11, 1981, p. B9.

26. *Guantánamo Gazette*, August 5, 1969, 1969 Command History, USNOA, Post-1946 Command File, GTMO, Box 1243.

27. Murphy, *History of Guantánamo Bay*, 1982 ed., http://www.nsgtmo.navy.mil/history/gtmohistoryvol2ch5.htm (accessed July 4, 2006).

28. 1966 Command History and 1967 Annual Report (PWC), USNOA, Post-1946 Command File, GTMO, Box 1245; U.S. Navy Public Works Center, 1967 Command History, USNOA, Post-1946 Command File, GTMO, Box 1245; and J. Gaona, "25 Years of Jamaican Independence Honored in Guantánamo Bay with Food, Music, and Dance," *Guantánamo Gazette*, August 6, 1987.

29. 1973 Command History, USNOA, Post-1946 Command File, GTMO, Box 1243.

30. Jamaica Information Services, "14,000 Jamaicans Benefited from Overseas Employment Programme Last Year," May 19, 2005, http://www.jis.gov.jm/labour/html/20050518t080000–0500_5708_jis_14_000_jamaicans_benefited_from_overseas_employment_programme_last_year.asp (accessed September 9, 2006).

31. "Some Overseas Hotel Workers Exempt from Visa Quota," May 19, 2005, http://www.jis.gov.jm/labour/html/20050518t080000–0500_5710_jis_some_overseas_hotel_workers_exempt_from_visa_quota.asp (accessed July 27, 2007).

32. "Jamaican Independence Day: GTMO Style," *Guantánamo Gazette*, August 12, 2005, http://www.nsgtmo.navy.mil/Gazette%20Online/archived

%20editions/2005/050812all.pdf (accessed July 4, 2006). This article has since been removed from the U.S. Navy's GTMO website. Also see, "Forty-Five Years of Independence," *Guantánamo Gazette*, August 10, 2007, for another account of Jamaican Independence celebrations on the base, http://www.cnic.navy.mil/navycni/groups/public/@pub/@southe/@guantanamobay/documents/document/cnip_021001.pdf (accessed August 23, 2007).

33. "GTMO Celebrates Philippine Independence Day," *Guantánamo Gazette*, June 22, 2007, http://www.nsgtmo.navy.mil/Gazette%20Online/archived%20editions/2007/070622all.pdf (accessed July 16, 2007); Honey Nixon, "A Celebration of Culture and Heritage," *Guantánamo Gazette*, June 23, 2006, http://www.nsgtmo.navy.mil/Gazette%20Online/archived%20editions/2006/060623all.pdf (accessed July 4, 2006); and "Welcome Aboard from the Command Master Chief," http://www.cnic.navy.mil/Guantanamo/AboutGTMO/WelcomeAboard/WelcomeAboard Welcome Aboard (accessed August 23, 2007).

34. 1967 Workforce Study, August 15, 1967, USNOA, Post-1946 Command File, GTMO, Box 1243.

35. Ibid.

36. María Cristina García, *Havana, U.S.A.: Cuban Exiles and Cuban Americans in South Florida, 1959–1994* (Berkeley: University of California Press, 1996), 37–45.

37. 1966 Command History, USNOA, Post-1946 Command File, GTMO, Box 1242. For exiled workers who were not Cuban citizens, the majority maintaining their British West Indian or Jamaican nationality, the U.S. military established an alternate route of migration to Jamaica. 1967 Workforce Study, USNOA, Post-1946 Command File, GTMO, Box 1243.

38. 1967 Workforce Study, August 15, 1967, USNOA, Post-1946 Command File, GTMO, Box 1243.

39. Ibid.

40. Murphy, *History of Guantánamo Bay*, 1982 ed.; Mason, *Across the Cactus Curtain*, 96; and Stacey Byington, "Cuban American Friendship Spans Many Years," *Guantánamo Gazette*, February 3, 2006, http://www.nsgtmo.navy.mil/Gazette%20Online/archived%20editions/2006/060203all.pdf (accessed on July 4, 2006).

41. "Americans, Cubans, Celebrate Friendship Day," *Guantánamo Gazette*, December 11, 1969, USNOA, Post-1946 Command File, GTMO, Box 1243.

42. "Qué pasa amigo," *Guantánamo Gazette*, December 11, 1970, USNOA, Post-1946 Command File, GTMO, Box 1243.

43. Mason, *Across the Cactus Curtain*, 96.

44. Stacey Byington, "Cuban American Friendship Spans Many Years," *Guantánamo Gazette*, February 3, 2006, http://www.nsgtmo.navy.mil/Gazette%20Online/archived%20editions/2006/060203all.pdf (accessed on July 4, 2006).

45. *Gitmo: Cold War Cuba*, dir. Ian Stuttard.

46. García, *Havana, U.S.A.*, 13–30. For a contemporary account by the director of the Cuban Refugee Program Welfare Administration, see John F. Thomas, "Cuban Refugees in the United States," *International Migration Review* 1 (Spring 1967): 46–57.

47. Max Frankel, "Guantánamo Base Offers Haven for Refugees from Cuban Crisis: Babies Wail and Grandmothers Worry as Navy Operates an Airlift for Those Caught Between Two Nations," *New York Times,* January 7, 1961, p. 2.

48. The 1903 Lease Agreement states: "Fugitives from justice charged with crimes or misdemeanors amenable to Cuban law, taking refuge within said areas, shall be delivered up by the United States authorities on demand by duly authorized Cuban authorities. On the other hand, the Republic of Cuba agrees that fugitives from justice charged with crimes or misdemeanors amenable to the U.S. law, committed within said areas, taking refuge in Cuban territory, shall on demand, be delivered up to duly authorized U.S. authorities."

49. 1967 Command History, USNOA, August 15, 1967, Post-1946 Command File, GTMO, Box 1243.

50. 1968 Command History, USNOA, March 3, 1969, Post-1946 Command File, GTMO, Box 1243.

51. 1967 Command History, USNOA, August 15, 1967, Post-1946 Command File, GTMO, Box 1243.

52. "81 of 150 Shoot Way Past Cuban Lines, Reach Guantánamo and Fly to Florida," *New York Times,* January 9, 1969, p. 1; and "Freedom Riders," *Time,* January 1, 1969, p. 31.

53. Juan de Onis, "Cubans Who Fled Tell of Desperation," *New York Times,* January 10, 1969, p. 1.

54. "Cuba: Who's Fooling Whom?" *Newsweek,* January 20, 1969, p. 44–45; and "*Newsweek* Hints U.S. Helped Cubans Flee," *New York Times,* January 13, 1969, p. 7.

55. "Why Some Will Risk All to Leave," *New York Times,* January 12, 1969, p. E7.

56. Jorge Oliva, "Guantánamo Bay," *Donde una llama nunca se apaga* (Havana: Ediciones Unión, 1998).

57. Reinaldo Arenas, *Before Night Falls* (New York: Penguin Books, 1992), 112.

58. Ibid., 141.

59. Ibid., 163–75.

60. García, *Havana, U.S.A.,* 46–80.

61. Robert Pear, "Carter Orders Move to Expel Criminals among the Refugees," *New York Times,* June 8, 1980, p. 1.

62. "Reagan to Move Cubans Out of Fort Chaffee," *New York Times,* July 9, 1981, p. A14.

63. "Koch on the Town," *New York Times,* March 24, 1982, p. A20.

64. David Binder, "101 Haitian Refugees Pose Painful Problem for U.S.," *New York Times,* September 1, 1977, p. 3.

65. Mireya Navarro, "Many Haitian Children View Camps Limbo as Permanent," *New York Times,* May 1, 1995; Elaine Sciolino, "U.S. Tells Haitians at Guantánamo They Must Go Home," *New York Times,* December 30, 1994; Michael Ratner, "How We Closed the Guantánamo HIV Camp: The Intersection of Politics and Litigation," *Harvard Human Rights Journal* 11 (Spring 1998): 187–220; and Neuman, "Anomalous Zones."

66. Alberto Pérez, "Wet Foot, Dry Foot, No Foot: The Recurring Controversy between Cubans, Haitians, and the U.S. Immigration Policy," *Nova Law Review* 28 (December 2004): 437–64; Alfredo A. Fernández, *Adrift: The Cuban Raft People,* trans. Susan Giersbach Rascón (Houston, TX: Arte Público, 2000); and Domingo M. Perera González, *Encierro, incertidumbre, y sexo* (Miami, FL: Spin Quality Printing, 2001).

67. 1967 Workforce Study, August 15, 1967, USNOA, Post-1946 Command File, GTMO, Box 1243.

68. Walter Knight, personal interview, Guantánamo, Cuba, November 22, 2004.

69. Derek Stedman, personal interview, Guantánamo, Cuba, October 15, 2004.

70. Victor Davis, personal interview, Guantánamo, Cuba, October 8, 2004.

71. Hernández, *La seguridad nacional de Cuba.*

72. 1966 Command History, U.S. Naval Investigative Service Office, USNOA, Post-1946 Command File, GTMO, Box 1244.

73. Ibid.

74. Ibid.

75. Mason, *Across the Cactus Curtain,* 94–95. In his 1984 account, Mason suggested that spying was possible on both sides and that this "encouraged intriguing speculation."

76. "Not Just Bugs and Boredom," *Guantánamo Gazette,* 1969, 1969 Command History, USNOA, Post-1946 Command File, GTMO, Box 1243.

77. 1967 Workforce Study, August 15, 1967, USNOA, Post-1946 Command File, GTMO, Box 1243.

78. Informe del equipo de la Escuela de Historia, "Guantánamo: Esquema de la historia de una ciudad."

79. Reynold Rassí, *Cuba: Nueva división político-administrativa* (Havana: Editorial Orbe, 1981); Raúl Cordovés, *Guantánamo en cifras* (Guantánamo: Combinado Poligráfico, 1985); and Isla, *Guantánamo: Primera trinchera antiimperialista de Cuba.*

80. Rassí, *Cuba: Nueva división político-administrativa.*

81. "Mortalidad infantil," *Granma,* January 3, 2005.

82. 1972 U.S. Naval Hospital Command History, Civilian Cooperation, USNOA, Post-1946 Command File, GTMO, Box 1244.

83. Donald P. Baker, "Cuban Commuters Work for U.S. Navy, Spend Their Pay in Communist Cuba," *Washington Post,* January 28, 1998, http://www.washingtonpost.com/wp-srv/inatl/longterm/cuba/stories/econo12898.htm (accessed July 3, 2006).

84. Walter Knight, personal interview, Guantánamo, Cuba, November 22, 2004.

85. Miguel Gómez (pseud.), personal interview, Guantánamo, Cuba, January 16, 2005. Miguel was ninety-three years old and had received his pension through a third party for only two years when I met him.

86. Juan González, personal interview, Guantánamo, Cuba, October 10, 2004.

87. Victor Davis, personal interview, Guantánamo, Cuba, October 8, 2004.

88. Derek Stedman, personal interview, Guantánamo, Cuba, October 15, 2004.

89. Walter Knight, personal interview, Guantánamo, Cuba, November 22, 2004.

90. Operations and Maintenance, Representative Projects, http://www.roe.com/om_projcts.htm (accessed July 16, 2007); and Burns and Roe Awarded Contract for Utility Services at the U.S. Naval Station, Guantanamo Bay, Cuba, May 11, 2006, http://www.roe.com/news_article.asp?ArticleID = 132 (accessed July 16, 2007). The base operating services contract is part of a joint venture, called BREMCOR, between Burns and Roe and Emcor Facilities Services. Burns and Roe Awarded Base Operating Contract at U.S. Naval Base, Guantanamo Bay, Cuba, October 19, 2006, http://www.roe.com/news_article.asp?ArticleID = 138 (accessed July 17, 2007).

91. "GTMO Celebrates Philippine Independence Day," *Guantánamo Gazette,* June 22, 2007), http://www.nsgtmo.navy.mil/Gazette%20Online/archived%20editions/2007/070622all.pdf (accessed July 16, 2007.

92. Bob Lamb, "Service with a Smile," *Guantánamo Gazette,* April 22, 2005, http://www.nsgtmo.navy.mil/Gazette%20Online/archived%20editions/2005/050422all.pdf (accessed July 17, 2007). The 2005 *Guantánamo Gazette* has since been removed from the U.S. Navy's GTMO website; and Jobco, http://www.jobco.com.ph/jobs.html (accessed July 17, 2007). This website advertises food service jobs in Cuba for Filipino workers.

93. Derek Stedman, personal interview, Guantánamo, Cuba, October 15, 2004.

94. Walter Knight, personal interview, Guantánamo, Cuba, November 22, 2004.

EPILOGUE

1. David Phinney, "Blood, Sweat and Tears: Asia's Poor Build U.S. Bases in Iraq," Corpwatch, October 3, 2005, http://www.corpwatch.org/article.php?id = 12675 (accessed June 19, 2007); Mark Baker and Cynthia Banham, "Arroyo Pulls Out Troops to Save a Life," *Sydney Morning Herald,* July 15, 2004, http://www.smh.com.au/articles/2004/07/14/1089694429500.html?from = storylhs (accessed June 19, 2007); and "Family Prays as Deadline Passes," *TVNZ.co.nz,* July 12, 2004, http://tvnz.co.nz/view/news_world_story_skin/435533?format = html (accessed June 19, 2007).

2. "Manila Begins Iraq Troop Pullout," *CNN.com,* July 14, 2004, http://www.cnn.com/2004/WORLD/meast/07/13/philippines.hostage/ (accessed June 19, 2007); "Filipino Hostage Freed in Iraq," *CNN.com,* July 20, 2004, http://www.cnn.com/2004/WORLD/meast/07/20/iraq.philippines/index.html (accessed June 19, 2007); and "Cheers, Tears, and Beers as Hostage Goes Free," *China Daily,* July 20, 2004, http://www.chinadaily.com.cn/english/doc/2004–07/20/content_350080.htm (accessed June 19, 2007).

3. Rene Ciria-Cruz, "Philippines Leader Did the Right Thing by Pulling Out of Iraq," Pacific News Service, July 22, 2004, http://news.pacificnews.org/news/view_article.html?article_id = 455b78579638f795dabef23c9e409dbd (accessed August 24, 2007).

4. Diana Mendoza, "Released Filipino a Star, but Reality Bites Others," *Antiwar.com*, http://www.antiwar.com/ips/mendoza.php?articleid = 3154 (accessed June 19, 2007).

5. Max Boot, "The Iraq War's Outsourcing Snafu," *LA Times*, March 31, 2005; Ariana Eunjung Cha, "Iraq: Many Foreign Laborers Receive Inferior Pay, Food and Shelter," *Washington Post*, July 1, 2004; and Cam Simpson, "Iraq War Contractors Ordered to End Abuses," *Chicago Tribune*, April 24, 2006.

6. Cher S. Jimenez, "U.S. Outsources War to Filipinos," *Asia Times*, July 15, 2006, http://www.atimes.com/atimes/Southeast_Asia/HG15Aeo1.html (accessed August 19, 2006); and Pratap Chatterjee, "Doing the Dirty Work," *ColorLines*, July/August 2006, http://www.colorlines.com/article.php?ID = 139 (accessed August 24, 2007).

7. Pedro Salgado and José Fernández to Franklin Roosevelt, September 3, 1940, RG 59/811.34537/278, Box 3784.

8. "Powell Calls for Immediate Closure of Guantánamo," *ABCnews.com*, June 10, 2007 http://www.abcnews.go.com/Politics/wirestory?id = 3263904 (accessed June 29, 2007).

9. "Joint Chiefs Chairman: Close Guantánamo," *USA Today*, January 13, 2008, http://www.usatoday.com/news/world/2008–01–13-Guantanamo_N.htm (accessed March 13, 2008).

10. Gillem, *America Town*, 24. The Transnational Institute is initiating a project to map all foreign military bases throughout the globe. See http://www.tni.org/detail_page.phtml?&act_id = 17252&menu = 11e (accessed September 9, 2007).

11. Andrew Pollack, "Three U.S. Servicemen Convicted of Rape of Okinawa Girl," March 7, 1996, *New York Times*.

12. Garramore, "Rumsfeld, Myers Discuss Military Global Posture."

13. Henry, "Transforming the U.S. Global Defense Posture;" and Gillem, *America Town*, 269.

14. John Lindsay-Poland, "U.S. Military Bases in Latin America and the Caribbean," Foreign Policy in Focus, August 2004, http://www.fpif.org/briefs/vol9/v9no3latammil_body.html (accessed June 30, 2007); and Henry, "Transforming the U.S. Global Defense Posture."

15. Henry, "Transforming the U.S. Global Defense Posture."

16. Joseph Gerson, "U.S. Foreign Military Bases and Military Colonialism," American Friends Service Committee, http://www.afsc.org/newengland/pesp/Bases-Chapter.htm (accessed May 25, 2007); and Harkavy, "Thinking about Basing."

17. Harkavy, "Thinking about Basing."

18. Gillem, *America Town*, 31–32; "U.S. Troops Set for Bulgaria Base," BBC News, April 28, 2006, http://news.bbc.co.uk/2/hi/europe/4951726.stm (accessed September 9, 2007); and "Rice Signs U.S.-Romania Bases Deal," BBC News, December 6, 2005, http://news.bbc.co.uk/2/hi/europe/4504682.stm (accessed September 9, 2007).

19. Dana Priest, "Secret Prison System Detains High-Level Terrorism Suspects," *Washington Post*, November 2, 2005; and Dahlia Lithwick, "The 6th

Annual Year in Ideas: Redefining Torture," *New York Times,* December 10, 2006. Infuriated that its cover was at least partially blown, the U.S. government proposed a criminal investigation following the journalistic exposé. David Johnston and Carl Hulse, "CIA Asks Criminal Inquiry over Secret Prison Article," *New York Times,* November 9, 2005. By September 2006, President George W. Bush admitted that the CIA had been holding detainees in secret prisons. "Bush Admits to CIA Secret Prisons," BBC News, September 7, 2006, http://news.bbc.co.uk/2/hi/americas/5321606.stm (accessed August 24, 2007).

20. Jane Mayer, "The Black Sites: A Rare Look into the CIA's Secret Interrogation Program," *New Yorker,* August 13, 2007; Nick Hawton, "Hunt for CIA 'Black Site' in Poland," BBC News, December 28, 2006, http://news.bbc.co.uk/2/hi/europe/6212843.stm (accessed August 21, 2007); and Marcel Rosenbach and John Goetz, "New Report Cites Use of CIA Black Sites," Spiegel Online International, June 8, 2007, http://www.spiegel.de/international/world/0,1518,487325,00.html (accessed August 21, 2007).

21. William Langewiesche, "Welcome to the Green Zone: The American Bubble in Baghdad," *Atlantic Monthly,* November 2004, http://www.theatlantic.com/doc/print/200411/langewiesche (accessed June 28, 2007).

22. Brian Bennet, "Inside the Green Zone," *Time,* April 26, 2007.

23. Tom Engelhardt, "Can You Say 'Permanent Bases'?" February 14, 2006, http://www.tomdispatch.com/index.mhtml?pid = 59774 (accessed May 25, 2007); Green Zone, http://www.globalsecurity.org/military/world/iraq/baghdad-green-zone.htm (accessed June 29, 2007); and Barbara Slavin, "Giant U.S. Embassy Rising in Iraq," *USA Today,* April 19, 2006, http://www.usatoday.com/news/world/iraq/2006–04–19-us-embassy_x.htm (accessed June 29, 2007).

24. Engelhardt, "Can You Say Permanent Bases?"

25. P. W. Singer, *Corporate Warriors: The Rise of the Privatized Military Industry* (Ithaca, NY: Cornell University Press, 2003); P. W. Singer, "Corporate Warriors: The Rise of the Privatized Military Industry and Its Ramifications for International Security," *International Security* 26 (Winter 2001/2002): 186–220; Jeremy Schahill, *Blackwater: The Rise of the World's Most Powerful Mercenary Army* (New York: Nation Books, 2007); Kristen McCallion, *War for Sale! Battlefield Contractors in Latin America and the 'Corporatization' of America's War on Drugs,* 36 U. Miami Inter-Am. L. Rev. 317 (Winter/Spring 2005); Martha Minow, *Outsourcing Power: How Privatizing Military Efforts Challenges Accountability, Professionalism, and Democracy,* 46 B. C. L. Review 989 (September 2005); Wm. C. Peters, *On Law, Wars, and Mercenaries: The Case for Courts-Martial Jurisdiction over Civilian Contractor Misconduct in Iraq,* 2006 B. Y. U. L. Rev. 367 (2006); James R. Coleman, *Constraining Modern Mercenarism,* 55 Hastings L. J. 1493 (June 2004); Aaron E. Garfield, *Bridging a Gap in Human Rights Law: Prisoner of War Abuse as 'War Tort,'* 27 Geo. J. Intn'l L. 725 (Summer 2006); and Mark W. Bina, *Private Military Contractor Liability and Accountability after Abu Ghraib,* 38 J. Marshall L. Rev. 1237 (Summer 2005).

26. Alan Feuer, "For an Iraq Contractor, Duty, and then Death," *New York Times,* August 8, 2007.

27. Schahill, *Blackwater;* James Glanz and Floyd Norris, "The Reach of War: Questions, Pledges, and Confrontations; Report Says Iraq Contractor Is Hiding Data from U.S.," *New York Times,* October 28, 2006.

28. Phinney, "Blood, Sweat and Tears;" and "Private Warriors," *Frontline,* http://www.pbs.org/wgbh/pages/frontline/shows/warriors/view/ (accessed June 29, 2007).

29. "Imperial Life in the Emerald City: Inside Iraq's Green Zone: An Interview with Rajiv Chandrasekaran," September 29, 2006, http://www.democracynow .org/article.pl?sid = 06/09/29/151212 (accessed July 28, 2007).

30. Barbara Slavin, "Giant U.S. Embassy Rising in Iraq," *USA Today,* April 19, 2006, http://www.usatoday.com/news/world/iraq/2006–04–19-us-embassy _x.htm (accessed June 29, 2007).

31. Mike Drummond, "On U.S. Base, Iraqis Must Use Separate Latrine," August 3, 2007, http://www.mcclatchydc.com/homepage/story/18685.html (accessed August 13, 2007).

32. Bennett, "Inside the Green Zone."

33. Cha, "Iraq: Many Foreign Laborers Receive Inferior Pay, Food and Shelter"; and Phinney, "Blood, Sweat and Tears."

34. David Phinney," Asian Workers Trafficked to Build U.S. Embassy in Baghdad," Corpwatch, October 26, 2006, http://www.alternet.org/story/43444/ (accessed June 19, 2007).

35. Cha, "Iraq: Many Foreign Laborers Receive Inferior Pay, Food and Shelter."

36. David Rohde, "Indian Contract Workers in Iraq Complain of Exploitation," *New York Times,* May 7, 2004.

37. Nicola Smith, " 'Kidnapped' Filipinos Build U.S. Embassy," *Times Online,* August 5, 2007, http://www.timesonline.co.uk/tol/news/world/iraq/article2199263 .ece (accessed August 24, 2007).

38. Cam Simpson, "Desperate for Work, Lured into Danger," *Chicago Tribune,* October 9, 2005; Cam Simpson, "Into a War Zone, on a Deadly Road," *Chicago Tribune,* October 9, 2005; and Cam Simpson, "Rescue Spares Some Workers: 'They Told Us That We Had to Go to Iraq,' " *Chicago Tribune,* October 10, 2005.

39. Cam Simpson, "Rescue Spares Some Workers"; and Simpson, "Iraq War Contractors Ordered to End Abuses," *Chicago Tribune,* April 23, 2006.

40. Ben Gilbert, "Underdogs of War, Part II," Marketplace (radio broadcast), June 12, 2006, http://marketplace.publicradio.org/shows/2006/06/12/ PM200606127.html (accessed August 8, 2006).

41. Simpson, "Iraq War Contractors Ordered to End Abuses."

42. Nicola Smith, " 'Kidnapped' Filipinos Build U.S. Embassy."

43. Caroline Brothers, "Migrants Fall into Hardship in Iraq," *International Herald Tribune,* May 11, 2007; Pratap Chatterjee, "Doing the Dirty Work"; and David Phinney, "Gulf Catering Wins More Business," May 17, 2007, http:// www.davidphinney.com/pages/labor_trafficking/ (accessed July 27, 2007). Phinney reported that KBR has denied that its subcontractors compel their

employees to work "against their will," but Middle Eastern subcontracting firms have refused to answer further questions.

44. Phinney, "Blood, Sweat and Tears;" Phinney, "Asian Workers Trafficked to Build U.S. Embassy in Baghdad"; Cha, "Iraq: Many Foreign Laborers Receive Inferior Pay, Food and Shelter"; and Rohde, "Indian Contract Workers in Iraq Complain of Exploitation."

45. Rick Rocamora, "Made for Al Qaeda," *Newsbreak,* August 5, 2002, http://www.inq7.net/nwsbrk/2002/aug/05/nbk_5-1.htm (accessed August 19, 2006); and Jimenez, "U.S. Outsources War to Filipinos."

Selected Bibliography

ARCHIVES

CUBAN ARCHIVAL COLLECTIONS

Cuban National Archive, Havana

Secretaría de la Presidencia.

Elvira Cape Provincial Library, Santiago de Cuba

Guantánamo Municipal Museum

Guantánamo Provincial Archive

Apuntes Biográficos: Gustavo Fraga Jacomino.
Guantánamo Civil Registry.

Santiago de Cuba Provincial Archive

Fondos del Gobierno Provincial, Caimanera, 1943–48.

U.S. ARCHIVAL COLLECTIONS

Digital National Security Archive

Cuban Missile Crisis, 1962.

Hoover Institution Archives, Stanford University

Edward J. O'Donnell Papers.

U.S. National Archives and Records Administration (NARA), College Park, MD

Central Foreign Policy Files, 1964–66.

RG 59 State Department Decimal File.

RG 84 Foreign Service Posts of the State Department. Santiago de Cuba Consulate. Confidential Records.

RG 84 Foreign Service Posts of the State Department. Santiago de Cuba Consulate. General Records.

RG 181 Records of Naval Districts and Shore Establishments. Commander U.S. Naval Station, Guantánamo Bay, Cuba. Weekly Intelligence Summaries and Correspondence Files, 1949–55.

RG 181 Records of Naval Districts and Shore Establishments. U.S. Naval Station, Guantánamo Bay, Cuba. World War II Files.

U.S. Naval Historical Center, Navy Yards, Washington DC

U.S. Naval Institute's Oral History Collection.

U.S. Navy Operational Archives. Post-1946 Command Histories. Guantánamo Bay, Cuba.

Vertical Files. "Guantánamo."

NEWSPAPERS, PERIODICALS, AND RADIO BROADCASTS
CUBAN NEWSPAPERS AND PERIODICALS

Adelante (Havana)
Avance (Havana)
Diario de Cuba (Santiago de Cuba)
Diario de la Marina (Havana)
Granma (Havana)
Hoy (Havana)
Mujeres (Havana)
Prensa Libre (Havana)
La Revista Oriental (Santiago de Cuba)
Revolución (Havana)
Sierra Maestra (Santiago de Cuba)
Venceremos (Guantánamo)
El Vigilante (Guantánamo)
La Voz del Pueblo (Guantánamo)

U.S. NEWSPAPERS, PERIODICALS, AND RADIO BROADCASTS

Amsterdam News
Atlantic Monthly
Baltimore Sun
Boston Globe
Boston Review
Chicago Defender
Chicago Tribune

Christian Science Monitor
Esquire
Foreign Affairs
Guantánamo Gazette (GTMO daily newspaper, 1960s through the present)
The Indian (GTMO daily newspaper, 1950s)
International Herald Tribune
International Security
LA Times
Life
Marketplace
The Nation
National Catholic Review
National Geographic
National Public Radio
The New Internationalist
The New Republic
New York Times
New York Times Magazine
The New Yorker
Newsweek
Saturday Evening Post
Time
U.S. News and World Reports
The Washington Post

PRINTED PRIMARY AND SECONDARY SOURCES

Abdala Pupo, Oscar Luis. *La intervención militar norteamericana en la contienda independentista cubana, 1898.* Santiago de Cuba: Editorial Oriente, 1998.

Agamben, Giorgio. *State of Exception.* Trans. Kevin Attel. Chicago: University of Chicago Press, 2005.

Agee, Philip. *Inside the Company: CIA Diary.* New York: Stonehill, 1975.

Alexander, Robert J. *A History of Organized Labor in Cuba.* Westport, CT: Praeger, 2002.

Ameijeiras Delgado, Efigenio. *Más allá de nosotros: Columna 6 "Juan Manuel Ameijeiras," Segundo Frente Oriental "Frank País."* Santiago de Cuba: Editorial Oriente, 1984.

Anzaldúa, Gloria. *Borderlands/La Frontera.* San Francisco: Aunt Lute Books, 1999.

Arenas, Reinaldo. *Before Night Falls.* New York: Penguin Books, 1992.

Argote-Freyre, Frank. *Fulgencio Batista: From Revolutionary to Strongman.* New Brunswick, NJ: Rutgers University Press, 2006.

———. "In Search of Fulgencio Batista: An Examination of Pre-revolutionary Cuban Scholarship." *Revista Mexicana del Caribe* 11 (2001): 193–227.

Ayala, César J. *American Sugar Kingdom: The Plantation Economy of the Spanish Caribbean, 1898–1934.* Chapel Hill: University of North Carolina Press, 1999.

Bayly, C. A, Sven Beckert, Matthew Connelly, Isabel Hofmeyr, Wendy Kozol, and Patricia Seed. "AHR Conversation: On Transnational History." *American Historical Review* 111 (December 2006): 1440–64.

Bederman, Gail. *Manliness and Civilization: A Cultural History of Gender and Race in the United States, 1880–1917*. Chicago: University of Chicago Press, 1995.

Blight, James G., Bruce J. Allyn, and David A. Welch. *Cuba on the Brink: Castro, the Missile Crisis, and the Soviet Collapse*. New York: Pantheon Books, 1993.

Blight, James G., and Peter Kornbluh. *Politics of Illusion: The Bay of Pigs Invasion Reexamined*. Boulder, CO: Lynne Rienner, 1998.

Blum, John Morton. *V Was for Victory: Politics and American Culture during World War II*. San Diego: Harcourt Brace, 1976.

Bonsal, Philip W. *Cuba, Castro, and the United States*. Pittsburgh, PA: University of Pittsburgh Press, 1971.

Bosch Ferrer, Diego, and José Sánchez Guerra. *Rebeldía y apalencamiento: Jurisdicciones de Guantánamo y Baracoa*. Guantánamo: Centro Provincial de Patrimonio Cultural, 2003.

Bowman, Larry W., and Jeffrey A. Lefebvre. "The Indian Ocean and Strategic Perspectives." In *The Indian Ocean: Perspectives on a Strategic Arena*, ed. William L. Dowdy and Russell B. Trood, 413–35. Durham, NC: Duke University Press, 1985.

Bradley, Mark Philip. *Imagining Vietnam and America: The Making of Postcolonial Vietnam, 1919–1950*. Chapel Hill: University of North Carolina Press, 2000.

Brandt, Allan M. *No Magic Bullet: A Social History of Venereal Disease in the United States since 1880*. New York: Oxford University Press, 1987.

Brennan, Denise. *What's Love Got To Do With It? Transnational Desires and Sex Tourism in the Dominican Republic*. Durham, NC: Duke University Press, 2004.

Breuer, William B. *Sea Wolf: A Biography of John D. Bulkeley*. Novato, CA: Presidio, 1989.

Briggs, Laura. *Reproducing Empire: Race, Sex, Science, and U.S. Imperialism in Puerto Rico*. Berkeley: University of California Press, 2002.

Brittain, Victoria, and Gillian Slovo. *Guantánamo: Honor Bound to Defend Freedom*. London: Oberon Books, 2004.

Brock, Lisa, and Digna Castañeda Fuertes, eds. *Between Race and Empire: African-Americans and Cubans before the Cuban Revolution*. Philadelphia, PA: Temple University Press, 1998.

Bronfman, Alejandra. *Measures of Equality: Social Science, Citizenship, and Race in Cuba, 1902–1940*. Chapel Hill: University of North Carolina, 2004.

Burnett, Christina Duffy, and Burke Marshall, eds. *Foreign in a Domestic Sense: Puerto Rico, American Expansion and the Constitution*. Durham, NC: Duke University Press, 2001.

Butler, Judith. *Precarious Life: The Powers of Mourning and Violence*. London: Verso, 2004.

Carlson, David. "The Cuban War of Independence in Guantánamo, 1895–1898: A Regional Study of Insurgency and Intervention." Master's thesis, University of North Carolina, 2001.

Carr, Barry. "Identity, Class, and Nation: Black Immigrant Workers, Cuban Communism, and the Sugar Insurgency, 1925–1934." *Hispanic American Historical Review* 78 (February 1998): 83–116.

Carr, Roland T. *To Sea in Haste.* Washington DC: Acropolis Books, 1975.

Chailloux Laffita, Graciela. "La contribución antillana a la identidad cubana." *Debates Americanos* 12 (January–December 2002): 54–62.

Chailloux Laffita, Graciela, Roberto Claxton, and Robert Whitney. "I am the Caribbean: A West Indian Melting Pot in Cuba." In *Intra-Caribbean Migration: The Cuban Connection, 1898–Present.* Publication of the proceedings, University of the West Indies, Mona, Jamaica, June 14–16, 2001.

Challener, Richard. *Admirals, Generals, and American Foreign Policy, 1898–1914.* Princeton, NJ: Princeton University Press, 1973.

Chan, Sucheng. *Asian Americans: An Interpretative History.* London: Twayne, 1991.

Chang, Grace. *Disposable Domestics: Immigrant Women Workers in the Global Economy.* Cambridge, MA: South End, 2000.

Chang, Laurence, and Peter Kornbluh, eds. *The Cuban Missile Crisis, 1962: A National Security Archive Document Reader.* New York: New Press, 1998.

Chomsky, Aviva, Barry Carr, and Pamela Maria Smorkaloff, eds. *The Cuba Reader: History, Culture, and Politics.* Durham, NC: Duke University Press, 2003.

Chomsky, Aviva, and Aldo Lauria-Santiago, eds. *Identity and Struggle at the Margins of the Nation-State: The Laboring Peoples of Central America and the Hispanic Caribbean.* Durham, NC: Duke University Press, 1998.

Columna 18 "Antonio López Fernández," Segundo Frente Oriental "Frank País." *Hijos de su tiempo: Segundo Frente Oriental "Frank País."* Havana: Ediciones Verde Olivo, 1998.

Columna 20 "Gustavo Fraga," Segundo Frente Oriental "Frank País." *En la línea de fuego.* Santiago de Cuba: Editorial Oriente, 1998.

Conniff, Michael. *Black Labor on a White Canal: Panama 1904–1981.* Pittsburgh, PA: University of Pittsburgh Press, 1985.

Cordovés, Raúl. *Guantánamo en cifras.* Guantánamo: Combinado Poligráfico, 1985.

Cruz Díaz, Rigoberto. *Guantánamo Bay.* Santiago de Cuba: Editorial Oriente, 1977.

de Dios Noris, Marilis. "Efectos de la presencia de los marines yanquis en la ciudad de Guantánamo 1903–1952." Master's thesis, Universidad de Oriente, Cuba, May 2004.

de la Fuente, Alejandro. *A Nation for all: Race, Inequality, and Politics in Twentieth-Century Cuba.* Chapel Hill: University of North Carolina Press, 2001.

———. "Myths of Racial Democracy: Cuba, 1900–1912." *Latin American Research Review* 34, no. 3 (Fall 1999): 39–73.

Dean, Robert D. *Imperial Brotherhood: Gender and the Making of Cold War Foreign Policy.* Amherst: University of Massachusetts Press, 2001.

Dorr, Nicolás. "Confesión en el Barrio Chino." In *La Chacota,* 171–238. Havana: Editorial Letras Cubanas, 1989.

Ehrenreich, Barbara, and Alice Russell Hochschild. *Global Women: Nannies, Maids, and Sex Workers in the New Economy.* New York: Henry Holt, 2002.

Enloe, Cynthia. *Bases, Beaches, and Bananas: Making Feminist Sense of International Politics.* Berkeley: University of California Press, 1989.

Espiritu, Yen Le. *Home Bound: Filipino American Lives across Cultures, Communities, and Countries.* Berkeley: University of California Press, 2003.

Farber, Samuel. *The Origins of the Cuban Revolution Reconsidered.* Chapel Hill: University of North Carolina Press, 2006.

———. *Revolution and Reaction in Cuba, 1933–1960: A Political Sociology from Machado to Castro.* Middletown, CT: Wesleyan University Press, 1976.

Farnsworth-Alvear, Ann. *Dulcinea in the Factory: Myths, Morals, Men and Women in Columbia's Industrial Experiment, 1905–1960.* Durham, NC: Duke University Press, 2000.

Federación de Mujeres Cubanas. "La prostitución: Una enfermedad social curable, una experiencia importante de la Revolución Cubana." Unpublished report, Federación de Mujeres Cubanas, Havana, Cuba, 1988.

Fein, Seth. "Everyday Forms of Transnational Collaboration: U.S. Film Propaganda in Cold War Mexico." In *Close Encounters of Empire: Writing the Cultural History of U.S.–Latin American Relations,* ed. Gilbert Joseph, Catherine LeGrand, and Ricardo D. Salvatore, 400–50. Durham, NC: Duke University Press, 1998.

———. "New Empire into Old: Making Mexican Newsreels the Cold War Way." *Diplomatic History* 28 (November 2004): 703–48

Fernández, Alfredo A. *Adrift: The Cuban Raft People.* Trans. Susan Giersbach Rascón. Houston, TX: Arte Público, 2000.

Fernández Robaina, Tomás. "Marcus Garvey in Cuba: Urrutia, Cubans, and Black Nationalism." In *Between Race and Empire: African-Americans and Cubans before the Cuban Revolution,* ed. Lisa Brock and Digna Castañeda Fuertes, 120–28. Philadelphia, PA: Temple University Press, 1998.

Ferrer, Ada. *Insurgent Cuba: Race, Nation, and Revolution, 1868–1898.* Chapel Hill: University of North Carolina Press, 1999.

Fishkin, Shelley Fisher. "Crossroads of Cultures: The Transnational Turn in American Studies; Presidential Address at the American Studies Association, November 12, 2004." *American Quarterly* 57, no. 1 (2005): 17–57.

Fiskesjo, Magnus. *The Thanksgiving Turkey Pardon, the Death of Teddy's Bear, and the Sovereign Exception of Guantánamo.* Chicago: Prickly Paradigm, 2003.

Foley, Neil. *The White Scourge: Mexicans, Blacks, and Poor Whites in Texas Cotton Culture.* Berkeley: University of California Press, 1997.

Foner, Philip S. *The Spanish-Cuban-American War and the Birth of American Imperialism.* New York: Monthly Review, 1972.

Franqui, Carlos. *The Twelve.* Trans. Albert B. Teichner. New York: Lyle Stuart, 1968.

Fraser, Steven. *Labor Will Rule: Sidney Hillman and the Rise of American Labor.* Ithaca, NY: Cornell University Press, 1991.

Frederick, Rhonda D. *"Colón Man a Come": Mythographies of Panamá Canal Migration.* Lanham, MD: Lexington Books, 2005.

Friedman, Max Paul. *Nazis and Good Neighbors: The United States Campaign against the Germans of Latin America in World War II.* Cambridge: Cambridge University Press, 2003.

Fursenko, Aleksander, and Timothy Naftali. *"One Hell of a Gamble": The Secret History of the Cuban Missile Crisis, Khrushchev, Castro, and Kennedy, 1958–1964.* New York: W. W. Norton, 1997.

García, María Cristina. *Havana, U.S.A: Cuban Exiles and Cuban Americans in South Florida, 1959–1994.* Berkeley: University of California Press, 1996.

García-Pérez, Gladys Marel. *Insurrection and Revolution: Armed Struggle in Cuba 1952–1959.* Trans. Juan Ortega. Boulder, CO: Lynne Rienner, 1998.

Gatewood, Willard B., Jr. *"Smoked Yankees" and the Struggle for Empire, 1898–1902.* Urbana: University of Illinois Press, 1971.

Gellman, Irwin. *Roosevelt and Batista: Good Neighbor Diplomacy in Cuba, 1933–1945.* Albuquerque: University of New Mexico Press, 1973.

Gerson, Joseph, and Bruce Birchard, eds. *The Sun Never Sets: Confronting the Network of Foreign U.S. Military Bases.* Boston: South End, 1991.

Gillem, Mark L. *America Town: Building the Outposts of Empire.* Minneapolis: University of Minnesota Press, 2007.

Gilly, Adolfo. "A la luz relámpago: Cuba en octubre." In *Espejos de la guerra fría: México, América Central, y el Caribe,* ed. Daniela Spenser, 215–45. Mexico City: Centro de Investigaciones y Estudios Superiores, 2004.

Gilroy, Paul. *The Black Atlantic: Modernity and Double Consciousness.* Cambridge, MA: Harvard University Press, 2007.

Giovannetti, Jorge. "Black British Subjects in Cuba: Race, Ethnicity, Nation, and Identity in the Migratory Experience, 1898–1938." PhD diss., University of North London, 2001.

———. "The Elusive Organization of 'Identity': Race, Religion, and Empire among Caribbean Migrants in Cuba." *Small Axe* 10 (2006): 1–27.

Gleijeses, Piero. *Conflicting Missions: Havana, Washington, and Africa, 1959–1976.* Chapel Hill: University of North Carolina Press, 2002.

Glick Schiller, Nina, Linda Basch, and Cristina Blanc-Szanton. *Towards a Transnational Perspective on Migration: Race, Class, Ethnicity, and Nationalism Reconsidered.* New York: Annals of the New York Academy of Sciences, 1992.

Goodwin, Doris Kearns. *No Ordinary Time, Franklin and Eleanor Roosevelt: The Home Front in World War II.* New York: Simon and Schuster, 1994.

Gosse, Van. "The African American Press Greets the Cuban Revolution." In *Between Race and Empire: African-Americans and Cubans before the Cuban Revolution,* ed. Lisa Brock and Digna Castañeda Fuertes, 266–80. Philadelphia, PA: Temple University Press, 1998.

———. *Where the Boys Are: Cuba, Cold War America and the Making of a New Left.* London: Verso, 1993.

Grandin, Greg. *The Last Colonial Massacre.* Chicago: University of Chicago Press, 2004.

———. "Your Americanism and Mine: Americanism and Anti-Americanism in the Americas." *American Historical Review* 111, no. 4 (2006): 1042–66.

Greene, Julie. "The Labor of Empire: Recent Scholarship on U.S. History and Imperialism." *Labor: Studies in Working Class History of the Americas* 1 (Summer 2004): 113–29.

———. "Spaniards on the Silver Roll: Labor Troubles and Liminality in the Panama Canal Zone, 1904–1914." *International Labor and Working-Class History* 66 (Fall 2004): 78–98.

Guerra, Lillian. *The Myth of José Martí: Conflicting Nationalisms in Early Twentieth-Century Cuba.* Chapel Hill: University of North Carolina Press, 2005.

Hardt, Michael, and Antonio Negri. *Empire.* Cambridge, MA: Harvard University Press, 2000.

Harkavy, Robert E. "Thinking about Basing." *Naval War College Review* 58 (Summer 2005): 12–42.

Helg, Aline. *Our Rightful Share: The Afro-Cuban Struggle for Equality, 1886–1912.* Chapel Hill: University of North Carolina Press, 1995.

Henry, Ryan. "Transforming the U.S. Global Defense Posture." *Naval War College Review* 59 (Spring 2006): 13–28.

Hernández, Rafael. *La seguridad nacional de Cuba y la cuestión de la base naval de Guantánamo.* Havana: Centro de Estudios sobre América, 1988.

Hinckle, Warren, and William W. Turner. *The Fish is Red: The Story of the Secret War against Castro.* New York: Harper and Row, 1981.

Hodes, Martha. "Fractions and Fictions in the United States Census, 1890." In *Haunted by Empire,* ed., Ann Laura Stoler, 240–70. Durham, NC: Duke University Press, 2006.

———. "The Mercurial Nature and Abiding Power of Race: A Transnational Family Story." *American Historical Review* 108 (February 2003): 84–118.

Hoganson, Kristin. *Fighting for American Manhood: How Gender Politics Provoked the Spanish-American and Philippine-American Wars.* New Haven, CT: Yale University Press, 1998.

Hunt, Michael. *Ideology and U.S. Foreign Policy.* New Haven, CT: Yale University Press, 1987.

Hunter, Tera W. *To 'Joy My Freedom: Southern Black Women's Lives and Labors after the Civil War.* Cambridge, MA: Harvard University Press, 1997.

Ibarra, Jorge. "La inmigración antillana: ¿Desproletarización o desnacionalización del proletariado cubano o aceleración de las contradicciones sociales? ¿Disgregación y marginalización del antillano o progresiva integración de éste en las luchas de la clase obrera?" Paper presented at IV Encuentro de Historiadores Latinoamericanos y del Caribe, 1983. (Located in the José Martí National Library, Havana, Cuba.)

———. *Prologue to Revolution Cuba, 1898–1958.* Trans. Marjorie Moore. Boulder, CO: Lynne Rienner, 1998.

Informe del equipo de la Escuela de Historia, Universidad de la Habana. "Guantánamo: Esquema de la historia de una ciudad." Unpublished report, José Martí National Library, Havana, Cuba, May 1967.

Isla, Vicente, ed., *Guantánamo: Primera trinchera anti-imperialista de Cuba*. Havana: Editorial José Martí, 1988.

Jacobs, Seth. *America's Miracle Man in Vietnam: Ngo Dinh Diem, Religion, Race, and U.S. Intervention in Southeast Asia 1950–1957*. Durham, NC: Duke University Press, 2005.

Johnson, Chalmers. *Nemesis: The Last Days of the American Republic*. New York: Henry Holt, 2006.

———. *The Sorrows of Empire: Militarism, Secrecy, and the End of the Republic*. New York: Henry Holt, 2004.

Joseph, Gilbert, Catherine LeGrand, and Ricardo D. Salvatore, eds. *Close Encounters of Empire: Writing the Cultural History of U.S.–Latin American Relations*. Durham, NC: Duke University Press, 1998.

Kaplan, Amy. *The Anarchy of Empire in the Making of U.S. Culture*. Cambridge, MA: Harvard University Press, 2002.

———. "Black and Blue on San Juan Hill." In *Cultures of United States Imperialism*, ed. Amy Kaplan and Donald E. Pease. Durham, NC: Duke University Press, 1993.

———. "Homeland Insecurities: Reflections on Language and Space." *Radical History Review* 85 (Winter 2003): 82–92.

———. "Where Is Guantánamo?" *American Quarterly* 57 (September 2005): 831–58.

Kaplan, Amy, and Donald E. Pease, eds. *Cultures of United States Imperialism*. Durham, NC: Duke University Press, 1993.

Kelley, Robin. " 'But a Local Phase of a World Problem': Black History's Global Vision, 1883–1950." *Journal of American History* 86 (December 1999): 1045–77.

———. *Race Rebels: Culture, Politics, and the Black Working Class*. New York: Free Press, 1994.

Kelly, Mary Pat. *Proudly We Served: The Men of the USS Mason*. Annapolis, MD: Naval Institute Press, 1995.

Kelshall, Gaylord T. M. *The U-Boat War in the Caribbean*. Annapolis, MD: Naval Institute Press, 1994.

Kennedy, Robert F. *Thirteen Days: A Memoir of the Cuban Missile Crisis*. New York: W. W. Norton, 1968.

Klein, Christina. *Cold War Orientalism: Asia in the Middlebrow Imagination, 1945–1961*. Berkeley: University of California, 2003.

Knight, Franklin W. "Jamaican Migrants and the Cuban Sugar Industry, 1900–1934." In *Between Slavery and Free Labor: The Spanish-Speaking Caribbean in the Nineteenth Century*, ed. Manuel Moreno Fraginals, Frank Moya Pons, and Stanley L. Engerman, 94–116. Baltimore, MD: Johns Hopkins University Press, 1985.

Kofas, Jon V. *The Struggle for Legitimacy: Latin American Labor and the United States, 1930–1960*. Tempe: Arizona State University Press, 1992.

Kramer, Paul A. "The Darkness That Enters the Home: The Politics of Prostitution during the Philippine-American War." In *Haunted by Empire*, ed. Ann Laura Stoler, 366–404. Durham, NC: Duke University Press, 2006.

Kumar, Amitava. *Passport Photos*. Berkeley: University of California Press, 2000.

LaFeber, Walter. *America, Russia, and the Cold War, 1945–1992*. New York: McGraw Hill, 1993.

———. *Inevitable Revolutions: The United States in Central America*. New York: W. W. Norton, 1983.

———. *The New Empire: An Interpretation of American Expansion, 1860–1898*. 35th anniv. ed. Ithaca, NY: Cornell University Press, 1998.

———. *The Panama Canal: The Crisis in Historical Perspective*. New York: Oxford University Press, 1978.

Latham, Michael. *Modernization as Ideology: American Social Science and "Nation Building" in the Kennedy Era*. Chapel Hill: University of North Carolina Press, 2000.

LeGrand, Catherine. "Living in Macondo: Economy and Culture in a United Fruit Company Banana Enclave in Colombia." In *Close Encounters of Empire: Writing the Cultural History of U.S.–Latin American Relations*, ed. Gilbert Joseph, Catherine LeGrand, and Ricardo D. Salvatore, 333–68. Durham, NC: Duke University Press, 1998.

Levitt, Peggy. *Transnational Villagers*. Berkeley: University of California Press, 2001.

Lindsay-Poland, John. *Emperors in the Jungle: The Hidden History of the U.S. in Panama*. Durham, NC: Duke University Press, 2003.

Lipman, Jana K. "Between Guantánamo and Montego Bay: Cuba, Jamaica, Migration and the Cold War, 1959–62." *Immigrants and Minorities* 21 (November 2002): 25–51.

Little, Douglas. *American Orientalism: The United States and the Middle East since 1945*. Chapel Hill: University of North Carolina Press, 2002.

Llerena, Mario. *The Unsuspected Revolution: The Birth and Rise of Castroism*. Ithaca, NY: Cornell University Press, 1978.

López Jardo, Pedro A. *Guantánamo y "Gitmo": Detalles y eventos históricos relacionados con Guantánamo, la ciudad del Guaso, y la base naval de los EEUU*. Miami, FL: Ediciones Universal, 2000.

Love, Eric T. *Race over Empire: Racism and U.S. Imperialism, 1865–1900*. Chapel Hill: University of North Carolina Press, 2004.

Lundestad, Geir. "Empire by Invitation in the American Century." *Diplomatic History* 23 (Spring 1999): 189–217.

Lutz, Catherine. *Homefront: A Military City and the American 20th Century*. Boston: Beacon, 2001.

Major, John. *Prize Possession: The United States and the Panama Canal, 1903–1979*. Cambridge: Cambridge University Press, 1993.

Margulies, Joseph. *Guantánamo and the Abuse of Presidential Power*. New York: Simon and Schuster, 2006.

Martínez Incháusegui, Concepción, Felipa Suárez Ramos, and Sonia Maldonado González. *Punta de vanguardia: Historia de la Brigada de la Frontera*. Santiago de Cuba: Editorial Oriente, 1986.

Mason, Theodore K. *Across the Cactus Curtain: The Story of Guantánamo Bay*. New York: Dodd, Mead, 1984.

May, Ernest. *Imperial Democracy: The Emergence of America as a World Power.* Chicago: Imprint, 1961.

McAlister, Melani. *Epic Encounters: Culture, Media, and U.S. Interests in the Middle East, 1945–2000.* Berkeley: University of California Press, 2001.

McCaffrey, Katherine T. *Military Power and Popular Protest: The U.S. Navy in Vieques, Puerto Rico.* New Brunswick, NJ: Rutgers University Press, 2002.

McClintock, Ann. *Imperial Leather: Race, Gender, and Sexuality in the Colonial Contest.* New York: Routledge, 1995.

McCoy, Mary Ellene Chenevey. "Guantánamo Bay: The United States Naval Base and Its Relationship to Cuba." PhD diss., University of Akron, 1995.

McLeod, Marc. "Undesirable Aliens: Haitians and British West Indian Immigrant Workers in Cuba, 1898 to 1940." PhD diss., University of Texas, Austin, 2000.

———. "Undesirable Aliens: Race, Ethnicity, and Nationalism in the Comparison of Haitian and British Subjects." *Journal of Social History* 21 (Spring 1998): 599–623.

McPherson, Alan. "Courts of World Opinion: Trying the Panama Flag Riots of 1964." *Diplomatic History* 28 (January 2004): 83–112.

———. *Yankee No! Anti-Americanism in U.S.–Latin American Relations.* Cambridge, MA: Harvard University Press, 2003.

Mershon, Sherie, and Steven Schlossman. *Foxholes and Color Lines: Desegregating the U.S. Armed Forces.* Baltimore, MD: Johns Hopkins University Press, 1998.

Miller, Richard E. *The Messmen Chronicles: African Americans in the U.S. Navy, 1932–1943.* Annapolis, MD: Naval Institute Press, 2004.

Miranda Bravo, Olga. *Undesirable Neighbors: The U.S. Naval Base in Guantánamo Bay.* Ed. José H. Amilva Dalboys and Israel Fernández Pujol. Havana: Instituto Cubano del Libro, Editorial José Martí, 2001.

———. *Vecinos indeseables: La base yanqui de Guantánamo.* Havana: Editorial Ciencias Sociales, 1998.

Moon, Katherine H. S. *Sex among Allies: Military Prostitution in U.S.-Korean Relations.* New York: Columbia University Press, 1997.

Morley, Morris H. "The U.S. Imperial State in Cuba, 1952–1958." *Journal of Latin American Studies* 14, no. 1 (May 1982): 143–70.

Murphy, Marion Emerson. *The History of Guantánamo Bay.* U.S. Naval Base, Guantanamo Bay: District Publications and Printing Office Tenth Naval District, 1953 (updated 1982 edition available online at http://www.nsgtmo.navy.mil/htmpgs/gtmohistorymurphy.htm).

Neptune, Harvey. *Caliban and the Yankees: Trinidad and the United States Occupation.* Chapel Hill: University of North Carolina Press, 2007.

Neuman, Gerald L. "Anomalous Zones." *Stanford Law Review* 48 (May 1996): 1197–234.

Ngai, Mae M. *Impossible Subjects: Illegal Aliens and the Making of Modern America.* Princeton, NJ: Princeton University Press, 2004.

Oliva, Jorge. *Donde una llama nunca se apaga.* Havana: Ediciones Unión, 1998.

Paterson, Thomas G. *Contesting Castro: The United States and the Triumph of the Cuban Revolution.* New York: Oxford University Press, 1994.

Pelley, Patricia M. *Postcolonial Vietnam: New Histories of the National Past.* Durham, NC: Duke University Press, 2002.

Perera González, Domingo M. *Encierro, incertidumbre, y sexo.* Miami, FL: Spin Quality Printing, 2001.

Pérez, Alberto. "Wet Foot, Dry Foot, No Foot: The Recurring Controversy between Cubans, Haitians, and the U.S. Immigration Policy." *Nova Law Review* 28 (December 2004): 437–64.

Pérez, Louis A., Jr. *Cuba and the United States: Ties of Singular Intimacy.* Athens: University of Georgia Press, 1990.

———. *Cuba between Empires, 1878–1902.* Pittsburgh, PA: University of Pittsburgh Press, 1983.

———. *Cuba: Between Reform and Revolution.* New York: Oxford University Press, 1995.

———. *Cuba under the Platt Amendment, 1902–1934.* Pittsburgh, PA: University of Pittsburgh Press, 1986.

———. *On Becoming Cuban: Identity, Nationality, and Culture.* New York: HarperCollins, 1999.

———. *The War of 1898: The United States and Cuba in History and Historiography.* Chapel Hill: University of North Carolina Press, 1998.

Pérez de la Riva, Juan. "Cuba y la Migración Antillana, 1900–1931." In *La república neocolonial: Anuario de estudios cubanos.* Vol. 2. Havana: Editorial Ciencias Sociales, 1979.

———. "Una isla con dos historias." In *El Barracón: Esclavitud y capitalismo en Cuba.* Barcelona: Editorial Crítica, 1978.

Pérez Rubio, Ana Celia, Hazael Deulofeu Atencio, Luisa D'León Founier, and Joaquín Toirac Adames. "Historia local de Caimanera." Unpublished manuscript, February 22, 1995. (Located in the Guantánamo Provincial Archive.)

Pérez-Stable, Marifeli. *The Cuban Revolution: Origins, Course, and Legacy.* New York: Oxford University Press, 1999.

Pessar, Patricia. *From Fanatics to Folk: Brazilian Millenarianism and Popular Culture.* Durham, NC: Duke University Press, 2004.

Portel Vilá, Herminio. *Historia de la guerra de Cuba y los Estados Unidos contra España.* Havana: Publicaciones de la Oficina del Historiador de la Ciudad, 1949.

Pratt, Mary Louise. *Imperial Eyes: Travel Writing and Transculturation.* London: Routledge, 1992.

Queeley, Andrea. "A Dream Derailed? The English-Speaking Caribbean Diaspora in Revolutionary Cuba." PhD diss., City University of New York, 2007.

Quinsaat, Jesse, ed. *Letters in Exile: An Introductory Reader on the History of Pilipinos in America.* Los Angeles, CA: UCLA Asian American Studies Center, 1976.

Quintero Mena, Rolando E. "El caso Chicle: Un crimen del imperialismo yanqui que quedó impune." *El Managui, Sección de Investigaciones Históricas del Comité Provincial del PCC, Guantánamo* 4, no. 9 (1989): 3–12.

Rabe, Stephen G. *U.S. Intervention in British Guiana: A Cold War Story.* Chapel Hill: University of North Carolina Press, 2005.

Radosh, Ronald. *American Labor and United States Foreign Policy.* New York: Random House, 1969

Rassí, Reynold. *Cuba: Nueva división político-administrativa.* Havana: Editorial Orbe, 1981.

Ratner, Michael. "How We Closed the Guantánamo HIV Camp: The Intersection of Politics and Litigation." *Harvard Human Rights Journal* 11 (Spring 1998): 187–220.

Ratner, Michael, and Ellen Ray. *Guantánamo: What the World Should Know.* White River Junction, VT: Chelsea Green, 2004.

Renda, Mary. *Taking Haiti: Military Occupation and the Culture of U.S. Imperialism, 1915–1940.* Chapel Hill: University of North Carolina Press, 2001.

Reynolds, Bradley. "Guantánamo Bay, Cuba: The History of an American Naval Base and Its Relationship to the Formulation of U.S. Foreign Policy and Military Strategy toward the Caribbean, 1895–1910." PhD diss., University of Southern California, 1982.

———. "Guantánamo Bay, Cuba, U.S. Naval Base, 1898–." In *United States Navy and Marine Corps Bases Overseas,* ed. Coletta Paolo E. and K. Jack Bauer, 146–57. Westport, CT: Greenwood, 1985.

Roig de Leuchsenring, Emilio. *Cuba no debe su independencia a los Estados Unidos.* Buenos Aires: Hemisferio, 1965.

Rolph-Trouillot, Michel. *Silencing the Past: Power and the Production of History.* Boston: Beacon, 1997.

Romualdi, Serafino. *Presidents and Peons: Recollections of a Labor Ambassador in Latin America.* New York: Funk and Wagnalls, 1967.

Roorda, Eric Paul. *The Dictator Next Door: The Good Neighbor Policy and the Trujillo Regime in the Dominican Republic, 1930–1945.* Durham, NC: Duke University Press, 1998.

Rose, David. *Guantánamo: The War on Human Rights.* New York: New Press, 2004.

Rosenberg, Emily. *Financial Missionaries to the World: The Politics and Culture of Dollar Diplomacy, 1900–1930.* Cambridge, MA: Harvard University Press, 1999.

Rundstetler, Theresa. " 'Journeymen': Boxing, Race, and the Transnational World of Jack Johnson." PhD diss., Yale University, 2007.

Saar, Erik, and Viveca Novak. *Inside the War: A Military Soldier's Eyewitness Account of Life at Guantánamo.* New York: Penguin, 2005.

Salazar Parreñas, Rhacel. *Servants of Globalization: Women, Migration, and Domestic Work.* Stanford, CA: Stanford University Press, 2001.

Sánchez Guerra, José. *Los anglo-caribeños en Guantánamo, 1902–1950.* Guantánamo: Editorial el Mar y la Montaña, 2004.

———. *Mambisas guantanameras.* Guantánamo: Editorial el Mar y la Montaña, 2000.

Sánchez Guerra, José, and Wilfredo Campos Cremé. *La batalla de Guantánamo, 1898.* Havana: Ediciones Verde Olivo, 2000.

Sánchez Oliva, Iraida, and Santiago Moreaux Jardines. *La Guantanamera.* Havana: Editorial José Martí, 1999.

Sartori, Maria. "The Cuban Migration Dilemma: An Examination of the United States' Policy of Temporary Protection in Offshore Safe Havens." *Georgetown Immigration Law Journal* 15 (Winter 2001): 319–55.

Schahill, Jeremy. *Blackwater: The Rise of the World's Most Powerful Mercenary Army.* New York: Nation Books, 2007.

Scheina, Martin J. "The U.S. Presence in Guantánamo." *Strategic Review* (Spring 1976): 81–88.

Schwartz, Rosalie. *Pleasure Island: Tourism and Temptation in Cuba.* Lincoln: University of Nebraska Press, 1997.

Scott, James C. *Weapons of the Weak: Everyday Forms of Peasant Resistance.* New Haven, CT: Yale University Press, 1985.

Scott, Rebecca J. "The Provincial Archive as a Place of Memory: The Role of Former Slaves in the Cuban War of Independence (1895–98)." *History Workshop Journal* 58 (Autumn 2004): 149–66.

———. *Slave Emancipation in Cuba: The Transition to Free Labor, 1850–1899.* Princeton, NJ: Princeton University Press, 1985.

Sección de Historia del PCC de la Provincia Guantánamo. *Guantánamo: Apuntes para una Cronología Histórica.* Santiago de Cuba: Editorial Oriente, 1985.

Seigel, Micol. "Beyond Compare: Comparative Method after the Transnational Turn." *Radical History Review* 91(Winter 2005): 62–90.

Sims, Harold Dana. "Collapse of the House of Labor: Ideological Divisions in the Cuban Labor Movement and the U.S. Role, 1944–1949." *Cuban Studies* 21 (1991): 123–47.

———. *Latin America Between the Second World War and the Cold War, 1944–1948.* New York: Cambridge University Press, 1992.

Singer, P. W. *Corporate Warriors: The Rise of the Privatized Military Industry.* Ithaca, NY: Cornell University Press, 2003.

Smith, Neil. *American Empire: Roosevelt's Geographer and the Prelude to Globalization.* Berkeley: University of California Press, 2003.

Smith, Wayne. "The Base from the U.S. Perspective." In *Subject to Solution: Problems in Cuban-U.S. Relations,* eds. Wayne A. Smith and Esteban Morales Dominguez. Boulder, CO: Lynne Rienner, 1988.

Spalding, Hobart A. "U.S. and Latin American Labor: The Dynamics of Imperialist Control." *Latin American Perspectives* (Winter 1976): 45–69.

Spenser, Daniela, ed. "La crisis del Caribe: Catalizador de la proyección soviética en América Latina." In *Espejos de la guerra fría: México, América Central, y el Caribe,* ed. Daniela Spenser, 281–317. Mexico City: Centro de Investigaciones y Estudios Superiores, 2004.

———. *Espejos de la guerra fría: México, América Central, y el Caribe.* Mexico City: Centro de Investigaciones y Estudios Superiores, 2004.

Stade, Joan Bulkeley. *Twelve Handkerchiefs: The Global Journey of Alice Wood Bulkeley Through World War II and the Twentieth Century with an American Navy Hero.* Tucson, AZ: Patrice, 2001.

Stephens, Michelle A. "Black Transnationalism and the Politics of National Identity: West Indian Intellectuals in Harlem in the Age of War and Revolution," *American Quarterly* 50.3 (1998):592–608.

Stoler, Ann Laura. *Carnal Knowledge and Imperial Power: Race and the Intimate in Colonial Rule.* Berkeley: University of California Press, 2002.

―――., ed. *Haunted by Empire: Geographies of Intimacy in North American History.* Durham, NC: Duke University Press, 2006.

―――. *Race and the Education of Desire: Foucault's History of Sexuality and the Colonial Order of Things.* Durham, NC: Duke University Press, 1995.

―――. "Tense and Tender Ties: The Politics in North American History and (Post) Colonial Studies." *Journal of American History* 88 (December 2001): 829–65.

―――. "Working the Revolution: Plantation Laborers and the People's Militia in North Sumatra." *The Journal of Asian Studies* 47 (May 1988): 227–47.

Sturdevant, Sandra Pollock, and Brenda Stoltzfus. *Let the Good Times Roll: Prostitution and the U.S. Military in Asia.* New York: New Press, 1992.

Suárez, Felipa, and Pilar Quesada. *A escasos metros del enemigo: Historia de la Brigada de la Frontera.* Havana, Cuba: Ediciones Verde Olivo, 1996.

Suárez Findlay, Eileen. *Imposing Decency : The Politics of Sexuality and Race in Puerto Rico, 1870–1920.* Durham, NC: Duke University Press, 2000.

Swanger, Joanna Beth. "Land Rebellion: Oriente and Escambray Encountering Cuban State Formation, 1934–1974." Ph.D. Diss., University of Texas, Austin, 1999.

Sweig, Julia E. *Inside the Cuban Revolution: Fidel Castro and the Urban Underground.* Cambridge, MA: Harvard University Press, 2002.

Takaki, Ronald. *Strangers from a Different Shore: A History of Asian Americans.* New York: Penguin Books, 1989.

Thelen, David. "The Nation and Beyond: Transnational Perspectives on United States History." *Journal of American History* 86 (December 1999): 965–75.

Thomas, Hugh. *Cuba; or, The Pursuit of Freedom.* London: Eyre and Spottiswoode, 1971.

Thomas, John F. "Cuban Refugees in the United States," *International Migration Review* 1 (Spring 1967):46–57.

Toirac Adames, Joaquín. "Apuntes sobre el movimiento obrero en la base naval norteamericana." *El Managui: Sección de Investigaciones Históricas del Comité Provincial del PCC Guantánamo* (1988): 3–8.

Tosté Ballart, Gilberto. *Guantanamo: U.S.A. al Desnudo.* Havana: Editorial Ciencias Sociales, 1983.

Tyrrell, Ian. "American Exceptionalism in an Age of International History." *American Historical Review* 96 (October 1991): 1031–55.

―――. "Making Nations/Making States: American Historians in the Context of Empire." *Journal of American History* 86 (December 1999): 1015–44.

U.S. Bureau of Yards and Docks. *Building the Navy's Bases in World War II: History of the Bureau of Yards and Docks and the Civil Engineer Corps, Volumes I and II.* Washington DC: U.S. Government Printing Office, 1947.

Valdés Millán, Ana Daelé. "Presencia china en la ciudad de Guantánamo 1906–1960." Master's thesis, Universidad de Oriente, 2003.

Van Pelt, Robert Jan, and Deborah Dwork. *Auschwitz, 1270 to the Present.* New Haven, CT: Yale University, 1996.

Venegas Delgado, Hernán. *La región en Cuba: Un ensayo de interpretación historiográfica.* Santiago de Cuba: Editorial Oriente, 2001.

Vine, David. "The Bases of Empire: Expulsion and the Military on Diego Garcia." Ph.D. Diss., City University of New York, 2006.

Vitalis, Robert. *America's Kingdom: Mythmaking on the Saudi Oil Frontier.* Stanford, CA: Stanford University Press, 2006.

Von Eschen, Penny. *Satchmo Blows Up the World: Jazz Ambassadors Play the Cold War.* Cambridge, MA: Harvard University Press, 2006.

Waters, Robert and Gordon Daniels. "The World's Longest General Strike: The AFL-CIO, the CIA, and British Guiana." *Diplomatic History* 29 (April 2005): 279–308.

Weiner, Myron. "International Migration and Development: Indians in the Persian Gulf." *Population Development Review* 8 (March 1982): 1–36.

Wexler, Laura. *Tender Violence: Domestic Visions in an Age of U.S. Imperialism.* Chapel Hill: University of North Carolina Press, 2000.

White, Richard. *The Middle Ground: Indians, Empires, and Republics in the Great Lakes Region, 1650–1815.* Cambridge: Cambridge University Press, 1991.

Whitney, Robert. "The Architect of the Cuban State: Fulgencio Batista and Populism in Cuba, 1937–1940." *Journal of Latin American Studies* 32 (2000): 435–59.

———. *State and Revolution in Cuba: Mass Mobilization and Political Change, 1920–1940.* Chapel Hill: University of North Carolina, 2001.

Williams, William Appleman. *The Tragedy of American Diplomacy.* new ed. New York: W. W. Norton, 1988.

Winchell, Meghan Kate. "Good Food, Good Fun, and Good Girls: USO Hostesses and World War II." Ph.D. Diss., University of Arizona, 2003.

Wood, Bryce. *The Making of the Good Neighbor Policy.* New York: Columbia University Press, 1961.

Woods, Randall Bennett. *The Roosevelt Foreign-Policy and the 'Good Neighbor': The United States and Argentina, 1941–1945.* Lawrence: Regents Press of Kansas, 1979.

Wyden, Peter. *Bay of Pigs: The Untold Story.* New York: Simon and Schuster, 1979.

Yergin, Daniel. *The Prize: The Epic Quest for Oil, Money, and Power.* New York: Simon and Schuster, 1991.

Young, Robert J. C. *Postcolonialism: An Historical Introduction.* Oxford: Blackwell Publishing, 2001.

Yuh, Ji-Yeon. *Beyond the Shadow of Camptown: Korean Military Brides in America.* New York: New York University Press, 2002.

Zanetti, Oscar, and Alejandro García. *United Fruit Company: Un caso del dominio imperialista en Cuba.* Habana: Editorial Ciencias Sociales, 1976.

Žižek, Slavoj. *The Ticklish Subject: An Essay in Political Ontology.* New York: Verso, 1999.

Acknowledgments

Acknowledgments are too often long, and I fear mine are the same. As I traveled back and forth between New Haven, New York, Washington DC, Fairhaven, MA, Havana, Santiago de Cuba, and Guantánamo, I acquired countless intellectual and personal debts.

First, I must thank my *compañeros* and *compañeras* in Cuba. Their generosity and support for my research was incredible, and I am deeply indebted to them. As this is an era when very few Cuban scholars are granted access to U.S. archives and resources, I am even more grateful for the openness and access I received in Cuba. In Havana, I must thank Hernán Venegas and the Instituto de Historia. I would also like to thank Graciela Chailloux, Rafael Hernández, Samuel Furé Davis, Jorge Macle, Belkis Quesada, Ileana Sanz, and the Centro Juan Marinello. The gift of friendship is as important, and I would like to thank the families of Normita del Castillo Sotolongo, Rolando Milían, and Olga Castañeda for their warmth and welcome when I was alone.

In Santiago de Cuba, I would like to thank Olga Portuondo, Maria Eugenia Espronceda, Julia Zayas Casamayor, and the library staff at the Biblioteca Elvira Cape.

And Guantánamo, Cuba. After working in Guantánamo, Cuba, for several months, I cannot begin to thank my friends and colleagues in this regional capital, which receives few tourists and fewer researchers. I must thank José Sánchez Guerra and the *compañeras* at the Guantánamo Archive; Marguerita Canseco and the *compañeras* at the Guantánamo Provincial Library; Marilis de Dios Noris, a fellow historian of the base; Jorge Derrick and the British West Indian Centre; and Roberto Claxton and Father Carlos from the Episcopal church. I also must thank local *guantanamero* historians Héctor Tatty Borges and Luis Figueras Pérez. Without their aid and assistance this project would not have been possible. Equally, I thank the men and women who worked on the base and welcomed me into their homes and shared their stories with me about working for the U.S. military. *Gracias*.

From the outset, my advisors have been supportive of this project even when the logistical and archival hurdles initially seemed impenetrable. They have all read multiple drafts, listened to my questions, and helped me hone my arguments and my writing. Matthew Jacobson was as encouraging and thoughtful an advisor as one could hope for, Gilbert Joseph offered many hours of critical engagement and advice, Michael Denning helped sharpen the book's organization and scope, and Lillian Guerra provided me with invaluable mentoring and knowledge of Cuban history. In addition, I would like to acknowledge the Yale faculty who aided me as I began my research, including Seth Fein, John Lewis Gaddis, Paul Gilroy, and Jennifer Klein.

I would also like to thank the institutions that funded my research, including the Yale Graduate School, International Security Studies, Yale Center for International and Area Studies, Lamar Center for Frontiers and Borders, and the Council for Latin American Studies. I must also thank Harold Rose, Yale legal counsel, who helped facilitate the legal paperwork necessary for research in Cuba.

At Yale, I found a fulfilling intellectual, political, and emotional community. In particular, a shout-out belongs to the Transnationalist Working Group that met throughout 2005–2006 and to Theresa Runstedtler, who I believe has read more drafts of this manuscript than anyone else. Special thanks goes also to Michelle Chase, Amanda Ciafone, Lisa Pinley Covert, Tracey Graham, Brandi Hughes, Edward Kehler, Leah Mancina-Khagani, Manuella Meyer, Jessica Stites Mor, Bethany Moreton, Rebecca Peabody, Camilla Schofield, Anita Seth, Ashley Riley Sousa, Melissa Stuckey, and Jenifer Van Vleck. In addition, the Yale Graduate and Employee Student Organization was a constant source of community and political engagement. I am lucky to have been a part of such a dynamic and committed organization. It helped me imagine an intellectual world I wanted to belong to and challenged me to match my scholarship with political action.

I have also had the opportunity to be part of several collective endeavors that have informed this project. In particular, I would like to thank Cynthia Enloe, Catherine Lutz, David Vine, and our Bases Working Group for its cooperative and socially active collaboration. Temple University's International History Workshop and the Tepoztlán Institute for Transnational History of the Americas were also particularly valuable intellectual spaces. I would also like to thank the following scholars for speaking with me and assisting in the initial stages of this project: David Carlson, Audrey Charlton, Michael Donoghue, Ada Ferrer, Jorge Giovannetti, Martha Hodes, Amy Kaplan, Melani McAlister, Alan McPherson, Harvey Neptune, Melina Pappademos, Louis Pérez, Andrea Queeley, Julia Sweig, and Robert Whitney.

At St. Joseph's College, I would like to thank Phillip Dehne, Peter Maust, Raymond D'Angelo, Mirella Landriscina, and Maria Montoya for unmatched collegiality and support.

Also, a special thank you belongs to Niels Hooper at University of California Press, and to Suzanne Knott, Rachel Lockman, and Susan Silver for seeing this manuscript from draft stages to the printed page.

And to my friends and family, thank you for tolerating my many absences, the lack of email and phone communication, and my endless stories about Guantánamo. Thank you to Mirna Adjami, Elizabeth O'Brien, Wendy Pearlman, and Eileen Stevens for reading drafts and helping me write clearly. My parents, Evelyn Baum and Ken Lipman, are a constant source of love and support. Both of them read the manuscript cover to cover, and my mother made critical edits before it went to press. And finally, I thank Eli Feinstein, my amazing husband, who has been more enthusiastic and more patient with this project than anyone else, and Liza Feinstein, who first made her presence known in Santiago de Cuba and has kept us smiling ever since.

Index

Italicized page numbers refer to illustrations.

147–50, 152–53, 159; in World War II
era, 46, 54

wages, 9, 14; and Cold War unionism,
64, 71–72, 75, 78, 81–84, 86, 97–98,
257–58n66; and contract workers,
194; and Good Neighbor policy, 100,
130–33; in Iraq, 216, 222–23, 226; in
revolutionary era, 146, 155–61, *159*,
164, 167, 214; and water crisis (1964),
183, 185–86; in World War II era, 42,
47
war games, 32, 66, 178
War of Independence (1895–98), 21–23,
104, 118, 145, 242n9
War on Terror, 2–3, 226–27
Washington Post, 220, 289–90n19
water supply, 12, 33, 37, 75, 141–42,
181–90, 213, 221
Welles, Sumner, 27
West, Kenneth M., 30–31, 54–56
West Indian Democratic Association, 36,
122
West Indians, 1–2, 4, 45, 49, 15, 26, 43,
193, 196–97, 240n33, 244n36, 284n21,
285n37; and Cold War unionism, 61,
80–81, 96; and Good Neighbor policy,
100–101, 118, 126–27, 129, 133; in revolutionary era, 144, 150; in World War
II era, 36, 41, 43–45, 47–50, 53,
250n74. *See also* Jamaicans
"wet foot, dry foot policy," 207
Weyler, George, 52, 56, 58
"Where Is Guantánamo" (Kaplan), 4–5
"whitening," 26, 52
whites/whiteness, 8, 19–21, 26; and
Good Neighbor policy, 103, 116–23,

125–26, 129, 133; in World War II era,
35–36, 52. *See also* race
Wilson, Woodrow, 27
Winkleman Corporation. *See* Drake Winkleman Corporation
women, Cuban, 3, 6, 9, 14–16; and Cold
War unionism, 72, 81; and Good
Neighbor policy, 16, 100–103,
108–10, 112, 115–31, 142, 267n85;
and Missile Crisis (1962), 176, 180; as
permanent base residents, 201; in revolutionary era, 136, 164–66, 171–73;
and water crisis (1964), 186–88; in
World War II era, 36, 39, 42, 45, 49,
59–60
women, U.S., 101, 131, 177–80, 194
women's rights, 21, 27, 71–72
worker activism, 36, 64–65, 72–73,
84–86, 92–95, 99, 225
workers' rights, 68, 71–72, 77, 85–86,
98, 186, 191–92
Workforce Study (1967), 195, 200
working class, 36, 73, 123, 149, 175,
186, 191, 207, 214, 217. *See also* base
workers
World War II, 6–7, 9, 16, 29–60, 144,
222; and Cold War unionism, 65–66,
69–70, 73; and Good Neighbor policy,
103, 120, 126, 132, 266n69

Yateras River, 33, 37, 141
Young Communist League, 41, 69,
188
Your Navy Job (U.S. Navy), 79

Zarran Treas, Juan, 83–84
zones of tolerance, 113–14, 117

AMERICAN CROSSROADS

Edited by Earl Lewis, George Lipsitz, Peggy Pascoe, George Sánchez, and Dana Takagi

Text:	10/13 Sabon
Display:	Sabon, Akzidenz Grotesk
Cartographer:	Bill Nelson
Indexer:	Sharon Sweeney
Compositor:	Binghamton Valley Composition, LLC
Printer and binder:	Sheridan Books, Inc.